Springer Proceedings in Business and Economics

More information about this series at http://www.springer.com/series/11960

Tadeusz Dudycz • Grażyna Osbert-Pociecha •
Bogumiła Brycz
Editors

The Essence and Measurement of Organizational Efficiency

Springer

Editors
Tadeusz Dudycz
Wrocław University of Technology
Wrocław
Poland

Grażyna Osbert-Pociecha
Wrocław University of Economics
Wrocław
Poland

Bogumiła Brycz
Wrocław University of Technology
Wrocław
Poland

ISSN 2198-7246 ISSN 2198-7254 (electronic)
Springer Proceedings in Business and Economics
ISBN 978-3-319-21138-1 ISBN 978-3-319-21139-8 (eBook)
DOI 10.1007/978-3-319-21139-8

Library of Congress Control Number: 2015952648

Springer Cham Heidelberg New York Dordrecht London

Printed on acid-free paper

Springer International Publishing AG Switzerland is part of Springer Science+Business Media (www.springer.com)

Preface

The forerunners of economists considered the problem of efficiency long before our era. One of the first was Hesiod (gr. Hesiodos), who lived in the eighth century BC and was interested in efficiency due to the fact that he was a farmer. He was one of the initiators of economic thought. As a farmer, he was interested in efficiency at the level of producers and households. Subsequent Greek thinkers dealing with economic problems also considered efficiency at this level, not at the scale of society as a whole. Not surprisingly, therefore, the word "economics" derives from the Greek language. It was first used as the title of a book by Xenophon, *Oikonomikos*, and concerned efficiency at the level of manufacturers. Over time, they began to examine efficiency more broadly at the scale of whole societies and countries. Over the centuries, states and societies which achieved high efficiency, both at the level of individual organizations and the macroscale, have left us testimony of their high material and spiritual culture. Their complexity, scale, and sometimes even speed of realization are difficult to achieve, even given our present level of technology. With the development of civilization, methods of management underwent continuous transformation, characterized by progressive changes, which have allowed us to reach today's unprecedented dynamics of technological transformation, both economic and social. The source of these changes is the maelstrom of breakthroughs that ultimately lead to the modification of existing paradigms. Increasingly, there are opinions about the decline, or even the bankruptcy, of traditional economics, which, as a science, is based on the study of accuracy and repeatability. The modern era is characterized by rapid changes, which is not conducive to such study. In these conditions, models (including mathematical ones) based on accepted a priori assumptions lose their applicability, which is required to meet one of the most important challenges for economists, determining a path for rational development. In our currently dynamic and ambiguous reality, the pursuance of being rational, effective, and efficient still seems to be valid. There is a constant need to deepen our understanding of the concept of efficiency, further identify its dimensions and essence, recognize new conditions for efficiency, improve ways of measuring it, etc. The VI International Conference titled "Efficiency as a Source of the Wealth of Nations" was devoted to this objective (ESWN 2015). The conference served as a platform for researchers, business practitioners, and academics to discover different aspects underlying new approaches to efficiency and deliberated upon the causes of inefficiency. Each paper submitted to ESWN 2015 has gone through a stringent peer review process by members of the International Programme Committee. The conference resulted in a very fruitful discussion and exchange of thoughts. Finally, we would like to thank all the contributing authors, members of the Programme Committee, and the rest of the Organizing Committee for their highly valuable work in enabling the success of this sixth edition of ESWN.

Wrocław, Poland
March, 2015

Tadeusz Dudycz
Grażyna Osbert-Pociecha
Bogumiła Brycz

Contents

Identification of Performance Measurement Systems Applied in Polish Enterprises

Barbara Batóg, Jacek Batóg, Andrzej Niemiec, Wanda Skoczylas, and Piotr Waśniewski

Abstract The construction of an appropriate performance measurement system is an important objective that every company is facing today. Firms using sustained performance measurement systems in management achieve higher efficiency. An identification of solutions in performance measurement applied in Polish enterprises has been made and is based on the analysis of the existing relations between the size of the company, the economic sector, variables describing development strategy and measurements of its implementation, as well as the performance measurement organization. Dependences occurred among the variables: character and the frequency of applied aims measures, possession or not of a development strategy, indicators and economic-financial variables and the way of connecting exploited measures with the motivation system.

The source of the data for the contingency tables was a nationwide survey conducted by the CATI method, which was covered by 300 Polish companies (National Science Centre Project number N N115 436640 "Key indicators of performance management"). Identification was accomplished by the chosen statistical tests and measures.

Keywords Business efficiency • Performance measurement system (PMS)

1 Introduction

A company is successful, when the use of resources is efficient, is strategically well-targeted (effectiveness), and has the ability to respond the changes occurring in a given environment at any time. Nowadays, we can say "this company is performing better". Performance in this approach represents the aggregation of basic stages of activity, from intention to result (Lebas 1995). The important challenges in modern management are: "intentions" are strategic and long term oriented, but results come from operation processes. To manage both, a manager needs support. Often, it is a performance measurement system (PMS): strategy oriented, but referring to the

B. Batóg (✉) • J. Batóg • A. Niemiec • W. Skoczylas • P. Waśniewski
University of Szczecin, Szczecin, Poland
e-mail: barbara.batog@wneiz.pl; batog@wneiz.pl; andrzej.j.niemiec@gmail.com; wanda@wneiz.pl; wasniewski@wneiz.pl

T. Dudycz et al. (eds.), *The Essence and Measurement of Organizational Efficiency*, Springer Proceedings in Business and Economics, DOI 10.1007/978-3-319-21139-8_1

processes and their efficiency and effectiveness. Performance measurement in this case is defined as the process of quantifying the effectiveness and efficiency of actions (Neely et al. 1995).

Such systems should be based upon the strategic role of the company (Azzone et al. 1991; Bititci et al. 2000; Dixon et al. 1990; Eccles 1991; Grady 1991; Kaplan and Norton 1992; Kennerley and Neely 2003; Medori and Steeple 2000). It means that it should be mutually supportive and consistent with the business's goals, objectives, critical success factors and programmes (Dixon et al. 1990) and moreover should be used to challenge strategic assumptions (Bititci et al. 2001; Bourne et al. 2000) at any level of corporation (Lockamy 1991). Such a system consists of well-defined and measurable criteria for the organization (Globerson 1985).

Since performance measure is a metric to quantify this efficiency and effectiveness of operations (Neely et al. 1995), the ability to measure the performance of operations can be seen as an important prerequisite for improvement. This is why companies have increased the capabilities of their performance measurement systems (PMSs) over the last few years (Fawcett and Cooper 1998). While early PMSs were based on costing and accounting systems, today measuring performance in operations requires a more balanced set of financial and non-financial measures at various points along the supply chain (Andersson et al. 1989; Flapper et al. 1996; Fortuin 1988; Fransoo and Wouters 2000). In this case non-financial performance measures should be complementary alongside financial measures (Kaplan and Norton 1996). Even in this shape, performance measurement system allows managing a corporation's performance. To respond to a change it needs something more. In this case performance should be reported daily or weekly (Crawford 1988).

According to researchers in most developed countries, most PMSs are static. That is, they are not dynamic and sensitive to changes in the internal and external environment of the firm (Nudurupati and Bititci 2000; Kueng 2001; Marchand and Raymond 2008). As a result, the presented information is not relevant, up-to-date or accurate. A new class of PMSs have an integrated Management Information Systems (MIS) infrastructure. Hence, the lack of MIS support results in cumbersome and time-consuming data collection, sorting, maintenance and reporting (Marr and Neely 2002).

Pressure on the improvement of the organization, including its control function and evaluation of activity, causes great interest in the theory and practice of performance measurement systems (Haffer 2011). Performance measurement system is a base for managing the enterprise and thereby solutions applied in this field determines efficiency and effectiveness of the organizations (Spitzer 2010).

The research question of the article is what do PMSs look like in Poland? The aim of this article is to characterize PMSs in Poland. The source of the data for the contingency tables was based on a nationwide survey conducted by the CATI method, which was covered by 300 Polish companies.[1] Identification was accomplished by chosen tests and statistical measures.

[1] National Science Centre Project number N N115 436640 "Key indicators of performance management".

2 Characteristics of the Survey

The aim of the survey was to collect information on performance measurement systems in non-financial Polish enterprises. The representative survey was conducted in 2012 for the whole of Poland by means of CATI (Computer Assisted Telephone Interviews). The sample size was 300.

The cluster sampling was applied in two ways. In the first one the size of the enterprise separated groups and in the second one—the size of the enterprise and the economic section. In order to keep the structure of the firm's population the weights were computed on the base of data of the Central Statistical Office of Poland.

The total time of the interviews was 20 min. The interviewer asked questions to members of management boards, middle-level managers, and management accounting specialists. The starting point for the analysis was to identify the present level of performance measurement, and thus determine which level: strategic, operational or just individual employees corresponded to the solutions applied.

The identification required gathering opinions concerning the fact of having a strategy or not, and the way it is described. It means, whether the strategic objectives were measurable, how often they were measured and how the measurement system was organized.

Sustained performance measurement requires the use of performance indicators set in a financial perspective, as well as other separate fields, including a non-financial one. Identification of the PMS structure referred to the used financial indicators (universal in any type of business) perspective of non-financial ratings (customers, broadly defined as internal processes, learning and development, environmental protection, etc.) and specific measurement solutions in each of them. Respondents had to add other perspectives, relevant to their business, and the ways they used to measure performance. The evaluation was a two-pronged approach. In addition to an identification of the performance measures, their importance to the whole PMS was also assessed.

The following part of the research concerned questions such as: how PMS was developed, linkage with the motivation system, software and computer support.

The respondents were asked to express an opinion on the degree of satisfaction of their own performance measurement system and possibilities for its improvement.

The last part of the questionnaire was the respondent's particulars. From the PMS point of view, important attributes were: the size of the enterprise, including: size of employment and incomes, economic section, place of business, as well as the ownership and profits of the business in the last 3 years.

The internal consistency determines the quality of performance measurement systems and the fulfilment of its functions. Therefore, the scope of the undertaken research was an analysis of the relations between individual characteristics of performance measurement systems by means of selected tests and statistical measures.

3 Applied Methods

In the literature many measures of dependence between the pair of variables could be found—for example the contingency coefficient, Tschuprow's coefficient and Cramer's V. In order to calculate all these measures the bivariate frequency distributions in the form of contingency tables are necessary. The contingency tables were computed with weights keeping the structure of the firm's population. In the research Cramer's V was applied because the examined variables have different numbers of categories (data matrix has a different number of rows and columns). The chi-square test of independence was also used.

3.1 *Cramer's V Coefficient*

Cramer's V coefficient is a measure of association between two categorical variables X and Y. It varies from 0 (no association) to 1 (perfect association). The calculations are based on a contingency table for examined variables. Cramer's V coefficient is given in formula (1).

$$V = \sqrt{\frac{\chi^2/n}{\min((r-1)(s-1))}} \tag{1}$$

where:

n—number of observations,

$$\chi^2 = \sum_{i=1}^{r}\sum_{j=1}^{s}\frac{\left(n_{ij}-\hat{n}_{ij}\right)^2}{\hat{n}_{ij}}, \tag{2}$$

r—number of categories of variable X,
s—number of categories of variable Y,
n_{ij}—observed frequencies in category i of variable X and category j of variable Y,
$\hat{n}_{ij}$—expected frequencies calculated with the assumption of the independence of variables X and Y.

3.2 *Chi-Square (χ^2) Test of Independence*

The null hypothesis is that the row and column variables are independent of each other. The test statistic is given by Eq. (2) and has an χ^2 distribution with (r−1)(s−1) degrees of freedom. On the basis of the value of the test statistic the p-value is computed. If the p-value is less than the given significance level α the null hypothesis should be rejected. Rejecting the null hypothesis means accepting the alternative hypothesis that variables are dependent.

4 Empirical Results

For all meaningful pairs of variables Cramer's V coefficients were computed as well as the test statistics and p-values of the chi-square test of independence. The pairs for which the null hypothesis were rejected on the significance level $\alpha = 0.05$ are presented in Table 1. Chosen research questions are presented in Appendix.

Although the values of Cramer's V are not too high the dependences are statistically significant. It means that the distribution of one variable changes when the distribution of the second variable changes. On the basis of Table 1 the following dependences could be concluded:

- Size of the company (R1) and having strategy (O1)
- Size of the company (R1) and types of indicators (O3)
- Size of the company (R1) and who runs performance measurement (O7)
- Size of the company (R1) and kind of set of indicators (O8)
- Size of the company (R1) and the connection between indicators and the motivation system (O10)
- Economic section (S4) and having strategy (O1)
- Having strategy (O1) and a kind of set of indicators (O8)
- Having strategy (O1) and the connection between indicators and the motivation system (O10)
- Having strategy (O1) and the origin of the company's capital (S6)
- Having measures within strategy (O2) and levels the performance measurement (O5-0)
- Number of areas of indicators' application (O12) and age of company (S5)

Table 1 Cramer's V coefficient, test statistic χ^2 and p-value in case of rejecting the hypothesis of independence on the significance level $\alpha = 0.05$

Variables	Cramer's V	χ^2	p-value
R1—O1	0.37	40.01	0.0000
R1—O3	0.19	22.35	0.0010
R1—O7	0.24	35.09	0.0000
R1—O8	0.19	17.35	0.0266
R1—O10	0.13	9.69	0.0461
S4—O1	0.22	15.03	0.0103
O1—O8	0.25	14.82	0.0051
O1—O10	0.18	9.22	0.0099
O1—S6	0.17	8.30	0.0402
O2—O5-0	0.16	6.95	0.0309
O12a—S5	0.29	24.97	0.0001

Source: Own calculations

5 Interpretation of Results

As a result of the study it was found that the strategy has 38 % of Polish companies employing more than 10 persons. There has been a strong correlation between the size of the company and possession of the strategies. Over 78 % of the surveyed big companies have got established strategies, on the other hand only 34 % of small enterprises planned their development in the long term. Other found relationships have revealed a correlation between the section of a company and having the strategy. In manufacturing over 2/3 of firms have got a strategy of development, also in some sections of the services (L, M, and N) and in the retailing section more than a half of enterprises have got that. On the other hand there is a logistic section in which only 31 % think about developing a long term strategy. There is also a link between the size and types of measures used in the aims of the realization of control. The financial measures play a key role but the nonfinancial measures are becoming more significant along with the growth of the enterprises. 75 % of big companies use both financial and nonfinancial measures, and only 47 % of small enterprises do that.

Moreover, the relationship between the size of the company, having developed strategy and performance measures systems have been statistically significant. There is also a significant correlation of the size and measures applied in the companies—the larger the company, the complex solutions are more important, such as systems of ordered nonfinancial or/and financial measures (42 % of the answers of big companies). Over half of the small companies responses concern a set of unrelated measures (especially financial), which are not forming the system. Furthermore, 20 % of small and medium enterprises could not answer that question. These links are confirmed by a third correlation, between having a strategy and applied performance measures. Enterprises developing strategies are more likely to implement the advanced solutions in the form of systems (68 surveyed companies compared to 34 companies without long term strategies).

There is also a correlation between the size and organization of performance measurement in the companies. In small enterprises measurement is concentrated in the accounting department (55 % of answers); in medium ones measurement conducted by all units within their competences is more frequent (41–45). That option is also most significant for big companies (56 answers), which more often than others have pointed the necessity for performance measurement middle-management specialists.

Another tested relationship was the one between the size of the company and linking the performance measures with the motivation system. Nearly a half of small (47 %) and big (46 %) companies use the measures in their incentive systems for all employees, which were mentioned only by 28 % of medium firms. That group prefers linking measures to motivation systems only for chosen workers.

The next two examined relations concern having a strategy. The first aspect is linking it to using measures in motivation systems. It has been statistically proved, that companies with developed strategies are more likely to use performance measures in motivation systems, either for all employees or only for chosen ones. The second aspect is referring to the origin of the company's ownership. Most of the foreign capital, mixed capital and Polish national equity companies have a long term strategy for their development. Polish private equity firms are divided almost equally.

There is also a correlation between including measures in a company's aims (besides the descriptive part) and the level of performance measurement. Most companies measure the performance of a company as a whole, but the fact of including the measures in targets seems to have an influence on measuring the performance on the level of organizational units and individual employees.

The last discussed correlation is between the level of usage of performance measures and business experience (in years of existence). Many areas of application of performance measures are used especially by companies with a 10 years or more market history.

6 Conclusions

A generalization of the results of the conducted study about relationships between variables characterizing performance measurement systems of Polish enterprises is an image of a performance measurement system level, the principles of its functioning and institutionalization. This image varies depending on the size of the company or economic section.

The strategic level of performance measurement occurs in large enterprises. Often they are companies from industrial sections, services (L, M, N sections), trade and repair. They have developed a strategy and quantified targets using unstructured and structured systems of financial and non-financial measures (e.g. Balanced Scorecard). These firms also constantly monitor the realization of the aims and implement modifications as a basis for continuous refinement and improvement of their effectiveness. Measurements carried out at each position makes the whole company involved in the performance management process, especially when measures are associated with a motivation system.

A different situation occurs in small enterprises. Often they do not have a strategy and use as well financial measures as both groups of indicators. In most cases the motivation system for employees is related to financial measures. The measurement of performance is mostly in the hands of the chief accountant.

Elements of both presented performance measurement systems are those used in medium-sized enterprises. They also have often formulated a strategy. They measure targets using financial indicators or both groups of measures, but these indicators usually do not form a system. These measures are related to the motivation system only for selected employees.

Therefore the highest and most complete level of performance management characterizes large enterprises. The quality of these systems is relatively high. Many of them are based on the new class of PMSs with an integrated Management

Information Systems (MIS) infrastructure. Concluding, firms using sustained performance measurement systems in management achieve higher efficiency (Lingle and Schiemann 1996; Batóg et al. 2015).

The research in this range has not been yet realised in Poland. Main findings comprise important contribution in the field of performance measurement systems.

Appendix

Chosen research questions mentioned in the article:

R1. **Q:** Size of the company (enterprise)
A: Small, medium, big

O1. **Q:** Have You developed a strategy of Your company?
A:
1. Yes,
2. No

O2. **Q:** Does the company's strategy besides the descriptive part includes also company's aims measures?
A:
1. Yes, it does,
2. No, the aims of the strategy are expressed only descriptively

O3. **Q:** What types of measures are applied in Your company?
A:
1. Mainly or solely financial, e.g. profit, turnover, assets, profitability
2. Above all others non-financial, not expressed in money (currency), e.g. number of employed, work efficiency, number of clients, customer's loyalty, customer satisfaction, working time,
3. Both financial and nonfinancial
4. None of tchem.

O5. **Q:** On which levels the performance measurement is calculated by the company?
A:
1. The company as a whole,
2. Organizational units,
3. Individual employees.

O7. **Q:** In what way is the performance measurement in the company organized?
A:
1. a senior position was distinguished for the performance measurement
2. run only by the accounting department
3. conducted by all units within their competence

O8. **Q**: Are measures used in Your company form:

A:

1. a set of unrelated, other for each department, financial measures,
2. a set of unrelated, other for each department, financial and nonfinancial measures,
3. a set of unrelated, other for each department, nonfinancial measures,
4. ordered system of financial measures such as DuPont Model, ZVEI
5. create an orderly system of financial and nonfinancial measures, such as Balanced Scorecard, Performance Prism, EFQM
6. Do not know, hard to say

O10. **Q:** Are the performance measures or are they not related to motivation system in Your company?

A:

1. Yes, it is regarding all employees,
2. Yes, but is regarding only chosen groups of employees,
3. No

O12. **Q:** What is the aim of usage of performance measures in the company?

A:

1. To measure and assess the achievements of the company
2. To refine the vision and strategy
3. To explain the objectives and the integrate these measures with strategic management system
4. For planning, setting objectives and strategic decision-making
5. For internal communication
6. To improve systems for monitoring the strategy realisation and organizational learning
7. To improve operational processes such as increasing the employees productivity, improve the quality
8. To control the current economic activity
9. To motivate employees
10. For external reporting
11. To fulfill specific legal requirements and technology
12. Other aims

O12A. 1. few areas of application (0–5)
2. many areas of application (6–12)

S4. Are leading PKD section of Your company is: Manufacturing (B, C, D, E), Construction (section F), Trade and repair (G), Transportation and storage (H), Services I (I, J), Services II (L, M, N)?

S5. **Q:** Since when is the company conducting its activity?

A:

1. To 1 year
2. 1–3 years

3. 4–5 years
4. 6–10 years
5. 10 years and more
6. Don't know, hard to say

S6. **Q:** What is the origin of the company's capital:
A:
1. Polish private equity
2. Polish national equity
3. Foreign capital
4. Mixed capital

References

Andersson P, Aronsson H, Storhagen NG (1989) Measuring logistics performance. Eng Costs Prod Econ 17:253–262

Azzone G, Masella C, Bertele U (1991) Design of performance measures for time-based companies. Int J Oper Prod Manag 11(3):77–85

Batóg B, Batóg J, Niemiec A, Skoczylas W, Waśniewski P (2015) Zastosowanie metod klasyfikacyjnychw identyfikacji kluczowych indykatorów osiągnięć w zarządzaniu wynikami przedsiębiorstw, in print

Bititci U, Turner T, Begemann C (2000) Dynamics of performance measurement systems. Int J Oper Prod Manag 20(6):692–704

Bititci U, Suwignjo P, Carrie A (2001) Strategy management through quantitative modelling of performance measurement systems. Int J Prod Econ 69:15–22

Bourne M, Mills J, Wilcox M, Neely A, Platts K (2000) Designing, implementing and updating performance measurement systems. Int J Oper Prod Manag 20(7):754–771

Crawford K (1988) An analysis of performance measurement systems in selected just-in-time operations. Dissertation, University of Georgia

Dixon J, Nanni A, Vollmann T (1990) The new performance measurement challenge: measuring operations for world-class competition. Dow Jones-Irwin/APICS, Homewood, IL

Eccles RG (1991) The performance measurement manifesto. Harv Bus Rev 69(1):131–137

Fawcett SE, Cooper MB (1998) Logistics performance measurement, and customer success. Ind Mark Manag 27:341–357

Flapper SD, Fortuin L, Stoop PPM (1996) Towards consistent performance measurement systems. Int J Oper Prod Manag 16(7):27–37

Fortuin L (1988) Performance indicators—why where and how? Eur J Oper Res 34:1–9

Fransoo JC, Wouters MJF (2000) Measuring the bullwhip effect in a supply chain. Supply Chain Manag 5(2):78–89

Globerson S (1985) Issues in developing a performance criteria system for an organisation. Int J Prod Res 23(4):639–646

Grady M (1991) Performance measurement: implementing strategy. Manag Account 72 (12):49–53

Haffer R (2011) Samoocena i pomiar wyników działalności w systemach zarządzania. W poszukiwaniu doskonałości biznesowej. Wydawnictwo Naukowe Uniwersytetu Mikołaja Kopernika, Toruń

Kaplan R, Norton D (1992) The balanced scorecard—measures that drive performance. Harv Bus Rev 70(1):71–79

Kaplan R, Norton D (1996) Using the balanced scorecard as a strategic management system. Harv Bus Rev 74(1):75–85

Kennerley M, Neely A (2003) Measuring performance in a changing business environment. Int J Oper Prod Manag 23(2):213–229

Kueng P (2001) Performance measurement systems in the service sector – the potential of IT is not yet utilized. Internal working paper no. 01–05, Fribourg

Lebas M (1995) Oui, il faut définir la performance. Revue Française de Comptabilité 226

Lingle JH, Schiemann WA (1996) From balanced scorecard to strategy gauge, is measurement worth it? Manag Rev March:56–62. By: Haffer R, Samoocena i pomiar wyników działalności w systemach zarządzania. W poszukiwaniu doskonałości biznesowej, Wydawnictwo Naukowe Uniwersytetu Mikołaja Kopernika, Toruń, p 325

Lockamy A III (1991) A study of operational and strategic performance measurement systems in selected world class manufacturing firms: an examination of linkages for competitive advantage. Dissertation, University of Georgia

Marchand M, Raymond L (2008) Researching performance measurement systems – an information systems perspective. Int J Oper Prod Manag 28(7):663–686

Marr B, Neely A (2002) Balanced scorecard software report. Gartner, Inc. and Cranfield School of Management, Stamford .

Medori D, Steeple D (2000) A framework for auditing and enhancing performance measurement systems. Int J Oper Prod Manag 20(5):520–533

Neely A, Mills J, Gregory M, Platts K (1995) Performance measurement system design – a literature review and research agenda. Int J Oper Prod Manag 15(4):80–116

Nudurupati SS, Bititci US (2000) Review of performance management information systems (PerforMIS). Internal report, Centre for Strategic Manufacturing, DMEM, University of Strathclyde

Spitzer D (2010) Preface. In: Tyagi RK, Gupta P (eds) Strategiczna karta wyników firm usługowych. Wydawnictwo Profesjonalne PWN, Warszawa, pp 15–16

The Impact on the Organisational Effects of the Implementation of ERP and Selected Management Methods

Agnieszka Bieńkowska, Katarzyna Walecka-Jankowska, and Anna Zgrzywa-Ziemak

Abstract The aim of the article was the analysis of the relations of the coexistence of the Enterprise Resource Planning (ERP) and selected management methods: Benchmarking, Business Process Management (BPM), Business Process Reengineering (BPR), Balanced Scorecard (BSC), Competency-based Management (CBM), Customer Relationship Management (CRM), Knowledge Management (KM), Lean Management (LM), Outsourcing, Six Sigma, Total Quality Management (TQM). Contemporary organisations invest more and more in enterprise systems, including ERP systems, and high growth of these investments is still predicted. The complexity and dynamics of modern management systems in fact determine the simultaneous and sequential application of many management concepts and methods. In the main, however, the coexistence of implemented solutions should be beneficial for an organisation. The theoretical views on the relations of ERP and selected management methods have thus been empirically verified in the analysis of differences in the assessment of a number of effects of using the selected management methods in pairs with ERP as well as separately (business, efficiency, management, social and environmental effects) were investigated. One-way ANOVA was used for a sample of 167 Polish organizations.

Keywords ERP • Management methods • Organisational performance

1 Introduction

Contemporary organisations invest more and more in enterprise systems, including ERP systems, and high growth of these investments is still predicted. Enterprise resource planning (ERP) systems are found to be critical to organisational performance and survival (Liang and Xue 2004). Davenport (2000) underlines the ERP

A. Bieńkowska (✉) • K. Walecka-Jankowska • A. Zgrzywa-Ziemak
Faculty of Computer Science and Management, Wroclaw University of Technology, Wroclaw, Poland
e-mail: agnieszka.bienkowska@pwr.edu.pl; katarzyna.walecka-jankowska@pwr.edu.pl; anna.zgrzywa-ziemak@pwr.edu.pl

T. Dudycz et al. (eds.), *The Essence and Measurement of Organizational Efficiency*, Springer Proceedings in Business and Economics, DOI 10.1007/978-3-319-21139-8_2

systems' potential to greatly enhance organisational performance and establish competitive advantage (Liang and Xue 2004). According to Cebeci, ERP systems play a vital role in today's organisations in fulfilling their visions and strategies (Cebeci 2009).

However, installing an enterprise system is not merely a computer project, but an expensive and risky investment, which impacts on a firm's primary and support processes, its organisational structure and procedures, the existing legacy systems, and the personnel's roles and tasks (Aloini et al. 2012, p. 183).

It is understandable that a significant body of research on ERP systems has been focused on the reasons for implementation, the challenges of the implementation project itself and critical success factors in implementation (Laframboise and Reyes 2005). Some studies also investigate the impact of ERP implementation on organisational performance (Liang and Xue 2004; Galy and Sauceda 2014). Although much research has been conducted on ERP implementation issues, there are still too few studies related to the post-implementation phase, including estimating the impact of ERP on organisational results not only just after or even during implementation, but in the long term (i.e. Laframboise and Reyes 2005; Varzandeh and Farahbod 2010; Satzinger et al. 2011), and most of them are concerned only with financial performance (i.e. Katerattanakul et al. 2014). According to Aloini et al., ERP has wide-ranging, cross-functional (difficult to isolate) and 'long-term' impact on resources and competences (Aloini et al. 2012, p. 183).

The purpose of this article is to present the results of the empirical research on the impact of organisational effects on the interaction between ERP systems and selected management methods. Much research has been carried out in an attempt to understand ERP's success. The bulk of this research body consists of variance research, which seeks to identify success factors and utilise these factors in order to explain variation in ERP implementation outcomes (Satzinger et al. 2011, p. 401). However, there is relatively little empirical research on the effects of using ERP together with other management methods.

2 ERP Definitions

Gable (1998), Holsapple and Sena (1999) define ERP system variously as a software, integrated standard software package, enterprise system, enterprise-wide system, enterprise-business system, integrated vendor software and enterprise application system (Al-Mashari et al. 2003). Gable (1998) adds an additional perspective to the ERP system as one that presents a holistic view of the business from a single information and IT architecture (Al-Mashari et al. 2003). However, ERP is a way of doing business, not merely a software package, as it combines both business processes in the organisation and IT into one integrated solution (Al-Mashari et al. 2003). According to Satzinger et al. ERP is a process in which an organisation commits to using an integrated set of software packages for key information systems to improve the effectiveness and efficiency of the enterprise (Satzinger et al. 2011).

3 Empirical Research

The results of the study presented in this paper are part of the empirical research carried out by the Management and Marketing Systems Department of the Organisation and Management Institute of Wroclaw University of Technology in 2009. The aim of the study was defined very broadly: to explore the usage of management methods in Poland—in general and for various groups of organisations; to investigate the reasons for methods' implementation, the barriers to their implementation and their impact on organisational effects; and finally to explore the coexistence of management methods. A research tool was a survey questionnaire, which was addressed to enterprises functioning in Poland (differing in terms of business type, size and ownership form). The selection of the organisations was of a target-based character. We looked for those organisations that made use of one or more of the management methods under analysis and, at the same time, represented different types of activity, different sizes and forms of ownership. Only one survey was conducted, anonymously, in each company. The questionnaire was filled in by the employees who have a broad view of the whole enterprise (i.e. CEO, management team, quality specialists etc.). As a result of the research activities, 173 questionnaires were returned to the authors. However, for the final analysis, a sample containing 167 correctly filled-out questionnaires was accepted (Bieńkowska and Zgrzywa-Ziemak 2011). The empirical study concentrated on 13 selected contemporary management methods. The number of the enterprises that have implemented particular methods has been presented in Fig. 1. ERP was implemented in 49 enterprises.

Table 1 presents the structure of the enterprises that declared the implementation of ERP.

3.1 The Coexistence of ERP and Selected Management Methods

As can be observed in Fig. 2, ERP is usually connected with controlling, CRM, BPM and TQM implementation (in more than 50 % of cases) but statistical analyses showed that not every relationship is significant (Table 2). However, there is a large number of organisations that do not implement any of the analysed methods.

From the results presented in Fig. 2, it emerges that for each pair, the most numerous group in particular pairs is the situation in which neither of the methods is used. The results of the statistical analyses (the cross tabulations, chi-squared test)

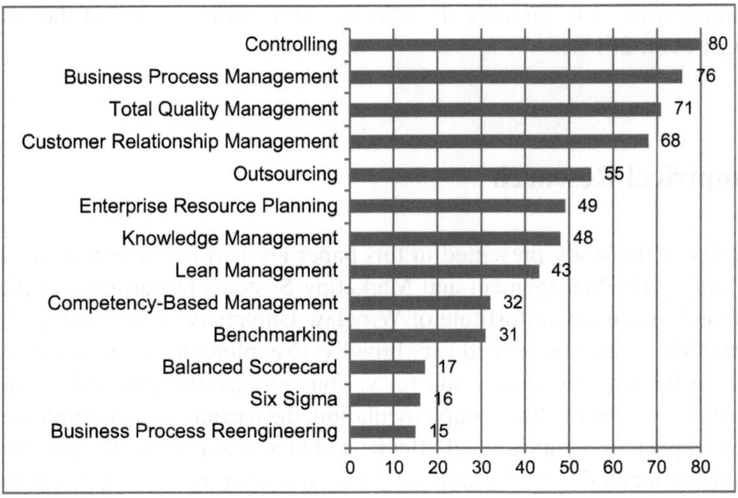

Fig. 1 The number of the enterprises which have implemented particular management methods (*Source*: Bieńkowska and Zgrzywa-Ziemak (2013))

Table 1 The structure of the analysed organisations using ERP in terms of their selected characteristics

	The number of researched organisations	The percentage of organisations using ERP (%)
Activity type		
Production	63	33.33
Service	54	24.07
Production-service	37	35.14
Commercial	13	16.67
Organisation size		
Up to 50 people	44	27.27
51–250 people	53	20.75
251–500 people	33	24.24
Above 500 people	37	48.65
Headquarters' location		
In Poland	139	26.62
Abroad	28	42.8
Total	167	29.34

Source: The authors' own study

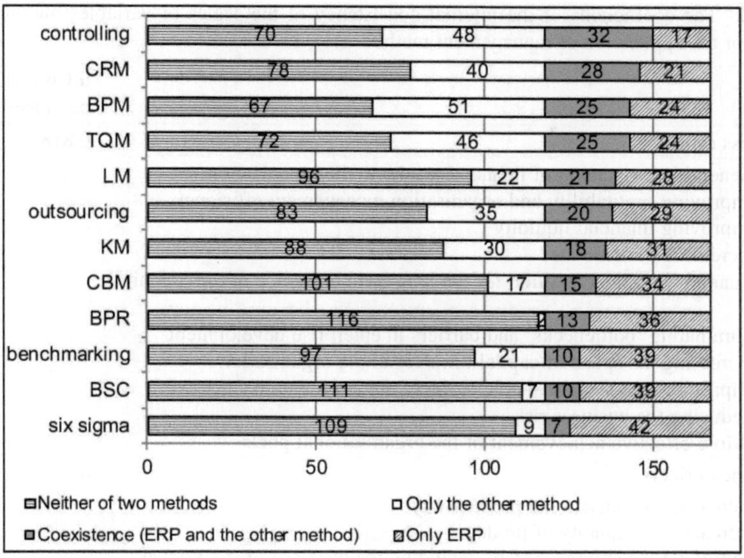

Fig. 2 The coexistence of ERP with particular management methods (*Source*: The authors' own study)

show that the differences in the groups are statistically significant for the following pairs: ERP-BSC, ERP-BPR, ERP-CRM, ERP-controlling, ERP-LM, ERP-CBM (presented in Table 2). The values calculated from the cross tabulations are under a great influence of the number of the coexistences of particular methods.[1]

3.2 *The Effects of ERP Usage*

Five groups of organisational effects were determined[2]: business, efficiency, management, social and environmental effects. The items that build the scale of each group of effects, together with the internal consistency factor (measured by Cronbach α parameter consistency), are presented in Table 2.

The enterprises that implemented ERP benefit from significantly greater business effects than those enterprises who do not use this method (Table 3 presents the statistical results).

[1] The authors realise that the major difficulty that occurred in the course of the study was the different number of the existence of particular methods in the organisations under study. This fact affects the 'potential' possibilities of the coexistence of these methods.

[2] 39 organisational results were listed by the research team. Each result was evaluated on the Likert's scale of 1–5 (from 'very negative' to 'very positive') by the respondents. The exploratory factor analysis was used to group the results. Factors satisfy the condition of normality (Kolmogorov–Smirnov test was used).

Table 2 The coefficients of the internal consistency of the scales of variables making up the effects of the application of management methods ($n = 167$)

Effects	α Cronbach parameter
Business effects	0.818
1. General improvement of financial results in the organisation 2. Improving profitability and organisation management efficiency 3. Improving financial liquidity 4. Increasing the revenues 5. Guaranteeing the condition for the long-term existence of the organisation 6. Eliminating 'bottlenecks' and barriers in enterprise development 7. Increasing the speed of capital turnover in the organisation 8. Improving organisational adaptation to environment changes 9. Reducing the business risk 10. More effective achievement of the organisational goals	
Efficiency effects	0.822
1. Increasing organisational productivity 2. Increasing the quality of products 3. Improving the storage system, including the decrease of stock level 4. Improving the timely rate of production orders 5. Decreasing the time of new product development 6. Implementing more ecologically friendly technologies 7. More effective and more rational organisational resources management 8. The decrease in functioning costs, the decrease of prodigality in the enterprise 9. Increasing work productivity	
Social effects	0.802
1. Increasing employees' motivation 2. Improving the satisfaction of employees 3. Improving the innovation and creativity of employees 4. Improving job involvement 5. Improving the competences of employees	
Management effects	0.762
1. Improving task coordination in management 2. More accurate decisions in the process of organisation management 3. Reducing the time of decision-making 4. Improving the competence and responsibility division on various levels of management 5. Improving the information flow in the organisation 6. Providing various levels of management with additional multidimensional information necessary in enterprise management 7. Improving the integration of employees and the cooperation between different organisational units	
Environmental effects	0.673
1. Improving communication between the organisation and environment 2. Increasing the synergy effect in cooperation with customers and/or business partners 3. Increasing customers' satisfaction 4. Improving relations with suppliers	

Source: Bieńkowska and Zgrzywa-Ziemak (2013)

Table 3 The use of ERP and business effects

	ERP implemented[a]	ERP not implemented	*t*-statistic	Significance level	Effect size measure[b]
Business effects	M = 3.87, SD = 0.47	M = 3.65, SD = 0.38	t(153) = −3.03	p = 0.003	g = 0.530

Source: the authors' own study

[a]*M* mean, *SD* standard deviation

[b]Hedges' g statistic was used (an effect size of 0.2 is a small effect, an effect size of 0.5 is a medium effect, and an effect size of 0.8 is a large effect; g can take values greater than 1)

The effects were even higher when ERP was implemented together with other researched management methods.

3.3 *The Effects of the Coexistence of ERP and Other Methods*

In order to investigate the relationship between the coexistence of selected management methods and the effects of their use, the analysis of variance method was performed. One-way ANOVA was used to determine whether the business effects depend on using a pair of management methods (ERP and another method), a single method or no method at all. Tukey post hoc test was used for multiple comparisons. All statistically significant relations between the coexistence of ERP with selected management methods and organisational effects are listed in Appendix.

The coexistence of ERP and other methods allowed—in some cases—all groups of effects to be better achieved. It should be noted that the use of ERP and other methods did not, in any of the cases, lead to a reduced assessment of organisational effects. Key research findings are as follows:

- In almost all the analysed methods—11 out of 12 (no significant relation is present in the case of BPR)—their use in conjunction with ERP brought greater business effects than in those cases where ERP was not implemented. Moreover, in as many as nine methods (out of 12), the implementation of the pair of methods with ERP led to greater business effects than the use of ERP only or any other method on its own (these methods were: BPM, LM, Controlling, CBM, Benchmarking, Six Sigma, BSC, Outsourcing and CRM). The implementation of ERP together with KM or TQM brings higher business effects than the use of KM or TQM only.
- The coexistence of ERP and TQM or BSC leads to higher efficiency effects than the implementation of ERP only. The results show that ERP supports CRM, because the efficiency effects are higher when a pair of methods is implemented than when CRM is used alone.

- The findings show that the social and management effects of the coexistence of ERP and KM, CBM or BSC are higher for the pairs of methods than when ERP is used alone (but not vice versa).
- The coexistence of ERP and CRM leads to significantly higher environmental effects than for either method used separately.
- The coexistence of ERP and BPR has no impact on the organisational effects.

4 Discussion and Conclusions

The research proved that using ERP significantly benefits the business effects responsible for overall condition of the entire organisation (including general improvement of financial results, profitability, revenues, adaptability etc.). This result correlates with numerous literature statements (Li et al. 2008; Cebeci 2009; Aloini et al. 2012). However, there was no significant relationship between ERP implementation and more specific effects—mainly efficiency and management effects. In the literature, attention is often directed to these kinds of benefits resulting from the use of ERP (Kale 2001; Hitt et al. 2002; McAfee 2002; Stratman and Roth 2002; Al-Mashari et al. 2003; Hendricks et al. 2007). On the other hand, the coexistence of ERP and other methods allowed better effects to be achieved—not only business effects, but also efficiency, management and environmental ones.

The results of the research point to the fact that the implementation of ERP together with controlling gives higher effects than for either method used separately. Among the assumptions of implementing ERP are, most of all, the increase in transparency and information relevance as well as the integration of the information resources of various enterprise functional areas (Al-Mashari et al. 2003; Hendricks et al. 2007; Aloini et al. 2012). Thus, ERP can constitute an important tool for improvement of decision-making process (Kluge and Kużdowicz 2011). Furthermore, the two methods used together, give an opportunity of basing decisions on the same information. However, the findings show that controlling also supports ERP.

Operations' coordination, which is the consequence of the use of the ERP system as well as having access to reliable information, is essential to achieve a given level of organisation efficiency in almost all conditions. However, it should be emphasised that the use of ERP in an organisation seems to support in particular the orientation process and this is the reason for the correlation with BPM. This is because, among other reasons, as claimed by Kieser and Walgenlach work in the ERP system is determined by the standard of task execution defined in the phase of process modelling, and system configuration can take place only in accordance with the adopted specifications (Kieser and Walgenlach 2003). The fundamental role that the process models play in the implementation and use of ERP systems in enterprises is stressed by Kasprzak (2005). The findings prove that ERP and BPM are complementary methods—the methods mutually support one another in achieving the organisational goals.

According to this study's research results the use of ERP together with BSC leads to an increase in nearly all effects (business, managerial, social as well as efficiency) in relation to the use of ERP on its own—without BSC. Management in a balanced way should provide the avoidance of the defects resulting from the phenomenon of suboptimalisation. Thus, the decisions made by the management members should be based on the data coming from different areas of the organisation and ERP allows for the aggregation of such information. 'Moreover, it is very important to match the ERP package objectives with business objectives' (Cebeci 2009, p. 8902). Balanced scorecard helps to define key objectives, benefits and expectations, thus the expectations for ERP are clear (Cebeci 2009).

The use of ERP together with TQM leads to higher efficiency and business effects. In the literature there are some who suggest that ERP can be used as an enabler for the implementation of effective TQM. Moreover, Li et al. examined the relationship between TQM and ERP implementation, operations management, customer satisfaction and firm's performance and they claim that those methods are complementary, due to the organisation of an enterprise's processes, and they believe that ERP plays an important role in high-level management and in the coordination of procedural quality functions (Li et al. 2008). Furthermore, in the view of Schniederjans and Kim (2003), TQM gives proper ERP support—corporate culture and organisational infrastructure (after: Kowalak 2009). Laframboise and Reyes believe that a successful implementation of ERP and TQM provides a potentially complementary resource leading to the competitive advantage (Laframboise and Reyes 2005). Schniederjans and Kim (2003) argued that change methods, such as BPR, and catalysts for change methods, such as TQM, must be aligned to support the implementation of ERP (after Laframboise and Reyes 2005). Jha and Joshi (2007) emphasized the relevance of TQM for the facilitation of ERP implementation (after Movahedi and Nouri Koupaei 2011).

In the context of quality there is another method that should be mentioned—Varzandeh and Farahbod studied the role of ERP among selected industries to achieve 'Six Sigma' quality (Varzandeh and Farahbod 2010). The new Six Sigma is data-driven and needs a reliable source of information. Enterprise resource planning would guide the organisations and provide them with a road map to better meet customers' needs with virtually zero dissatisfaction. The research findings prove that ERP and Six Sigma mutually support one another in achieving the business and management goals.

The analysis of the results shows that the coexistence of ERP and CRM leads to higher efficiency effects than using CRM alone. Order cycle times can be reduced, resulting in improved throughput, customer response times, and delivery speeds stemming from ERP implementation (McAfee 2002; Cotteleer and Bendoly 2006; Hendricks et al. 2007). But according to research results, ERP and CRM mutually support one another in achieving business goals. On the one hand, ERP systems provide the infrastructure that facilitates a long-term relationship with customers (Hendricks et al. 2007), on the other, it is possible that with the integration of ERP and CRM the IT system is more customer-oriented.

In the literature, ERP is often combined with KM (Bieńkowska et al. 2013). It is stressed that the integration of both methods gives special benefits (e.g. Metaxiotis 2009), that ERP implementation is a KM tool (e.g. Chan et al. 2009) or KM must be strategically and systematically incorporated into each implementation phase of ERP-implemented projects (McGinnis and Huang 2007). Pang-Lo found that the introduction of ERP and KM has a positive impact on organisational performance (Pang-Lo 2011). The research results state that implementation of ERP together with KM brings higher social effects than the use of ERP only; however, a reverse situation did not occur.

The coexistence of benchmarking and ERP leads to higher business and efficiency effects—these methods can be considered as complementary, they assist each other in achieving organisational goals. From the point of view of benchmarking (especially internal), the importance of ERP systems is enormous. They allow updated information to be generated from each functional area of the enterprise (Kowalak 2009) and from the organisational environment (Koslowski and Strüker 2011). On the other hand, the designers of ERP systems, by using the effects of the benchmarking analysis, can identify the weaknesses of the implemented systems and take actions to improve the efficiency of the whole organisation.

Moreover, CBM with ERP leads to achieving higher business and management effects than for either method used separately, and ERP paired with CBM leads to better social effects than when used on its own (however, a reverse situation did not occur). In relation to the CBM, what is definitely helpful is an HRM module, which allows for the flow of current information. The research results confirm this relationship with regard to the business and efficiency effects but do not support the conjecture on the management effects. This is puzzling, since in principle ERP managers should facilitate rational decision-making (in the CBM as well). On the other hand, CBM supports ERP in the field of orientation towards the employee, and therefore the employee's knowledge and skills. This translates to higher business, performance and management effects achieved by an organisation in which two methods coexist, rather than those achieved when only ERP is implemented (without CBM).

Contemporary organisations need to apply various management methods and concepts (Jagoda and Lichtarski 2003; Sułkowski 2004; Sobczak 2009; Szpitter 2011). The results of the research confirm this thesis—implementing two methods helps to achieve a synergistic effect, which would not be achieved if the concepts were used separately. In the view of the authors, the issues presented in the paper should be treated as an introduction to the discussion of the coexistence of ERP and other management methods. What seems to be particularly important is to indicate the methods, to determine the influence of the implementation of particular management methods on the efficiency of ERP itself and to define the model solutions in this respect. At the same time, changing perspective into more general one could bring interesting results in the field of the coexistence of contemporary management methods and, in particular, to the issue of determining the character of the relations of particular method pairs, as well as examining the order and scope of implementing the methods.

Other problems that need further investigation are the changes of the relations in time, the indication of the complementary methods, the consideration of their possible hierarchisation, the order of implementation, the possibility of the substitution use of methods (some methods can be more adjusted to the existing solutions in the organisation or to the organisational culture than others), the clear indication of which methods can be really considered contradicting, and how the character of the relations changes with time.

Appendix

See Table 4.

Table 4 Results of one-way ANOVA: the coexistence of ERP with selected management methods and organisational effects (only significant mean differences are included)

		N	M	SD	Sig. lev.	F statistic
Business effects						
ERP and BPM	No method	62	3.66	0.43	0.000	F(3,151) = 8.92; p < 0.001
	Only BPM	46	3.64	0.31	0.000	
	Only ERP	22	3.62	0.39	0.000	
	ERP and BPM	25	4.08	0.42	–	
ERP and KM	No method	81	3.63	0.37	0.001	F(3,151) = 4.99; p < 0.01
	Only KM	27	3.70	0.43	0.037	
	ERP and KM	18	4.03	0.56	–	
ERP and controlling	No method	64	3.61	0.37	0.000	F(3,151) = 6.84; p < 0.001
	Only controlling	44	3.70	0.40	0.014	
	Only ERP	15	3.61	0.42	0.014	
	ERP and controlling	32	3.99	0.44	–	
ERP and CRM	No method	71	3.62	0.39	0.000	F(3,151) = 5.72; p < 0.01
	Only CRM	37	3.71	0.36	0.032	
	Only ERP	20	3.70	0.44	0.062*	
	ERP and CRM	27	3.99	0.45	–	
ERP and CBM	No method	93	3.67	0.34	0.000	F(3,151) = 10.53; p < 0.001
	Only CBM	15	3.52	0.58	0.000	
	Only ERP	32	3.70	0.43	0.000	
	ERP and CBM	15	4.23	0.32	–	
ERP and TQM	No method	69	3.67	0.40	0.021	F(3,151) = 3.82; p < 0.05
	Only TQM	39	3.62	0.36	0.013	
	ERP and TQM	25	3.94	0.54	–	

(continued)

Table 4 (continued)

		N	M	SD	Sig. lev.	F statistic
ERP and benchmarking	No method	90	3.62	0.38	0.000	F(3,151) = 8.37; p < 0.001
	Only benchmarking	18	3.78	0.35	0.012	
	Only ERP	37	3.76	0.42	0.003	
	ERP and benchmarking	10	4.26	0.44	–	
ERP and BPR	No method	106	3.64	0.38	0.008	F(3,151) = 4.47; p < 0.01
	ERP and BPR	13	4.03	0.43	–	
ERP and outsourcing	No method	77	3.64	0.39	0.001	F(3,151) = 5.28; p < 0.01
	Only outsourcing	31	3.68	0.36	0.014	
	Only ERP	27	3.74	0.46	0.068*	
	ERP and outsourcing	20	4.04	0.43	–	
ERP and six sigma	No method	100	3.65	0.39	0.001	F(3,151) = 5.86; p < 0.01
	Only six sigma	8	3.59	0.16	0.008	
	Only ERP	40	3.80	0.46	0.030	
	ERP and six sigma	7	4.26	0.31	–	
ERP and BSC	No method	102	3.65	0.39	0.000	F(3,151) = 8.26; p < 0.001
	Only BSC	6	3.63	0.24	0.008	
	Only ERP	37	3.75	0.43	0.001	
	ERP and BSC	10	4.29	0.34		
ERP and LM	No method	90	3.65	0.35	0.000	F(3,151) = 8.86; p < 0.001
	Only ERP	26	3.66	0.40	0.000	
	Only LM	18	3.64	0.52	0.001	
	ERP and LM	21	4.12	0.42	–	
Efficiency effects						
ERP and BPM	No method	64	3.71	0.51	0.048	F(3,154) = 3.86; p < 0.05
	Only BPM	48	3.62	0.52	0.009	
	Only ERP	23	3.62	0.46	0.030	
	ERP and BPM	23	4.02	0.42	–	
ERP and controlling	No method	66	3.59	0.52	0.052*	F(3,154) = 2.65; p = 0.051
	ERP and controlling	30	3.88	0.50	–	
ERP and CRM	No method	73	3.70	0.54	0.098*	F(3,154) = 2.71; p < 0.05
	Only CRM	39	3.63	0.46	0.044	
	ERP and CRM	26	3.96	0.48	–	
ERP and CBM	No method	97	3.69	0.51	0.020	F(3,154) = 3.39; p < 0.05
	Only CBM	15	3.57	0.56	0.023	
	Only ERP	32	3.70	0.46	0.056*	
	ERP and CBM	14	4.10	0.41	–	

(continued)

Table 4 (continued)

		N	M	SD	Sig. lev.	F statistic
ERP and TQM	No method	71	3.62	0.56	0.011	F(3,154) = 3.52; p < 0.05
	Only ERP	23	3.65	0.38	0.085*	
	ERP and TQM	23	4.00	0.52	–	
ERP and benchmarking	No method	92	3.66	0.52	0.005	F(3,154) = 3.81; p < 0.05
	Only benchmar.	20	3.74	0.47	0.074*	
	Only ERP	36	3.71	0.44	0.028	
	ERP and benchmar.	10	4.21	0.45	–	
ERP and six sigma	No method	103	3.67	0.53	0.025	F(3,154) = 2.83; p < 0.05
	ERP and six sigma	7	4.22	0.31	–	
ERP and BSC	No method	106	3.66	0.52	0.003	F(3,154) = 4.26; p < 0.01
	Only ERP	36	3.71	0.43	0.017	
	ERP and BSC	10	4.23	0.45	–	
LM and ERP	No method	91	3.64	0.52	0.013	F(3,154) = 3.59; p < 0.05
	LM and ERP	20	4.01	0.48	–	
Management effects						
ERP and BPM	No method	64	3.68	0.50	0.092*	F(3,155) = 2.80; p < 0.05
	Only BPM	47	3.63	0.49	0.043	
	Only ERP	23	3.61	0.43	0.081	
	ERP and BPM	25	3.94	0.46	–	
ERP and KM	No method	83	3.62	0.53	0.013	F(3,155) = 3.32; p < 0.05
	Only ERP	31	3.65	0.40	0.063	
	ERP and KM	17	4.02	0.51	–	
ERP and CBM	No method	97	3.64	0.49	0.002	F(3,155) = 4.95; p < 0.01
	Only ERP	33	3.63	0.41	0.005	
	ERP and CBM	15	4.12	0.42	–	
ERP and benchmarking	No method	91	3.65	0.49	0.018	F(3,155) = 2.97; p < 0.05
	Only benchmarking	20	3.67	0.51	0.072	
	Only ERP	38	3.69	0.45	0.056	
	ERP and benchmark.	10	4.13	0.39	–	
ERP and six sigma	No method	102	3.66	0.49	0.016	F(3,155) = 3.12; p < 0.05
	Only six sigma	9	3.62	0.58	0.064	
	Only ERP	41	3.71	0.44	0.046	
	ERP and six sigma	7	4.22	0.39	–	
Management effects						
ERP and BSC	No method	105	3.65	0.48	0.004	F(3,155) = 4.04; p < 0.01
	Only ERP	38	3.67	0.43	0.012	
	ERP and BSC	10	4.20	0.41	–	

(continued)

Table 4 (continued)

		N	M	SD	Sig. lev.	F statistic
LM and ERP	No method	91	3.67	0.50	0.024	F(3,155) = 3.41; p < 0.05
	Only ERP	28	3.62	0.44	0.034	
	Only LM	20	3.60	0.47	0.040	
	LM and ERP	20	4.01	0.42	–	
Social effects						
ERP and KM	Only ERP	31	3.50	0.51	0.031	F(3,157) = 3.40; p < 0.05
	ERP and KM	18	3.92	0.56	–	
ERP and CBM	No method	96	3.60	0.50	0.021	F(3,157) = 4.22; p < 0.01
	Only ERP	34	3.49	0.55	0.007	
	ERP and CBM	15	4.01	0.42	–	
ERP and BSC	No method	106	3.62	0.52	0.020	F(3,157) = 3.51; p < 0.05
	Only ERP	39	3.53	0.53	0.009	
	ERP and BSC	10	4.12	0.45	–	
Environmental effects						
ERP and CRM	Only ERP	21	3.49	0.40	0.019	F(3,155) = 4.40; p < 0.01
	ERP and CRM	28	3.96	0.46	–	
Only ERP	Only CRM	36	3.89	0.54	0.042	F(3,155) = 4.40; p < 0.01
	Only ERP	21	3.49	0.40	–	
	ERP and CRM	28	3.96	0.46	0.019	

*Slightly outside the significance level

References

Al-Mashari M, Al-Mudimigh A, Zairi M (2003) Enterprise resource planning: a taxonomy of critical factors. EJOR 146(2):352–364. doi:10.1016/S0377-2217(02)00554-4

Aloini D, Dulmin R, Mininno V (2012) Risk assessment in ERP projects. Inf Syst 37(3):183–199. doi:10.1016/j.is.2011.10.001

Bieńkowska A, Zgrzywa-Ziemak A (2011) Współczesne metody zarządzania w przedsiębiorstwach funkcjonujących w Polsce – identyfikacja stanu istniejącego. In: Hopej M, Kral Z (eds) Współczesne metody zarządzania w teorii i praktyce. Oficyna Wydawnicza PWr, Wrocław, pp 211–252

Bieńkowska A, Zgrzywa-Ziemak A (2013) Rezultaty stosowania TQM wspólnie z innymi metodami zarządzania. PN UE we Wrocławiu 277:120–133

Bieńkowska A, Walecka-Jankowska K, Zgrzywa-Ziemak A (2013) Zarządzanie wiedzą i inne metody – efekty współwystępowania. Przegląd Organizacji 9:10–16

Cebeci U (2009) Fuzzy AHP-based decision support system for selecting ERP systems in textile industry by using balanced scorecard. Expert Syst Appl 36:8900–8909. doi:10.1016/j.eswa.2008.11.046

Chan EWL, Walker DHT, Mills A (2009) Using a KM framework to evaluate an ERP system implementation. J Knowl Manag 13(2):93–109. doi:10.1108/13673270910942727

Cotteleer MJ, Bendoly E (2006) Order lead-time improvement following enterprise information technology implementation: an empirical study. MIS Q 30(3):643–660

Davenport TH (2000) Mission critical: realizing the promise of enterprise systems. HBSP, Boston

Gable G (1998) Large package software: a neglected technology. J Glob Inf Manag 6(3):3–4

Galy E, Sauceda MJ (2014) Post-implementation practices of ERP systems and their relationship to financial performance. Inf Manag 51(3):310–319. doi:10.1016/j.im.2014.02.002

Hendricks KB, Singhal VR, Stratman JK (2007) The impact of enterprise systems on corporate performance: a study of ERP, SCM, and CRM system implementations. J Oper Manag 25:65–82. doi:10.1016/j.jom.2006.02.002

Hitt LM, Wu DJ, Zhou X (2002) Investment in enterprise resource planning: business impact and productivity measures. J Manag Inf Syst 19(1):71–98. doi:10.1080/07421222.2002.11045716

Holsapple C, Sena M (1999) Enterprise system for organizational decision support: a research agenda. In: Proceedings of AMCIS

Jagoda H, Lichtarski J (2003) O istocie i ewolucji współczesnych koncepcji i metod zarządzania przedsiębiorstwem. Przegląd Organizacji 1:3–6

Jha VS, Joshi H (2007) Relevance of total quality management (TQM) or business excellence strategy implementation for enterprise resource planning (ERP) – a conceptual study. In: Proceedings of the 12th international conference on information quality. MIT, Cambridge

Kale V (2001) SAP R/3. Przewodnik dla menedżerów [SAP R/3. A guide for managers]. Helion, Gliwice

Kasprzak T (2005) Organizacja zorientowana na procesy biznesu – modelowanie referencyjne. In: Kasprzak T (ed) Modele referencyjne w zarządzaniu procesami biznesu. DIFIN, Warszawa

Katerattanakul P, Lee JJ, Hong S (2014) Effect of business characteristics and ERP implementation on business outcomes: an exploratory study of Korean manufacturing firms. Manag Res Rev 37(2):186–206. doi:10.1108/MRR-10-2012-0218

Kieser A, Walgenlach P (2003) Organisation. Schäffer-Poeschel, Stuttgart

Kluge PD, Kużdowicz P (2011) Rachunek kosztów i pomiar dokonań w cyklu zarządzania przedsiębiorstwem wspomaganym systemem ERP. In: Nowak E, Nieplowicz M (eds) Rachunek kosztów i dokonań, vol 182, PN UE we Wrocławiu. Wydawnictwo UE we Wrocławiu, Wrocław, pp 228–237

Koslowski DKT, Strüker J (2011) ERP on demand platform. Bus Inf Syst Eng 3(6):359–367

Kowalak R (2009) Benchmarking jako metoda zarządzania wspomagająca controlling przedsiębiorstwa. Wydawnictwo UE we Wrocławiu, Wrocław

Laframboise K, Reyes F (2005) Gaining competitive advantage from integrating enterprise resource planning and total quality management. J Supply Chain Manag 41(3):49–64. doi:10.1111/j.1055-6001.2005.04103005.x

Li L, Markowski C, Xu L, Markowski E (2008) TQM – a predecessor of ERP implementation. Int J Prod Econ 115:569–580. doi:10.1016/j.ijpe.2008.07.004

Liang H, Xue Y (2004) Coping with ERP-related contextual issues in SMEs: a vendor's perspective. J Strateg Inf Syst 13:399–415. doi:10.1016/j.jsis.2004.11.006

McAfee A (2002) The impact of enterprise information technology adoption on operational performance: an empirical investigation. Prod Oper Manag J 11(1):33–53

McGinnis TC, Huang Z (2007) Rethinking ERP success: a new perspective from knowledge management and continuous improvement. Inf Manag 44:626–634. doi:10.1016/j.im.2007.05.006

Metaxiotis K (2009) Exploring the rationales for ERP and knowledge management integration in SMEs. J Enterp Inf Manag 22(1/2):51–62. doi:10.1108/17410390910922822

Movahedi MM, Nouri Koupaei M (2011) A framework for applying ERP in effective implementation of TQM. Middle-East J Sci Res 10(4):489–495

Pang-Lo L (2011) Empirical study on influence of critical success factors on ERP knowledge management on management performance in high-tech industries in Taiwan. Expert Syst Appl 38(8):10696–10704. doi:10.1016/j.eswa.2011.02.045

Satzinger JW, Jackson R, Burd SD (2011) Systems analysis and design in a changing world. Cengage Learning, Boston

Schniederjans MJ, Kim GC (2003) Implementing enterprise resource planning systems with total quality control and business process reengineering: survey results. IJOPM 23(4):418–429

Sobczak T (2009) O koncepcjach i metodach w naukach o zarządzaniu w Polsce. Przegląd Organizacji 10:6–9

Stratman JK, Roth AV (2002) Enterprise resource planning (ERP) competence constructs: two-stage multi-item scale development and validation. Decis Sci 33(4):601–628. doi:10.1111/j.1540-5915.2002.tb01658.x

Sułkowski Ł (2004) Problem niewspółmierności koncepcji w zarządzaniu. Przegląd Organizacji 4:6–8

Szpitter AA (2011) Koncepcje zarządzania – próba klasyfikacji. Przegląd Organizacji 10:9–12

Varzandeh J, Farahbod K (2010) Comparative and strategic role of ERP in six sigma quality. ASBBS Annu Conf Las Vegas 17(1):511–516

Industry Concentration and Performance: Case of Life Insurance Industry

Zuzana Brokešová, Tomáš Ondruška, Erika Pastoráková, and Jana Péliová

Abstract Industry concentration is traditionally used as a measure of the competition in the industry. If the concentration of the industry increases then small number of firms can dominate the industry, which could on the one hand increase the prices for customers. But it is not necessarily a negative situation as with the increase in firm size they may be able to benefit from economies of scale. Therefore, higher concentrated market may cause higher prices as well as higher profits and performance. This is likely to occur in industries with high fixed costs and scope for specialization as life insurance industry. Based on this assumption, we decided to reveal the presence of a link between the changes in the industry concentration and market performance. For the purpose of the analysis, we use life insurance industry data from the Slovak Republic during the period 1993–2012. During analyzed period, this industry has developed from monopolistic market with one dominant insurance company and few very small ones to competitive market with 19 insurance companies offering life insurance products in 2012. Our model proved that decreasing life insurance industry concentration increases profit and performance of the industry.

Keywords Industry concentration • Industry performance • Life insurance

1 Introduction

Life insurance is broadly defined as a "deferred consumption". Therefore, it can provide the necessary financial resources in case of change in the individual consumption due to, e.g. death or illness (Greene and Trieschmann 1988). In particular, individuals typically have three motives to buying life insurance products: the desire to smooth consumption over time, bequests, and tax advantages (Melnic and Everitt 2008). However, research conducted by Hammond et al. (1967) shows that one of the main incentive for purchasing life insurance is to secure dependents against the financial losses that would jeopardize household in the event of death

Z. Brokešová (✉) • T. Ondruška • E. Pastoráková • J. Péliová
University of Economics in Bratislava, Bratislava, Slovakia
e-mail: zuzana.brokesova@euba.sk; tomas.ondruska@euba.sk; erika.pastorakova@euba.sk; jana.peliova@euba.sk

T. Dudycz et al. (eds.), *The Essence and Measurement of Organizational Efficiency*, Springer Proceedings in Business and Economics, DOI 10.1007/978-3-319-21139-8_3

of the breadwinner. Therefore, efficiently functioning life insurance market could help to sustain the wealth of society.

In the Slovak Republic, the importance of life insurance started to grow slowly after the origin of Republic in 1993. While non-life insurance dominated among Slovak population for more than decade, since 1995 and during the first decade of new millennium the role of life insurance has started increasing faster and more dynamically. After all, the life insurance consumption exceeded the non-life insurance measured by the amount of gross written premium in 2008 for a first time. This increased interest and newly elicited demand also flew into the changes on the supply side of life insurance. The structure of the Slovak insurance market varied significantly during this period. From the starting point, when only 6 life insurance companies[1] operated on this market in 1993, to 19 insurance companies offering life insurance products in 2012. Market structure was developed from monopolistic market with the one dominant insurance company and few very small in 1993 to medium concentrated and competitive market in 2012. However, have these significant changes in competition also affected the performance of the industry? And does lower concentration evoke higher performance?

The main aim of the paper is to reveal the presence of a link between the changes in the industry concentration and market performance. For the purpose of the analysis, we use life insurance industry data from the Slovak Republic during the period 1993–2012.

The remainder of the paper is organized as follows. In the first section, we provide the basic theoretical background as well as a literature review and results of previous research. In the second part, we discuss the methodology used and the data. The next two sections cover the main results, their analysis and the resulting conclusions.

2 Literature Review

Industry concentration is traditionally used as a measure of the market structure and the competition in the industry. If the concentration of the industry increases then small number of firms can dominate the industry and they are able to create externality in the form of monopoly power. This change could on the one hand increase the prices for customers but is not necessarily a negative situation as with the increase in firm size they may be able to benefit from economies of scale. This is likely to occur in industries with high fixed costs and scope for specialization as life insurance industry. According to Weiss (1974) and Choi and Weiss (2005), collusive behaviour should be more frequently observed in highly concentrated market, since only a relatively small number of firms must agree to collude. Therefore,

[1] As a life insurance company, we consider all insurance companies that offer life insurance products on the market.

higher concentrated market may causes higher prices as well as higher profits and performance (Ellickson 2014). However, in the economic theory this relation is not so apparent.

The Structure Conduct Performance (SCP) hypothesis explains performance via conduct market structure (Mason 1939; Bain 1951). Seminal work in this area is done by Bain (1951), who expects that concentrated markets encouraged oligopolistic behaviour among the competitors. Further research supports his assumptions about the existence of relation between market structure and market performance. However, direction of this relation lacks consensus and varies across the literature.

Empirical investigation of SCP paradigm was mainly implemented on the banking system data (e.g. Smirlock 1985; Goldberg and Rai 1996; Berger and Hannan 1998; Maudos 1998) and there is only a few studies, which analyse insurance industry data (e.g. Cummins et al. 1972; Weiss 1974; Jung 1987; Carroll 1993; Chidambaran et al. 1997; Bajtelsmit and Bouzouita 1998; Choi and Weiss 2005; Pope and Ma 2008; Bikker 2012). Only one of them, Cummins et al. (1972), focuses on life insurance industry at our knowledge. In addition, banking studies are primarily focused on individual companies, while majority of the insurance studies use country aggregated data (Carroll 1993; Bajtelsmit and Bouzouita 1998; Chidambaran et al. 1997). Results of these studies are ambiguous. For example, Bajtelsmit and Bouzouita (1998) focus on automobile insurance and their results show positive and significant relation between market performance and market concentration. On contrary, Cummins et al. (1972) find also statistical significant but inverse relation between market concentration and market performance. According to their analysis of the U.S. life insurance industry, these variables are inversely related, which indicates a positive relationship between market concentration and profitability. However, these results are weaker in comparison to banks and non-life insurers.

3 Methodology and Data

In the research, we focus on the verification of the SCP hypothesis in the data of the Slovak life insurance industry during the period from 1993 to 2012. We use a linear regression model on a country level with robust standard errors. Data are log-log transformed for interpretation as elasticity.

Model specification is as follows:

$$\pi_t = \beta_0 + \beta_1 \mathrm{HHI} + \beta_2 \mathrm{gGWP} + \varepsilon_t \tag{1}$$

where t refers to time, $t \in (1, 2, \ldots, 20)$, ε_t refers to unobservable random disturbance and β_0, β_1, β_2 are regression coefficients of key explanatory variables used to evaluate SCP hypothesis. We use underwriting profit in life insurance industry in Slovak Republic (π_t) as a dependent variable. In our analysis, it represents an indicator of market performance, while underwriting profit is a profit

Table 1 Descriptive statistics

Variable	N	Mean	St. Dev	Min	Max
π_t	20	162,173.1	150,363.7	−23,927.15	581,774.8
HHI	20	2858.97	2196.60	1231.27	7271.63
gGWP	19	1.17	0.15	0.94	1.55

that insurance companies obtain from direct insurance services, i.e. earned premium remaining after deduction of paid claims and administrative costs linked to life insurance. By this profit, we can approximate real profit from life insurance products in Slovak insurance market while these values are adjusted from non-direct insurance operations of insurance companies. As for log transformation, positive values are required and this assumption is not fully applicable to all values, we have to add a constant to all observations. Life insurance market concentration approximated by the Herfindahl-Hirschman index (HHI) represents an explanatory variable. Herfindahl-Hirschman index is a sum of squared market shares of firms, where increased value of index represents increased market concentration as well. According to the U.S. Department of Justice, market with a result of less than 1000 to be a competitive marketplace while a result of 1800 or greater indicated highly concentrated marketplace (Rhoades 1993). In the estimation, we also incorporate a control variable for market growth—growth of Gross Written Premium. However, the role of market growth varies based on the barriers to entry (Choi and Weiss 2005). When the barriers to market entry are low the market growth entices new insurers to enter the market. But on the other hand, when the barriers to market entry are significantly high then the growth of market evoke increasing in profitability of insurance companies.

As SCP hypothesis predicts, simultaneous cause-and-effect relationship between market structure and market performance (Choi and Weiss 2005), Augmented Durbin-Wu-Hausman (DWH) test are conducted for the Eq. (1) to determine whether the suspect variables are endogenous. In the time series sample, we rejected presence of unit root by Augmented Dickey–Fuller test ($p < 0.001$). Serial correlation in regressions were rejected by Durbin–Watson statistic ($p > 0.05$).

Dataset is obtained from the database of the National Bank of Slovakia (NBS 2014) and descriptive statistics are shown in Table 1.

4 Results and Discussion

The life insurance industry has developed dynamically in the Slovak Republic during the analyzed period, which was driven mainly by socio-economic, law and institutional changes. Step by step with these changes arose the integration efforts of Slovak Republic into international organizations like OECD, NATO and the European Union. Necessary harmonization of the legislation and integrated financial services supervisions had a major impact on the changes that occurred in the private insurance industry. Since 1995, the role of life insurance has started increasing faster and more dynamically. Changes in needs of population started to turn mainly property and liability coverage oriented insurance market on to market offering wide variety of life insurance products.

Improving life insurance industry performance also motivated new insurance companies for enter to the market. Market benefited not only by the entry of new specialized foreign companies that brought new know-how and labor opportunities but also by the increased competition between new and established companies. Efficiency and competition on the life insurance sector are important not only for companies but also for households to keep premiums low and innovation and quality high (Bikker 2012). Those changes did not result only in the increased number of insurance companies but in overall benefits in supply as well as demand for life insurance products. Attractiveness of the life insurance had increased especially during the years 2006 and 2011, when clients could use tax advantage of life insurance. Entrant insurance companies offering life insurance products brought also new types of policies for consumers with wider coverage and services that were usual in developed economies. Majority of these "new" companies were subsidiary firms of international companies with foreign capital. Turning point in the Slovak insurance industry was the merge of the dominant insurance company Slovenská poisťovna, a.s. (with life insurance market share 28.32 % in 2002 followed by Kooperativa poisťovňa, a.s. with 11.86 %) and Allianz poisťovňa, a.s. (with life insurance market share 5.43 % in 2002) in 2003. The life insurance market share of new merged Allianz—Slovenská poisťovňa, a.s. was 30.08 % in 2003. But its market share in life insurance was decreasing during the following years and nearly equalized the share around 20 % with the Kooperativa poisťovňa, a.s. in 2012. However, half of the life insurance market according to gross written premium was controlled by three insurance companies.

Main indicators of life insurance market development as gross written premium, share of life insurance, insurance penetration and density are shown in reduced form of 4 years periods in Table 2 (OECD 2014). Chosen period is illustrated by not only growing numbers of entities offering life insurance products but also by the increase in the gross written premium, share of life insurance, insurance penetration and density.

From Table 2, it is evident that during the analyzed period, the gross written premium in life insurance industry has increased by almost 18 times. Also the share of the life insurance on the whole industry has risen from less then quarter in 1993 to more than 55 % in 2012. Market performance measured as underwriting profit of life insurance industry has increased, while life insurance market concentration measured by Herfindahl-Hirschman index has decreased.

In Table 3, we can see inverse relation between market performance and market structure. Due to identified endogeneity, with respect to the concentration variables and gross written premium growth in Eq. (1) by Augmented Durbin-Wu-Hausman (DWH) test, we decided conduct Instrumental variables (2SLS) regression. In this model, we assumed that market concentration in life insurance industry (ln_HHI) is

Table 2 Indicators of life insurance industry in the Slovak Republic

Variable	1993	1997	2001	2005	2009	2012
Gross written premium (millions EUR)	65.43	156.79	457.41	731.33	1062.10	1165.6
Share of life insurance (%)	23.47	26.94	42,90	42.50	52.39	55.13
Insurance penetration (%)	0.38	0.51	0.94	1.85	1.69	1.63
Insurance density (EUR)	12.28	29.13	85.02	135.75	196.02	215.55
Market share of foreign life insurance companies in the domestic market	N/A	25.14	55.95	92.43	91.56	90.20
Underwriting profit (thousands EUR)	−16.23	24.18	151.88	295.89	221.38	122.31
Herfindahl-Hirschman index	7272	5199	1739	1391	1377	1231
Number of life insurance companies	6	22	22	21	17	19

Table 3 Regression results

$\ln\pi_t$	Instrumental variables (2SLS) regression
lnHHI	−2.713257***
	(0.8076294)
lngGWP	1.405165
	(1.436591)
Constant	32.09582***
	(5.870782)
R-squared	0.6602
Prob > chi2	0.0031

Note: Regarding the instrumental variables (2SLS) regression: Instrumented: lnHHI, Instruments: lnGWP, lngIC, ** and *** denote significance at the 5 and 1 % level, respectively

in relation with the amount of gross written premium in life insurance industry (lngGWP) and the yearly change of absolute value of life insurance companies (lngIC). We decided to implement this variable mainly due to fact that traditional SCP hypothesis omits the possibility of insurance companies to entry the market (Choi and Weiss 2005). However, due to the observed development in Slovak Republic, the number of insurance companies varies during this period. The industry has also witnessed tremendous growth in the number of life insurance entities, mainly between 1993 and 1996, when their number more than doubled.

Model shows that with decreasing market concentration increases profit, which supports the results of Cummins et al. (1972). Our results also support empirical evidence of Zhang and Zhu (2005) and Sliwinski et al. (2013) that monopolistic insurance markets are less developed than competitive and also the level of performance of the market is significantly lower. Therefore, the social and economic transformations, the break-up of monopolies and growing competition in the Slovak Republic have contributed to the increase of life insurance industry performance.

5 Conclusions

The paper examines the relationships between the changes in the industry concentration and market performance. For the purpose of the analysis, we use life insurance industry data from the Slovak Republic during the period 1993–2012. We performed Instrumental variables (2SLS) regression to identify the statistically significant relation between the development of market concentration and market performance. Model proved that decreasing market concentration increases profit, which supports previous results of Cummins et al. (1972). In addition, our results support empirical evidence of Zhang and Zhu (2005) and Sliwinski et al. (2013) that monopolistic insurance markets are less developed than competitive and likewise the level of performance of the industry is significantly lower. Improving of the Slovak life insurance industry performance caused several changes in the market. As the positive changes in life insurance industry during the analyzed period, we consider: increased market share and gross written premium; growth in the number of insurance entities and increased competitiveness; wider coverage and services; and better performance. On the other hand, changing conditions caused also the negative consequences on the market performance linked primarily with fusions and acquisitions. These increase the market concentration, which according to our results may lead to the decrease of market performance and affects life insurance companies as well as their clients. Regulation authorities, therefore, should be very careful with the mergers and acquisitions permission in the area of life insurance.

It is important to note that while in the manufacturing industry, the benefits of merger and acquisition transactions lie primarily on the acquisition of know-how as well as on mutual research and development to reduce costs, in case of life insurance companies and other financial institutions mergers and acquisitions are on the front burden the enhance of a market position and gain of the potential of the clients. This is the reason why the interest of the regulators should be concerned on the fusions and acquisitions and moreover our results are confirming that the monopolistic markets cause less efficiency and performance from which neither insurance companies nor clients benefit. For the better performance of the insurance industry, as the significant part of the economy, is necessary to focus on the effects of the fusions and acquisitions to the market structure.

The main limitation of our paper is the aggregated character of used dataset, where the results are based on very few observations. Therefore, our current results about the presence of relation between market structure and market performance development are not robust. However in the further research, we would like to confirm our results by extended model based on individual companies' data and incorporation of the analysis of efficiency changes role in this relation. In addition, deeper analysis of endogeneity among analyze variables will be in the area of our further interest.

Acknowledgments This paper is part of a research project No. 1/0431/14 entitled 'Insurance Relationship as a Key Element of the Insurance Sector Operation in the Context of Socio-economic Changes' and project No. 1/0849/15 entitled 'Economic and social aspects of the information asymmetry in the insurance market' provided by the Ministry of Education, Science, Research and Sport of the Slovak Republic.

References

Bain JS (1951) Relation of profit-rate to industry concentration: American manufacturing, 1936–1940. Q J Econ 65(3):293–324

Bajtelsmit VL, Bouzouita R (1998) Market structure and performance in private passenger automobile insurance. J Risk Insur 65(3):503–514

Berger AN, Hannan TH (1998) The efficiency cost of market power in the banking industry: a test of the "Quiet Life" and related hypotheses. Rev Econ Stat 80(3):454–465

Bikker JA (2012) Performance of the life insurance industry under pressure: efficiency, competition and consolidation. https://ideas.repec.org/p/dnb/dnbwpp/357.html. Accessed 3 Oct 2014

Carroll AM (1993) An empirical investigation of the structure and performance of the private workers' compensation market. J Risk Insur 60(2):185–207

Chidambaran NK, Pugel TA, Saunders A (1997) An investigation of the performance of the U.S. property-liability insurance industry. J Risk Insur 64(2):371–381

Choi BP, Weiss MA (2005) An empirical investigation of market structure, efficiency, and performance in property-liability insurance. J Risk Insur 72(4):635–673

Cummins JD, Denenberg HS, Scheel WC (1972) Concentration in the U.S. life insurance industry. J Risk Insur 39(2):177–199

Ellickson PB (2014) Market structure and performance. In: Wright JD (ed) International encyclopedia of the social and behavioral sciences, 2nd edn. Elsevier, Oxford

Goldberg LG, Rai A (1996) The structure-performance relationship for European banking. J Bank Finance 20(4):745–771

Greene MR, Trieschmann JS (1988) Risk and insurance. South-Western, Chicago

Hammond JD, Houston DB, Melander ER (1967) Determinants of household life insurance premium expenditures: an empirical investigation. J Risk Insur 34(3):397–408

Jung BD (1987) Market structure, conduct, and performance of the U.S. property and liability insurance industry: a theoretical and empirical examination. Dissertation, University of Texas at Austin

Mason ES (1939) Price and production policies of large-scale enterprise. Am Econ Rev 29(1): 61–74

Maudos J (1998) Market structure and performance in Spanish banking using a direct measure of efficiency. Appl Financ Econ 8(2):191–200

Melnic EL, Everitt BS (eds) (2008) Encyclopedia of quantitative risk analysis and assessment, vol 3. Wiley, New York

NBS (2014) Statistika poistovní a penzijnych fondov. http://www.nbs.sk/sk/statisticke-udaje/statistika-poistovni-a-penzijnych-fondov. Accessed 26 Oct 2014

OECD (2014) Insurance indicators. http://stats.oecd.org/Index.aspx?QueryId=25437#. Accessed 20 Oct 2014

Pope N, Ma YL (2008) The market structure–performance relationship in the international insurance sector. J Risk Insur 75(4):947–966

Rhoades SA (1993) The Herfindahl-Hirschman index. Fed Reserv Bull 79(3):188–189

Sliwinski A, Michalski T, Roszkiewicz M (2013) Demand for life insurance – an empirical analysis in the case of Poland. Geneva Paper Risk Insur Issues Pract 38(1):62–87

Smirlock M (1985) Evidence on the (non) relationship between concentration and profitability in banking. J Money Credit Bank 17(1):69–83

Weiss LW (1974) The concentration-profits relationship and antitrust. In: Goldschmid HJ, Mann HM, Weston JF (eds) Industrial concentration: the new learning. Little Brown, Boston, pp 184–233

Zhang C, Zhu N (2005) Determinants of the development of insurance in China under the globalization. http://www.cerdi.org/uploads/sfCmsContent/html/200/Zhang_31.pdf. Accessed 26 Oct 2014

Communication Infrastructure and Enterprise Effectiveness

Maria Fic and Mariusz Malinowski

Abstract The objective of this article is to define the relationship between the development level of communication infrastructure and the effectiveness of enterprises in individual voivodeships in Poland. First, we describe communication infrastructure as a subsystem of economic infrastructure, and discuss the impact of communication infrastructure on the functioning of enterprises. Next, we empirically analyse the relationship between the development of communication infrastructure and the effectiveness of enterprises. The problem of the measurement of enterprise effectiveness, although studied in numerous research analyses, has not been comprehensively solved. In this article we attempt to create a synthetic measure of economic effectiveness of enterprises, seizing on an earlier selected set of diagnostic variables. The application of synthetic measures that use one aggregate indicator instead of a series of variables to describe objects, enables us to quantify the multidimensional nature of economic operations and systematize them in a linear way. Our analysis covers all 16 Polish voivodeships. The methodological approach is based on Hellwig's method, correlation and spatial autocorrelation analysis. The main criterion of variable selection was completeness and availability of data for the period 2003–2011.

Keywords Effectiveness of enterprises • Communication infrastructure • Synthetic measures

1 Introduction

The effectiveness of enterprises depends on both internal and external factors of their functioning. Infrastructure constitutes an irreplaceable and universal regional resource, which can be used by entities operating in various industries to increase their effectiveness and competitive potential. The specific characteristics of communication infrastructure (transport and communications) in a given region (e.g. capital intensity, spatial immobility, long period of formation) makes it a strategic resource for enterprises operating in this region. Without a certain

M. Fic, Ph.D. (✉) • M. Malinowski, Ph.D.
Wrocław University of Technology, Wrocław, Poland
e-mail: maria.fic@pwr.wroc.pl; malinowski.mariusz@op.pl

T. Dudycz et al. (eds.), *The Essence and Measurement of Organizational Efficiency*,
Springer Proceedings in Business and Economics, DOI 10.1007/978-3-319-21139-8_4

minimum level of infrastructure, the functioning of any enterprise becomes practically impossible. This element determines the usage of other factors, that define the effectiveness of entities located in the area. Largely, it results from the fact that classical manufacturing factors, as distinguished by Smith and Ricardo, including capital, natural and human resources (among others mineral resources), are usually characterized by significant mobility, and the effectiveness of these resources, depends on the infrastructure.

In a knowledge based economy, universal and constant access to information becomes particularly significant. Nowadays, information becomes a strategic resource in economic processes. The spatial character of enterprise activity implies the need to create conditions that improve the circulation of information between individual market entities. In view of the need to respond effectively to the market needs, as well as adjust the market offer, rapid circulation of information gains special significance. With increasing competition, obtaining information as well as its fast circulation determines the smooth functioning of the market. Communication infrastructure plays thus a very important role in enterprise activity, since, enabling access to information, determines not only the efficiency of enterprise functioning, but also their existence (e-commerce). The aim of this article is to identify the relationship between communication infrastructure and enterprise efficiency. First, we describe communication infrastructure as a subsystem of economic infrastructure and discuss the impact of communication infrastructure on the functioning of enterprises. Next, we conduct an empirical analysis of the relationship between the level of development of communication infrastructure and enterprise effectiveness. Our analysis encompasses all 16 Polish voivodeships. We use the Hellwig's method, as well as correlation and spatial autocorrelation analysis. The main criterion of variable selection was completeness and availability of data for 2003–2011. We used data from the Local Database of the Central Statistical Office, and from the Financial results of economic entities (Central Statistical Office).

2 Communication Infrastructure and Effectiveness of Enterprises

When defining infrastructure, authors often emphasize the fact that it is a vital prerequisite for socio-economic activity. Dziembowski presents a very broad definition of infrastructure as the long term tangible assets enabling the functioning of institutions and economic entities, as well as providing adequate living conditions for the population (Dziembowski 1985). Kupiec et al. define infrastructure as public equipment essential to ensure adequate functioning of the national economy, appropriately distributed in space along with historically developed and characteristic relations between its individual elements (Kupiec et al. 2005). According to Tarr infrastructure can be perceived as a certain structural and network system (roads and highways, waste treatment systems, water supply systems and sewage system, electric lines and gas networks, telecommunications networks), connecting cities and metropolitan areas and enabling social and economic activity (Jacobson and Tarr 1994).

We can assume that infrastructure constitutes a set of equipment and facilities which are essential for social and economic activities, as well as a set of institutions organizing the functioning of business entities. Economic literature distinguishes between social and economic/business infrastructure. Social infrastructure includes equipment and institutions that directly meet the needs of society and ensures appropriate living conditions. Kupiec et al. define social infrastructure as a set of equipment essential above all for satisfying society needs and providing adequate living conditions (Kupiec et al. 2004). Social infrastructure consists of subsystems that provide services associated with the social sphere in terms of, for example, education, science, health care, public administration, culture, recreation, social welfare, safety and social organizations.

In contrast with social infrastructure, economic infrastructure provides mainly displacement functions. Grzywacz calls it economic "innervation", and looks at transport equipment as its basic element that enables and increases the exchange of information, material substances and people (Grzywacz 1982). Kupiec et al. distinguish between different elements of economic infrastructure: communication systems (transport and communications), energy (electricity, heat, gas) and water systems (Kupiec et al. 2005). According to Godlewska, economic infrastructure is a set of communication, energy and water systems, while social infrastructure consists of the institutions of civil service (Godlewska 2001).

It is worthwhile to note that in the literature, "communication" and "transport" are often used interchangeably in the context of bridging distances (the same applies to transport and communication infrastructure). According to the author both notions are complementary to each other, rather than synonyms. In accordance with the encyclopedic definition of communication, it is a technique of people and cargoes transport as well as information transmission (communication) (Kalisiewicz 1995). Hence, this article considers transport (transport infrastructure) and communication (communication infrastructure) as two communication subsystems.

Infrastructure equipment has a particular role in the theory of Porter in the context of obtaining a competitive advantage and efficiency improvement of a conducted activity. Based on research, the author identifies four domestic (or local) elements that have an impact on the localization advantage of a given country (region), support economic growth and innovations and improve enterprise effectiveness (Porter 2001): conditions of production; strategy and competition; demand; the existence of other sectors. Infrastructure elements, defining conditions of production, play here an important role.

Literature shows that the notion of effectiveness is unambiguous and multidimensional.

Effectiveness generally comes down to comparing revenues from a business activity to its costs. Samuelson and Nordhaus identify effectiveness with a lack of waste and losses, i.e., such use of resources that contributes to reaching maximum satisfaction level given expenditure and technology (Samuelson and Nordhaus 2004). What is more important, the concept of effectiveness in economics is considered not only in the context of business functioning, but also from a perspective of distribution of wealth in the society. Contemporary economics (welfare) often appeals to the effectiveness in Pareto sense. Allocation is effective in Pareto's meaning, if no further reallocation is possible, which would improve the position of some people without any harmful effects for others (Begg et al. 2007).

Regarding the enterprise effectiveness concept, it is possible to distinguish between its two dimensions—operational and strategic. Effectiveness in the operational sense comes down to recommendation to do much better than others do in the same industry, implementing the same business activity concept. The strategic dimension refers to acting in a different way fulfilling a unique business target (Szymańska 2010). Bielski draws attention to the fact that among numerous attempts to define organizational effectiveness, it is fundamentally possible to distinguish between two interpretations of this notion: purpose-based and system-based. The first one stresses intentional character of business enterprises and treats them as artificial systems. The second one treats them as natural systems, similar to life forms (Bielski 1996).

Effectiveness is a relative category because its evaluation depends on (Malik 2001): scope of effects taken into account on the expenditure and revenues side; identification of all effects in the specific business activity; and adopted reference criteria.

There are not only different definitions of effectiveness, but also different criteria for its evaluation. By considering the multi-aspect nature of effectiveness, Bielski distinguishes between its following dimensions (Bielski 1996):

- In-kind effectiveness— refers to accomplishment of the genotype organization function. Indicates to what extent the organization is effective in satisfying determined social needs or to what extent its external objectives are fulfilled.
- Economic effectiveness—includes criteria expressing the relation between effects and expenditure.
- System effectiveness—determines whether the given system may exist in certain surrounding.
- "Political" effectiveness—refers to relations of the organization with its surrounding.
- Political effectiveness—refers to the organization effectiveness in strengthening/infringement of existing social and political governance in a particular country.
- Cultural effectiveness—refers to the ability of the organization to strengthen its values and norms, which enable it to preserve its cultural identity.
- Behavioral effectiveness—concerns criteria such as work satisfaction, intensity of internal conflicts, employee morale, etc. It expresses the interests of participants in the organization and is mainly used for the evaluation from their point of view.

Economic effectiveness (often treated as the fundamental evaluation dimension of business efficiency) seems to be easier to define.

In economic literature effectiveness is interpreted as the ratio of obtained effects to disbursed production factors (Marciniak 2005). Hence, in economic terms the efficiency evaluation refers to the relationship between expenditure and effects. The general way of building indicators, used to analyze its size, may take the form of the following formats (Adamczyk 1995): difference in effects and expenditure, quotient of effects and expenditure, quotient of difference between effects and expenditure to incurred expenditure.

The problem of the measurement of enterprises effectiveness has not been completely solved despite numerous research analyses. In principle, the effectiveness measurement methods are based on three approaches (Szymańska 2010):

- Indication—analyzes relations between different indicators (profitability and productivity ratios).
- Parametric—determines technical relations between expenditures and production, determining the maximum quantity of product that can be obtained given a specified expenditure level. This approach distinguishes between the SFA (*Stochastic Frontier Approach*), TFA (*Thick Frontier Approach*), or DFA methods (*Distribution Free Approach*).
- Nonparametric—applies linear programming procedures, (the issue of randomness and potential measurement errors are not considered). Here it is possible to distinguish the DEA (*Data Envelopment Analysis*) and FDH methods (*Free Disposal Hull*).

Since the external environment becomes more and more turbulent, it is advisable to expand the effectiveness analysis with an analysis of nonfinancial factors.

According to Bielski it is not possible to determine the best effectiveness indicator. Its choice is subjective, and it depends on a range of criteria such as values, preferences, and interests of the business owner. Bielski argues that it is not possible to apply a single effectiveness criterion, nor it is possible to create a universal, multi-criterion evaluation system. Such a system must be created individually, taking into consideration the genotype of the organization, a set of current objectives and the hierarchy of their importance recognized by the leadership (Bielski 2004). In Szczepańska's view the creation of universal indicators to measure business effectiveness, which could be used in every enterprise, is significantly impeded due to (Szczepańska 2009): selection problems resulting from the multitude of indicators; the potential lack of appropriate (interdisciplinary) knowledge; relatively high changeability of financial measures; and the information cost.

In this article we attempt to create a synthetic measure of enterprise effectiveness based on a set of diagnostic variables. The application of synthetic measures based on an aggregate indicator instead of a series of variables allows us to measure the multidimensional nature of business effectiveness and organise its different aspects in a linear way. In the context of the multi-criterion system of evaluation of the enterprise effectiveness, such an approach may constitute a certain simplification, but at the same time it may be a starting point to a more comprehensive analysis.

Effectiveness measures (partial) combine information concerning both company's expenditure and its economic performance. These measures can be a starting point to evaluate the status quo and/or determine future actions (Świetlik 2005). The indicator analysis is particularly useful when evaluating the following (Skowronek-Mielczarek and Leszczyński 2008): economic situation (among others wealth, funds rotation), capital situation (among others invested capital structure), cash flow and profitability. According to Skowronek-Mielczarek and Leszczyński it is necessary to assign a special significance to the profitability and liquidity analysis. These two areas of activity evaluation enable us to diagnose the scale and level of profits, which the company brings to their owners, as well as what its solvency is and ability to generate financial flows (Skowronek-Mielczarek and Leszczyński 2008).

Transport development has a particular impact on enterprises and it may impinge on their effectiveness. Among others, it affects: location decisions concerning business activity (which largely determines its success or failure); decisions concerning further investment or delocalization; the process of production (dependent on the supply of raw materials and semi-finished products); the size and structure of the production assortment (the transport infrastructure contributes to the expansion of markets; in addition, the structure of production assortment may be determined by access to specialist transport means, such as, for example, tank cars, or river barges); the stocks level; the products quality (transport infrastructure (in particular its quality) often affects the quality of delivered products (e.g. food, glass products), as well as production materials); the cost of produced goods; employees' productivity (insufficiently developed transport infrastructure causes congestion, which may cause employees delays, as well as their physical tiredness and stress).

According to Grzywacz the benefits, which transport infrastructure creates, can be measured easily and (they are quickly perceptible), or they can be difficult to estimate. The first group of benefits includes: reduction in transport costs, reduction in the number of accidents, and time savings. The benefits that are difficult to estimate encompass open access to new export (import) markets, increased economic cooperation, labour flows from the surplus to deficit areas (Grzywacz 1982).

Infrastructure constitutes a specific link between the buyer and the seller, or between the supplier and the seller. The road transport infrastructure plays a particular role because its network density is much higher than that of the rail infrastructure, or the infrastructure of the inland water transport. It is the only type of transport infrastructure that enables "*door-to-door*" delivery.

Development of transport infrastructure and increase of its quality standards, determines to a large extent transport costs, which often constitute a significant element of total business activity costs, thus affecting management results. According to Anderson the share of transport costs in production costs for enterprises in the USA fluctuates from 3 % (production of leather and leather goods) to the average of 7–9 % (production of rubber and plastic, textile industry and metallurgical processing) and 27 % (refined petroleum products, glass industry and stonemasonry) (Domańska 2006). According to Godlewska, the share of transport costs in total production costs amounts to 6–8 % (Godlewska 2001). Transport, to a different degree, determines production costs of individual goods. In particular, it affects the production of construction materials, characterized by a low processing level and requiring a lot of cargo handling operations. Moreover, transport determines the costs of import or production of energy raw materials, ceramics and glass, or wood. To a lesser degree, transport affects production costs of highly processed products (among others medicines, electronic products, clothes) (Grzywacz and Burnewicz 1989).

The impact of road infrastructure on productivity has been analyzed by Stephan. The author carried out an analysis (applying three different methods) of the impact of road infrastructure on the production size in the manufacturing sector in 11 German Lands over the period 1970–1993. He found a strong positive correlation between expansion of road infrastructure and productivity in manufacturing sector. Existing developmental disproportions in individual regions in the road infrastructure explain a part of existing productivity difference between eastern and western lands. However, the author emphasized the existence of other exogenous factors that may also be relevant in this respect (Stephan 1997).

Logistics plays an important role in determining enterprise effectiveness. Logistics is defined as a process including planning, coordination and control, both in terms of time and space in order to effectively achieve objectives of the organization. These activities apply to spatial and temporal distribution of goods that are an element of the organisational process (Krawczyk 2001). Their effectiveness is determined by the density and quality of transport infrastructure in the region. It is often emphasized that these activities, to a significant degree, affect business profitability. The profitability ratio of an enterprise (ROA) is expressed as a quotient of the net financial result and the enterprise assets, and it depends on the effectiveness of management. As the effectiveness of management increases, which manifests itself, inter alia, with a more efficient policy of assets turnover, the profitability ratio increases. Since effective asset management determines business profitability, the requirements of enterprises with regard to the quality of transport services and transport infrastructure have been constantly growing.

A study carried out by Morash, Dröge and Vickery shows that there is a positive correlation between enterprise effectiveness (measured by indicators such as ROA, ROI and ROS), and the intensity of supplies, the quality of logistic processes and the level of logistic costs (that significantly depend on the transport infrastructure) (Morash et al. 1996). Skowronek and Sarjusz-Wolski explain the multi-dimensional impact of logistic processes on operating costs, assets productivity, labour productivity and return on invested capital, with the following factors (Skowronek and Sarjusz-Wolski 2003):

- Logistic processes involve fixed assets such as buildings and stock storages, means of transport, machinery, and equipment used for products handling and storage. Maintenance of these assets is costly and it is also associated with potential losses from alternative capital investment.

- Processes of physical flow of goods, as well as information processes, require a significant number of employees, which generates high labour costs.
- Stocks as an element of assets has a significant impact on results, since there are costs and investments associated with it.

The role of saturation of individual regions with the communications infrastructure has been rising. Technological progress that materialized in the field of communications over the last couple of decades, has contributed significantly to a quantitative and qualitative change in business operations. Large quantity and variety of information is a feature of modern enterprises. Communications infrastructure is thus more important as determining access to information affects not only the effectiveness of enterprises, but also enables their functioning (e-business). With regard to spatial character of business activities, fast information circulation gains special significance as it enables an effective response to the market needs and a quick adjustment of the market offer. Enterprises function in a global competition environment but they also operate in conditions of rising cooperation, often on international level. Such market conditions often trigger a need to seek for new ways of distribution as well as fast and effective transfer of information (as well as funds and goods). Communication solutions become a chance for survival and development in a turbulent environment. However, their effective use is subject to the quality of regional communication infrastructure.

L. Kupiec defines communication as knowledge and practical human activity in the field of human communication and social contacts, using accessible technical means (Kupiec et al. 2005). The main task of communication is a transmission of information (as well as intangible assets) within a specified time. The media of information may take both a material (such as paper) and intangible (e.g. radio waves) form.

Taking into account the definition of the communication concept, we can assume that the communications infrastructure consists of objects, devices and facilities enabling transmission of information, goods and other intangible assets; as well as institutions performing this type of activity. Within the area of communication (communications infrastructure), we can distinguish two subsystems, i.e. postal communication and telecommunication (Table 1).

For centuries postal services have remained a relatively universal and competitive form of communication. Generally, postal services include two types of services. The first one consists of shipment of all sorts (both national and international). The second one relates to additional services encompassing, inter alia, banking and insurance services. Performing these services requires a use of facilities and equipment of infra- as well as supra-structural character, i.e. postal administrative and service facilities (among others transceiver facilities), means of transport and technical equipment, post office equipment (sorting machines, shipping equipment).

Apart from enabling transport between business entities, postal operators impact the enterprises effectiveness through promotional activities (especially direct marketing) and support for market researches.

Table 1 Communication services

Postal services	Telecommunication services
Mail	Landline telephone services
Advertising mail	Mobile phone services
Addressless mail	Telegraph services
Money transfers	Internet services
Postal parcels	Radio communication services
Palette parcels	Satellite communications services
Press distribution and other services (insurance and banking services)	Other telecommunication services

Source: Own elaboration based on Kupiec et al. 2005

Direct marketing carried out by a postal operator, plays a special role when directly accessing a specific, specialized groups of recipients, or when strengthening the brand image and customer loyalty (e.g., by sending a written thank you letter for using the offer). It can also be applied as a kind of an "introduction" initiating a direct contact.

Currently, the primary instrument used in direct marketing by postal operators is *a direct mail service*. Mail used in direct marketing can have a named or unnamed addressee and it includes among others: letters, leaflets, folders, booklets, catalogues, digital media, sent via mail to potential customers (Garbarski et al. 2000). High selectivity is an undoubted advantage of this technique (mail can be addressed to a specific recipient group); this mail can also be highly individualized.

Postal services can provide support for marketing research conducted by economic entities. One of the methods of obtaining economic information (e.g. from experts in a given field) is questionnaires, which can be sent by post. Postal surveys are of particular relevance, when enterprises want to ensure anonymity of respondents, and when the sample of respondents is dispersed geographically (practically, enterprises are not limited geographically). In this method the postal operator participates in the delivery and receipt of questionnaire forms.

Public postal operators can also be regarded as a shadow banking system. Using postal infrastructure, they provide a series of simple and accessible banking services that enable enterprises to obtain credit, make deposits, service their accounts, for example, via Internet. Moreover, public postal operators offer insurance products (including accident insurance).

Additionally, public postal operators offer a wide range of other financial services. Enterprises can seize on a full service of postal orders, sent both per traditional main, as well as electronically. Based on automated cash handling processes, public postal operators offer cash processing service, including collection of money from an indicated point, transporting and sorting processes, authenticity control, payment to a designated bank account. Enterprises can also benefit from services of collecting and transport of both money as well as and other materials containing classified information, or hazardous materials (such as weapons).

Therefore, postal services directed to enterprises are not only limited to postal shipments. A well-developed network of postal institutions, which offers financial and banking services for enterprises, can constitute a certain (to a limited extent) competition for other financial institutions (banks) that offer business support.

Technological progress and change in communication forms have resulted in telecommunication (where the communication medium has an immaterial form (e.g. electromagnetic waves) becoming a substitute for and/or complement to traditional postal services.

According to Leffa communication networks reduce fixed costs associated with obtaining information, as well as variable costs associated with the market share. Telecommunication contributes to an increase in the efficiency of business activities, since:

- It reduces the costs associated with allocation to different economic sectors.
- As the cost of communication decreases, the optimal search level rises, and the quantity and quality of available information increases, contributing to better decisions.
- Lower costs of obtaining information result in an increase in arbitrage opportunities, and raise the financial markets efficiency, reducing capital costs.
- Lower costs of information result in better information about the probability distribution of prices, reducing uncertainty or converting it into risk (Raczyński 2007).

Technological progress has led to telephony and information technology becoming strategic telecommunications areas. Nowadays, the most quickly developing telecommunications subsystem is mobile telephony.

The increasing popularity of this telecommunication form results above all from practically unrestricted mobility and price attractiveness of offered services. Mobile telephony has also a number of other advantages, such as, for example: the possibility to add various services (mobile marketing, mobile payments, banking transactions), a wide tele-service range (including short text messages, telefax, e-mail), diversity of functions carried out on mobile phones (including calendar, notebook), the ease of data transmission.

It is hard to imagine enterprises functioning without support of Internet solutions. Bednarczyk points out that the success of enterprises to a large degree depends on identifying and seizing on opportunities in virtual space, rather than in real surroundings (Bednarczyk 1999). On the one hand, the telecommunications infrastructure constitutes a catalyst of economic cooperation, and creating networks, on the other—it leads to the creation of so-called creative spaces, the shaping of which becomes an important task of regional policy. Marciniak observes that the access to broadband Internet becomes crucial, generating positive spillovers for labour productivity (Marciniak 2011).

Next to mobile networks, Internet is the biggest telecommunications network in the world. It is often considered a special type of communication medium, not only supporting electronic communication, but also creating conditions for functioning and development of business enterprises. The rising role of Internet in business results from its specific characteristics, and among them (Społeczeństwo informacyjne w Polsce. Wyniki badań statystycznych z lat 2006–2010): the lack of bureaucratic restrictions, the possibility of cooperation of international specialists, global reach and high flexibility. Internet creates a special space, which has a significant impact on entities functioning in the market environment. It constitutes a platform for the sale of both standard and innovative products and services, it determines relations between individual economic entities, and may affect the shape of enterprises strategy. As a global information network, it provides conditions for functioning in the international environment for all companies, regardless of their size.

Unquestionably, through the use of Internet, enterprises have started operating in a different environment than a classical one. There are new areas that enable the search and exchange of information, as well as carrying out transactions. The Internet impact on the business activity can be illustrated by a ICDT model (Information, Communication, Distribution, Transactions). In this model the traditional market space is expanded to include a virtual space, consisting of four segments (Szapiro and Ciemniak 1999):

- Virtual space of information that includes new channels, which enable transmission of, and access to, information about business activities
- Virtual space of communication, enabling entities to build relations, exchange opinions and ideas
- Virtual space of distribution, including new distribution channels for products and services (among others digital products, and tele-consulting services)
- Virtual space of transaction, associated with enabling enterprises to initiate and carry out economic transactions.

Access of enterprises to computer networks, connected to Internet, determines electronic exchange of information (transmission via websites or automatic data exchange), as well as supports automation of business processes, which is particularly important in the context of optimization of many business process. Fereńc claims that in order to transition from a work- and capital-based economy to a knowledge-based economy, access to information and communications technologies becomes essential, and additional investment in infrastructure is needed (especially telecommunications infrastructure). The effect of the development of electronic communication is: an increase in productivity and labour mobility, reduced production costs, better product quality and adaptation to consumer needs as well as new a release of new products (Fereńc 2008). Further positive effects of the development of electronic communication (Internet) include: acceleration of order processing (by reduction in the time of information circulation), shorter clearing time, reduction in the cost of stocks (by supporting the delivery chain management), facilitation of order processing and payment formalities (electronic cash transfer), creation of new distribution channels, creation of conditions that support implementation of new organizational structures (especially network structures), creation of the corporate brand and consumer views, and internal and external integration of business processes. To this list, Szapiro and Ciemniak add, for example, growing importance of the law of rising incomes, increase in the bargaining power of consumers, reduction in of cost of the supplier change, breakdown of the chain value into smaller units (Szapiro and Ciemniak 1999).

What is particularly important in this study is that Internet enables enterprises to significantly reduce their transaction costs (among others by reducing the number of business trips and limiting the volume of traditional correspondence). James distinguishes four main effects of Internet on transaction costs: simplification of order processing, new trade possibilities, services trade between countries, further reduction in transaction time (James 2002). Research by Garicano and Kaplan confirms the positive Internet impact on the transaction costs reduction. The authors show that a shift from physical car auctions to online auctions contributes to a reduction in transaction costs up to 80 % (Garicano and Kaplan 2001). The reduction in transaction costs is possible through application of Internet solutions that imply lower costs of information acquisition and no need of physical contact between both parties of the transaction (contract is concluded via Internet). The reduction of the costs of control of the contract execution is also possible (monitoring using specialized information systems with access to Internet).

3 Communication Infrastructure and the Economic Effectiveness of Enterprises: A Statistical Analysis

Enterprise effectiveness is determined by a series of various factors, concerning both individual features of the enterprise, as well as the environment in which it functions. Enterprises are open systems, and their development to a significant degree is determined by external factors, including infrastructure. We analyse the external factors based on the following premises (Gabrusewicz 2002): relations of an enterprise with its environment are primary to processes occurring inside the entity; environment is a source of economic entity's power as well as the recipient of their activity results; results of entities that conduct business activity are determined by the external environment. Nowadays changes in the more distant environment that concern economic (including infrastructure), technological, political, legal, social or cultural factors, have a significant impact on the functioning and development of enterprises. It is hard to disagree with the fact that what occurs inside entities, which conduct business activity, is a consequence of changes occurring in their environment. In consequence, it is the external environment rather than enterprise's internal resources that is more often considered a factor determining enterprises success (or failure).

In the analysis of voivodeships' spatial variation resulting from differences in communication infrastructure, we deal with a number of research objects described by a set of different variables. Therefore it is hard to express them using a single measure (this also applies to measuring effectiveness in a given region). To study the relationship between the effectiveness of enterprises and the quality of communication infrastructure in individual regions, we apply a taxonomical method based on synthetic measures of development (SMD).

One of the most popular methods of linear ordering is Hellwig's method. The synthetic measures of development are a method whereby to describe objects, instead of using many variables, we use a single aggregate indicator. This facilitates the analysis of similarities of the studied objects and their linear systematization. The value of SMD increases as the distance between a given object and a common pattern, an artificially defined object, characterized by optimal properties (maximum values of stimulant and minimal values of destimulant features) decreases.

For research purposes, we propose 15 specific indicators, which reflect access of enterprises to communication infrastructure in individual voivodeships:

1. Road transport infrastructure: K_{11}—average weighted indicator of the public roads density; K_{12}—average weighted indicator of the public roads density with hard surface; K_{13}—average weighted indicator of the public roads density with hard improved surface; K_{14}—average weighted indicator of the highways density; K_{15}—average weighted indicator of the expressways density; K_{16}—immediate renovation needs indicator for national roads.
2. Rail transport infrastructure: K_{21}—average weighted indicator of railway lines density; K_{22}—average weighted indicator of electrified railway lines density; K_{23}—average weighted indicator of two- and more railway lines density.
3. Air transport infrastructure: K_{31}—average weighted indicator of the airports density; K_{32}—air mobility indicator.
4. Postal infrastructure: K_{41}—average weighted indicator of the postal institutions density.
5. Telecommunications infrastructure: K_{51}—average weighted indicator of the telephone lines density; K_{52}—average weighted indicator of the BTS GSM-1800 base stations density; K_{53}—average weighted indicator of the BTS GSM-900 base stations density.

Due to the multi-aspect nature of the enterprise efficiency, it is necessary to use a significant number of measures. We need to remember that too many variables can distort and even block the effective objects classification (Młodak 2006). Complexity and the multi-aspect nature of the enterprises efficiency implies a need to use synthetic measures. In order to determine the effectiveness of enterprises in the region, a set of 15 potential variables was used. We divide them into five groups:

1. Revenues and costs of business activity: P_{11}—net financial result per one employee; P_{12}—revenue from business activity per one employee; P_{13}—the ratio of costs to revenues.
2. Return on business activity: P_{21}—profitability ratio of gross turnover; P_{22}—profitability ratio of net sales; P_{23}—return on assets; P_{24}—profitability ratio of current assets; P_{25}—return on equity.

3. Cash Flow of business activity: P_{31}—financial liquidity indicator of the first degree; P_{32}—financial liquidity indicator of the second degree; P_{33}—financial liquidity indicator of the third degree.
4. Debt of business activity: P_{41}—long-term debt ratio; P_{42}—short-term debt ratio; P_{43}—ratio of liabilities to assets (with regard to supplies and services).
5. Productivity: P_{51}—gross value added per one employee.

The selection of variables was largely determined by the availability and completeness of data for all objects and their validity. The included specific variables are indicative rather than absolute, which allowed us, to a certain extent, to avoid interferences associated with some objects exhibiting certain features blurring the analysis (e.g., much greater area than the other objects). In order to obtain a final set of diagnostic variables, we analyse the degree of their correlation with other variables in used the study. We have also examined the level of variability of individual variables since a low level of variability would be of low analytical value. We used a classical variation coefficient. From the set of potential variables that illustrate the level of communication infrastructure in the region, we eliminated those, for which the value of the variation coefficient was smaller than an arbitrary threshold of 10 % (the variable with the variation coefficient of below 10 % were qualified as quasi-constant). Since the variability of all measures describing the level of communication infrastructure was relatively high, all of them were included in further analysis. From the set of variables, describing the enterprise effectiveness, we eliminated variables: P_{13}, P_{33}, P_{42} and P_{43}.

Apart from variation, an important criterion in variables selection is their correlation. Two highly correlated variables provide similar information, so it is recommended to eliminate one of them. One of the selection methods is the so-called method of inverse correlation matrix. For each subgroup of variables, we calculate an inverse correlation matrix. A variable with a highest diagonal value that exceeds the threshold value was eliminated ($r^* = 10$). This way, the K_{12} variable was eliminated from the set of potential decision variables that describe the communication infrastructure. Similarly, the P_{22} and P_{23} variables were eliminated from the set of variables that describe the enterprises effectiveness. For every variable we determined its character (in terms of the direction of its impact)—as a stimulant, destimulant or nominant.

In the case of the communication infrastructure indicators, almost all variables were qualified as stimulants (the higher the impact, the better). Out of all variables, only the K_{16} variable—immediate renovation needs indicator for national roads, was qualified as a destimulant (the smaller the impact, the better). None of the variables were qualified as nominant (Table 2).

In the case of the enterprise effectiveness variables, the P_{41} variable was qualified as a destimulant, and the P_{31} and P_{32} variables—as nominants. The remaining variables were qualified as stimulant.

Silesian, Lower Silesian and Lesser Poland voivodeships are characterized by the highest levels of SMD communication infrastructure—the values of individual diagnostic variables are high. The smallest SMD values of communication

Table 2 Synthetic measures of the communication infrastructure and enterprises effectiveness over the period 2003–2011

	SMD communication infrastructure					SM effectiveness of enterprises				
J.p.	2003	2005	2007	2009	2011	2003	2005	2007	2009	2011
DS	0.409	0.442	0.423	0.423	0.380	0.263	0.376	0.382	0.436	0.375
KP	0.233	0.268	0.269	0.269	0.239	0.342	0.126	0.137	0.239	0.195
LB	0.102	0.136	0.125	0.114	0.094	0.177	0.067	0.083	0.205	0.175
LS	0.281	0.287	0.302	0.282	0.292	0.224	0.310	0.251	0.317	0.128
ŁD	0.260	0.273	0.305	0.269	0.286	0.258	0.165	0.232	0.357	0.252
MP	0.348	0.378	0.355	0.367	0.409	0.249	0.305	0.309	0.386	0.220
MZ	0.212	0.313	0.312	0.333	0.291	0.172	0.284	0.323	0.508	0.120
OP	0.322	0.330	0.316	0.292	0.264	0.210	0.258	0.248	0.607	0.317
PK	0.118	0.118	0.108	0.109	0.110	0.216	0.181	0.058	0.193	0.133
PL	0.017	0.025	0.036	0.046	0.046	0.364	0.178	0.248	0.190	0.053
PM	0.215	0.251	0.280	0.311	0.300	0.455	0.408	0.303	0.457	0.225
SL	0.512	0.553	0.600	0.621	0.630	0.689	0.393	0.324	0.233	0.340
ŚK	0.201	0.217	0.238	0.257	0.263	0.235	0.140	0.389	0.300	0.182
WM	0.160	0.119	0.120	0.129	0.191	0.379	0.216	0.050	0.045	0.024
WP	0.313	0.390	0.395	0.391	0.330	0.378	0.341	0.233	0.467	0.235
ZP	0.197	0.209	0.248	0.275	0.259	0.048	0.018	0.075	0.084	0.138
Min	0.017	0.025	0.036	0.046	0.046	0.048	0.018	0.050	0.045	0.024
Max	0.512	0.553	0.600	0.621	0.630	0.689	0.408	0.389	0.607	0.375
ŚR.	0.244	0.269	0.277	0.280	0.274	0.291	0.235	0.228	0.314	0.195
SD	0.122	0.135	0.138	0.140	0.137	0.146	0.118	0.114	0.157	0.097

Source: Own elaboration based on BDL GUS (www.stat.gov.pl), ULC (www.ulc.gov.pl), Bilansowe wyniki finansowe podmiotów gospodarczych 2004–2012, www.uke.gov.pl

Indications: *J.p.* spatial unit, *DS* Lower Silesian Voivodeship, *KP* Kuyavia-Pomerania Voivodeship, *LB* Lublin Voivodeship, *LS* Lubusz Voivodeship, *ŁD* Lodzkie Voivodeship, *MP* Lesser Poland Voivodeship, *MZ* Masovian Voivodeship, *OP* Opole Voivodeship, *PK* Subcarpathian Voivodeship, *PD* Podlaskie Voivodeship, *PM* Pomeranian Voivodeship, *SL* Silesia Voivodeship, *ŚK* Świętokrzyskie Voivodeship, *WM* Warmia-Masuria Voivodeship, *WP* Greater Poland Voivodeship, *ZP* West Pomerania Voivodeship, *MIN* minimum value, *MAX* maximum value, *ŚR* arithmetic average, *SD* standard deviation

infrastructure were observed in Eastern Poland voivodeships (Podlaskie, Subcarpathian, Lublin). We conclude that in terms of the level of the development of communication infrastructure we can distinguish between the west part (characterized by a much higher development level of communication infrastructure) and the eastern part (where communication infrastructure in individual regions is much less developed).

The highest values of SMD in the enterprise effectiveness were identified in the Silesia, Lower Silesia and Pomeranian voivodeships. The relatively small SMD values of the enterprises effectiveness were recorded in the Mazovian voivodeship. The "shadow of the large city" phenomenon can be a cause of such a state (which is

Table 3 Values of Spearman's rank correlation coefficient between synthetic measures of communication infrastructure development and enterprises effectiveness

Description	2003	2004	2005	2006	2007	2008	2009	2010	2011
Correlation coefficient	0.279	0.541	0.644	0.779	0.588	0.479	0.641	0.659	0.650

Source: Own study

particularly visible in this voivodeship). A considerable part of the entire socio-economic potential of the voivodeship cumulates in the capital city (large enterprises (international corporations), comprehensive economic infrastructure, numerous business institutions, educational units). This makes the neighbouring districts relatively less attractive for businesses.

To study the relationship between the level of infrastructure in the region and the enterprises effectiveness, a correlation analysis was carried out. To eliminate the negative impact of possible outliers, a nonparametric Spearman's rank correlation coefficient was applied (Zeliaś 2000):

$$r_s = 1 - \frac{6\sum_{i=1}^{n} d_i^2}{n^3 - n}. \qquad (1)$$

where:

d_i—difference between ranks (subsequent numbers) of X and Y;
n—number of elements in the sample.

Table 3 shows the values of correlation coefficients between the synthetic measures of the level of communication infrastructure development and the enterprise effectiveness.

The analysis shows that there is a positive correlation between individual regions' communication infrastructure and the effectiveness of enterprises. We observe a high degree of correlation at the significance level of $p < 0.05$. The critical value of the correlation coefficient at the significance level 0.05 amounts to r^* $0.05(16) = 0.5029$. The calculated value of the correlation coefficient for the entire analyzed period fluctuated between 0.279 and 0.779, and almost in the entire analyzed period (apart from data for 2003 and 2008) exceeded the critical value.

In the evaluation of enterprise effectiveness it is essential not only to determine the measures of enterprise effectiveness, but also to ensure that they are compliant with the requirements of rational management. Under certain conditions, business activity may show extensive or intensive management features. Extensive management aims at higher incomes and bigger profits as a result of increased involvement of foreign capital or equity, both in terms of value, quantity and time. Intensive management aims to achieve an increase in sales revenue and profit per unit of resources, especially by effective technical-organizational progress. It is associated with higher productivity and profitability, as well as higher efficiency of fixed assets and turnover (Bednarski et al. 1998). It is worthwhile to analyze the spatial variation character of enterprise management with regard to regional communication infrastructure. This—as already mentioned—determines the use of remaining factors in the management process. A synthetic analysis can be conducted based on a standard model. For example, for a deepened evaluation of management efficiency it is possible to use a set of the following indicators (Bednarski et al. 1998):

$$\mathrm{iMR} < \mathrm{iPM} < \mathrm{iPR} < \mathrm{iZP} < \mathrm{iZM} < \mathrm{iZR}$$

where:

i—dynamics index,
MR—average investment of capital components (fixed assets and turnover) per employee,
PM—assets turnover,
PR—productivity per employee,
ZP—sales profitability,
ZM—wealth profitability,
ZR—labour profitability per employee.

It should be noted that there may appear different deviations from the above model that depend on the life cycle of the organization or its external environment (Bławat 1999).

Table 4 presents a system of economic indicators that is used to evaluate the management effectiveness over three periods: 2003, 2007–2008, and 2010–2011.

The results show that in 2003–2011 in individual voivodeships, the standard indicators dynamics system (annual values) most often was not fully compatible. This suggests that the enterprises' functioning in individual regions does not comply with requirements of the intensive management. In the entire analyzed period, symptoms of intensive management in five voivodeships—Lubusz, Mazovian, Opole, Podlaskie and West Pomeranian were observed at most twice. We did not observe any similarities between the frequency of intensive management symptoms (desired from a rational management point of view), and the quality of the communication infrastructure. On the other hand, we can assume that the existing gap in the quantity and quality of individual infrastructure elements (also in the regions with favourable values of synthetic measures of communication infrastructure), reduces the chances to achieve high economic results compliant with requirements of rational management.

It is worthwhile to emphasize that enterprises often conduct trans-regional activity. For this reason, "infrastructure clusters", which are clusters of bordering regions characterized by a high infrastructure development level, gain particular importance. Therefore, we conduct analysis of spatial correlation (autocorrelation), which enables us to determine the relationship between voivodeships with regard to communication infrastructure development, as well as it enables us to identify voivodeships clusters that are similar with regard to infrastructure development level.

Table 4 Synthetic management evaluation

J.p.	Model of economic indicators (data in %) 2003–2004	2007–2008	2010–2011	SGI 2003–2011
DS	105.9 > 105.0 < 111.2 < 287.9 < 302.2<320.1	111.4 > 94.2 < 104.9 > 62.9 > 59.3 < 66.0	111.2 > 96.8 < 107.7 < 151.5 > 146.7 < 163.2	0
KP	107.0 > 105.2 < 112.6 < 219.0 < 230.5 < 246.6	107.9 > 98.3 < 106.1 > 66.4 > 65.3 < 70.5	109.0 > 102.4 < 111.7 < 107.0 < 109.6 < 119.5	0
LB	100.9 < 107.7 < 108.7 < 295.3 < 318.1 < 320.9*	91.1 < 112.7 > 102.6 > 75.8 < 85.4 > 77.8	110.5 > 102.4 < 113.2 < 141.5 < 145.0 < 160.1	1
LS	106.1 < 106.4 < 112.9 < 403.5 < 429.2 < 455.5*	110.5 > 93.7 < 103.5 > 43.1 > 40.4 < 44.6	104.8 > 104.2 < 109.2 > 85.2 < 88.8 < 93.0	2
ŁD	106.4 > 101.8 < 108.3 < 244.1 < 248.5 < 264.5	109.0 > 97.9 < 106.7 > 83.4 > 81.7 < 89.0	112.8 > 99.2 < 111.8 > 88.3 > 87.5 < 98.7	0
MP	103.4 < 105.4 < 108.9 < 312.6 < 329.5 < 340.5*	110.4 > 95.5 < 105.5 > 79.3 > 75.7 < 83.6	112.6 > 99.1 < 111.6 > 88.8 > 88.0 < 99.1	1
MZ	103.9 < 106.5 < 110.7 < 717.0 < 763.7 < 793.5*	98.5 < 101.2 > 99.7 > 56.2 < 56.9 > 56.0	106.4 > 103.3 < 110.0 > 64.7 < 66.9 < 71.2	2
OP	108.8 < 112.1 < 122.0 < 437.7 < 490.7 < 534.1*	108.4 > 101.4 < 109.9 < 112.8 < 114.4 < 124.0	98.9 < 114.3 > 113.0 > 98.8 < 112.9 < 111.6	2
PK	107.0 > 101.7 < 108.7 < 240.7 < 244.7 < 261.7	111.9 > 99.3 < 111.0 > 56.0 > 55.6 < 62.2	118.5 > 94.3 < 111.7 > 99.6 > 94.0 < 111.3	0
PL	106.0 < 107.1 < 113.6 < 143.6 < 153.8 < 163.0*	114.9 > 93.4 < 107.3 > 62.9 > 58.8 < 67.5	109.5 > 98.3 < 107.7 > 93.4 > 91.9 < 100.6	2
PM	106.5 < 108.2 < 115.2 < 176.3 < 190.7 < 203.0*	107.4 > 102.5 < 110.2 > 56.3 < 57.8 < 62.0	114.7 > 105.2 < 120.7 > 83.2 < 87.6 < 100.5	1
SL	110.6 < 113.1 < 125.1 > 92.1 < 104.1 < 115.2	102.7 < 105.0 < 107.8 > 60.2 < 63.2 < 64.9	109.7 > 102.1 < 112.0 > 110.8 < 113.1 < 124.1	0
ŚK	108.2 > 103.6 < 112.1 < 221.3 < 229.3 < 248.1	115.0 > 96.0 < 110.4 > 85.5 > 82.1 < 94.4	109.9 > 101.2 < 111.3 > 95.8 < 97.0 < 106.6	0

WM	98.5 < 110.4 > 108.7 < 134.5 < 148.5 < 146.2	111.6 > 95.2 < 106.2 > 54.2 > 51.6 < 57.5	107.1 > 105.3 < 112.8 > 79.4 < 83.7 < 89.6	1
WP	103.5 < 107.5 < 111.2 < 221.1 < 237.7 < 246.0*	111.3 > 96.8 < 107.7 > 74.2 > 71.8 < 79.9	110.6 > 100.6 < 111.3 > 85.2 < 85.8 < 94.8	1
ZP	101.5 < 106.4 < 108.0 < 2149.8 < 2287.8 < 2321.7*	114.9 > 96.6 < 111.0 > 44.9 > 43.4 < 49.9	104.0 < 107.5 < 111.8 > 105.8 < 113.7 < 118.3	2

Source: Own elaboration based on Bilansowe wyniki finansowe podmiotów gospodarczych 2004–2012
Indications: as in Table 2; SGI—Number of intensive management symptoms in 2003–2011
(*) indicates intensive management symptom

In the subject literature spatial autocorrelation is defined as correlation between realisations of the same variable in different locations. This means that the value of the variable determines and simultaneously is determined by its realisations in other locations. There are two variants of spatial correlation relations, i.e., positive and negative autocorrelation. The positive autocorrelation is regarded as spatial collection of high or low values of the observed variables. However, the negative autocorrelation means that high values are adjacent to low, and low to high (Suchecki 2010).

Analysis of this type defines the neighborhood structures with so-called spatial weights. They are calculated on the basis of a matrix of distance or neighborhood. For purposes of this article, as the main criterion of proximity we adopt the common border between the neighborhood of the first order.

We distinguish two types of measures used for spatial correlation analysis—global and local measures. Global measures are one-numerical indices of spatial autocorrelation or general regional resemblance. Local statistics, computed for each area, enable us to answer the question whether the given region is surrounded by regions that are similar—or different (Kopczewska 2007).

To analyze the relationship between the values of synthetic measures of the communication infrastructure development in individual voivodeships, with the values of these indicators in adjacent voivodeships, we calculate Moran's I statistics (global and local).

The Moran's I global statistics is a basic statistic used in the spatial autocorrelation analyses which takes the following form (Suchecki 2010):

$$I = \frac{1}{\sum_{i=1}^{n}\sum_{j=1}^{n} w_{ij}} \cdot \frac{\sum_{i=1}^{n}\sum_{j=1}^{n} w_{ij}(x_i - \overline{x})(x_j - \overline{x})}{\frac{1}{n}\sum_{i=1}^{n}(x_i - \overline{x})^2} \tag{2}$$

where:

x_i—value recorded in n regions or locations ($i = 1, 2, \ldots, n$),
$\overline{x}$—average in all analysed regions,
w_{ij}—elements of spatial weights matrix.

In order to find a global autocorrelation share for each of the analyzed locations, the Moran's I_i local statistics was used, as a part of so-called local indicators of spatial association (LISA). Moran's Ii local statistics is given by (Suchecki 2010):

Table 5 Values of Moran's I global statistics over 2003–2011

Description	2003	2004	2005	2006	2007	2008	2009	2010	2011
Correlation coefficient	0.38*	0.34*	0.27*	0.26*	0.28*	0.24*	0.21*	0.19*	0.23*

Source: Own elaboration
Indications: *Statistically significant values at the level of $p < 0.05$. Significance tests of global statistics were based on histogram permutation analysis of randomization test, and hypotheses verification was based on the values of pseudo-significance level

$$I_{i(w)} = \frac{(x_i - \overline{x})\sum_{j=1}^{n} w_{ij}^{*}(x_j - \overline{x})}{\sum_{i=1}^{n}(x_i - \overline{x})^2} \tag{3}$$

Table 5 presents the values of Moran's I global statistics, calculated for synthetic measures of the communications infrastructure development.

The values of Moran's I global statistics calculated for the synthetic measures of the communications infrastructure development over 2003–2011 fluctuated between 0.19 and 0.38, and in the entire analyzed period they were statistically significant (at significance level of 0.05). Therefore, we conclude that there exists positive spatial autocorrelation. However, it is possible to interpret the obtained moderate values of Moran's I global statistics as a quite weak "tendency" to cluster voivodeships with similar development level of communication infrastructure. Moreover, in the analyzed period, a downward trend in the value of the calculated statistics was evident, which we interpret as gradual deterioration of spatial relations between individual voivodeships in terms of the communication infrastructure.

In order to visualize the local spatial relations (clusters), we draft scatter charts of Moran's I global statistics for 2003 and 2011 (Fig. 1).

The concentration of points (corresponding to individual voivodeships) in the left bottom and right upper chart quadrant, confirms the existence of a positive spatial autocorrelation. The relatively even distribution of points in the first and third quadrant of the coordinate system shows that the tendency to group objects of similar values in neighboring areas. Both in 2003 and 2011 certain untypical objects were identified (located in the second and fourth quadrant). In 2003 these were West Pomeranian and Świętokrzyskie voivodeships, however in 2011 atypical observations were identified in Opole, Świętokrzyskie, West Pomeranian (fourth quadrant) and Masovian and Pomeranian (second quadrant) voivodeships.

The next stage of the study was to analyze the structure of the studied spatial variables in the entire area, with a use of local correlation coefficients (Table 6).

Analyzing the value of Moran's I_i local statistics calculated for SMD communication infrastructure, we find that only in Lublin and Opole voivodeships this statistic takes positive values and is statistically significant. This implies that these

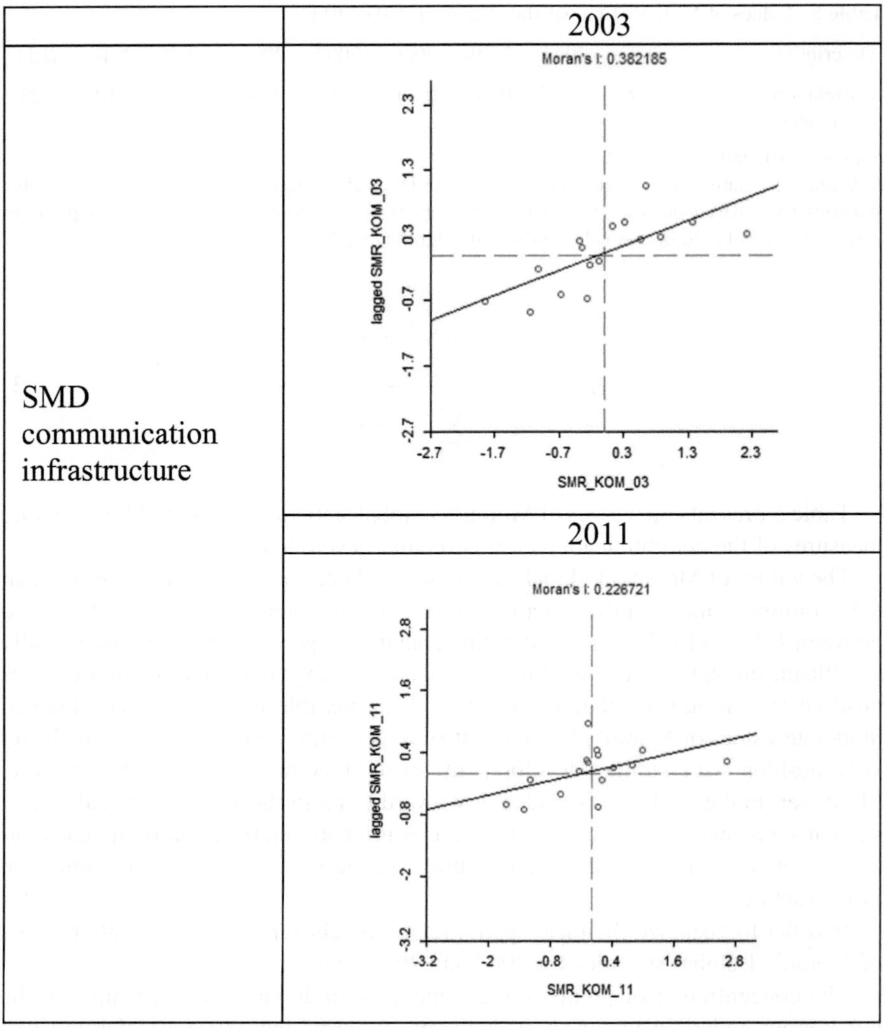

Fig. 1 Moran's I global statistics scatter chart of synthetic measurements of the communication infrastructure development in 2003 and 2011 (*Source*: Own study based on BDL GUS (www.stat.gov.pl), ULC (www.ulc.gov.pl, www.uke.gov.pl)

voivodeships are adjacent to voivodeships with similar SMD values of the communication infrastructure. However, in the case of the Mazovian voivodeship, almost in the entire analyzed period a negative value of Moran's I_i local statistics was observed (statistically significant at the level of $p < 0.05$). Therefore, we conclude that this voivodeship is adjacent to regions with much different SMD values of the communication infrastructure. In the case of remaining voivodeships the Moran's I_i local statistics for the analyzed variable assumed positive values, however they weren't statistically significant.

Table 6 Values of Moran's I_i local statistics for synthetic measures of the communication infrastructure development over 2003–2011

J.p.	2003	2005	2006	2007	2008	2009	2010	2011
DS	0.69	0.63	0.40	0.46	0.37	0.30	0.12	0.12
KP	0.01	0.00	0.01	0.00	0.00	0.00	0.00	−0.01
LB	1.02*	0.74*	0.81*	0.82*	0.86*	0.79*	0.87	0.93*
LS	0.16	0.08	0.00	0.10	0.07	0.01	0.00	0.05
ŁD	0.06	0.02	0.03	0.11*	0.02	−0.05	−0.07*	0.04
MP	0.23	0.16	0.19	0.16	0.17	0.21	0.37	0.44
MZ	0.17*	−0.23*	−0.15**	−0.17**	−0.19**	−0.27**	−0.23**	−0.08*
OP	0.69**	0.49**	0.35**	0.31**	0.25*	0.09*	−0.05*	−0.07*
PK	0.23	0.21	0.28	0.33	0.39	0.30	0.24	0.16
PL	1.31	1.08*	1.22	1.15	1.07	1.05	1.05	1.00
PM	0.03	0.02	−0.03	0.00	−0.03	−0.02	−0.03	−0.03
SL	0.71	0.47	0.43	0.45	0.28	0.27	0.36	0.60
ŚK	−0.04	−0.07	−0.03	−0.05	−0.05	−0.03	−0.02	−0.02
WM	0.42	0.46	0.34	0.43	0.32	0.31	0.22	0.24
WP	0.14	0.17	0.17	0.18	0.15	0.13	0.06	0.04
ZP	−0.08	−0.13	−0.11	−0.07	−0.08	−0.01	0.00	−0.03

Source: Own elaboration based on BDL GUS (www.stat.gov.pl), ULC (www.ulc.gov.pl, www.uke.gov.pl)
Indications: as in Table 2
*Statistically significant values at the level of $p < 0.05$
**Statistically significant values at the level of $p < 0.01$

4 Conclusion

Taking into consideration the spatial aspect of enterprises' functioning, external conditions determining the enterprises effectiveness (including infrastructure) play a particular role. The conducted research shows a high correlation between indicators of the communication infrastructure and measures of the enterprises effectiveness in individual voivodeships. This is because precisely the economic infrastructure elements (including communication infrastructure) determine an efficient functioning of enterprises.

Due to specific characteristics of communication infrastructure (e.g. capital intensity and low susceptibility to changes), we can assume that it constitutes a necessary, but insufficient factor to improve the efficiency of economic activities in the region. Further analysis of enterprise effectiveness is needed to assess the impact of regional infrastructure, and its multidimensional perspective, which has so far been limited due to the availability of data.

References

Adamczyk J (1995) Efektywność przedsiębiorstw sprywatyzowanych. Akademia Ekonomiczna, Kraków
Bank Danych Lokalnych GUS (2014) www.stat.gov.pl/bdl. Accessed 12 Nov 2014
Bednarczyk M (1999) Wpływ otoczenia komunikacyjnego na redefinicje strategii konkurencyjnej polskich przedsiębiorstw. In: Materiały z konferencji: Konkurencyjność przedsiębiorstw wobec wyzwań XXI wieku, Wyd. AE im. Oskara Langego we Wrocławiu, Wrocław, 8–10 października
Bednarski L, Borowiecki R, Duraj J, Kurtys E, Waśniewski T, Wersty B (1998) Analiza ekonomiczna przedsiębiorstwa. Wyd. Akademii Ekonomicznej im. Oskara Langego we Wrocławiu, Wrocław
Begg D, Fischer S, Dornbusch R (2007) Mikroekonomia. PWE, Warszawa
Bielski M (1996) Organizacje. Istota, struktury, procesy. Wyd. Uniwersytetu Łódzkiego, Łódź
Bielski M (2004) Podstawy teorii organizacji i zarządzania. Wyd. C.H. Beck, Warszawa
Bilansowe wyniki finansowe podmiotów gospodarczych 2004–2012. GUS, Warszawa
Bławat F (1999) Analiza ekonomiczna. Politechnika Gdańska, Gdańsk
Domańska A (2006) Wpływ infrastruktury transportu drogowego na rozwój regionalny. PWN, Warszawa
Dziembowski Z (1985) Infrastruktura jako kategoria ekonomiczna. Ekonomista 4(5):725–739
Fereńc M (2008) Uwarunkowania prawne i regulacyjne rozwoju infrastruktury telekomunikacyjnej w Polsce. Instytut Łączności – Państwowy Instytut Badawczy, Warszawa
Gabrusewicz W (2002) Podstawy analizy finansowej. PWE, Warszawa
Garbarski L, Rutkowski I, Wrzosek W (2000) Marketing. Punkt zwrotny nowoczesnej firmy. PWE, Warszawa
Garicano L, Kaplan SN (2001) The effects of business-to-business E-commerce on transaction cost. J Ind Econ XLIX(4):463–485
Godlewska H (2001) Lokalizacja działalności gospodarczej. Wybrane zagadnienia. WSHiFM, Warszawa
Grzywacz W (1982) Infrastruktura transportu. Wyd. KiŁ, Warszawa
Grzywacz W, Burnewicz J (1989) Ekonomika transportu. Wyd. KiŁ, Warszawa
Jacobson CD, Tarr JA (1994) Ownership and financing of infrastructure: historical perspectives (A background paper for the 1994 world development report). Carnegie Mellon University
James J (2002) Information technology, transactions costs and patterns of globalization in developing countries. Rev Soc Econ 60(4):507–519
Kalisiewicz D (ed) (1995) Nowa encyklopedia powszechna PWN, Tom 3. PWN, Warszawa
Kopczewska K (2007) Ekonometria i statystyka przestrzenna z wykorzystaniem programu R-Cran. CeDeWu, Warszawa
Krawczyk S (2001) Zarządzanie procesami logistycznymi. PWE, Warszawa
Kupiec L, Gołębiowska A, Wyszkowska D (2004) Gospodarka przestrzenna. Tom VI. Infrastruktura społeczna. Wyd. Uniwersytetu w Białymstoku, Białystok
Kupiec L, Gołębiowska A, Truskolaski T (2005) Gospodarka przestrzenna. Tom VII. Infrastruktura ekonomiczna. Wyd. Uniwersytetu w Białymstoku, Białystok
Malik K (2001) Ekonomiczno-ekologiczna efektywność gospodarowania w warunkach rynkowych. In: Piontek E (ed) Ekonomia a rozwój a rozwój zrównoważony. T.1. Teoria i kształcenie. Wyd. Ekonomia i Środowisko, Białystok, p 181
Marciniak S (ed) (2005) Makro- i mikroekonomia. Podstawowe problemy. PWN, Warszawa
Marciniak M (2011) Rozwój przedsiębiorczości szansą polskich obszarów wiejskich. Instytut Obywatelski, Warszawa
Młodak A (2006) Analiza taksonomiczna w statystyce regionalnej. Difin, Warszawa
Morash E, Dröge C, Vickery S (1996) Strategic logistics capabilities for competitive advantage and firm success. J Bus Logist 17(1):1–22
Porter ME (2001) Porter o konkurencji. PWE, Warszawa

Raczyński M (2007) Telekomunikacja, wzrost gospodarczy i nierówności. In: Woźniak MG (ed) Nierówności społeczne a wzrost gospodarczy. Zeszyt nr, vol 10. Wyd. Uniwersytet Rzeszowski, Rzeszów, pp 369–380
Samuelson PA, Nordhaus WD (2004) Ekonomia, Tom 2. PWN, Warszawa
Skowronek C, Sarjusz-Wolski Z (2003) Logistyka w przedsiębiorstwie. PWE, Warszawa
Skowronek-Mielczarek A, Leszczyński Z (2008) Analiza działalności i rozwoju przedsiębiorstwa. PWE, Warszawa
Społeczeństwo informacyjne w Polsce. Wyniki badań statystycznych z lat 2006–2010. (2010) GUS, Warszawa
Stephan A (1997) The impact of road infrastructure on productivity and growth: some preliminary results for the German manufacturing sector. Wissenschaftszentrum Berlin für Sozialforschung, Berlin
Suchecki B (ed) (2010) Ekonometria przestrzenna. Metody i modele analizy danych przestrzennych. Wyd. C.H. Beck, Warszawa
Świetlik W (2005) Analiza działalności gospodarczej przedsiębiorstw. Wyższa Szkoła Ekonomiczna, Warszawa
Szapiro T, Ciemniak R (1999) Internet – nowa strategia firmy. Difin, Warszawa
Szczepańska K (2009) Koszty jakości dla inżynierów. Placet, Warszawa
Szymańska E (2010) Efektywność przedsiębiorstw – definiowanie i pomiar. Roczniki Nauk Rolniczych. Seria G, T. 97, Z. 2(2010):152–164
Urząd Komunikacji Elektronicznej (2014) www.uke.gov.pl. Accessed 14 Nov 2014
Urząd Lotnictwa Cywilnego (2014) www.ulc.gov.pl. Accessed 14 Nov 2014
Zeliaś A (2000) Metody statystyczne. PWE, Warszawa

The Influence of Intellectual Capital Performance on Value Creation in Slovak SMEs

Marian Holienka, Anna Pilková, and Miroslava Kubišová

Abstract The intellectual capital has been stressed to play a crucial role in determining firm performance in current knowledge economies. Theoretical works as well as several empirical studies have declared its importance as a value creation driver. The aim of our study is to challenge these paradigms in the context of SMEs in Slovakia. Therefore, we examine the relationship between intellectual capital (measured using financial data through VAIC^{TM}) and firm value creation (using the ROCE measure as the most appropriate value creation proxy in this context). Also, we control for the effect of firm size and leverage in this relation. We based our analysis on 2011 financial statements of 3311 Slovak SMEs operating in ten different industrial sections. The data have been obtained from a business information portal (CRIBIS Universal Register). To examine the relation between intellectual capital and value creation while accounting for industry effects we constructed a set of regression models and analysed the explanatory power of intellectual capital performance in firm value creation. Our results suggest, that intellectual capital performance represents a significant value creation driver in each of the examined industries, and its explanatory power exceeds in all cases but one the explanatory power of control variables. Therefore, our results confirm the paradigm of intellectual capital importance for value creation also in the context of small and medium size companies (SMEs) in Slovakia.

Keywords Intellectual capital • Performance • Value creation • SMEs • VAIC^{TM} • ROCE

1 Introduction

Intellectual capital is frequently perceived as one of the key value drivers in the new economy wherein knowledge-based firms are crucial for economic development (Sveiby 1997; Edvinsson 1997; Lynn 1998). A core strategy for gaining a competitive advantage by a firm is the use of knowledge as a resource base. As such, value

M. Holienka (✉) • A. Pilková • M. Kubišová
Faculty of Management, Comenius University in Bratislava, Bratislava, Slovakia
e-mail: marian.holienka@fm.uniba.sk

T. Dudycz et al. (eds.), *The Essence and Measurement of Organizational Efficiency*, Springer Proceedings in Business and Economics, DOI 10.1007/978-3-319-21139-8_5

is thereby created for shareholders and stakeholders. It is clear that formulation of an adequate strategy is a very important component in the value creation process. Equally important is value management process in which relevant intellectual capital management is a serious challenge. Part of this challenge, on macro level, is also measurement of the contribution of intellectual capital to the economy. OECD (2008), in its report, stresses the importance of this issue, stating that the bias towards tangible assets in measuring investments is likely to result in inefficient policymaking, inappropriate allocation of resources by managers, as well as increased cost of capital for investors. However, OECD (2008) also emphasises that potential inclination toward understanding intellectual assets as investments, instead of expenses, will have to face considerable challenges related to measurement and valuation of such assets.

At a micro level, the impact of intellectual capital performance on a firm's value creation can be measured from both short term and long term perspectives. From a short term perspective it can be measured with selected financial performance ratios as proxies of value creation, such as ROA, ROE or sales to total assets. Also, as suggested in this paper, value creation indicators especially developed in the context of value-based management, such as ROCE, may be employed for this purpose. On the other hand, the long term perspective can be best measured by stock value dynamics. The issues addressed above are rather comprehensive and represent a considerable challenge for all types of companies but especially for SMEs. In many economies, similar to Slovakia, SMEs play a critical role in their development. In Slovakia, SMEs include 99.9 % of the companies (in the entire European Union this share is 99.8 %), account for 71.8 % of total employment (in the EU it is 67.5 %) and 41.3 % of GDP in non-financial industries (SBA 2014). Even though SMEs have their specific characteristics and managerial issues, they must also use knowledge as a source of competitive advantage particularly in turbulent times. Thus, in our paper we have investigated the role of intellectual capital in value creation of Slovak SMEs, operating in different industries.

In Sect. 2 of this paper, we discuss the context of intellectual capital and value creation in SMEs. In Sect. 3, we present the data and methods used in our research. Section 4 presents the results of our analysis and Sect. 5 discusses and concludes on the findings as well as their implication.

2 Intellectual Capital and Value Creation in SMEs

The most frequently used definition characterizes the concept of intellectual capital as any knowledge convertible into value (Edvinsson 1997). In line with this definition, the essence of intellectual capital is the value creation. More specifically, intellectual capital can be understood as a complex of intangible property, knowledge, skills, processes, applied experience and technologies used in organizations to ensure a competitive advantage on the market (Papula and Volna 2011). Thanks to superior competitiveness, companies are able to achieve desired financial

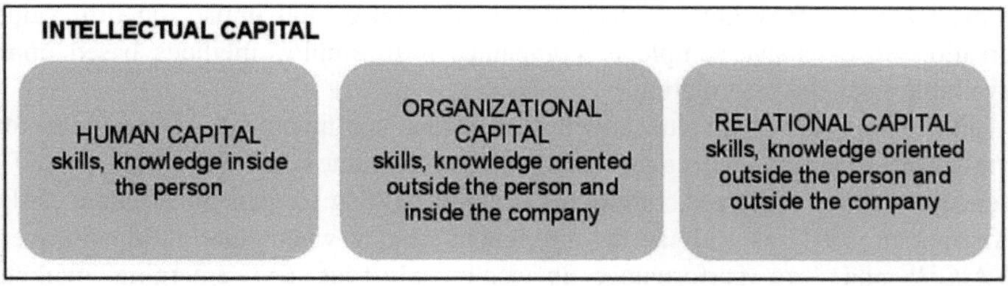

Fig. 1 Intellectual capital components (*Source*: Papula and Volna (2011))

performance and create value to their shareholders. According to literature (Edvinsson 1997; Sveiby 1997; Stewart 1998; Bontis 2002; Mouritsen et al. 2002; Pablos 2003), intellectual capital consists of three main components: human capital, organizational capital and relational capital. As can be seen in Fig. 1 [adapted from Papula and Volna (2011)] human and organizational capital both represent knowledge oriented towards internal environment of the organization, in contrast to relational capital which contains knowledge items oriented outside the organization, to its external environment.

To this date, a considerable amount of empirical research on intellectual capital and its relation to financial performance of the company has been published. Whereas some of the results are ambiguous (Javornik et al. 2012; Iazzolino and Laise 2013), many studies have confirmed positive relationship of intellectual capital and firm performance (e.g. Chen et al. 2005; Clarke et al. 2011; Alipour 2012; Mondal and Ghosh 2012; Pilkova et al. 2013; Holienka and Pilkova 2014). On the other hand, to our knowledge, no empirical research had so far focused its attention to relationship between intellectual capital and value creation represented by ROCE indicator.

Intellectual capital is a complex phenomenon. A lot of questions remain unanswered due to complexity of its measurement in empirical research as well as business practice. To a great extent, the approach used in intellectual capital performance measurement depends on the particular perspective or the purpose. As a result, researchers have developed a number of different methods in an attempt to overcome the limitations and irrelevance of traditional measures. In 2010, Sveiby presented a comprehensive analysis of 42 identified measurement methods (Sveiby 2010). According to his classification, intellectual capital measurement methods can be grouped into four main categories: direct intellectual capital evaluation methods, scorecard methods, market capitalization methods, and return on assets methods. The first two methods attempt to identify intellectual capital components and create some index to quantify them. On the contrary, the second two methods are based on decomposition of certain parameters. The value added intellectual coefficient (VAIC™), an indicator developed by Pulic (1998, 2000, 2004, 2008), is the only method that does not quite fit any of the four categories, while it is closest to ROA measurement methods (Sveiby 2010). Each of the intellectual capital measurement methods has its own pros and cons. In our opinion, the best and most pragmatic way how to study the intellectual capital impact on firm value creation on extensive sample of companies is to employ methods based upon available financial information.

Pulic proposed the value added intellectual coefficient as an indicator for measuring performance in a knowledge economy context. However, his VAIC™ concept has been criticized both for his assumptions (e.g. Zeghal and Maaloul 2010; Andriessen 2004) as well as for ambiguous results when relationship between VAIC™ and firm performance in some industries and emerging markets (e.g. Chan 2009; Puntillo 2009). According to Iazzolino and Laise (2013), part of this criticism can be contributed to misunderstandings resulting from the different meanings that Pulic gives to the terms of human capital (HC) and structural capital (SC) in comparison to Scandia Navigator. Further, they expressed belief that the connection created between the notions of value added and that of value creation in a knowledge economy context created by Pulic is the main attribute contributing to the strength of his proposal. On the contrary, they think that the main weakness is the attempt to position VAIC™ as a performance measurement criterion alternative (or rival) to the existing ones. In their opinion, VAIC™ can be viewed as an innovative indicator of intellectual capital efficiency that complements the existing measurement of the firm performance as multidimensional concept. With respect to its both advantages and disadvantages, we consider VAIC™ as the most appropriate intellectual capital performance measure to be used in the empirical investigation on financial statements data on an extensive sample of SMEs. Therefore, we will employ VAIC™ indicator in our analysis.

Measurement of firm value creation is, similarly to intellectual capital performance, a rather comprehensive issue. There exist several approaches using different metrics to capture how firms manage to create value for their stakeholders and shareholders (Bausch et al. 2009). Among the wide range of metrics, considerable attention has been paid to return on capital employed (ROCE) indicator. ROCE is a financial ratio which characterises the overall excellence of a business. It is considered a central concept in financial analysis which expresses the firm's capacity to obtain profit from its own capitals and borrowed ones, which have been invested in activities. The ratio is indeed widely used by managers and investors in SMEs for indicating how successfully businesses are utilising their assets. The nature of ROCE, its calculation and analysis serve as a reliable measure of corporate performance. Its extensive exploitation started with Stern/Stuart EVA concept's introduction (Stern et al. 1996). The use of ROCE performance measurement is of interest not only because of what it measures, but also because, unlike most indicators, it can, in principle, be applied across the full range of a body's operations and be compared between bodies (Rutherford 2002). As a result, ROCE often serves as a powerful tool for comparison of a company's performance with competitors or with the industry average. It consequently enables comparisons of the relative profitability, as one of the key financial value drivers, of different departments and the different kinds of products. In addition, these returns can be used to compare returns available from different projects that the company might undertake. Due to the above mentioned arguments, we consider ROCE indicator as the most appropriate firm value creation proxy in relation to intellectual capital performance. Thus, we will apply this indicator in our analysis.

As seen in above mentioned review, both theoretical grounding as well as previous empirical research suggest that intellectual capital should play a considerable role in determining SMEs performance leading to value creation. Moreover, the assumption that recent financial crisis have emerged formulation and implementation of new business strategies that put more effort on improvement of intellectual capital usage, further supports this premise. However, we have not found any quantitative analysis-based empirical evidence explaining the relation between intellectual capital performance and firm financial performance measured by ROCE as a proxy for value creation.

3 Research Methods and Data

3.1 Sample

Our analysis is based on data from financial statements of 3311 Slovak small and medium-sized enterprises operating in ten industrial sections for year 2011. To obtain this sample we have used a commercial database of business information portal CRIBIS Universal Register operated by CRIF—Slovak Credit Bureau. The data in the database have been collected by the vendor from the official Company register collection of documents and from the official Business bulletin. The original dataset comprised of 6211 companies with available data from financial statements. To obtain the final sample for our analysis, we applied several selection criteria to this dataset. Firstly, we have selected only small and medium-sized enterprises in accordance to EU definition (EC 2005), applying the financial thresholds (because of missing information on number of employees and the autonomy of the enterprise these criteria were omitted). Secondly, we eliminated all companies with zero turnover, zero or missing staff costs or negative equity. Thirdly, we have selected only the industrial sections (adhering to the SK NACE Rev. 2 statistical classification using the aggregated level of industry sections) for which we had at least 100 companies in the remaining sample. Finally, we have eliminated the cases with extreme values of independent and dependent variables. This filtering procedure resulted into the final sample of 3311 SMEs from ten industrial sections. Despite the limited representativeness of this sample resulting from the character of the original data based on convenience sampling, its considerable size and broad coverage of different industries enables certain generalization of the findings. The distribution of industrial sections in our sample is displayed in Table 1.

Table 1 Industry distribution of the research sample

Industry section	SK NACE	Sample size
Agriculture, forestry and fishing	A	329
Manufacturing	C	828
Construction	F	294
Wholesale and retail trade, repair of motor vehicle and motorcycle	G	922
Transportation and storage	H	175
Information and communication	J	115
Real estate activities	L	119
Professional, scientific and technical activities	M	240
Administrative and support service activities	N	129
Human health and social work activities	Q	160
Total		3311

3.2 Variables

As a dependent variable measuring firm value creation we used the Return on capital employed (ROCE) indicator. This return performance measure expresses the firm's capacity to obtain profit from the capital invested in business activities. The ratio is indeed widely used by managers and investors in SMEs for indicating how successfully businesses are utilising their assets (Burja 2013). Also, it belongs to the most frequently applied value-based management measures (Bausch et al. 2009). ROCE was calculated as a ratio of NOPAT (net operating profit after taxes) and capital employed (Eq. 1).

$$\begin{aligned}\mathrm{ROCE} &= \mathrm{NOPAT}/\mathrm{CE}\\ &= (\mathrm{EBIT}^{*}(1-\text{tax rate}))/(\text{fixed assets}+\text{working capital})\end{aligned} \tag{1}$$

To measure the level of intellectual capital performance in the firm we applied the VAIC™ indicator developed by Pulic (1998, 2000, 2004, 2008). This coefficient measures how much and how efficiently intellectual capital and capital employed create value (Pulic 2004). Thus, it is calculated as a sum of intellectual capital efficiency coefficient (ICE) and capital employed coefficient (CEE). The first component comprises indicators of human capital efficiency (HCE) and structural capital efficiency (SCE). HCE shows the value added (VA, the difference between the total output and the total input that represents the new wealth created) created by the human capital in the company (HC, total labour costs considered as the investment to knowledge workers). SCE measures the share of structural capital in the creation of value added (human and structural capital in this formula are inversely proportional). The latter component (CEE) act as an indicator of asset value efficiency, and it represents the value added created by one unit of capital of a company. The calculation formulas are provided in Eqs. (2, 3, 4, and 5).

$$\mathrm{HCE} = \mathrm{VA}/\mathrm{HC} \tag{2}$$

$$\mathrm{SCE} = (\mathrm{VA} - \mathrm{HC})/\mathrm{VA} \tag{3}$$

$$\mathrm{CEE} = \mathrm{VA}/\mathrm{CE} \tag{4}$$

$$\mathrm{VAIC}^{\mathrm{TM}} = \mathrm{ICE} + \mathrm{SCE} = (\mathrm{HCE} + \mathrm{SCE}) + \mathrm{CEE} \tag{5}$$

To control for the impact of other variables that may explain the observed relationship with SME value creation measured by ROCE, we have included two control variables in our analysis: firm size and firm leverage. Firm size was calculated as the natural logarithm of the book value of total assets. Firm leverage was calculated as a ratio of total debt and book value of total assets.

3.3 Methods

In order to examine the relationship between intellectual capital performance as measured by VAIC™ indicator and firm value creation represented by ROCE, we created a set of 10 regression models (one for each analysed industrial section) using forward stepwise regression analysis. This method allows for adding variables into the model at each step in the regression until the best regression model is achieved (Munkova et al. 2012). The final model enables us to estimate the contribution that each of the predictive variables makes toward explaining the variability in ROA, the dependent variable. After obtaining final regression models for each industry, we summarized the results on the relationship between IC performance and value creation across these industries to generalize the findings of our analysis.

Our assumptions regarding the statistical methods used in our analysis were also tested for appropriateness. We constructed a plot of standardized residuals and independent variables to test the linear relationship between dependent variable and independent variables and heteroscedasticity. This test proved the appropriateness of our models. To test for normality we constructed a normal plot of residuals. To confirm the independence of residuals we applied the Durbin-Watson test for independence and serial correlation. In most cases, the serial correlation value was close to 0 and values of Durbin-Watson statistics were close to 2, which indicates independence of residuals. Outliers in our data were eliminated already in sample selection procedure (by eliminating cases with extreme values of dependent and independent variables), therefore in our case the model input data contained no outliers. Finally, to test for multicollinearity we used correlation analysis. The results of above mentioned test methods confirmed the appropriateness of the statistical method used.

4 Results

In this section, we present the results of our analysis. Main descriptive statistics of the VAIC™ variable in different industrial sections is presented in the appendix of this paper. The results of the regression analysis performed in order to examine the contribution of VAIC™ and control variables to the variability explanation of dependent variable ROCE are presented in Tables 2 and 3. For each model we present the overall model parameters (adjusted coefficient of determination, F value and Durbin-Watson statistics) and different predictor variables, their significance and explanatory power.

The results presented in Tables 2 and 3 clearly demonstrate that VAIC™ (as an indicator of intellectual capital performance) is a significant predictor variable for dependent variable ROCE (as a firm value creation proxy) in case of all 10 analysed industrial sections. Moreover, in each of the presented models but one (related to industrial section L—real estate activities), the VAIC™ was the predictor variable with the highest explanatory power. This indicates that none of the control variables (firm size or leverage) had higher impact on ROCE than intellectual capital performance measured by VAIC™. In most cases, the model parameters

Table 2 Overview of regression—modelling ROCE, industry sections A to H

Dependent: ROCE	Section A	Section C	Section F	Section G	Section H
Independent					
VAIC (BETA)	0.413 (p=0.000)	0.393 (p=0.000)	0.577 (p=0.000)	0.365 (p=0.000)	0.324 (p=0.000)
Lev. (BETA)	0.163 (p=0.000)	0.087 (p=0.006)	0.103 (p=0.030)	0.151 (p=0.000)	
Size (BETA)	−0.305 (p=0.000)	−0.140 (p=0.000)	−0.094 (p=0.047)	−0.282 (p=0.000)	−0.219 (p=0.002)
F (ANOVA)	57.736	60.490	52.865	88.735	18.771
Adj. R-sq.	0.342	0.177	0.347	0.222	0.170
D-W st.	1.633	1.904	1.832	1.868	1.931

Table 3 Overview of regression—modelling ROCE, industry sections J to Q

Dependent: ROCE	Section J	Section L	Section M	Section N	Section Q
Independent					
VAIC (BETA)	0.547 (p=0.000)	0.241 (p=0.006)	0.345 (p=0.000)	0.396 (p=0.000)	0.618 (p=0.000)
Lev. (BETA)		0.265 (p=0.002)	−0.127 (p=0.037)		
Size (BETA)		−0.339 (p=0.000)			
F (ANOVA)	48.222	11.516	19.302	23.571	97.534
Adj. R-sq.	0.293	0.211	0.133	0.150	0.378
D-W st.	2.014	1.574	2.001	2.275	1.972

(Durbin-Watson statistics and F value) were acceptable. The adjusted coefficients of determination show that the models explained on average 24.23 % of ROCE variance. While in few cases the percentage of explained variance was rather low (e.g. 13.3 % in case of section M—Professional, scientific and technical activities), the models with higher adjusted R-sq. values explained considerable variance of dependent variable ROCE (e.g. 37.8 % in case of section Q—Human health and social work activities, or 34.7 % in case of section F—Construction).

5 Discussion and Conclusion

The findings of our analysis indicate a somewhat consistent pattern across almost all investigated industrial sections. The important role of intellectual capital performance in predicting firm's value creation has been clearly established. Therefore, even small and medium-sized companies should consider intellectual capital as an important asset and pay serious attention to issues of its management in order to increase their competitiveness and achieve superior performance in terms of value creation.

At the same time, our findings also proved that the strength of relation between intellectual capital performance and SME value creation differs in some industries. In particular, the explanatory power of the model and the VAIC™ predictor value were considerably high in sections Q (Human health and social work activities), F (Construction), A (Agriculture, forestry and fishing) and J (Information and communication). Looking at these sections individually, we may find arguments for the strong relationship between examined variables in the business specifics of the particular industries. Namely, human health and social work section as well as agriculture, forestry and fishing section may include broad scope of different activities with naturally divergent levels of intellectual capital utilisation. Within these sections, companies performing more sophisticated and more intellectual capital-intensive activities may create significantly higher value added and thus differentiate from their competitors in terms of value creation. Similar logic may apply to the construction industry section. While some activities within this industry are more intellectual capital-intensive and create higher value added leading to superior value creation, other activities may face intense competitive pressure on production efficiency leading to lower value added margins with considerable amounts of capital employed and thus also to lower creation of value to their owners. Finally, in case of information and communication services industry, we assume that the generally high knowledge intensity and human capital importance in these activities imply the strong relation of intellectual capital performance and financial performance in terms of value creation to firm stakeholders.

On the contrary, the model explanatory power and VAIC™ predictor value was relatively lower (in comparison to other industries), but at the same time still considerable especially in case of sections M (Professional, scientific and technical activities), N (Administrative and support service activities), H (Transportation and storage) and C (Manufacturing). Similarly to previously mentioned set of industries, also in these cases we attribute the results to business specifics in these industries. Particularly, in case of professional, scientific and technical activities, we assume that the level of intellectual capital intensity in such businesses would be generally relatively high irrespective the actual financial performance in terms of value creation. Usually, value creation in such fields has rather long-term character, so the long-term value creation effects may not be completely covered by our examination focused at the same year for both variables. Secondly, in case of administrative and support service activities, we may expect the general pressure on efficiency especially in usage of human resources to be a part of industry standards, resulting to generally high and more convergent levels of intellectual capital utilisation. Finally, we may assume that in industries related to manufacturing or transportation and storage a considerable mass of market players strongly focuses on achieving operational excellence via process innovation, sophisticated production and logistics systems and operations management proficiency. Thus, the value added achieved within such set of competitors may exhibit more convergent rates than within industries with greater differences in intellectual capital utilisation. This assumption is empirically supported by mean values of financial indicators of economic activities in Slovakia for 2011 (CRIF—Slovak Credit Bureau 2012), where e.g. section A (Agriculture, forestry and fishing) exhibits almost twice greater spread between upper and lower quartile of the value added in earnings indicator compared to section C (Manufacturing) or H (Transportation and storage).

Our findings on the significant relation between VAIC™ measure of intellectual capital and ROCE as a proxy for firm value creation can be understood in the context of two rather contradictory streams in intellectual capital research.

As previously mentioned, one stream of interpretation of relationship between financial performance measures (such as ROA, EVA or ROCE) and Pulic's VAIC™-based perspective on firm intellectual capital performance argues that these two categories of indicators reflect substantially different dimensions of firm performance and therefore should be perceived as co-existing indicators representing two views on performance, according to perspective employed to describe this contextual concept (Iazzolino and Laise 2013). This interpretation is against findings how intellectual capital (in terms of VAIC™) implies financial performance and value creation (e.g. performance expressed with ROCE). Even though our approach violates the very fundaments of this perspective, we argue that our findings contribute to its debate. If we consider value creation-based and intellectual capital-based approaches as two different perspectives of the multidimensional concept of firm performance, our findings suggest that under certain circumstances, these two dimensions are subjects of mutual convergence at firm level. Therefore, we may argue that in case of high value creating companies the financial (in this case value creation) and intellectual capital dimensions of performance reflect the similar intra-firm performance drivers.

On the contrary, there is still a substantial research stream that considers intellectual capital measured by VAIC™ model as the potential predictor of overall firm performance. So far, researchers have investigated the relationship among VAIC™-based measures and overall performance measures (such as ROA, ROE etc.) with inconsistent results (Javornik et al. 2012; Iazzolino and Laise 2013). Thus, additional research is necessary to further clarify these results. Our findings that established the importance of intellectual capital performance for value creation in the context of Slovak SMEs therefore contribute to this research stream.

They are in line with similar previous studies in the same national context (Pilkova et al. 2013; Holienka and Pilkova 2014). Moreover, they offer an explanation of ambiguousness of this relationship in different contexts by proposing an argument on its industry specific nature. We took into consideration industry specifics by analysing different industries separately. While the explanatory power of VAIC™ as a value creation predictor was considerable for all of the ten industrial sections we studied, the strength of this relation differed. This finding definitely advocates that while intellectual capital performance may be commonly important overall firm value creation driver across industrial sections, industry specifics play significant role in the strength of this relation.

Based on our findings on the significant relation between intellectual capital performance and value creation in SMEs, we may derive certain implications for SMEs management. Similar to our results, also these implications will be industry specific by nature. In some industries, a considerable value creation effect can be achieved by focusing on highly intellectual capital-intensive activities instead of less sophisticated and more efficiency-focused businesses. Thus, SMEs that aim to create superior value in the context of divergently knowledge-intensive environment should focus themselves preferably to high sophisticated activities and organize entire business models around this focus. On the contrary, in industries where intellectual capital utilisation proficiency is widely spread and is a part of industry standards, it is a must for a company to keep up with these industry patterns if it wants to remain competitive in terms of value creation. Therefore, while in some industries a systematic focus on intellectual capital is an option for SMEs to achieve superior value creation, in other industries it is already an absolute necessity for SMEs to survive and remain competitively profitable.

Acknowledgements Authors would like to thank to CRIF—Slovak Credit Bureau for providing access to CRIBIS Universal Register data used in this study.

Appendix

See Table 4.

Table 4 Descriptive statistics summaries for VAIC™ in different industries

Section	A	C	F	G	H
N	329	828	294	922	175
Mean	3.033	2.584	2.663	2.844	3.412
Median	2.741	2.350	2.379	2.436	3.020
Std. Dev.	1.212	1.009	1.167	1.332	1.467
Section	J	L	M	N	Q
N	115	119	240	129	160
Mean	3.040	2.931	3.054	3.163	3.142
Median	2.697	2.442	2.637	2.808	3.107
Std. Dev.	1.324	1.800	1.429	1.510	0.854

References

Alipour M (2012) The effect of intellectual capital on firm performance: an investigation of Iran insurance companies. Meas Bus Excell 16(1):53–66

Andriessen D (2004) IC valuation and measurement. Classifying the state of the art. J Intellect Cap 5(2):230–242

Bausch A, Hunoldt M, Matysiak L (2009) Superior performance through value-based management. In: Bausch A, Schwenker B (eds) Handbook utility management. Springer, Berlin, pp 15–36

Bontis N (ed) (2002) World congress on intellectual capital readings. Butterworth Heinemann, Boston, MA

Burja C (2013) Analysis model for return on capital employed. Annals – Economy Series, vol 1. Constantin Brancusi University, Faculty of Economics, Targu Jiu, pp 82–87

Clarke M et al (2011) Intellectual capital and firm performance in Australia. J Intellect Cap 12 (4):505–530

Chan KH (2009) Impact of intellectual capital on organizational performance: an empirical study of companies in the Hang Seng Index (Part 2). Learn Organ 16(1):22–39

Chen M et al (2005) An empirical investigation of the relationship between intellectual capital and firms' market value and financial performance. J Intellect Cap 6(2):159–176

Edvinsson L (1997) Developing intellectual capital at Skandia. Long Range Plan 30(3):266–373

European Commission (2005) The new SME definition. User guide and model declaration. Publications Office of the EU, Luxembourg

Holienka M, Pilkova A (2014) Comparing impact of intellectual capital on firm performance before and after crisis. In: Caganova D, Cambal M (eds) Proceedings of the 6th European conference on intellectual capital, Trnava

Iazzolino G, Laise D (2013) Value added intellectual coefficient (VAIC). A methodological and critical review. J Intellect Cap 14(4):547–563

Javornik S et al (2012) The efficiency of intellectual capital investments as a potential leading indicator. Int Bus Econ Res J 11(5):535–558

Lynn B (1998) Intellectual capital. CMA Mag 72(1):10–15

Mondal A, Ghosh S (2012) Intellectual capital and financial performance of Indian banks. J Intellect Cap 13(4):515–530

Mouritsen J et al (2002) Developing and managing knowledge through intellectual capital statements. J Intellect Cap 3(1):10–29

Munkova D et al (2012) Impact of cognitive-individual variables on process of foreign language learning. Proc Soc Behav Sci 46(1):5430–5434

OECD (2008) Intellectual assets and value creation—synthesis report. OECD, Paris

Pablos POD (2003) Knowledge management projects: state of the art in the Spanish manufacturing industry. Int J Manuf Technol Manag 14(4):297–310

Papula J, Volna J (2011) Intellectual capital as value adding element in knowledge management. In: Knowledge as business opportunity. In: Proceeding of the conference of the International School for Social and Business Studies, Celje

Pilkova A et al (2013) The influence of intellectual capital on firm performance among Slovak SMEs. In: Proceedings of the 10th international conference on intellectual capital, knowledge management and organizational learning (ICICKM), Washington, DC

Pulic A (1998) Measuring the performance of intellectual potential in the knowledge economy. Paper presented at the 2nd world congress on the management of intellectual capital, Hamilton, Jan 1998

Pulic A (2000) VAIC™ – an accounting tool for IC management. Int J Technol Manag 20 (5–8):702–714

Pulic A (2004) Intellectual capital – does it create or destroy value? Meas Bus Excel 8(1):62–68

Pulic A (2008) The principles of intellectual capital efficiency – a brief description. Croatian Intellectual Capital Center, Zagreb

Puntillo P (2009) Intellectual capital and business performance from Italian banking industry. Electron J Corp Financ 4(2):97–115

Rutherford BA (2002) Design and implementation of return on capital employed performance indicators within a trading regime: the case of executive agencies. Financ Account Manag 18 (1):73–101

SCB—Slovak Credit Bureau (2012) Mean values of financial indicators of economic activities in Slovak Republic for year 2011. SCB—Slovak Credit Bureau, Bratislava

Slovak Business Agency (2014) The report on state of SMEs in Slovakia. Slovak Business Agency, Bratislava

Stern JM, Stewart GB, Chew DH (1996) EVA: an integrated financial management system. Eur Financ Manag 2(2):223–245

Stewart T (1998) Intellectual capital. Nicholas Breadley, London

Sveiby KE (1997) The new organisational wealth: managing and measuring knowledge based assets. Berrett-Kohler, San Francisco

Sveiby KE (2010) Methods for measuring intangible assets. http://www.sveiby.com/articles/IntangibleMethods.htm. Accessed 4 Dec 2014

Zeghal D, Maaloul A (2010) Analyzing value added as an indicator of intellectual capital and its consequences on company performance. J Intellect Cap 11(1):39–60

Entrepreneurial Environment and Economic Growth: What Affects the Productiveness of Business Activity at Macro Level?

Marian Holienka, Anna Pilková, and Nataliia Ostapenko

Abstract The purpose of this article is to define the factors of the entrepreneurial environment which could drive productive entrepreneurial activity from the macroeconomic perspective. The main research question therefore is to identify, what are the main environmental drivers of productive entrepreneurial activity and what is its effective sectorial structure. Our analysis is based on 2013 Global Entrepreneurship Monitor (GEM) data obtained through an adult population survey and national expert survey. In our investigation we employ PATH-analysis, SEM model and multiple regression analysis to empirically define the effective structure of entrepreneurial activity for the performance of an economy and the environmental factors that impact it. This approach empirically examines the directions of influence in the above mentioned relationships. In addition, the robustness of our findings was checked by repeating our analysis on a different sample (2010 GEM data on 59 economies) and by multiplying regression analysis for separate variables of entrepreneurial activity effectiveness, and our results were confirmed. Our findings suggest that of all the different environmental enablers, access to infrastructure (both physical and commercial) is the most influential attribute of entrepreneurial environment affecting economic performance at a macro level and the effective sectorial structure of business activities. Overall, the main drivers of the productiveness of entrepreneurship are: access to infrastructure, rule of law, effective government programs and market openness and dynamics.

Keywords Entrepreneurship • Environment • Efficiency • Productivity • SEM-model • Infrastructure

1 Introduction

Entrepreneurship is an important phenomenon in national economies, because it helps to stimulate economic growth and to reduce unemployment. However, as can be seen from actual economic development, this phenomenon does not always

M. Holienka (✉) • A. Pilková • N. Ostapenko
Faculty of Management, Comenius University in Bratislava, Bratislava, Slovakia
e-mail: marian.holienka@fm.uniba.sk; anna.pilkova@fm.uniba.sk; natayal107@mail.ru

T. Dudycz et al. (eds.), *The Essence and Measurement of Organizational Efficiency*, Springer Proceedings in Business and Economics, DOI 10.1007/978-3-319-21139-8_6

perform its functions sufficiently. In some economies it considerably contributes to economic growth, while in others its potential in these terms is not fully exploited.

As stated by Baumol (1990) entrepreneurial activity can be productive, unproductive or even destructive, depending on the institutional environment of the national economy. Formal and informal institutions stimulate entrepreneurial potential and shape the behaviour and actions of entrepreneurs, who therefore conduct their business activities in certain ways. This concept has also been confirmed by work of De Soto (1989) who proved that imperfect institutions could be the main factor which drives business into the shadow economy. Thus, the institutional environment affects the productivity of business activities at an aggregate national level. Proper institutional framework should determine the productive structure of entrepreneurial activities, which could in turn accelerate economic growth. On the other hand, when institutional framework leads to an unproductive structure of entrepreneurial activity, the effect on economic growth could be neutral or even inverse.

The main aim of this research is to define the major elements of the institutional framework that lead entrepreneurship into productive behaviour in terms of effective sectorial structure leading to productiveness at a macro-economic level. As part of this effort we need to define the proxies of productive entrepreneurship and the major factors which affect it.

Section 2 of our paper describes research literature that links entrepreneurial environment with the shape of entrepreneurial activity as well as entrepreneurship to economic growth, and attempts to establish the key factors affecting these relationships. Section 3 describes the methodology of our research and Sect. 4 presents an analysis of our findings. Finally, in Sect. 5 we discuss our findings, and in Sect. 6 we conclude on them and deal with the limitations of our approach.

2 Literature Review

Entrepreneurial activity has been established as one of the key drivers of macro-economic outcomes, e.g. in terms of productiveness. Entrepreneurs may contribute to growth through a diverse range of behaviours, including innovation, combination of resources and increased competitive pressures (Valliere and Peterson 2009). According to Schumpeter (1934, 1950), an entrepreneur is someone who finds new combinations of resources and creates products that did not previously exist. He is a disruptive force in an economy, because the introduction of these new combinations leads to the obsolescence of others. Thus, entrepreneurship is the main factor in promoting economic growth and its instrument is innovation. Martin et al. (2010) concluded that entrepreneurship has a positive effect on economic growth through public investments. Kreft and Sobel (2005) showed a one-way causal relationship running from entrepreneurship to economic growth. However, causality between entrepreneurial prevalence and economic growth has not been conclusively established.

Entrepreneurial activity is fundamentally influenced by economic and socio-cultural influences in the environment in which it is formed and executed (e.g. Krueger et al. 2000; Stenholm et al. 2013). According to the rules of the game concept introduced by Baumol (1990), the environment influences not only the quantitative aspect of entrepreneurial activity, but mainly its qualitative allocation. He hypothesizes that the set of rules (instead of the supply of entrepreneurs or nature of their objectives) helps to dictate the ultimate effect on the economy via the allocation of entrepreneurial resources. Several researchers have confirmed this hypothesis with empirical evidence (e.g. Sobel 2008). The understanding of the concept of the entrepreneurial environment nowadays increasingly builds on the theory of institutions, traditionally concerned with how individuals, groups or organizations achieve their legitimacy by conforming to the rules of institutional environments (Bruton et al. 2010). The institutions are humanly devised constraints that shape human action (North 1990), i.e. behaviours and interactions of and between individuals, groups and organizations. One of such interactions is also entrepreneurship, since enterprise behaviour is understood as a reaction to the institutional framework (Amoros 2009). Thus, the theory of institutions offers the appropriate base to understand the entrepreneurial environment concept. Institutions can be generally divided into formal institutions in the form of formalized rules and the entire legal framework, and informal institutions, representing constraints which originate in socially transferred information as a part of culture (North 1990). Different classification derived from entrepreneurship perspective and introduced by Scott (1995) recognizes three institutional pillars: regulative, normative and cognitive. In addition, Stenholm et al. (2013) suggested also considering the so called conducive dimension to this classification.

Through its influence on entrepreneurial activity, which is the main driver of economic growth, the national institutional framework should therefore affect economic outcomes in terms of productiveness. According to Baumol (1990), a good institutional environment leads enterprising efforts into productive outcomes. In turn, productive entrepreneurship is the fundamental source of economic growth and wealth creation (Sobel 2008). Institutions create constraints and incentives that encourage entrepreneurs to move from unproductive to productive activities, and ultimately improve the overall economic well-being of society (North 1990). Economic growth and the development of institutions is a highly interdependent process at the macro level (Aixala and Fabro 2008; Jankauskas and Seputiene 2009; Rodrik 2000). As stated by Hare (2001), institutional environments affect the behaviour of enterprises in different ways, and the results of changes in their behaviour lead to different economic outcomes. Many authors attribute differences between the growth rates of different economies to their institutional frameworks (Reynolds et al. 1999; Zacharakis et al. 2000; Henderson 2002). For example, Broadman et al. (2004) found that economic growth in the emerging economies of Eastern Europe was impeded by the absence of effective market-based institutions to protect property rights and to ensure fair competition. Such arguments stress the importance of policymakers' efforts in creating favourable environments for productive entrepreneurial actions. The factors affecting entrepreneurial efforts are directly influenced by government actions in constructing and maintaining a supportive environment, as well as by societal norms toward entrepreneurship (Bruton et al. 2010). The impact of the management of any sphere of the national economy directly depends on the quality of the formed institutional environment, its adequacy to the present level of socio-economic and industrial relations in society (Golovko 2011; Rehak et al. 2014). Of course, the starting lines in these policymakers' efforts differ across economies. Institutional environments have been formed for a long time and are dependent on the previous development of the country (North 1990). Both formal regulations and informal institutions are based on the cultural traditions of the society, which in turn have an effect on the choice of the trajectory of socio-economic development and the macroeconomic structural model (Nureev 2010). Building on these assumptions, we will focus our investigation on understanding the relationship between the institutional framework of the entrepreneurial environment (with particular emphasis on regulatory pillar), entrepreneurial activity and the productiveness of economies.

3 Methodology

In this section of our paper we describe the data and variables used as well as the testing methods employed in our analysis.

3.1 Data

Our study is based on the Global Entrepreneurship Monitor (GEM) project datasets for 2013. GEM is the world's largest academic study that analyses various aspects of entrepreneurial attitudes, activity and aspirations as well as entrepreneurial environments in the involved countries. It uses harmonized methodology to collect data from representative samples of adult individuals (through adult population surveys—APS) and from samples of national experts (through national expert surveys—NES) to compute a set of aggregate national-level variables. In 2013, the project included 70 countries with approximately 197,000 interviewed individuals, which corresponds after extrapolation to three quarters of the world's population and 90 % of the world's GDP (Amoros and Bosma 2014).

Our analysis was based on national-level APS and NES data for 2013, comprising 65 economies involved in the GEM project. Thus, our sample included a variety of economies in different stages of economic development and different regional contexts, supporting the robustness of our findings. We preferred cross-country analysis instead of an intra-country approach following the recommendations of Bruton et al. (2010), who defined the questionable universal applicability of findings on the institutional impact to a wide set of environments as the main drawback of using a sample of only one given country. Finally, to further check the robustness of our findings we repeated the analysis with 2010 APS and NES national-level data from 59 GEM project member countries.

3.2 *Variables*

As a proxy of business activity productiveness at the national level we used the GDP per capita (PPP) indicator. To characterize entrepreneurial activity in search for its productive structure we employed the GEM project national-level variables derived from adult population surveys. Namely, we adopted GEM indicators of entrepreneurial activity (both early-stage and established), its main motives and sectorial structure (excluding extractive industries), indicators of intrapreneurial activity, and indicators of market expansion, internationalization, job creation and innovation aspirations within early-stage and established entrepreneurial activity. To determine the entrepreneurial environment of the analysed economies, the GEM project national-level variables based on national expert surveys were used. Namely, these included the indicators assessing the state of particular dimensions of the entrepreneurial environment.

3.3 *Methods*

To test the causal relationships between the entrepreneurial environment, entrepreneurial activity and productiveness of economies, and to define the productive structure of entrepreneurship leading to better economic outcomes, we used path-analysis and the SEM-model.

For this purpose we firstly performed a correlation analysis to find the main cross-correlated parameters for entrepreneurial activity corresponding to productiveness at the macroeconomic level.

Secondly, to identify the main factors of entrepreneurial environment which could stimulate the development of productive entrepreneurial activity, we used multiple regression analysis with method of steep selection.

4 Results

In this section we present our results using SEM-model and regression analysis, as well as a robustness check of our findings.

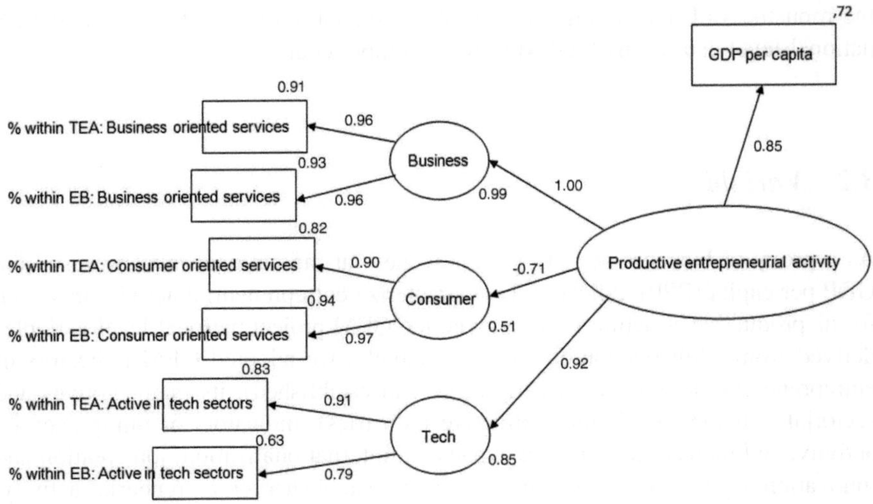

Chi-square = 11.422	CFI = 0.997
Degrees of freedom = 10	RMSEA = 0.47
Probability level = 0.326	PCLOSE = 0.455
CMIN/DF = 1.142	

Fig. 1 SEM-model of "productive entrepreneurial activity" and model FIT

4.1 SEM-Model and Regression Results

To define what structure of entrepreneurial activity is productive from the national economy perspective, the entire set of GEM project variables characterizing entrepreneurial activity at national levels were tested on regressions and correlations with GDP per capita (PPP). The relevant variables were selected and further used in the SEM-model. Figure 1 demonstrates the model explanation of proxy for entrepreneurial activity productiveness that could lead to accelerating economic development.

According to our results, the latent variable named "productive entrepreneurial activity" positively affects GDP per capita and explains 72 % of its variance (R^2 is 0.72). This latent variable is in relation with three additional latent variables characterizing sectorial attributes of entrepreneurial activity—share of business oriented services (factor for both TEA and EB), share of consumer oriented services (factor for both TEA and EB) and share of enterprises active in technology sectors (factor for both TEA and EB). Model Fit is acceptable and the model is well specified. According to these results, there are three factors of productive entrepreneurship which affect economic growth, namely the share of entrepreneurial activity engaged in business oriented services (with positive impact), the share of entrepreneurial activity engaged in technology sectors (with positive impact) and the share of entrepreneurial activity in customer oriented services (with negative impact).

A greater share of entrepreneurship active in technology sectors has the potential to accelerate economic growth because in general it exhibits higher levels of productivity and added value in comparison to non-technology businesses. This assumption is in line with the theory of endogenous economic growth by Romer (1990), who noted that growth is driven by technological change that arises from intentional investment decisions made by profit-maximizing agents and gave an endogenous explanation of the source of this technological change. Decisions by entrepreneurs to start technology ventures could accelerate growth at the macro level if these decisions are widespread inside one country. The opposite effects of entrepreneurial activities in business oriented services versus consumer oriented services could be in our opinion explained by general differences in productivity, value added, innovativeness and scope of businesses in these sectors. While business oriented services in general are characterized by a constant pressure on productivity and value added, are more frequently innovative and have implicitly higher growth potential, the latter group of entrepreneurial activities are usually replicative by nature, small in scope, and exhibit lower productivity and value added by their activities.

To test which factors could drive, affect and accelerate the "productive entrepreneurial activity" latent variable, we constructed the second SEM-model containing additional factors representing the different conditions of entrepreneurial environments, with the potential impacts on the latent variable. Results of this modelling are displayed in Fig. 2.

As can be seen on Fig. 2, the second model contains additional factors of the entrepreneurial environment derived from national expert surveys variables, namely: government support—latent variable for summary variables characterizing government programs, government policies in terms of bureaucracy and taxes as well as in terms of concrete policies, priority and support; infrastructure—latent variable consisting of summary variables assessing access to physical infrastructure and services as well as to professional and commercial infrastructure; and non-latent variable—summary variable assessing for financial environment related to entrepreneurship. From these variables, access to infrastructure was found to have a major impact on "productive entrepreneurial activity" variable. In total, all three variables explained 50 % of variance in "productive entrepreneurial activity" ($R^2 = 0.5$). A regression analysis was further performed to examine the significance of these impacts. The results are presented in Table 1.

From the regression analysis results (Table 1) it is obvious that access to infrastructure had the greatest impact on the "productive entrepreneurial activity" latent variable, with the level of significance being 0.001. On the other hand, the impact of the remaining factors of entrepreneurial environment on productive entrepreneurship proved insignificant. Therefore, our results suggest that access to infrastructure (in terms of both physical and commercial infrastructure) is more important for productive entrepreneurship than the availability of financial recourses or government support initiatives (in terms of policies and programs)

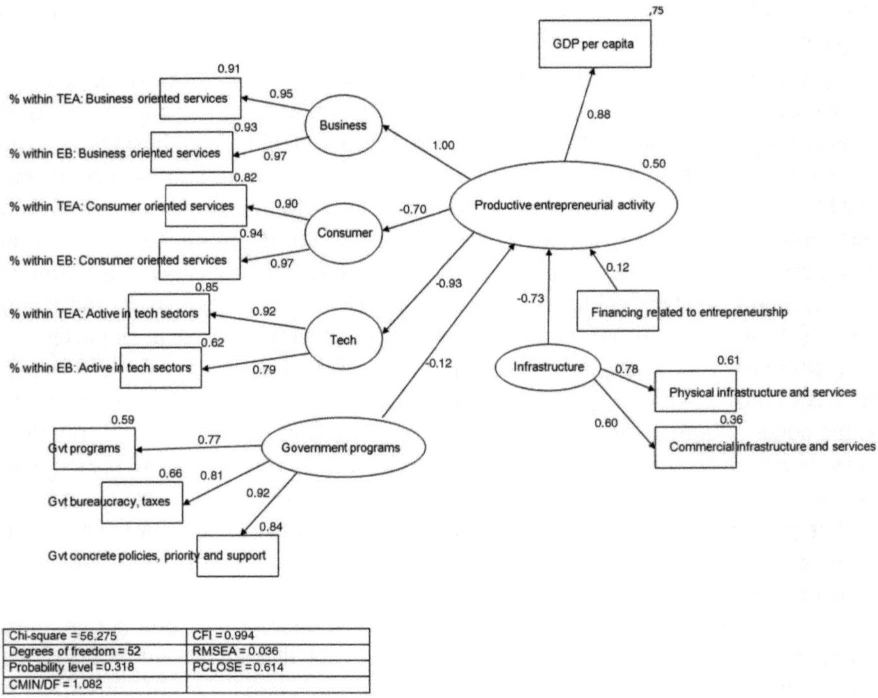

Fig. 2 SEM-model of causal relationship between environment, "productive entrepreneurial activity" and productiveness of economies and model FIT

Table 1 Regression weights

			Estimate	S.E.	C.R.	P
Productive e-ship	←	Govt. programs	−0.783	1.142	−0.686	0.493
Productive e-ship	←	Fin. environment	0.649	1.435	0.452	0.651
Productive e-ship	←	Infrastructure	4.352	1.329	3.274	0.001
Business services	←	Productive e-ship	5.491	0.680	8.069	0.000
Cons. services	←	Productive e-ship	−5.045	0.912	−5.532	0.000
Tech. e-ship	←	Productive e-ship	1.000			
GDP_per_capita	←	Productive e-ship	6.745	0.943	7.153	0.000

regarding entrepreneurship. Finally, productive entrepreneurial activity was found to have a significant impact on economic outcomes measured by GDP per capita.

4.2 Robustness Checks

To test the robustness of our findings we replicated the above mentioned analyses using 2010 GEM data. Results of this analysis are presented in Fig. 3.

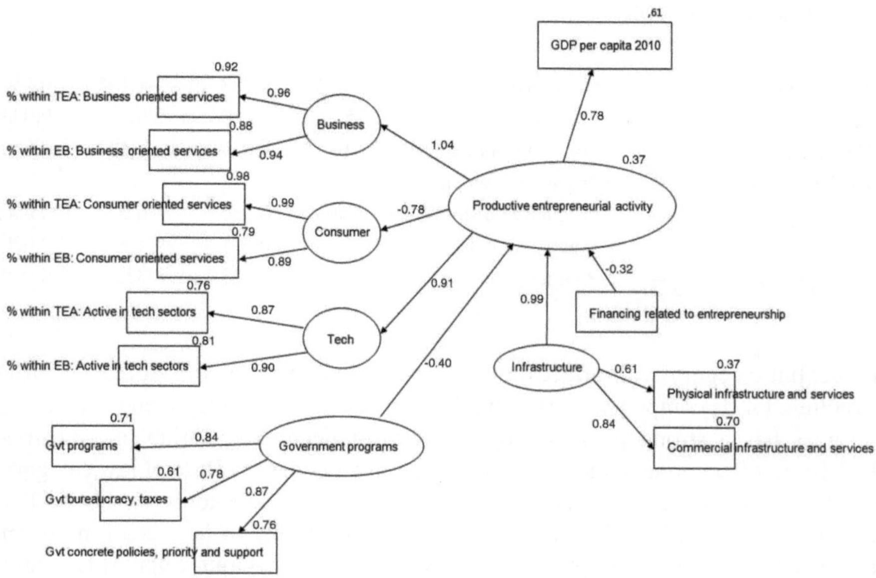

Chi-square = 66.699	CFI = 0.981
Degrees of freedom = 56	RMSEA = 0.361
Probability level = 0.155	PCLOSE = 0.061
CMIN/DF = 1.191	

Fig. 3 SEM-model of causal relationship between environment, "productive entrepreneurial activity" and productiveness of economies for 2010 GEM data and model FIT

As can be seen from the SEM-model in Fig. 3, the strong impact of the productive entrepreneurial activity latent variable on the productiveness of economies measured by GDP per capita ($R^2 = 0.61$) as well as signs of this impact have also been identified in 2010. Thus, it confirms our findings on 2013 data presented in Figs. 1 and 2. In addition, access to infrastructure (both physical and commercial) was found to have the greatest impact on productive entrepreneurship from all entrepreneurial environment factors. Table 2 presents regression weights for this model.

Estimates from multiple regression analysis also confirm the impact of physical and commercial infrastructure on the productive entrepreneurship indicator ($p = 0.043$). In turn, the productive entrepreneurial activity latent variable confirms its significant impact on GDP per capita.

In addition, as a second robustness check of our results we also performed multiple regression analysis of separate entrepreneurship environment components on separate productive entrepreneurship indicators. Results of this analysis are presented in Appendix. The influential factors can be grouped into seven categories: Rule of Law, Financial resources availability, Access to infrastructure, Government programs, Market openness and dynamics, Education, training and R&D transfer and Cultural and social norms. The largest (in terms of number of factors) and most

Table 2 Regression weights

			Estimate	S.E.	C.R.	P
Productive e-ship	←	Govt. programs	−10.284	8.983	−1.145	0.252
Productive e-ship	←	Infrastructure	52.751	26.101	2.021	0.043
Productive e-ship	←	Fin. Environment	−8.708	7.039	−1.237	0.216
Business services	←	Productive e-ship	1.000			
Cons. services	←	Productive e-ship	−1.106	0.166	−6.677	0.000
Tech. e-ship	←	Productive e-ship	0.294	0.031	9.464	0.000
GDP_per_cap	←	Productive e-ship	1.025	0.123	8.332	0.000

influential category with effect on all dependent variables is the Access to infrastructure. Of its components, particularly easy access to good legal and accounting services has a strong positive impact on most dependent variables. Anti-trust legislation effectiveness and enforcement, grouped under the Rule of law category, exhibited a predictably strong positive impact on most dependent variables. This finding is in line with wide acknowledgement of the rule of law as an important factor influencing the entrepreneurial activity and its behaviour. Support for entrepreneurship by science parks and business incubators has a positive impact on productive entrepreneurship variables. This is in line with the theory of endogenous growth and the importance of technology. Support of national culture towards individual success affirmed its positive impact on consumer oriented business. Thus, according to our findings, this particular element of national culture does not affect entrepreneurship in all sectors, and due to its influence on less innovative and growth-oriented activities, it does not automatically lead to productive entrepreneurial activity. Finally, the availability of financial resources showed a negative impact on most of the separate productive entrepreneurship indicators. Thus, it confirms the results of our SEM-models (Figs. 2 and 3).

5 Discussion

Our results of the latent factor of "productive entrepreneurial activity" contribute to work by Stel et al. (2005), who found out that TEA (total early-stage entrepreneurial activity) rates play positive roles in developed countries, and the impact of entrepreneurship in highly developed economies may indicate that entrepreneurial activity is important in the process of the commercialization of new (technological) knowledge. In addition, Stel et al. (2005) found that the TEA rate has a negative effect on GDP growth for developing countries. On the contrary, in developed countries TEA may reflect more innovative entrepreneurs in new sectors (for instance software companies). Thus, these findings explain our results in terms of technology entrepreneurship importance for productive entrepreneurial activity related to high levels of GDP per capita.

By defining "productive entrepreneurship" our results complement Sobel's work (2008), wherein we found that better institutional structures affect productive entrepreneurship. Moreover, we contributed to the definition of productiveness (in relation to entrepreneurial activity). Sobel used indicators of venture capital investments per capita, rate of patents per capita, rate of sole proprietorship growth, and establishment birth rate as proxies for productiveness. However, we propose other explanations and variables for the measurement of productive entrepreneurship. Unlike Sobel, we abstain from focussing on the overall quantity of entrepreneurial activity, since in our opinion it does not refer to productiveness by itself. As stated by Wong et al. (2005), having a higher degree of entrepreneurship or new business creation prevalence does not guarantee enhanced economic performance and faster rates of economic growth. They have confirmed the insignificance of the overall TEA rate and suggest that at the microeconomic level, only certain activities and functions of entrepreneurs may stimulate growth. As the analysis of Wong et al. (2005) was conducted at the aggregate macroeconomic level, they were not able to distinguish between these different roles of entrepreneurs, but they called for further empirical investigation.

Regarding regulations, Stenholm et al. (2013) concluded that a supportive regulative environment would be a decisive factor in factor- and efficiency-driven economies, since in these countries it is a necessity for any type of entrepreneurial activity to emerge. While these authors stress the importance of the regulative pillar in affecting the entry rate to entrepreneurial activity (i.e. quantity of entrepreneurship), we concluded that government programs and government policies (in terms of bureaucracy and taxes as well as in terms of concrete policies, priority and support) could affect productive types of entrepreneurship.

As far as infrastructure is concerned, Levie and Autio (2007) could not find support for their hypothesis about the positive impact of the extent and quality of business and commercial services and accessible physical infrastructure (work space, utilities, etc.) on the rate of entrepreneurial activity. However, our analysis related to the productiveness of entrepreneurship showed that access to infrastructure was found to have a major impact on productive entrepreneurial activity.

Regarding the rule of law, the results of our analysis confirm Baumol's (1990) statements that institutions providing for secure property rights, a fair and balanced judicial system, contract enforcement, and effective constitutional limits on the government's ability to transfer wealth through taxation and regulation, reduce the profitability of unproductive political and legal entrepreneurship. Thus, under this incentive structure, creative individuals are more likely to engage in the creation of new wealth through productive market entrepreneurship. Kreft and Sobel (2005) concluded that an environment of low taxes, low regulations, and secure private property rights is a necessity to encourage the kind of entrepreneurial activity that is vital to produce economic growth. In our results, the "rule of law" also plays an important role in affecting productiveness of entrepreneurial activity.

In addition, our results confirm Sobel's (2008) suggestions which conclude that rather than focusing on expanding government programs like subsidized loans, workforce education, or programs aimed at increasing 'entrepreneurial inputs' as a way to foster productive entrepreneurship, a better path is through institutional reform. This reform should constrain or minimize the government's role, lowering the return to unproductive types of entrepreneurship, because government programs too often encourage entrepreneurial individuals to devote their efforts toward figuring out how to obtain transfers or subsidies, rather than devoting those efforts toward satisfying consumers and creating wealth. Government programs have a controversial impact on entrepreneurship in our results. Also, Kreft and Sobel (2005) in their investigation of three policy variables identified that only one variable has significant influence on the entrepreneurial growth, namely the presence of state death taxes. Finally, Levie and Autio (2007) stated that entrepreneurship policy was negatively associated with high-expectation entrepreneurial activity (in terms of the expected number of created jobs). In addition the authors could not support their hypothesis about the positive impact of the quality of government programs on the level of entrepreneurial activity.

According to our results vocational, professional and continuing education support towards entrepreneurship, as well as the support of the science and technology base for the creation of world-class new-tech ventures both have negative impacts on the productive entrepreneurial activity. It could contribute to the work of Stenholm et al. (2013), who concluded that a conducive dimension—environments providing support and interplay between innovation, skills, and resources—play a positive role in fostering entrepreneurial activity. Our results also show the important role of higher education systems, but rather by general support to entrepreneurship than in fostering productive types of entrepreneurial activity. On the contrary, our findings in relation to higher education oppose the findings by Levie and Autio (2007). They argue that providing entrepreneurship education and training at higher-level educational institutions will influence the career decisions of those individuals who are likely to possess the kind of skills, competencies and social capital required to launch high-growth ventures, at a crucial time of their personal and professional development.

Finally, as far as entrepreneurial financing is concerned, Levie and Autio (2007) stated that financing does not exhibit significant influence on any of the dependent variables. In this case, our results are in line with their findings, because in our results the availability of financial resources plays a negative role in both SEM-models (Figs. 1 and 2) as well as in separate regressions (Appendix).

As far as limitations are concerned, we see the sample size (65 countries in 2013 and 59 countries in 2010) and usage of the same type of datasets as the main limitations of our research. On the other hand, we consider the GEM project with its special focus on entrepreneurship mapping activity, attitudes and aspirations of individuals as well as assessing environmental conditions as the most appropriate data source for this type of investigation.

Another limitation could result from the omission of certain variables, notable through the correlation of errors in Fig. 1 between GDP per capita and latent variables of consumer oriented services and activity in technology sectors, and in Fig. 2 between errors in GDP per capita and latent variable of consumer oriented services and between error in GDP per capita and latent variable of government programs. These results could be justified by the influence of stage of transition and economic development on these institutional attributes. Therefore, we recommend that further works should consider these questions. Errors in regressions for business oriented services and active in technology also correlate to errors of explanation of GDP per capita.

Finally, Acs (2007) clearly indicated that the ratio of opportunity-to-necessity entrepreneurship is a key indicator of economic development, which was found to rise with the increasing involvement in opportunity-based entrepreneurship and decreasing share of necessity-based entrepreneurship. In our analysis, opportunity and necessity entrepreneurship were excluded from the model because they exhibited too predictive an impact. However, it should be noted that they were significant in impacting on economic growth (opportunity entrepreneurship exhibited a positive impact while necessity entrepreneurship had a negative impact).

6 Conclusion

According our analysis of the causal relationships between the entrepreneurial environment, entrepreneurial activity and productiveness of economies, we can conclude that access to infrastructure (both physical and as well as professional and commercial), protection of property rights, easy access to good legal and accounting services and support for entrepreneurship by science parks and business incubators are the main drivers of productive entrepreneurship behaviour. These factors could re-orient entrepreneurial activity at a macro-level towards the effective structure from the point of view of macroeconomic effectiveness. The effective structure explaining productive entrepreneurial activity and leading to economic growth is characterized by the share of early-stage and established activity in business-oriented services (the opposite of consumer-oriented services) and in technology sectors.

We also pay close attention to reverse causality in our work. It is therefore possible to conclude that economic growth drives institutional development, which in turn enhances the effectiveness of the entrepreneurship environment, which in turn affects the productiveness of entrepreneurial activity.

Appendix

See Table 3.

Table 3 Multiple regression results summary for separate variables of productive entrepreneurial activity (step selection method)

	% within EB: business oriented services	% within TEA: business oriented services	Within EB: consumer oriented services	% within TEA: consumer oriented services	% within EB: active in technology sectors (high or medium)	% within TEA: active in technology sectors (high or medium)
$R^2 =$	0.89	0.85	0.76	0.66	0.78	0.74
(constant)	−9.261	−11.765	78.192	65.977	−2.305	−0.347
Rule of law						
Anti-trust legislation effect. and enforcement	10.380	5.107	−19.010	−9.207	3.045	
Quick access to permits and licenses					1.356	
Financial resources availability						
Avail. of fin. from private individuals		−7.091				−3.010
Availability of financing through IPOs					−2.037	
Availability of financing from gvt subsidies						1.976
Access to infrastructure						
Easy access to good legal and accounting services	16.832	15.561	−16.973	−12.958		3.792
Easy access to good banking services	−7.839	−4.703			−1.284	
Quality of phys. infrastructure		3.107				
Easy access to good subcontr., suppliers and consultants					2.756	
Quick access to utilities						1.242

(continued)

Table 3 (continued)

	% within EB: business oriented services	% within TEA: business oriented services	Within EB: consumer oriented services	% within TEA: consumer oriented services	% within EB: active in technology sectors (high or medium)	% within TEA: active in technology sectors (high or medium)
Government programs						
Adequate number of govt. support progr. for e-ship			13.413			
Support for e-ship by science parks and bus. incub.	8.355	3.994	−12.078			
Market openness and dynamics						
Affordable costs of market entry	−11.558		13.696			
Market openness				11.848		
Dynamics of consumer markets					1.656	
Education, training and R&D transfer						
Vocational, prof. and cont. educ. support towards e-ship	−5.445	−8.155			−3.080	−3.425
Support of science and tech. base for creation of world-class new-tech ventures	−9.243					
Avail. of support for researchers for commerc. of their ideas	5.722					
Efficient transfer of new tech, science and knowledge from research to bus.			15.295			

(continued)

Table 3 (continued)

	% within EB: business oriented services	% within TEA: business oriented services	Within EB: consumer oriented services	% within TEA: consumer oriented services	% within EB: active in technology sectors (high or medium)	% within TEA: active in technology sectors (high or medium)
Cultural and social norms						
Support of nat. culture towards individual success				6.950		

References

Acs ZJ (2007) How is entrepreneurship good for economic growth? Innovations 1(1):97–107

Aixala J, Fabro G (2008) Does the impact of institutional quality on economic growth depend on initial income level? Econ Aff 28(3):45–49

Amoros J (2009) Entrepreneurship and quality of institutions a developing-country approach. World Institute for Development Economics Research (UNU-WIDER), Helsinki, p 23

Amoros JE, Bosma N (2014) Global entrepreneurship monitor 2014 global report. Global Entrepreneurship Research Association, London

Baumol WJ (1990) Entrepreneurship: productive, unproductive, and destructive. J Polit Econ 5:893–921

Broadman HG et al (2004) Building market institutions in South Eastern Europe: comparative prospects for investment and private sector development. World Bank Publications, Washington, DC

Bruton GD et al (2010) Institutional theory and entrepreneurship: where are we now and where do we need to move in the future? Entrepren Theor Pract 34(3):421–440

De Soto H (1989) The other path: the economic answer to terrorism. Perseus Books, New York

Golovko MV (2011) About efficiency of the institutional environment of small business. http://www.erce.ru/internet-magazine/magazine/28/404

Hare PG (2001) Institutional change and economic performance in the transition economies. Paper presented at the UNECE Spring Seminar, UNECE, Geneva, 7–8 May 2001

Henderson J (2002) Building the rural economy with high-growth entrepreneurs. Fed Reserv Bank Kans City Econ Rev 87(3):45–70

Jankauskas V, Seputiene J (2009) The impact of the institutional environment on the economic development. Ekonomika 87:141–153

Kreft S, Sobel R (2005) Public policy, entrepreneurship, and economic growth. Cato J 25 (3):595–616

Krueger NF et al (2000) Competing models of entrepreneurial intentions. J Bus Ventur 15:411–432

Levie J, Autio E (2007) Entrepreneurial framework conditions and national-level entrepreneurial activity: seven-year panel study. Paper presented at the third global entrepreneurship research conference, George Mason University, Washington, DC, 1–3 Oct 2007

Martin M, Picazo M, Navarro J (2010) Entrepreneurship, income distribution and economic growth. Int Entrepren Manag J 6(2):131–141

North DC (1990) Institutions, institutional change and economic performance. Cambridge University Press, Cambridge

Nureev RM (2010) Institutional environment of the Russian business – the effect of a rut. http://uisrussia.msu.ru/docs/nov/leontief/2010/Nureev.pdf

Rehak J, Kohnova L, Kovacicova Z (2014) Inclusive entrepreneurship of disadvantaged groups in Europe. In: Social cohesion as a tool for eliminating disparities in the society. Ekonom, Bratislava, p 105

Reynolds PD, Hay M, Camp SM (1999) Global entrepreneurship monitor. Kauffman Center for Entrepreneurial Leadership, Kansas City

Rodrik D (2000) Institutions for high-quality growth: what they are and how to acquire them. NBER working paper no. 7540. NBER, Cambridge

Romer P (1990) Endogenous technological change. J Polit Econ 98(5):71–102

Schumpeter JA (1934) The theory of economic development. Harvard University Press, Cambridge

Schumpeter JA (1950) Capitalism, socialism and democracy. Harper and Row, New York

Scott WR (1995) Institutions and organizations. Sage, Thousand Oaks

Sobel R (2008) Testing Baumol: institutional quality and the productivity of entrepreneurship. J Bus Ventur 23(6):641–665

Stel A, Carree M, Thurik R (2005) The effect of entrepreneurial activity on national economic growth. Discussion paper no. 405 on entrepreneurship, growth and public policy. Max Planck Institute for Research into Economic Systems, Jena

Stenholm P, Acs Z, Wuebker R (2013) Exploring country-level institutional arrangements on the rate and type of entrepreneurial activity. J Bus Ventur 28:176–193

Valliere D, Peterson R (2009) Entrepreneurship and economic growth: evidence from emerging and developed countries. Entrepen Reg Dev 21(5–6):459–480

Wong P, Ho Y, Autio E (2005) Entrepreneurship, innovation, and economic growth: evidence from GEM data. Small Bus Econ 24(3):335–350

Zacharakis AL, Bygrave WD, Shepherd DA (2000) Global entrepreneurship monitor, national entrepreneurship assessment, United States of America. Kauffman Center for Entrepreneurial Leadership, Kansas City

A Value-Oriented Quantitative Model for Strategy Formulation Regarding Strategic Business Units

Michał J. Kowalski and Łukasz Biliński

Abstract Since dozens of years multi-business companies have constituted the dominant form of business organization. Years of research on their management led to the creation of Corporate Portfolio Management (CPM) concept, in which science have taken and lost interest alternately. Regardless of emerging and overturned concepts, contemporary research studies confirm that 2/3 of companies regularly use CPM tools and perceive CPM as the best way to build value. Unfortunately, despite years of scientific attention, recent studies also indicate that the CPM application is hampered by the lack of appropriate metrics and instruments. Managers express their dissatisfaction with the results they obtain using CPM in comparison to the effort they make.

The aim of the article is to propose a model supporting strategy formulation for strategic business units. The basis of the algorithm is a developed Rappaport's model of threshold margin. This article presents an application based on the mathematical model, previously developed by authors. The authors describe, step by step, quantitative measurement tools, on the basis of which development strategies for business units focused on maximizing enterprise value may be formulated. The proposed tools indicate, in which situations is it possible to maximize value through development, sale or divestment of strategic business units. The application includes financial constraints limiting the ability to increase enterprise value. The article presents the results of simulation for exemplary strategic business units.

Keywords Setting up strategy • Corporate portfolio management • Value creation

1 Present State of Knowledge

The history of portfolio management dates back to the period after World War II. Then, multi-business companies became a common organizational form in the world (Nippa et al. 2011). At the end of the 1980s, multi-business companies included on average 30 business units (Pidun et al. 2011). Despite passing dozens

---

M.J. Kowalski (✉) • Ł. Biliński
Wroclaw University of Technology, Wroclaw, Poland
e-mail: Michal.Kowalski@pwr.edu.pl

T. Dudycz et al. (eds.), *The Essence and Measurement of Organizational Efficiency*, Springer Proceedings in Business and Economics, DOI 10.1007/978-3-319-21139-8_7

of years since establishing first multi-business structures and questions put forward in literature about the need for creating such types of structures, often challenging the effects of diversification or proposing alternative methods of value creation using corporate centers or structures based on private-equity (Landau and Bock 2013), the companies, both large and small, still conduct diverse forms of activities involving many the so-called strategic business units (SBUs).

The research conducted by Pidun et al. on a sample of 1403 companies shows that from among large listed companies 25 % have 15 various SBUs, and the vast majority manage on average 9 SBUs (Pidun et al. 2011). Diversification is still a commonly applied tool of risk management and value creation (MMC 2007). For this reason, companies for which value creation is the main strategic objective build investment portfolios and create structures consisting of business units. Setting up strategy for business units is still one of the key elements of value based management (VBM). Ill-consider decisions, such as investing in "unattractive" businesses or delayed divestment can contribute to destroying previously build value as well as permanently weaken the company. Appropriate analytical tools are necessary to manage multi-business structures, and therefore the concept of Corporate Portfolio Management (CPM) was developed. CPM is supposed to support managers evaluating activities of business units, determining business units' future market position (Antczak 2010) and building proper, value-oriented business portfolios. There are many different definitions of portfolio and portfolio management depending on the context and application in a given area of knowledge. In finance, a portfolio is a collection of investments held by an investor, in marketing it is a collection of organizational clients, whereas in strategic management a collection of products and services provided by a company. Generally, portfolio management means centralized management of one or more portfolios, which includes identifying, prioritizing, authorizing, managing and controlling projects, programs and other related work to achieve specific strategic business objectives (PMI 2013). In the context of business value creation, CPM is defined as managing and coordinating a group of diversified business units to provide growth in value of the whole company.

Analyzing the present state of knowledge concerning CPM as a concept supporting pursuit of growth in value, two major directions of research can be distinguished:

- Methods resulting from strategic management, including research based on product life cycle and different portfolio matrix concepts.
- Methods focused on risk management, from among which we can distinguish attempts to apply to multi-businesses the concepts previously reserved to manage securities portfolio, methods aiming to measure risk at the level of SBU, simulative methods.

The product life cycle presents changing financial position of the SBU in time, passing through four key stages: introduction, growth, maturity and decline (Griffin 2004). The analysis of each phase, in particular its cash consequences, enables adjusting a proper strategy that ensures business growth (IBM 2009).

Determination of the current phase of a business unit improves management quality and counteracts opposing effects of business cycles (Dzikevicius and Vetrov 2013).

Among portfolio methods we should indicate, first of all, the BCG matrix (BCG growth-share matrix) (Seeger 1984), which refers directly to the product life cycle phases. It is one of the most popular and commonly used SBU evaluation techniques. Equally popular is McKinsey matrix (McKinsey industry attractiveness-business strength matrix) used, above all, by pharmaceutical concerns to evaluate projects in portfolio (Bode-Greuel and Nickisch 2008). Other popular concepts are the ADL matrix (Hofer and Schendel 1978) and much later developed the financial strategy matrix (Hawawini and Viallet 1998). The former includes the share of business in the market, product life cycle phases and relations between them, and the latter focuses on value metrics and value creation.

Among CPM tools, we can find in the literature many methods based on risk management. Many authors emphasize the need for decomposition of the company into separate business units and individual measurement of risk for each of them. Martin and Titman (2008) show that application of many discount rates, adapted to the risk level, affects significantly better allocation of the firm's capital. MMC (2007) indicates that the risk level of a single SBU will be different from that of the whole company. Among SBU risk measurement methods, the most often applied are modifications of CAPM model (Bhattacharya and Galpin 2011), and 3FM model (three-factor model) (Estrada 2011). Estrada (2011) estimates the level of SBU risk, and hence provides more reliable estimation of an asset's required return, taking into account the size of the company and market capitalization to book value. Among the most often applied risk management methods in CPM, we should indicate models based on the Markowitz's concept (Rutkauskas et al. 2011), VaR (Serban et al. 2013) and Monte Carlo simulation (Hertz 1968).

During many years of research, attempts were made aiming to determine the impact of the level of diversification on the company's financial situation and the company's ability to create value (Matusik and Fitza 2012). However, conclusions of these research are very ambiguous. Empirical evidence also indicates a vague answer whether diversification contributes to value destruction or creation (Nippa et al. 2011). On the one hand, companies try to benefit from diversification building portfolios of units which cash flows are not correlated, generating in this way larger returns per one risk unit (Green 2008). Nippa et al. (2011) draws attention to a number of benefits from the effect of scale and intelligent allocation of the firm's capital. Companies use mature SBUs to fund less developed units and, as a result of diversification, obtain the possibility of searching for new investments. On the other hand, several research proved that companies diversified in terms of business units tend to create lower value than companies from a uniform segment (Green 2008). Danger related to diversification consists in the lack of appropriate knowledge and resources that the parent company could transfer to business units to support their actions in effective value creation (Goold et al. 1998). Lack of market knowledge increases risk of an investment error, which may exemplify numerous analyses of ineffective mergers and acquisitions (Green 2008) and expansive actions towards new markets (Goold et al. 1998). The inverted-U model was developed to define the level of diversification that is the best in terms of business value creation (Nippa et al. 2011). However, the problem of the impact of diversification on the enterprise value still seems to be unsolved.

Despite great interest of both researchers and practitioners, we should indicate that CPM concept encountered a wave of research criticism. The grounds for portfolio methods were challenged and it was indicated that they contributed to simplifying difficult strategic decisions, thereby exposing multi-businesses to significantly greater risk (Pidun et al. 2011). Attention was also paid to the negligence of some SBU evaluation criteria. Prepared on the basis of portfolio methods analyses and recommendations did not reflect real companies' performance (Goold et al. 1998). Building portfolio based on incorrect information is a serious threat to the multi-business company and may result e.g. in deterioration of financial liquidity. Incorrect use of CPM evaluation tools by managers who were manipulating the companies' financial data to increase their attractiveness was also criticized (Pidun et al. 2011). Researchers challenge the usefulness of the BCG matrix and the product life cycle as well. Nippa et al. (2011) demonstrated that the actual application of the BCG matrix and knowledge concerning this concept tend to mislead managers and contribute to incorrect decision-making.

2 Relevance of the Subject and Research Problem

Despite a long history of research and above indicated criticism, CPM seems still one of the most important and very current management concepts. Surveys conducted by Pidun et al. (2011) indicate that as much as 60 % of companies take actions to integrate CPM into long-term planning processes, while 40 % of disinvestments and 23 % of acquisitions are a result of CPM analyses. PMI surveys conducted in 2012 show that 53 % of the investigated companies apply CPM regardless of industry (PMI 2013). The same surveys indicated that only 5 % of companies do not use CPM techniques and tools for business management (Pidun et al. 2011). Moreover, we can indicate research proving that CPM increases management quality and effects. Research carried out by PWC indicates that the companies which implemented CPM methods enjoyed 36 % increase in on-time realization of investment projects, 19 % decrease in the probability of exceeding budget, 18 % increase in achieving major strategic objectives and 36 % increase in ROI (PMI 2013).

Vast part of largest companies, 59 % investigated in PMI surveys, indicate as their main objective of using CPM value creation for shareholders in the long term (PMI 2013). Growth in the value seems the most important task for CPM. Bode-Greuel and Nickisch (2008) show that portfolio management maximizes company value through appropriate allocation of capital. Building portfolios also enables achieving main corporate objectives and creating shareholder value (Smith and Sonnenblick 2013). Companies seek in the CPM concept sources of support for investment decisions and answers to the question in which business units to invest to achieve growth in value. SBU selection is the main criterion of interest in CPM for 89 % of companies, 78 % of which prefer using quantitative criteria (Pidun et al. 2011). PMI surveys also indicate that 45 % of companies seek in CPM a way to increase the value of ROI (PMI 2013). CPM becomes also a very important element of business management at the time of crisis, as shown by Dzikevicius and Vetrov (2013). It may support overcoming effects of business cycles that expose the company to financial instability and loss of liquidity (Dzikevicius and Vetrov 2013). In addition, CPM is used as a tool supporting decision-making in the area of mergers and acquisitions (Green 2008). Much research also relates to the application of CPM in a specific environment. Bode-Greuel and Nickisch (2008) indicate that pharmaceutical companies create portfolios of innovative units, focused on developing and development of new drugs, and suggest tools to maximize the value of R&D projects. CPM objectives other than value creation include: growth in customer satisfaction (79 % companies), reduction in costs (59 % companies) (PMI 2013).

The literature proposes organizational forms alternative to multi-business, where traditional business units are replaced by conglomerates created of corporate centers and private—equity firms (Landau and Bock 2013), or where clustering techniques are used (Serban et al. 2011). These forms, however, require decision-making with regard to the directions of growth, investment and effective portfolio management, therefore, it appears that these alternative business forms may derive from the research on CPM.

The above mentioned research confirms on the one hand a very large interest in CPM on the part of business practitioners, but at the same time it indicates lack of appropriate analytical tools, management techniques and knowledge that would improve efficiency and quality of portfolio management. IBM Software Group research (2009) illustrates the scale of the problem. Only 21 % of the analyzed portfolios were determined as high value structures, only 25 % managers declared that they are able to select effectively investment priorities and evaluate SBU, and as many as 75 % of companies have too much business units in the portfolio in relation to available funds for financing their growth (IBM 2009). Despite years of research on CPM, a view emerges that there are no clear tools, methods and metrics that support evaluation of SBUs and portfolio management. Managers who deal with building portfolios feel disappointed because the effects remain unsatisfactory in relation to their work and intellectual effort put into the application of these methods (Pidun et al. 2011). We are still lacking proper indicators to evaluate companies, metrics and instruments fostering more efficient portfolio management. For example, Green (2008) indicates that General Electric applies more than 600 various SBU evaluation metrics. Muller et al. (2008) draws attention to the lack of sufficient quantitative tools and clear algorithms of action in CPM and that the achievements in this field do not bring about any expected results.

Lack of effective CPM methods and indicated defects affect the quality of managers' work and make them often take unjustified decisions. Green (2008) indicates that many managers consider company's sale as a personal defeat and recognition of their lack of competences. Companies reward employees who develop businesses; however, there are no tools that would indicate circumstances under which sale or divestment of SBU may create company value. As a result, portfolios contain SBUs that may cause destruction of the value. The relevant moment for their divestment is often overlooked (Green 2008). General aversion to selling business units is prevailing, and consequently, boards focus on "repairing" SBUs that are the source of value destruction, instead of withdrawing capital immediately from them (Nippa et al. 2011). The reasons for such a state of affairs can be traced back to the lack of tools allowing reliable reporting of information on SBUs, and tools measuring their ability to generate value (Li and Tiwari 2009).

In view of the present state of knowledge and numerous unresolved problems, further searching for methods supporting CPM seems necessary. Multi-business is still the most popular form of activity (Landau and Bock 2013) and a tool of value creation, however, CPM existing instruments seem insufficient. It is necessary to seek further methods and metrics supporting SBU evaluation and portfolio management. The formulation of the criteria of SBU selection to investment portfolio, assessment of potential of SBU's value growth, criteria for selection of portfolio strategy, identification of premises encouraging search for possibilities of strategic alliance or acceptance of the divestment strategy seem issues worth of scientific exploration. The algorithmic and quantitative methods are necessary; they will support SBU system reporting and indicate clear criteria of making decision relevant in terms of value.

The article is organized as follows. In Sect. 3, we present the mathematical model of fundamental value of SBU based on income approach. In Sect. 4, the results of conducted simulations are presented. We designate the area of value creation and the area of destroying value, and factors describing strategic position of SBU. In Sect. 5, we propose the algorithm of analysis and selection of SBU strategy focusing on value creation and show its application for two cases. We summarie our findings in conclusions.

3 Methods

When developing our SBU portfolio management model, we assumed that the main objective of the company is the growth of value. The value is created at the level of smallest managerial decisions, and therefore the value will depend on the ability to build value of a particular SBU. Each business unit is different and for this reason requires a separate analysis. Our objective is to propose a model for this analysis. As the main tool for drawing conclusions, we used our previously prepared mathematical model (Kowalski and Świderski 2012).

The model is based on the income paradigm of the value. We assume that the company value is determined by its ability to generate free cash flow to firm in the future or, otherwise, by capital and ability to generate residual income in the future. Residual income is defined as surplus of profit after tax above the cost of involved capital. Thus, as the basis for our research, we adopted the well-established in science and practice discounted cash flow (DCF) valuation model. We selected the model based on discounting cash flows rather than residual income, thus it is the following relation:

$$EV = PV\,FCF_1 + PV\,FCF_2 + \cdots + PV\,FCF_n + RV \tag{1}$$

where:

EV—enterprise value,
PV FCF_n—present value free cash flows in year n,
RV—residual value rate.

When defining cash flows, we based on free cash flow to firm. We also conducted their decomposition by adjustment of EBIT (Fernandez 2013). We assumed that flow in n-year can be presented in accordance with the equation:

$$\mathbf{FCF_n = EBIT_n - TAX_n + DA_n - CAPEX_n \pm dWCR_n} \tag{2}$$

where:

EBIT—earnings before deducting interest and taxes,
TAX—tax paid,
DA—depreciation and amortisation rate,
CAPEX—capital expenditures,
dWCR—delta working capital requirement.

Then we conducted decomposition of the model into value drivers. We referred to the well-established in science works in this respect. The basis for our research was the value drivers model by Rappaport (1986), which indicates seven factors affecting the enterprise value (seven drivers of shareholder value). After performing analyses, we conducted decomposition of our model, including the following value drivers:

- ROS—return on sales,
- d—sales growth ratio (sales dynamic),
- FAP—fixed assets productivity,
- T—tax rate,
- CCC—cash conversion cycle in days,
- AR—amortisation rate,
- n—years of growth,
- k—cost of capital.

Additionally, in our model we assume parameters that determine the SBU's starting position.

- S_0—sales in year 0
- BO—value of fixed assets in a year 0.

Sales in year 0 determine the current value of SBU, but also affects future growth in value. Taking into account competitors force, market potential, product life cycle, S_0 has influence on model parameters, such as sales growth ratio (d) and years of growth (n). State of fixed assets in a year 0 (BO) may be also one of SBU's value drivers. If SBU has more assets than resulting from the current sales (S_0) and fixed assets productivity (FAP), SBU can generate sales growths without incurring capital expenditures in subsequent years. This factor was included in our model.

While formulating the mathematical model, we made the following assumptions, presented in detail in our paper from 2012 (Kowalski and Świderski 2012). We made earnings before interest and taxes (EBIT) dependent on revenues and return on sales (ROS). Revenues in subsequent years were determined using a recurrent relation with the assumption that sales dynamics is constant throughout the whole analysis period, therefore, $S_n = S_0 \cdot d^n$. We modeled demand for working capital on the basis of cash conversion cycle in days (CCC). In our model, demand for cash related to incremental fixed assets depends on (1) economic life of these assets determined by amortization rate (AR), (2) on fixed assets productivity (FAP) and (3) on state of fixed assets in a year 0 (BO). We assumed that SBU must have constant fixed assets productivity. As a result, SBU expenditures on fixed assets concern reproduction of used assets and permit sales growth. We assumed that it is possible to determine the period when SBU is able to pursue growth. Years of growth (n) constitutes one of value drivers in our model. After this time, free cash flows will be constant. SBU will no longer generate further changes in cash flows, it will enter the phase of generating constant, recurring cash flows. We assume the possibility of generating constant cash flows to infinity, in accordance with the basic assumptions of the DCF method (Fernandez 2013). To model the value resulting from free cash flows after the phase of growth the Gordon model was used, assuming that constant growth rate in perpetuity will not be executed ($g = 0$) (Fernandez 2013).

In the model, we assume constant cost of capital. We also assume that, when evaluating SBU's strategic position, fixed and optimal structure of SBU's capital should be considered and that SBU is able to maintain it throughout the years of its growth. It means that if SBU growth requires additional capital, it is possible to increase SBU financing without changes in its capital structure. In our model we do not analyze the structure of financing and its impact on SBU value. These issues are the object of extensive research, but in our model we did not refer to them. In our research we are interested in enterprise value (EV), the company's total value (debt and equity) for all claimants: creditors and equityholders. We analyze the impact of adopted strategies on enterprise value, but do not refer to their impact on value of equity. Therefore, in our deliberations we do not refer to whether SBU is financed from debt or from equity.

Finally, after considering adopted components, the mathematical model describing the enterprise value assumes the following form:

$$
\begin{aligned}
EV &= PVFCF_1 + PVFCF_2 + \cdots + PVFCF_n + RV \\
&= \left[(1-T)\cdot S_0\cdot ROS - \frac{S_0}{FAP}\right]\cdot\sum_{i=1}^{n}\frac{d^i}{(1+WACC)^i} - \frac{CCC\cdot S_0}{365} \\
&\cdot\sum_{i=1}^{n}\frac{d^i-d^{i-1}}{(1+WACC)^i} + BO_1\cdot(AR+1) \\
&\cdot\sum_{i-1}^{n}\frac{(-AR)^{i-1}}{(1+WACC)^i} + \frac{S_0}{FAP}\cdot(AR+1) \\
&\cdot\sum_{i=1}^{n-1}\left[d^i\cdot\sum_{j=t+1}^{n}\frac{(-AR)^{j-t-1}}{(1+WACC)^j}\right] + \frac{(1+T)\cdot S_0\cdot d^n\cdot ROS}{WACC\cdot(1+WACC)^n}
\end{aligned}
\tag{3}
$$

We implemented our mathematical model into computer program. Using a spreadsheet, the model served us to carry out simulation on the basis of which we proposed the algorithm to formulate strategy for SBU to maximize enterprise value.

In the first place, we carried out simulations, which purpose was to identify relation between the enterprise value of SBU and factors adopted in the model. We designated the area of value creation and the area of destroying value and the impact of particular parameters on their range. We analyzed the impact of sales dynamics on the value creation ability. We designated threshold points, namely sales growth rate that ensures growth in the value, which we called the minimum value creation rate (MVCR). We carried out simulations aiming to specify the impact of particular value drivers on SBU's ability to increase value and MVCR.

Our approach refers to works of Rappaport from the 1980s who for the first time treated a new sale as an investment. In his works Rappaport formulated the term of threshold margin, i.e. the minimum acceptable operating return on incremental sales from the point of view of value creation. The concept of Rappaport was based on the aftertax operating cash flow perpetuity (the annuity model of earnings before interest and tax of incremental sales) and the required investment outlay for fixed and working capital occurred at the end of the period. The Rappaport's model was many times modified and verified by other researchers. Among others by Balachandran et al. (1986), who draws attention to additional value drivers such as weighted average economic life of depreciable assets. On the other hand, Dudycz (2005) points out that expenditures on additional working capital and fixed assets should be made at the beginning rather than at the end of the first examined year and that capital expenditures may require restoration. He modified the Rappaport's model accordingly. Our work is compliant with this research trend, constituting the extension of the basic Rappaport's model mainly through supplementation of the model with other value drivers. The use of computer program and data processing made it possible to carry out more extended simulations.

We carried out our simulations for a statistical SBU. For this purpose, we used the Damodaran database from January 2014. We analyzed 6022 European listed companies. We didn't analyze companies that run financial, insurance or similar business. For this reason, we excluded from the sample companies belonging to the following sectors: Bank, Banks (Regional), Brokerage and Investment Banking, Financial Services, Non-bank & Insurance, Reinsurance, Thrift. For each company from the final sample, we designated the value for all value drivers used in the model. Then we indicated the average values of value drivers, and obtained the following results:

- D = 109.41 % (sales growth ratio, sales dynamic),
- FAP = 1.99 (fixed assets productivity),
- WACC = 7.39 % (weighted average cost of capital),
- AR = 7.45 % (amortisation rate),
- N = 10 (years of growth),
- TAX = 19 % (tax rate),
- ROS = 7.988 % (return on sales).

We assumed these values as parameters of a statistical SBU, for which we carried out simulations. We assumed in our simulations that S_0 is 114.39 cash units. We adopted this value because then the enterprise value of SBU under lack of further growth (d = 1) is 100, which is an easy point of reference for the conclusions and subsequent analyses. In our model, revenues in year 0 do not have impact on the results of simulations. We assumed, at the same time, that SBU does not have surpluses or shortages of fixed assets. The value of initial fixed assets results directly from the adopted value S_0 and FAP, thus in the case of our statistical SBU, given $S_0 = 114.4$ and FAP = 1.99 BO has the value 53.19.

On the basis of the prepared model and the simulation results we developed the algorithm to formulate SBU's strategy.

4 Analysis of SBU's Value Creation Ability: Conclusions from the Conducted Simulations

In the first place, we present the effects of our analyses, i.e. the relation between sales dynamics, return on sales and enterprise value. We designated the area of value creation and the area of destroying value. We also designated the threshold point, at which sales growth ensures value growth. Conclusions from these analyses enabled us to formulate an equation that designates minimum value creation rate. Our proposal is a developed concept of threshold margin of Rappaport (1981).

Next, we present conclusions from computer simulations concerning the impact of particular value drivers on SBU's ability to increase value and on minimum value creation rate. We also determined the way particular value drivers determine shape and range of the area of value creation and of destroying value.

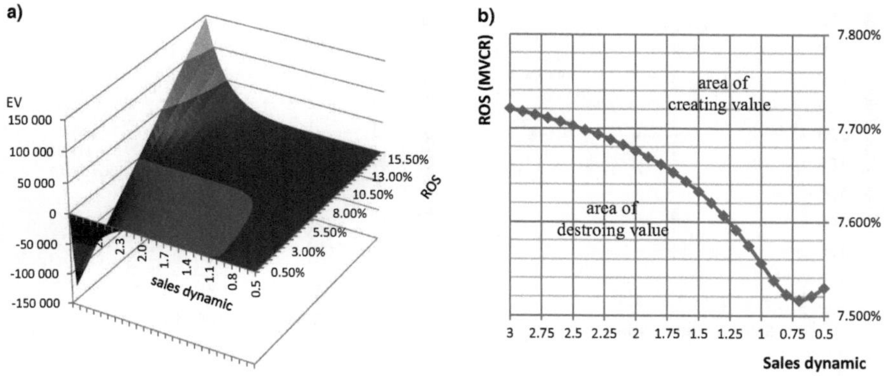

Fig. 1 Area of destroying value and value creation

4.1 Analysis of Relations Between Sales Dynamics, ROS and SBU's Value

Our analyses indicate that high sales dynamics may contribute to destroying SBU's value if, at the same time, the level of return on sales is not adequate. It is possible to designate the area of value creation and the area of destroying value as the relation between EBIT and sales dynamics. Figure 1 presents this type of relation for our statistical SBU. The visualization indicates the dependence of the value on sales and sales dynamics. The figure depicts that for part of combinations between ROS and sales dynamics, increase in sales causes decrease in the enterprise value. Figure 1a presents relation between ROS, sales dynamic and EV and Fig. 1b MVCR as a function of sales dynamics.

When ROS is below MVCR the SBU is the area of destroying value. The second one area is the area of value growth. In this zone, the SBU reaches the return required for financing of the assumed growth dynamics, modelled by sales growth ratio. Thus, to grow value by increasing sales dynamics, it is necessary to achieve appropriate return on sales (MVCR). Figure 2 presents the impact of sales value on the enterprise value. The presented curves illustrate the following situations:

- ROS on average amounting to 7.988 %,
- ROS equal to 50 % of the average, i.e. 3.999 %,
- ROS equal to 96 % of the average, i.e. 7.678 %.

In our simulations, SBU's MVCR amounts to 7.56 %, at sales growth ratio equal to 109.41 and values of the remaining parameters as indicated before (Fig. 2a). The SBU is in the area of value creation, because return on sales exceeds minimum value creation rate (ROS > MVCR). Provided the parameters describing the SBU are maintained, additional sales will be translated into value growth. Moreover, assuming increasing sales dynamics in spite of the fact that MVCR grows, MVCR will never exceed ROS recorded by the SBU. As a result, sales growth ratio for the analyzed SBU is always in the area of value creation. However, in the case of SBU

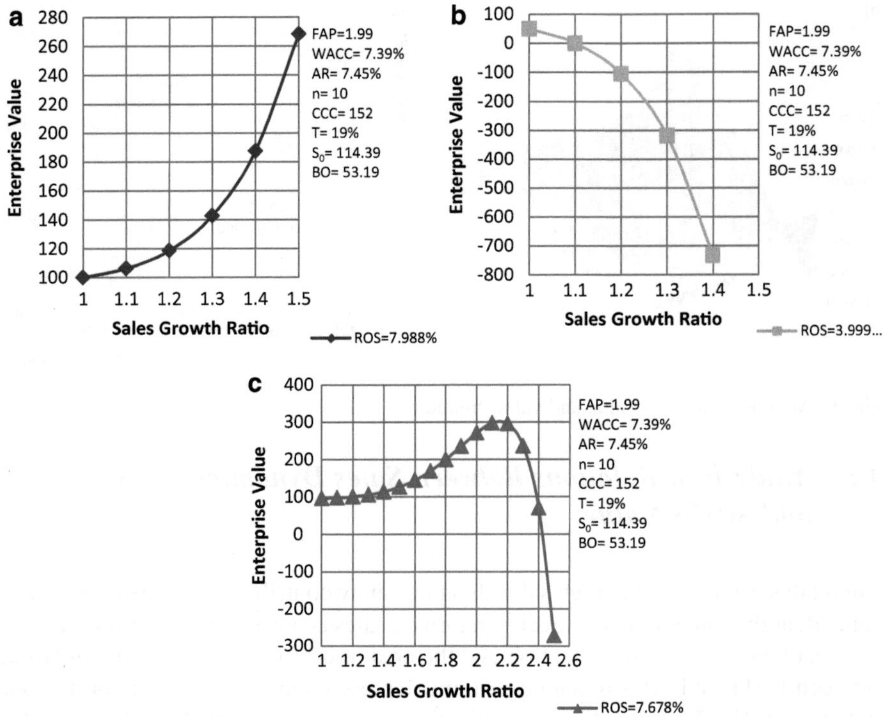

Fig. 2 Impact of sales dynamics on enterprise value

achieving ROS of 50 % of the average ROS, i.e. 3.999 %, ROS has the value below MVCR, and then each growth in sales will destroy the value. The situation is depicted in Fig. 2b. Additional sales dynamics increases and at the same time the value decreases. On the other hand, in the case of SBU achieving ROS 96 % of the average ROS, i.e. 7.678 % (Fig. 2c) at growth in sales dynamics, growing MVCR exceeds ROS. Thus, there is maximum sales growth ratio that guarantees value creation: in this case it is 210 %.

The value of sales growth ratio in which SBU reaches the maximum value is a significant parameter when determining the strategy. We will designate it as d max. Analytical designation of d max is possible only for two periods of growth. Then d max is:

$$\mathrm{d\,max} = \frac{-\left[(1-\mathrm{T})\cdot \mathrm{ROS} - \frac{1}{\mathrm{FAP}}\right]\cdot(1+\mathrm{WACC}) + \frac{\mathrm{CCC}}{365}\cdot \mathrm{WACC} - \frac{\mathrm{AR}+1}{\mathrm{FAP}}}{2\left[(1-\mathrm{T})\cdot \mathrm{ROS} - \frac{1}{\mathrm{FAP}} - \frac{\mathrm{CCC}}{365} + \frac{(1-\mathrm{T})\cdot \mathrm{ROS}}{\mathrm{WACC}}\right]} \tag{4}$$

In other cases, the most common use of the indicated proposal to designate d max are numerical methods and simulations. Having d max, it is possible to determine EV max, i.e. the maximum value achievable by SBU. In the analyzed cases, it is

Table 1 Parameters of average SBU for various ROS

Parameter	Statistical SBU (basic ROS)	SBU with 50 % basic ROS	SBU with 96 % basic ROS
ROS	7.998 %	3.999 %	7.678 %
MVCR	7.56 %	7.56 %	7.57 %
d max	None	1.0	2.1
EV przy d = 1	100	49.86	95.99
EV max	Infiniti	49.86	296.82

(1) for SBU with ROS of 50 %: 49.86, (2) for SBU with ROS of 96 %: 296.82. Summary of the calculation and conclusions are shown in Table 1.

The previously indicated value drivers have a large impact on the SBU's value. Chart 3 shows the influence of changes in the value of a given driver on the dependence of sales dynamics and EV. The driver selected by us is fixed assets productivity, which we increased by 25 and 50 %.

In all the indicated cases, improvement in FAP affects value growth. With the same sales dynamics, in each of the cases SBU obtains a higher value. In the case of SBU with 96 % ROS, a change in FAP modifies essentially its strategic position (Fig. 3c). With a better use of fixed assets, SBU moves beyond the area of destroying value. With FAP higher by 25 % of its basic value, sales growth (regardless of its scale) causes additional growth in value, contrary to the starting situation.

4.2 *Impact of Value Drivers on MVCR, d max and EV max*

Each of the designated value drivers (sales dynamics, weighted cost of capital, years of growth, amortization rate, cash conversion cycle in days, fixed assets productivity) affects the SBU's strategic situation. Change in any of these drivers affects EV and MVCR. They cause reduction or increase in SBU's value and influence MVCR and shape of the area of value creation and destroying value, but the scale of their impact is different. The relations are presented in Fig. 4.

The conducted analyses enabled us to state that EV and MVRC show the lowest sensitivity to changes in amortization rate and years of growth. Similar research was carried out by Miller and Mathisen (2004) who designated mathematical equations illustrating similar relations for profitability, growth, and capital intensity.

When evaluating the SBU's strategic situation, a similar analyses to the presented ones should be carried out. Such analyses will indicate attainable growth in the value depending on activities taken on defined drivers. Additionally, the analyses may indicate actions that will enable to shift SBU's position between the area of value creation and destroying value. This kind of thinking focuses

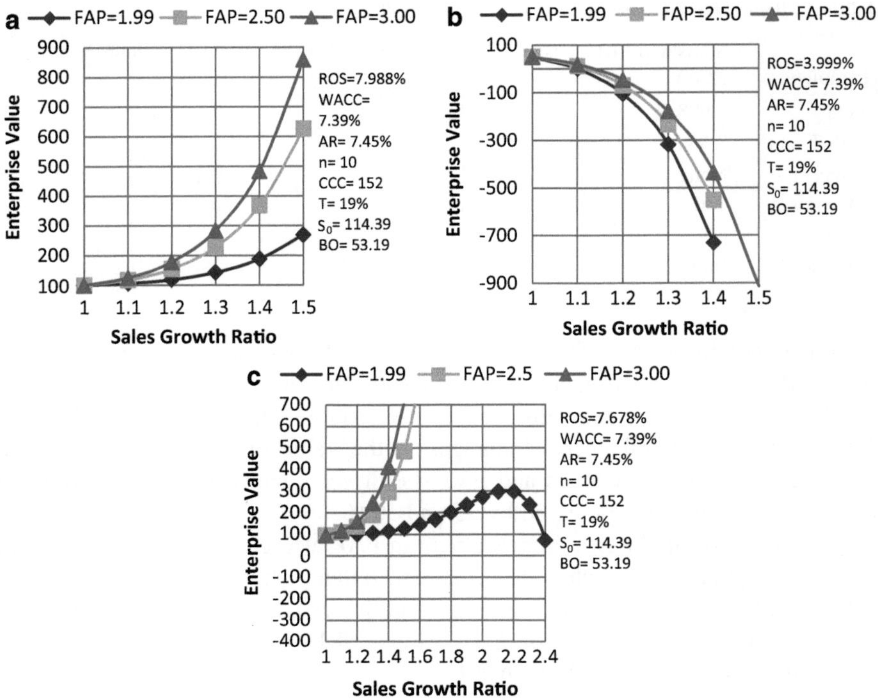

Fig. 3 Impact of FAP on the relation between d and EV

managers' attention on costs of growth and decrease in these costs. For an SBU, sales growth may not influence value growth at given values of drivers, while, for instance, reduction in demand for working capital or improvement in use of fixed assets can change this situation and the SBU will be able (at the unchanged value of ROS) execute value growth with growth in sales. The proposed analysis indicates this type of relations and enables their quantitative measurement.

4.3 Restrictions and Costs of SBU's Growth

During the analyses of an SBU and evaluation of its value creation ability, special attention should also be paid to costs related to its maintenance in the company portfolio and costs of the implementation of a specific strategy. For instance, strategy to increase sales dynamics can contribute to significant increase in SBU value, but in the short term it may require significant expenditures. Many researchers point out to financial feasibility while collecting the investment portfolio. Hawawini and Viallet (1998) analyzed SBU's ability to self-sustainable growth, and in their matrix of financial strategy they introduce self-sustainable growth rate (SGR), by means of which they determine financial feasibility of the

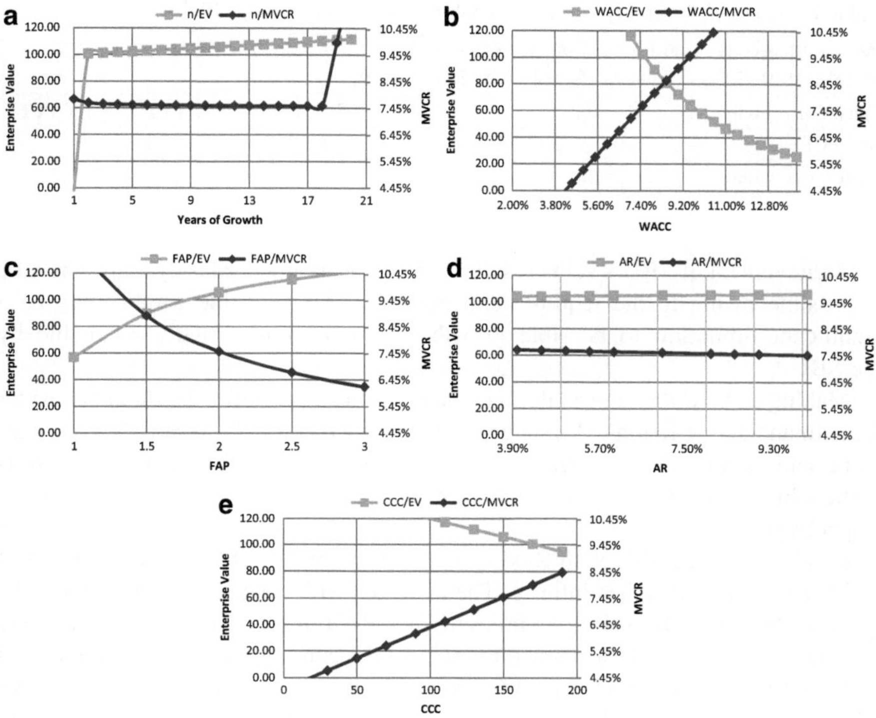

Fig. 4 Impact of value drivers on MVCR and enterprise value

strategy. Rappaport (1981) when analyzing SBUs also indicates the necessity to estimate financial possibilities to execute the agreed strategic plans.

For the purpose of simulations and analyses of business units, we adopted two variants:

- if $\sum_{1}^{n-1} \mathrm{PV\,FCFF} > 0$ the SBU has the ability to self-sustainable growth,
- if $\sum_{1}^{n-1} \mathrm{PV\,FCFF} < 0$ in the period of detailed forecast the SBU does not have the ability to self-sustainable growth and requires capital expenditures for its growth.

Table 2 presents FCFF values generated by analyzed SBU and its financial feasibility to execute the adopted strategy.

Our statistical SBU does not have the ability to self-sustainable growth for the taken strategy and sales dynamics, the sum of discounted future cash flows in the growth period is also negative. It means that in order to obtain approx. 105 cash units of enterprise value, it is necessary to spend within the next 10 years 11 cash units.

Table 2 Assessing the ability to self-sustainable growth of an average SBU

Value drivers: d = 1.09 FAP = 1.99, WACC = 7.39 %, AR = 7.45 %, CCC = 152, n = 10, TAX = 19 %, ROS = 7.998 %, S_0 = 114.39, BO = 53.19											
Years of growth	1	2	3	4	5	6	7	8	9	10	∑ PV FCFF
PV FCFF	−2	−1	−1	−1	−1	−1	−1	−1	−1	−1	−11
Enterprise value											105.32

Achievement of SBU's value resulting from the assumed sales dynamics may be impossible owing to the required expenditures. The available capital may be a significant limitation to possible growth rate and value actually attainable by the SBU.

Making an SBU strategy analysis in the investment portfolio, we should consider these financial restrictions. We suggest designating quantitatively SBU's maximum value and maximum sales dynamics, which are accessible by pursuing the self-sustainable strategy of growth. We mark them as EV max*and d max*, respectively.

For the analyzed SBU with ROS amounting to 7.998 %, EV max does not exist and the d max approaches infinity. The analyzed SBU reaches the ability to self-sustainable growth for sales dynamics 107.82 % (d max*). Then enterprise value EV max* equals 104.41 cash units, the sum of the current value of future free cash flows in the growth period is then 0. Every increase in sales dynamics, i.e. above 107.82 %, means loss of ability to self-sustainable growth and, at the same time, the possibility of additional growth in the value but with additional investments.

5 Model of Strategy Formulation for SBU

Starting management analysis of potential companies, in the context of Value Based Management, we should determine the attractiveness of business units and their ability to build additional value. In order to do it, after collecting historical data and calculating forecasts, we have to define value drivers for SBUs. We suggest designating drivers such as:

1. d—sales growth ratio (sales dynamic),
2. WACC—weighted average cost of capital,
3. n—years of growth,
4. AR—amortisation rate (measured by the average amortisation rate),
5. CCC—cash conversion cycle in days,,
6. FAP—fixed assets productivity,
7. S_0—sales in year 0,
8. ROS—return on sales,
9. BO—value of fixed assets in year 0,
10. T—tax rate.

5.1 Determination of SBU's Value Drivers

The tools determining the above drivers should be sought in the existing state of knowledge, using finance, strategic and marketing management concepts. We suggest starting from designating the assumed business growth period (n). The growth period is the time, after which it should be assumed that SBU will enter the phase of generating recurring annual FCFF. Determination of FCFF depends on the phase of SBU life cycle and period of economic life of product or service, on which it is based (Griffin 2004). When determining SBU's years of growth, Porter five forces analyses may be useful. It determines the economic situation of the company and the sector in which it operates. We can also use the BCG matrix. The issue of determining SBU's years of growth is analyzed by Mills (2005). He finally indicates the lack of one uniform method that designates the period of competitive advantage and the period of planning actions of the company. Decisions on the length of growth are largely based on intuitive thoughts of experienced managers or are accidental (Mills 2005). Then, key value drivers should be specified, starting from sales growth ratio (d) and return on sales (ROS). We should consider that the proposed model is based on average values that should be adopted in the assumed years of growth. When determining d, we can use historical CAGR, or refer to comparable companies. When determining WACC, we should take into account the target, optimal rather than current structure of financing. While determining other drivers affecting cost of SBU growth, we should use historical data as well as consider the effects of planned operational restructuring.

The determination of value drivers is not easy but they are of crucial importance for drawing conclusions about SBUs' strategy. We do not aim at providing universal recipes for estimation of SBU's value drivers, because they probably do not exist. We want to emphasize that prediction of SBU's value drivers during SBU strategic position evaluation is highly subjective. The accuracy of their predictions proves the qualifications of the manager. It will be probably determined by both management tools but also manager intuition. In addition, assessment of value drivers will depend on the context of a specific investor. One investor, when evaluating SBU's strategic position, may not notice the possibilities of changes in the value of a given driver in relation to its historical values, resulting from financial statements. In turn, another one may see potential that is unattainable for others, maybe integration of SBU with other processes of the investor will make it possible to increase ROS or decrease CCC. Therefore, strategic position and SBU's growth potential may vary depending on the context of analysis and investor.

5.2 *Algorithm of Evaluating SBU in the Value Creation Process*

In Fig. 5 we present an algorithm for analysis and selection of SBU strategy focused on value creation. The proposed model is a quantitative tool that supports portfolio

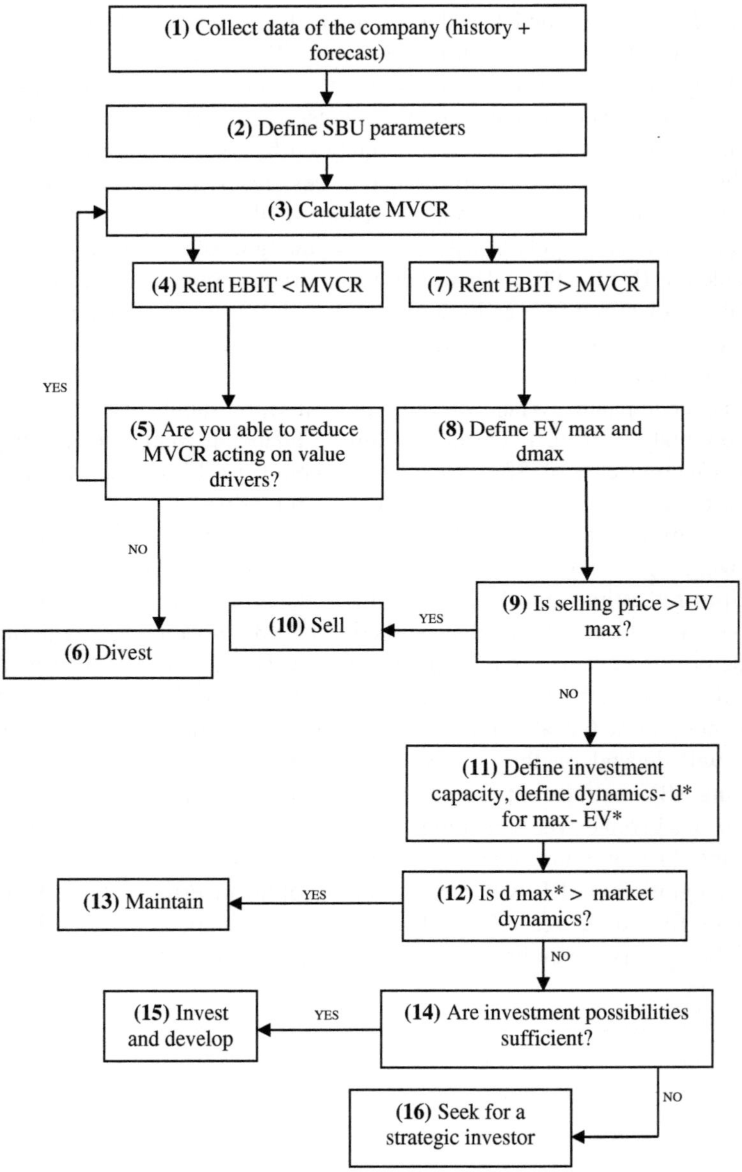

Fig. 5 SBU evaluation scheme

analysis. In the following steps, we suggest measuring parameters based on our mathematical model and suggest an SBU strategy on the basis of defined quantitative criteria. The algorithm concentrates on value creation for SBUs' owners—multi-business company.

The first step (1) is collection of historical and planning data about SBU. In the second (2) step value drivers are determined, indicated in Sect. 5.1, i.e. years of growth, return on sales, sale dynamics, weighted average cost of capital, amortization rate, cash conversion cycle, productivity of fixed assets, effective tax rate, sales in year 0 and value of fixed assets in year 0. Then (3) we suggest calculating MVCR and comparing it with ROS. Two cases are possible: ROS is below MVCR or above it. In the first case (4), SBU is in the area of destroying value. In such conditions, increase in SBU value by its growth (increasing sales) is not possible. Incremental sales will cause decrease in the value. A strategy for SBU is to change its unfavorable position. As indicated in Sect. 4, actions on value drivers may change SBU's strategic position. Assuming that change in ROS may be impossible, to shift SBU to the area of value creation it is necessary to take action on other drivers that determine relations between ROS and MVCR, in accordance with the logic we presented in Fig. 4. Operational actions having effect on, for example, CCC, FAP, AR may decrease MVCR and change SBU strategic position. In step (4) we should specify their feasibility and impact on SBU's strategic position, re-comparing MVCR with ROS. If none of the analyzed initiatives shift SBU to the area of value creation (7) the strategy of divestment or sale (of SBU) (5) seems justified; this unit does not ensure potential for long-term value growth and should be eliminated from the investor's portfolio. In the case when ROS exceeds MVCR (7), SBU is in the area of value creation. In this situation, we suggest defining threshold parameters, namely the maximum value SBU is able to generate (EV max) with maximum sales dynamics (d max) (8). This analysis will permit to specify the location of SBU in the area of value creation and destroying value. If ROS is high enough, SBU may be beyond the area of destroying value. Then EV max and d max approach infinity, and potential of SBU's value growth is described as indefinite. In other situations, the analysis will indicate SBU's possible value growth through sales growth strategy. The designated EV max value may be crucial when evaluating possible acquirer's offers concerning SBU. The present owner of SBU should seriously consider an offer when the price exceeds the designated EV max (9). It means that another investor, taking into account its scale of operations, integration with its processes or other competitive advantages, is able to achieve for SBU better value of drivers, unattainable for the present owner. In this situation, selling strategy of SBU maximizes portfolio value (10). In the next step, we suggest analyzing the SBU ability to self-sustainable growth and define necessary investments (11). We suggest specifying the SBU sales dynamics that is able to achieve without generating additional demand for cash (d max*), and the value it reaches at this dynamics (EV max*). In the next step, we suggest comparing the obtained threshold values with the market possibilities. We suggest confronting d max* with sales growth dynamics accepted by the market (12). Two situations are possible; if market dynamics is below d max*, SBU is able to develop and generate growth in

Table 3 Strategy proposals on the basis of the prepared algorithm

Type of strategy	Short characteristics
Sell the SBU	Sell the SBU if you manage to find a buyer, and the offered price is higher than the attainable maximum value of business Price > EV max
Divest	Withdraw cash from business unit (liquidation or divestment), if SBU is in the area of destroying value ROS < MVCR and, at the same time, you do not notice a possibility to change this relation by actions on value determinants
Maintain	Enable growth of SBU by way of self-sustainable growth, in the situation when SBU is in the area of value creation ROS > MVCR and market growth dynamics enables SBU self-sustainable growth dmax* > market dynamics
Invest and develop	Invest in SBU growth, in the situation when SBU is in the area of value creation ROS > MVCR, and market growth dynamics requires additional investments dmax* < market dynamics, and direction of investing in SBU is attractive taking account of alternative possibilities, and you have required capital
Strategic investor, alliance (merger)	Find the possibility of strategic alliance, in the situation when SBU is in the area of value creation ROS > MVCR, and market growth dynamics requires additional investments, dmax* < dynamics, on the other hand, the direction of investing in SBU is not attractive taking account of alternative possibilities, and/or you do not have capital required for growth

value without sustaining additional expenditures, the growth strategy should be assumed (13). Otherwise, the market requires sales dynamics that exceeds limits of self-sustainable growth and additional investments are necessary (14). Further analysis of SBU's position and selection of strategy will depend on financial owner possibilities, alternative available investments and their value creation potential. The investor must specify whether it has a desire and opportunities to fund and invest in growth in value of the analyzed SBU. If the answer is positive, the strategy of maintaining SBU in the investment portfolio, however with additional expenditures, will be implemented (15). Otherwise, when the investor does not have funds for financing SBU growth required by the market, seeking alternative sources of growth is justified, e.g. through a strategic investor (16). Table 3 sums up the proposed strategies and criteria of their selection.

The analysis of strategic situation of SBU is a continuous process. Perception of value drivers may and probably will change over time. For this reason, the analysis of SBU's strategic position should be a constant CPM action.

5.3 *Examples of SBU Analyzes*

On the basis of the analysis of data contained in long-term financial plans of a certain Multi-Business Company, we completed calculations and selected strategy

Table 4 Simulation for SBU 1

Value drivers: d = 1.14, WACC = 10 %, n = 5, FAP = 2, CCC = 60, AR = 15 %, MVCR = 7.019 %, ROS = 7.200 %, TAX = 19 %	
EV	2959
EV at d = 1.00	2871
d max	2.50
EV max	4438
$\sum_{1}^{n-1} PV\,FCFF$	−527
d max*	1.10
EV max* at d max*	2932
Market sales dynamic	1.15
Strategy	Invest and develop

for two SBUs. On their example, we will present the possibility of applying the proposed algorithm. For each of SBUs we present relation between EV and d. We determined limitations resulting from self-sustainable growth, i.e. d max* and EV max* (Table 4).

The calculations indicate that SBU 1 is in the area of value creation. While executing the assumed dynamics of 14 % growth in sales YOY, it reaches the value of 2959 cash units, with the value amounting to 2871 cash units with no sales growth, i.e. d = 100 %. Therefore, possible growth in the value is minimal and is only 3.1 %. This situation is confirmed in the relation between ROS and MVCR. In spite of the fact that SBU is in the area of value creation, surplus of ROS above MVCR is small. Additional sales requires high expenditures and, as a result, EV/d curve rises at a small pace (Fig. 6). The hypothetic maximum value of SBU is 4438 cash units (EV max), at the growth dynamics (d max) equal to 250 % YOY. Attention should be paid to very large investment costs related to the planned growth. The sum of the present values of cash flows in the years of growth is 527 cash units. SBU requires large capital expenditures. Taking account of the possibilities of self-sustainable growth, the estimated d max* is 110 %, and the value of SBU (EV max*) is 2932 cash units. This is a result similar to the initial enterprise value. Market analyses made it possible to specify growth dynamics accepted by the market at about 15 % YOY. It additionally complicates SBU's strategic situation. The market enables growth that exceeds growth dynamics resulting from the calculation of SBU's capacity to create value. At the adopted levels of value drivers, growth of SBU means high capital expenditures, providing insignificant growth in value. The analysis of internal conditions of the analyzed group indicates that involving capital in SBU is ineffective in relation to alternative possibilities. The investor opts for the strategy of seeking strategic alliance. Additionally, the investor counts on the fact that that the strategic decision will enable an operational change in SBU in the form of growth in ROS or change in drivers affecting the costs of growth, for instance it will reduce the demand for additional working capital or fixed assets. This change would make it possible to pursue sales

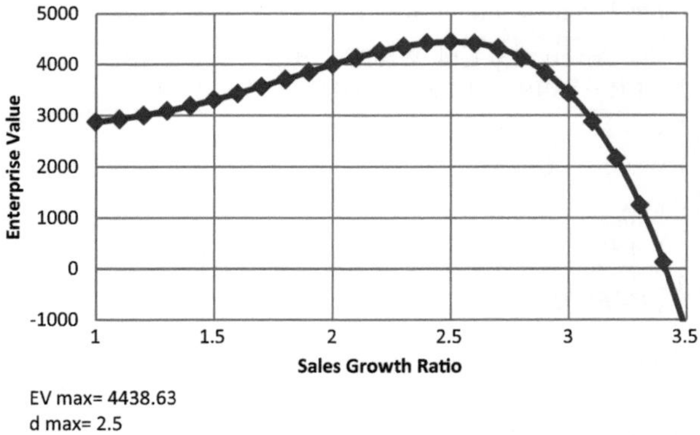

Fig. 6 Impact of sales dynamics on the value of SBU 1

Table 5 Simulation for SBU 2

Value drivers: d = 1.24, WACC = 14 %, n = 6, FAP = 4, CCC = 80, AR = 12 %, MVCR = 6.839 %, ROS = 6.700 %, TAX = 19 %	
EV	1676
EV at d = 1.00	1732
$\sum_{1}^{n-1} PV\,FCFF$	−1213
d max*	1.00
EV max* at d max*	1732
Market sales dynamic	1.13
Strategy	Seek for a strategic investor

growth awaited by the market with more dynamics growth in the value and lower capital expenditures. Until finding the possibility of alliance, the investor assumes a growth strategy by self-sustainable growth of SBU, assuming the strategy of selective growth in sales and limiting average sales dynamics to 10 %, i.e. d max* (Table 5).

The analyses conducted for SBU2 indicate that it is in the destructing area, ROS < MVCR. Therefore, each additional sale destroys the value, and the SBU reaches maximum value when it does not develop, i.e. for d = 100 % and 1732 cash units. The expected sales growth (d) equals 124 % and allows the SBU to achieve value of 1676 cash units, i.e. 3.2 % below the baseline. At such values of drivers, the development of SBU is pointless for value creation of the multi-business group. As long as the SBU is in the area of destructing value, estimation of EV max* and d max* is impossible, additional sales requires expenditures, which exceed additional margins from the sale. The analysis of the strategic situation of the SBU has focused board actions on reducing MVCR. The designated strategic goal is to reduce the cash conversion cycle in days (CCC) by 50 %. Assuming that the values of the other drivers will stay at present level, MVCR reduction will amount to 5.157 %, and the SBU will be shifted to the area of value creation. The dependence of d from the EV or SBU2 is presented in Fig. 7.

Fig. 7 Impact of sales dynamics on the value of SBU 2

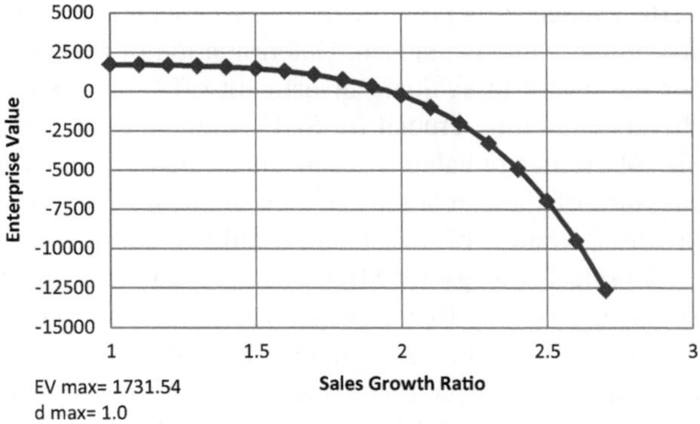

6 Conclusions

Contemporary science indicate that multi-business is still the dominant business organizational form. At the same time the literature emphasizes that despite many years of research, there is still deficit in tools supporting portfolio and multi-business structure management. Recent survey of managers concluded that there is a significant lack of quantitative tools that support decision-making concerning SBU selection to investment portfolio, setting up SBU development strategy or divestment. In our paper we propose an algorithm for SBU strategy selection based on value creation paradigm and prepared our own mathematical model. Our studies take part in a wide spectrum of research concerning value drivers and relation between them. In our model, we used nine value drivers that determine SBU strategic position, and affect its future directions of development. On the basis of the model, we conducted computer simulations and determined quantitative criteria for SBU strategy selection, assuming as the basic criterion growth in value of the multi business company. We do not propose tools to determine values of model parameters (value drivers), in our opinion they depend on the skills and intuition of the manager, but we indicate relations between them and their influence on SBU strategy selection.

As many research have shown, sales increase does not have to cause value growth of SBU and the whole portfolio. We have already indicated that it is possible to determine the area of value creation and the area of destroying value, i.e. to determine such values of drivers for which sales increase creates value or destroys it, respectively. Strategy for SBU should be set up on the basis of SBU position between these two areas. To find the position, it is necessary to calculate minimum value creation rate (MVCR), i.e. such ROS, which, taking into account other value drivers, guarantees value creation by sales growth. The relation between enterprise value and sales dynamics constitutes crucial element of SBU management. For a given SBU, the maximum available value may be enclosed within certain range. It is possible then to calculate maximum sales dynamics for which maximum value is reached. Determination of maximum available value is crucial for the owner to evaluate investment offers and SBU sales. Interacting on value drivers is, in turn, crucial for SBU potential to create value, MVCR value and the size of the area of value creation and destroying value, and it is possible quantitative measure of these relations. If it is impossible to shift SBU to the area of value creation, strategy of divestment should be considered.

To select strategy for SBU, it is necessary to assess its feasibility. In order to do so, SBU's ability to create growth should be verified. It is possible to assess maximal available sales dynamics for SBU through the strategy of self-development. We compare the assessed sales dynamics with the dynamics of market to verify if SBU development will require additional expenditures. This information, which additionally contains data about the owners ability to finance SBU development and compares it with alternative investments, will be the foundation of accepting SBU strategy or a stimulus to look for additional development sources, including merge.

References

Antczak S (2010) Metody portfelowe w planowaniu strategicznym jednostek biznesu. Zeszyty Naukowe Uniwersytetu Przyrodniczo- Humanistycznego w Siedlcach 87:68–82

Balachandran BV, Nagarajan NJ, Rappaport A (1986) Threshold margins for creating economic value. Financ Manag 15(1):68–77

Bhattacharya U, Galpin N (2011) The global rise of the value-weighted portfolio. J Financ Quant Anal 46(3):737–756

Bode-Greuel KM, Nickisch KJ (2008) Value-driven project and portfolio management in the pharmaceutical industry: drug discovery versus drug development-commonalities and differences in portfolio management practice. J Commer Biotechnol 14(4):307–325

Dudycz T (2005) Zarządzanie wartością przedsiębiorstwa. Polskie Wydawnictwo Ekonomiczne, Warszawa

Dzikevicius A, Vetrov J (2013) Investment portfolio management using the business cycle approach. Bus Theory Pract 14(1):58–63

Estrada J (2011) The three-factor model: a practitioner's guide. J Appl Corp Finance 23(2):77–84

Fernadez P (2013) Valuation and common sense, 2nd edn. http://www.slideshare.net/robszold/book-valuation-and-common-sense-2nd-edition-for-upload-opt. Accessed 6 Jan 2015

Goold M, Campbell A, Alexander M (1998) Corporate strategy and parenting theory. Long Range Plan 31(2):308–314

Green J (ed) (2008) Corporate portfolio management roundtable. J Appl Corp Financ 20(2):8–31

Griffin RW (2004) Podstawy zarządzania organizacjami. PWN, Warszawa

Hawawini G, Viallet C (1998) Finance for executives: managing for value creation. South-Western Publishing Company, Tennessee

Hertz DB (1968) Investment policies that pay off. Harv Bus Rev 46(1):96–108

Hofer CW, Schendel D (1978) Strategy formulation: analytical concepts. West Publishing Company, St. Paul

IBM Software Group (2009) The IBM register. http://www.ibm.com/us/en/. Accessed 21 Nov 2014

Kowalski M, Świderski M (2012) Wpływ wzrostu sprzedaży na wartość przedsiębiorstwa. Prace Naukowe Uniwersytetu Ekonomicznego we Wrocławiu 252:248–262

Landau C, Bock C (2013) Value creation through vertical intervention of corporate centres in single business units of unrelated diversified. Long Range Plan 46(1–2):97–124

Li CW, Tiwari A (2009) Incentive contracts in delegated portfolio management. Rev Financ Stud 22(11):4681–4714

Martin J, Titman S (2008) Single vs. multiple discount rates: how to limit "influence costs" in the capital allocation process. J Appl Corp Finance 20(2):79–83

Matusik SF, Fitza MA (2012) Diversification in the venture capital industry: leveraging knowledge under uncertainty. Strateg Manag J 33(4):407–426

Marsh and Mclennan Companies (2007) The MMC register. http://www.mmc.com. Accessed 17 Oct 2014

Miller TW, Mathisen RE (2004) Drivers of the value of the firm: profitability, growth, and capital intensity. J Account Finance Res 12(6):70–79

Mills RW (2005) Dynamika wartości przedsiębiorstwa dla przedsiębiorców. Ośrodek Doradztwa i Doskonalenia Kadr sp. z o.o, Gdańsk

Muller R, Martinsuo M, Blomquist T (2008) Project portfolio control and portfolio management performance in different contexts. Proj Manag J 39(3):28–42

Nippa M, Pidun U, Rubner H (2011) Corporate portfolio management: appraising four decades of academic research. Acad Manag Perpect 25(4):50–66

Pidun U, Rubner H, Kruhler M, Untiedt R (2011) Corporate portfolio management: theory and practice. J Appl Corp Finance 23(1):63–76

Project Management Institute (2013) The PMI register. http://www.pmi.org/default.aspx. Accessed 18 Dec 2014

Rappaport A (1981) Selecting strategies that create shareholder value. Harv Bus Rev 59:139–149

Rappaport A (1986) Creating shareholder value: a guide for managers and investors. Simon and Schuster, New York

Rutkauskas AV, Lapinskaite-Vvohlfahrt I, Stasytyte V (2011) Marketing portoflio management in a spectrum of marketing assets interaction to maximize holder's utility. Econ Eng Decis 22(5):485–493

Seeger JA (1984) Reversing the images of BCG's growth share matrix. Strateg Manag J 5(1):93–97

Serban F, Stefanescu V, Ferrara M (2011) Portfolio optimization and building of its efficient frontier. Econ Comput Econ Cybern Stud Res 2:125–137

Serban F, Stefanescu V, Ferrara M (2013) Portfolio optimization in the framework mean-variance-VaR. Econ Comput Econ Cybern Stud Res 1:61–79

Smith D, Sonnenblick R (2013) From budget-baset to strategy-based portfolio management: a six-year case study. Res Technol Manag 56(5):45–51

[illegible] M, S[illegible] (20[illegible]) [illegible] portfolio [illegible]
[illegible] C (2013) [illegible]
[illegible] (2009) [illegible] portfolio [illegible]
Martin J, [illegible] (200[illegible]) [illegible] capital allocation process [illegible]
[illegible] MA [illegible] capital [illegible] Strateg Manag J [illegible]
Marsh and McLennan Companies (2007) [illegible]. Accessed 17 Oct 2014
Miller TW, [illegible] (200[illegible]) [illegible] growth, and capital intensity [illegible] Finance [illegible]
Mills RW (2005) [illegible]
[illegible] management [illegible]
[illegible] (201[illegible]) [illegible] management [illegible] research [illegible]
[illegible] theory and practice [illegible]
Project Management Institute (2013) [illegible]. Accessed 17 Dec 2013
Rappaport A (1981) Selecting strategies that create shareholder value. Harv Bus Rev 59(3):139–147
Rappaport A (1986) Creating shareholder value: the new standard for business performance. Simon and Schuster, New York
[illegible] (201[illegible]) [illegible] management [illegible] shareholder [illegible]
[illegible] (19[illegible]) [illegible] shareholder value [illegible]
[illegible] (201[illegible]) [illegible] Technol [illegible]
[illegible] (201[illegible]) [illegible] management [illegible]
[illegible] R (201[illegible]) [illegible] management [illegible] case study [illegible]

The Impact of Intellectual Capital Efficiency on the Profitability of Agricultural Enterprises

Magdalena Kozera

Abstract The aim of this article is to examine whether the efficiency of generation of added value from intangible resources in agricultural enterprises is related to their financial performance.

According to conventional wisdom, the economic efficiency of agricultural enterprises is a function of the use of owned balance sheet and non-balance sheet resources, which are referred to as intellectual capital. One of the measures describing the effects of the use of these resources is the Value-Added Intellectual Coefficient (VAIC™) developed by Pulić. Similarly to profitability indicators used in financial analysis, it is based on companies' source data (balance sheet and income statement). This enables the study of the relationship between VAIC and its derivatives and corporate profitability measured with the indicators of the Return On Assets (ROA) and Return On Equity (ROE). The paper makes reference to a wide range of publications on the efficiency of use of intellectual capital and its impact on the financial results in non-agricultural sectors and it presents the results of a study on a group of Polish agricultural enterprises.

The results confirmed a correlation between the VAIC™ and profitability indicators, pointing to the growing importance of intellectual capital in agricultural enterprises, which justifies further research.

The research shows that intellectual capital is important to generate value added and results in enterprises. So far researchers of the agricultural sector have been disregarding this issue. The study proves the thesis that financial results are strongly related to the efficient use of non-balance sheet resources of intellectual capital.

Keywords Intangible resources • Intellectual capital • VAIC™ • Agricultural enterprise • Efficiency • Profitability

The study was financed from the funds of the National Science Centre under project No. 2011/03/B/HS4/02032 'Value Added of the Intellectual Capital of Polish Agricultural Enterprises'.

M. Kozera (✉)
Faculty of Economics and Social Sciences, Poznan University of Life Sciences, Poznan, Poland
e-mail: mkozera@up.poznan.pl

T. Dudycz et al. (eds.), *The Essence and Measurement of Organizational Efficiency*, Springer Proceedings in Business and Economics, DOI 10.1007/978-3-319-21139-8_8

1 Introduction

The contemporary market blurs differences in the performance of enterprises in various branches. More and more often this situation also concerns agriculture, which is an integral link in agribusiness and the entire economy. Similarly to other business entities, the business operating in agriculture wants to be successful and this is usually manifested by favourable economic results. In this context it is important to fully use one's resources—both conventional resources and the resources which some business managers are not fully aware of. These are intangible resources of intellectual capital which were developed from the knowhow, skills and experience owned and applied in an enterprise. In spite of the holistic and developmental character of the research on this form of capital, it is more widely applied only to a fragmentary and limited extent. However, it is both researchers of economics, accounting and finance and researchers of management and sociology that are engaged in the research on intellectual capital. The main premise for this research is an attempt to determine the impact of the intangible resources of intellectual capital on the efficiency of agricultural enterprises, including the aspect of the new management paradigm allowing for corporate social responsibility.

The article determines the efficiency of use of intellectual capital to generate value added with the VAIC™ method in selected agricultural enterprises in the Greater Poland region. The article also specifies the relation between the efficiency of use of intellectual capital to generate value added and the profitability of agricultural enterprises measured with the indicators of the return on assets and equity.

2 About the Measurement of Efficiency of Resources

Efficiency is one of essential, commonly applied categories in the assessment of human activity. Regardless of the fact whether it is considered in the economic, social, organisational or individual aspect, it concerns all sectors and entities in the economy. In spite of its commonness it is still the subject of continuous research and investigations. New methods and models measuring efficiency are still being developed.

Economic sciences usually consider two approaches to efficiency: the economic approach (which is related to research based on the theory of economics) and the organisational approach (which is related to organisation and management sciences and which identifies the synergic effect of organisation) (Bojanes and Latruffe 2008). The research resulting from the theory of economics mostly involves optimised allocation of resources. It is related with the strategic management of resources so as to generate the economic value over a period of time, which will guarantee that the return on investment will be above average (Farrell 1957; Charnes et al. 1978; Helfert 2004; Fried et al. 2008).

This research paves the way for considerations concerning the role of the resources which have not been noticed or fully appreciated so far. These resources include all non-balance sheet intangible resources which contribute to the generation of the value of an enterprise. Intellectual capital is the flagship of these resources (Edvinsson 1997; Bontis 1998; Sullivan 2000; Lev 2003; Stewart 2007). For many years researchers have been conducting multidimensional studies on the efficient use of this capital in enterprises. These studies are directly related to the organisational approach, but they do not reject the economic approach completely. It is caused by the fact that researchers see the sources of efficiency in the benefits resulting from the functioning of specific interaction systems within complex organisation systems (Piekarz and Stabryła 1989). The availability of ready-to-use measurement tools, such as the indicators applied in classic economic analysis, is an important advantage. These are key tools assessing the progress made by an enterprise to maximise its value (Petty and Guthrie 2000; Williams 2001; Sierpinska and Jachna 2004). Thus, they could be the point of reference in the determination of the usefulness of other indicators expressing the involvement of unconventional resources (which are not considered in accounting standards) in the generation of value added in an enterprise (Bontis et al. 2000).

In spite of the fact that agricultural enterprises operate under similar external conditions, they achieve different effects of management. The causes of this diversification should be sought in individual internal conditions in these enterprises, especially in the ways their resources are used. Studies point to considerable differences both in technical efficiency and financial performance (Muntean 2005; Kulawik and Józwiak 2007; Kulawik 2008; Bojanes and Latruffe 2008). On the other hand, it is noteworthy that in spite of enormous theoretical and empirical, domestic and foreign accomplishments (Hallam 1993; Färe et al. 1985; or Coelli 1995), in fact, there is not one commonly recognised standard for measuring efficiency in agriculture. This means that the analysis of the sources of efficiency and differences in efficiency is still a challenge both to scientists and practitioners.

It is necessary to stress the fact that agriculture is the branch whose efficiency may be affected by fortuitous events and by natural climatic conditions, especially in a short period of time, and it may also be affected by various instruments of protective or interventional agricultural policy, such as subsidies and direct payments.[1] This might lead to a bizarre situation when the enterprises which are inefficient in the market (making a loss without subsidies) may be formally profitable (with subsidies) (Kulawik 2008). Undoubtedly, these factors complicate the measurement of efficiency in agricultural enterprises both in an individual approach and in a branch approach and they also limit the area of potential use of these measurements.

Taking different conditions of operation into consideration, classic methods of financial analysis are used to assess the efficiency of an agricultural activity. They

[1] The issue of the demoralising role of subsidies in Polish agriculture was brought up by Józwiak (2010), who indicated the demotivating character of area payments.

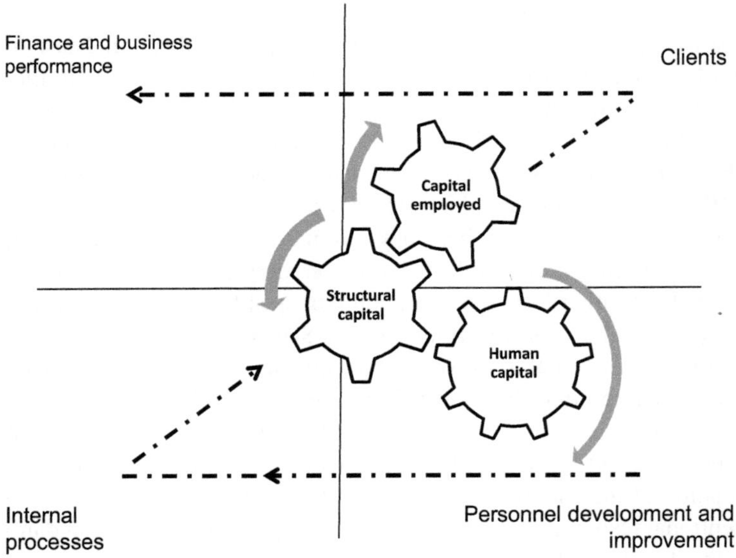

Fig. 1 The influence of the elements of intellectual capital on the creation of business performance (*Source*: based on Pietrzak (2003))

enable assessment of the following indicators: overall cost effectiveness, cost effectiveness in sales, ROA, ROE or Total Asset Turnover (TAT) (Szymańska 2007; Kulawik 2008). All of the indicators listed as well as other indicators used in the financial analysis of enterprises have contractual nature. They are also burdened with numerous methodological problems resulting from their construction, which causes difficulties in their interpretation (Sierpinska and Jachna 2004).

Being aware of the limitations outlined above, the author analysed the impact of intellectual capital on the business results achieved by agricultural enterprises. One of the sources of inspiration for the research was 'Theory Z' in the Halifax enterprise, where the role of intellectual capital was presented as a network of influences on the financial results of an enterprise (Pietrzak 2003) (Fig. 1).

The efficiency of intellectual capital was determined with the VAIC™ method developed by Pulić (2000). It gives a possibility to determine the degree of use of this capital in an enterprise and to identify the areas which particularly contribute to the generation of value added in this enterprise. This indicator is based on the information from the same financial reports of an enterprise (balance sheet and profit and loss account) which are used to calculate traditional indicators in financial analysis, such as ROA and ROE. Therefore, it can be compared with these indicators. In contrast to the classic indicators of the profitability of balance sheet resources, the VAIC™ method enables assessment of the total efficiency of tangible and intangible resources on the basis of current performance and it points to the role of the elements of intellectual capital (employees and organisation) in the generation of value added. The method makes an important assumption where remuneration of the staff is treated as an investment outlay rather than costs. This

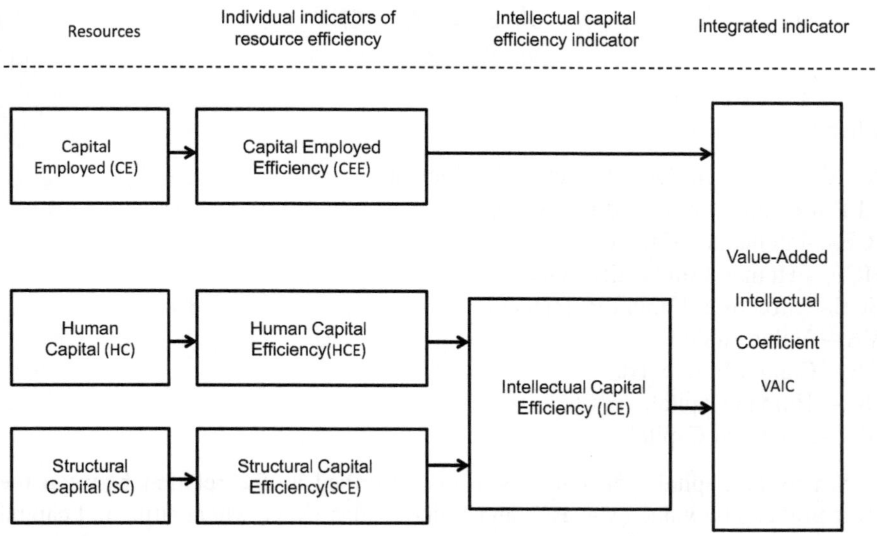

Fig. 2 The algorithm of generation of intellectual value added

simplification causes a wide range of procedural and methodological reservations (Andriessen 2004), but they do not discredit this method (Iazzolino and Laise 2013). Iazzolino and Laise make references to consultations with Pulić and they emphasise that although remunerations and other outlay on employees are equivalent to the time, knowledge, skills and experience given, they do not clearly reflect the value of intellectual capital, but they could be regarded as a substitute of this capital. Due to the methodological ambiguity about regarding intellectual capital as a resource influencing the efficiency of management Pulić proposed to measure its effects. This concept assumes that the generation of value added in an enterprise is not only the effect of the resources of capital employed but also the effect of intellectual capital (human and structural capital). This assumption is similar to 'Theory Z'. The VAIC™ is calculated as the sum of individual efficiencies of these capitals (Fig. 2).

The idea of Pulić's concept is shown in the following formula:

$$\mathrm{VAIC_t} = \mathrm{CEE_t} + \mathrm{ICE_t} = \mathrm{CEE_t} + \mathrm{HCE_t} + \mathrm{SCE_t} \tag{1}$$

Individual efficiencies are calculated according to the following formulas[2]:

$$\mathrm{CEE_t} = \mathrm{VA_t}/\mathrm{CE_t} \tag{2}$$

[2] Detailed methodological remarks concerning the calculation procedure and elements of discussion on the premises for selection of the method and the conditions of its use can be found in the author's earlier publications, e.g. Kozera (2014), Kozera and Kalinowski (2012), Kozera and Parzonka (2010), Other authors' publications: Tan et al. (2008), Stahle and Stahle (2011).

$$\mathrm{HCE_t = VA_t/HC_t} \tag{3}$$

$$\mathrm{SCE_t = SC_t/VA_t} \tag{4}$$

where:

$VAIC_t$—Value-Added Intellectual Coefficient,
CEE_t—Capital Employed Efficiency,
ICE_t—Intellectual Capital Efficiency,
HCE_t—Human Capital Efficiency,
SCE_t—Structural Capital Efficiency,
VA_t—Value Added,
CE_t—Capital Employed,
HC_t—Human Capital,
SC_t—Structural Capital.

Structural Capital Efficiency (SCE) is described as the relation between the structural capital value (VA–HC) and Value Added (VA), where structural capital is interpreted as the difference between value added and human capital. Publications on the measurement of an enterprise's capacity to generate value added also list other measures resulting from the use of individual indicators of resource efficiency obtained in VAIC™ calculations, e.g.:

1. Intellectual Capital Efficiency (ICE)—it shows the efficiency of use of intellectual resources, i.e. human capital and structural capital:

$$\mathrm{ICE_t = HCE_t + SCE_t}, \tag{5}$$

2. Best Practice Index (BPI)—it shows an enterprise through the prism of the use of capital employed and human capital in the generation of value added:

$$\mathrm{BPI = CEE + HCE} \tag{6}$$

The starting point for all these calculations is to determine Value Added (VA), which is defined as the difference between the results of the enterprise's operational activity and its outlay (reduced by the costs of employment and depreciation):

$$\mathrm{VA_t = OUT_t - IN_t = OP_t + HC_t + D_t + A_t} \tag{7}$$

where:

OUT_t—sales income in year 't',
IN_t—outlay, i.e. all expenses except those concerning human capital in year 't',
OP_t—operational activity income in year 't',
HC_t—labour costs in year 't',
D_t—write-downs (resulting from the predictions that particular components of assets will bring no economic profit in the future) in year 't',
A_t—depreciation in year 't'.

In practice, usually there are no write-downs. This means that value added can be calculated according to the following formula:

$$VA_t = OP_t + HC_t + A_t \quad (8)$$

The determination of individual indicators, ranging from Value Added (VA) through the values of Human Capital (HC), Structural Capital (SC) and Capital Employed (CE) is based on the information from the balance sheet and profit and loss account. Thus, it has the advantage of credibility and verifiability. Apart from that, it enables assessment of the relation between the obtained VAIC™ values and such indicators as Return On Assets (ROA) and Return On Equity (ROE). The method of calculation of these indicators is directly related with the actions taken by enterprises to achieve the best results possible.

3 Study Results

In the knowledge-based economy traditional measures of the performance of enterprises, e.g. increase or decrease in income/profit, do not reflect their real capacity to generate values or to use both tangible and intangible resources efficiently. Apart from that, these measures do not show which value an enterprise generates for investors, employees, local community, local government and other entities (which participate in generation of the value to various extents).

The leading hypothesis assumed in this study says that the more capable agricultural enterprises are of using their tangible and intangible resources to generate value added, the more profitable they are. This hypothesis was tested by means of the following three component hypotheses:

1. The more capable agricultural enterprises are of using their total resources of capital employed and intellectual capital to generate value added, the more profitable they are;
2. The more capable agricultural enterprises are of using their intellectual capital resources (ICE) to generate value added, the more profitable they are;
3. The more capable agricultural enterprises are of using their total resources of capital employed and human capital (BPI), the more profitable they are.

These hypotheses result from the author's previous studies on the role and importance of intellectual capital in agriculture (Kozera and Gołaś 2008; Kozera and Parzonka 2011; Kozera 2010, 2011, 2012, 2014; Kozera and Kalinowski 2012). They also result from recent publications discussing the issues of seeking the relation between the financial performance of enterprises and their intellectual capital. Some of these publications clearly confirm the presence of this dependence (Chen et al. 2005; Ahangar 2011; Mu Shun Wang 2011), but others reject it (Firer and Williams 2003; Bayatiani and Khodamipor 2013). There are numerous indications that specific socioeconomic conditions in enterprises and countries affect their performance. Thus, it is impossible to definitely accept or reject the hypothesis that intellectual capital is strongly related with value added generated in an enterprise (Bayatiani and Khodamipor 2013). The latter observations encourage intensification of the research on this subject, especially in the agricultural sector, which has been disregarded so far. It is part of a broader context of developing research on the efficiency of agribusiness enterprises.

The research on the relation between the efficiency of use of intellectual capital to generate value added in enterprises and financial profitability was conducted on a sample of 32 agricultural enterprises in the Greater Poland region. The enterprises were organised as limited liability companies. From 2002 to 2011 they ran their business activity continuously, kept full accountancy and made financial reports. All the enterprises participated in 'Ranking 300', i.e. a list of 300 best agricultural enterprises, which has been regularly prepared by the Institute of Agricultural and Food Economics since 1996 (http://www.ierigz.waw.pl/prace-badawcze/ranking-300/historia-i-zasady). The condition for being qualified for the research group was continuous business activity and access to complete financial reports during the ten-year period from 2002 to 2011.

In 2002 the total current value of net assets in the enterprises was 241.1 million zlotys. The enterprises almost tripled this value to 665.1 million zlotys in 2011. They doubled the value added they generated (in current prices) from 93.3 million zlotys in 2002 to 208.1 million zlotys in 2011 and they multiplied their nominal net profit from 8.8 million zlotys in 2002 to 67.8 million zlotys in 2011. The efficiency of use of the resources, measured with the indicators of value added generated and return on assets, increased at a much slower rate than the nominal value of the resources (which did not allow for changes in the financial value over time). Tables 1 and 2 show the basic financial performance and indicators of the efficiency of invested resources calculated for an average enterprise.

A statistical linear regression model was used for assessment of the relation between the efficiency of intellectual capital resources and profitability of assets. The model enables determination of the regression function for the empirical data under study. The method of least squares was used for the estimation of straight line parameters. The method enables determination of the degree of its fitting and the strength of interrelation which is the subject of correlation analysis (Aczel 2000).[3]

[3] This relation is measured with the coefficient of determination R^2, which shows to what extent the estimated regression line renders the values of the phenomena under study. When $R^2 = 1$, the variability of X fully explains upon the variability of Y. In this case, which usually does not occur in economic practice, the numerical data describing a real situation would be placed exactly on the regression line. When the regression line does not explain anything, $R^2 = 0$; there is no linear correlation between variables X and Y. Between the extreme values are R^2 values, which show how precisely the regression line fits the results of observation and to what extent the variation in one variable will probably cause variation in the other variable. The greater the R^2 value is, the greater the fitting is and the greater the confidence in regression is. It is usually assumed that if the R^2 value is less than 0.5, the relation between the variables is minimal (Aczel 2000).

Table 1 The average economic potential of agricultural enterprises (1000 zlotys)

Year	Gross assets	Net assets	Labour costs	Depreciation	Net profit	Value added
2002	11,113	7535	536	2153	277	2967
2003	11,824	8120	592	2055	247	2894
2004	13,827	9888	642	2139	1394	4175
2005	16,018	11,694	713	2253	1325	4291
2006	17,813	12,963	790	2324	1157	4270
2007	19,874	14,623	893	2588	1389	4870
2008	21,433	15,761	946	2865	1182	4993
2009	22,566	16,792	1042	2957	1091	5090
2010	24,988	18,876	1069	3093	1628	5789
2011	26,872	20,786	1164	3220	2120	6505

Table 2 The average indicators of the efficiency of use of intellectual capital resources and profitability ratios

Year	CEE	HCE	SCE	ICE	BPI	VAIC	ROA	ROE
2002	0.69	1.62	0.37	1.99	2.31	2.68	2.49	3.68
2003	0.62	1.67	0.36	2.04	2.29	2.65	2.09	3.04
2004	0.60	2.57	0.49	3.06	3.18	3.66	10.08	14.09
2005	0.52	1.98	0.41	2.39	2.49	2.90	8.27	11.33
2006	0.47	2.37	0.49	2.86	2.84	3.33	6.49	8.92
2007	0.46	2.31	0.50	2.81	2.77	3.27	6.99	9.50
2008	0.41	2.01	0.41	2.43	2.42	2.83	5.52	7.50
2009	0.39	1.94	0.44	2.38	2.33	2.77	4.84	6.50
2010	0.39	2.31	0.47	2.78	2.70	3.17	6.51	8.62
2011	0.38	2.21	0.49	2.70	2.59	3.08	7.89	10.20

If we assume that the final effects of a business activity (profit/loss, value added, return on assets) are the resulting values of assets owned and intellectual resources employed (stimulating tangible resources and initiating economic processes), we can assume that Return On Assets (ROA) and Return On Equity (ROE)[4] are dependent variables. The following indicators were assumed as independent variables: value-added intellectual coefficient (VAIC™) and its modifications, i.e. Intellectual Capital Efficiency (ICE) and best Business Practice Index (BPI).

The graphic image of the level and variation in these indicators in different types of configurations (Fig. 3) is shown by a relatively parallel course of the curves expressing their value. They are dominated by the indicator of the human capital efficiency. The rate of variation in all the parameters is the resultant of strong fluctuations in the HCE, slow increase in the structural capital efficiency (SCE) and regular decrease in the capital employed efficiency (CEE). In spite of natural and

[4] In other studies on efficiency authors suggested that the cost effectiveness of production and cost effectiveness of sales could also be used as variables (Cf. Kulawik 2008).

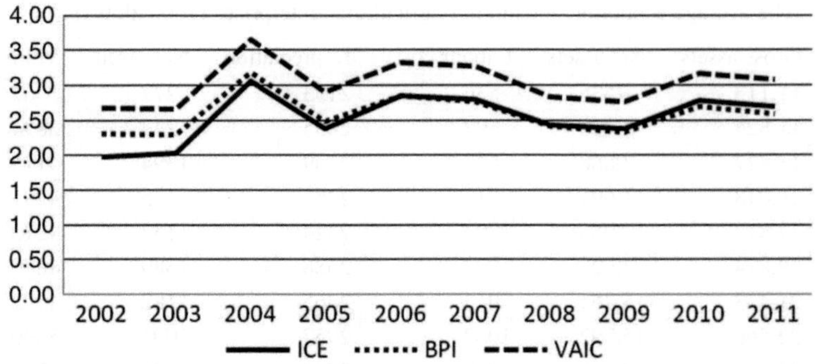

Fig. 3 Variation in intellectual capital performance indicators

conjunctural changes in the conditions of running an agricultural business during the decade under study, the role of non-balance sheet intangible resources in the generation of value added remained at a constantly high level and it was decisive to the retention of a stable position in the market, which was undergoing dynamic changes. The interrelation and strength of these bonds was determined by means of tools of data analysis in Excel spreadsheet.

The following regression functions were assumed in the research:

$$\mathrm{ROA} = \mathrm{a}_0 + \mathrm{a}_1\ \mathrm{VAIC\ and\ ROE} = \mathrm{a}_0 + \mathrm{a}_1\ \mathrm{VAIC} \tag{9}$$

$$\mathrm{ROA} + \mathrm{b}_0 + \mathrm{b}_1\ \mathrm{ICE\ and\ ROE} = \mathrm{b}_0 + \mathrm{b}_1\ \mathrm{ICE} \tag{10}$$

$$\mathrm{ROA} = \mathrm{c}_0 + \mathrm{c}_1\ \mathrm{BPI\ and\ ROE} = \mathrm{c}_0 + \mathrm{c}_1\ \mathrm{BPI} \tag{11}$$

The coefficients of correlation between the volume of profitability ratios and the VAIC™ and its derivatives calculated for each of the 32 enterprises for the 2002–2011 period indicate that there is a significant relation between the two parameters. More than 80 % of the enterprises under study were characterised by the coefficient of correlation $R^2 > 0.51$, and for more than 60 % of them—$R^2 > 0.81$ both for the ROA and ROE. Figure 4a, b show the mean values calculated for all of the agricultural enterprises in the group under study for the 2002–2011 period. Both the diagram and the numerical data on which it is based point to the fact that there is a significant relation between the variation in the return on assets and variation in the intellectual capital efficiency and it has significant influence on the generation of value added in the agricultural enterprises under study. The values of $R^2 = 0.6593$ and 0.6808 point to the fact that about 70 % of the variation in the return on assets can be explained with the variation in the efficiency of combined tangible and intangible resources of an enterprise (VAIC = CEE + ICE), where the efficiency of intangible resources (intellectual capital) is decisive.

The correlation between profitability and efficiency of generation of value added is also confirmed by R^2 values for the ICE and BPI. However, the greater R^2 value for the ICE (0.7142 vs. the ROA and 0.7020 vs. the ROE, respectively) points to the fact that the variation in the return on assets is better explained by the variation in

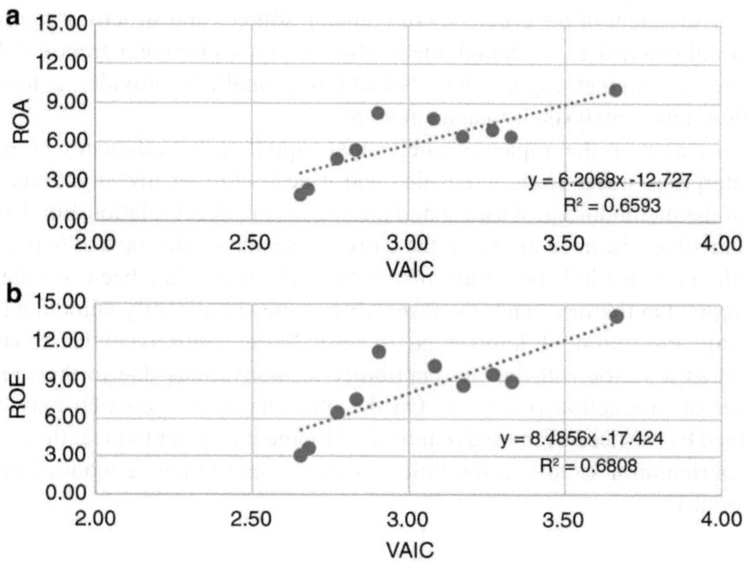

Fig. 4 (**a**) The scatter plot and regression line for the ROA and VAIC. (**b**) The scatter plot and regression line for the ROE and VAIC

the human capital efficiency and structural capital efficiency than by the variation in the capital employed efficiency and human capital efficiency (R^2 for the PBI is 0.6314 vs. the ROA and 0.6630 vs. the ROE, respectively). It is the consequence of the share of individual efficiency ratios, i.e. VAIC: CEE, HCE and SCE, where the human capital efficiency and structural capital efficiency were predominant. The mean value of the $VAIC_{2002–2011} = 3.04$ was composed of 16.2 % of the capital employed efficiency and 83.8 % of intellectual capital efficiency. As results from these calculations, based on the 10-year period of continuous agricultural business activity and various fortuitous, favourable and unfavourable natural and socioeconomic conditions, 70 % of the variation in the cost-effectiveness of the agricultural enterprises under study, which was measured with the return on assets and return on equity, can be explained by the variation in the intellectual capital efficiency in those enterprises.

4 Summary and Conclusions

The findings prove that the assumed research hypotheses were justified. They confirm the fact that at least in the agricultural enterprises which are leaders in technological and organisational progress the level of cost-effectiveness can be explained with the increased human capital efficiency and structural capital efficiency, which were much greater than the capital employed efficiency. In spite of the imperfections in the VAIC™ method, which were listed above, the method enables assessment of the efficiency of human resources and structural resources in agricultural enterprises. Although the method does not provide a precise definition of the terms 'human capital' and 'structural capital', it provides a tool for a multiple-criteria analysis of management results.

The research on the impact of intellectual capital on the efficiency in agribusiness enterprises needs to be intensified and it needs further investigations both in terms of the methodological aspect and the cause-and-effect relationship. Undoubtedly, it involves the need to extend the current research workshop and to practically verify the need for holistic nature of the research, which has been postulated for many years. On the one hand, the research may be significantly stimulated by the increasing absorption of knowledge in agriculture. Until recently it has been regarded as a sector with low susceptibility to innovations due to the biological character of production processes. On the other hand, the research may also be stimulated by the need of more dynamic development in order to meet the standards in non-agricultural sectors in the Polish economy and in the economies in developed countries.

References

Aczel AD (2000) Statystyka w zarządzaniu. Wydawnictwo Naukowe PWE, Warsaw, 493–494

Ahangar RG (2011) The relationship between intellectual capital and financial performance: an empirical investigation in an Iranian company. Afr J Bus Manag 5(1):88–95

Andriessen D (2004) Making sense pf intellectual capital. Designing a method for the valuation of intangibles. Elsevier Butterworth-Heinemann, Oxford

Bayatiani NN, Khodamipor A (2013) Investigating relationship between intellectual capital and financial variables of companies listed in Tehran stock exchange. Int Res J Appl Basic Sci 4 (4):825–828

Bojanes S, Latruffe L (2008) Measure of farm business efficiency. Ind Manag Data Syst 108 (2):258–270

Bontis N (1998) Intellectual capital: an exploratory study that develops measures and models. Manag Decis 36(2):63–76

Bontis N, Keow WCC, Richardson S (2000) Intellectual capital and business performance in Malaysian industries. J Intellect Cap 1(1):85–100

Charnes A, Cooper WW, Rhodes E (1978) Measuring the efficiency of decision-making units. Eur J Oper Res 2(6):429–444

Chen MC, Cheng SJ, Hwang Y (2005) An empirical investigation of the relationship between intellectual capital and firms market value and financial performance. J Intellect Cap 6 (2):159–176

Coelli TJ (1995) Recent developments in frontier modelling and efficiency measurement. Aust J Agric Econ 39(3):19–245

Edvinsson L (1997) Developing intellectual capital at Skandia. Long Range Plan 30(3):320–373

Färe R, Grosskopf S, Knox Lovell CA (1985) The measurement of efficiency of production. Kulwer Nijhoff Publishing, Dordrecht

Farrell MJ (1957) The measurement of productive efficiency. J R Stat Soc Ser A Gen 120 (3):253–290

Firer S, Williams SM (2003) Intellectual capital and traditional measures of corporate performance. J Intellect Cap 4(3):348–360

Fried HO, Lovell CAK, Schmidt SS (2008) Efficiency and productivity. The measurement of productive efficiency and productivity growth. Oxford University Press, New York, 3–91

Hallam A (1993) Empirical studies of size, structure, and efficiency in agriculture. Size, structure, and the changing face of American agriculture. Westview, Boulder, 204–231

Helfert AE (2004) Techniki analizy finansowej. Wydawnictwo PWE, Warsaw

Iazzolino G, Laise D (2013) Value added intellectual coefficient (VAIC). A methodological and critical review. J Intellect Cap 14(4):547–563

Józwiak W (2010) Polskie gospodarstwa rolnicze w pierwszych latach członkostwa-kwestie efektywności i konkurencyjności. Instytut Ekonomiki Rolnictwa i Gospodarki Żywnościowej-Państwowy Instytut Badawczy, Warsaw

Kozera M (2010) Kapitał intelektualny agrobiznesu. Ekonomika i organizacja Przedsiębiorstwa 8:17–24

Kozera M (2011) Intellectual capital in agriculture – measurement and determinants. Acta Sci Pol Oeconomia 10(3):83–95

Kozera M (2012) Kapitał intelektualny w rolnictwie- zrozumieć, zmierzyć, zastosować. In: Dudycz T, Osbert-Pociecha G, Brycz B (eds) Efektywność – konceptualizacja i uwarunkowania, vol 262. Prace Naukowe Uniwersytetu Ekonomicznego we Wrocławiu, Wrocław, 177–187

Kozera M (2014) Efektywność wykorzystania kapitału intelektualnego w przedsiębiorstwach rolniczych Wielkopolski. In: Tomaszuk A (ed) Przedsiębiorczość i Zarządzanie, vol XV, issue 6, Wydawnictwo Społecznej Akademii Nauk, Łódź, 165–179

Kozera M, Gołaś Z (2008) Istota kapitału intelektualnego jako potencjalnego czynnika konkurencyjności agrobiznesu. RN SERiA vol X, issue 1, Warsaw, 186–189

Kozera M, Kalinowski S (2012) Intellectual capital – non-material element of farm businesses economic success. In: Management – leadership – strategy – competitiveness. Proceedings of the international conference on management of human resources 2012, Szent Istvan University, Godollo, 405–413

Kozera M, Parzonka M (2010) Zasoby kapitału intelektualnego przedsiębiorstwa rolniczego i jego zmiany. Roczniki Naukowe Stowarzyszenia Ekonomistów Rolnictwa i Agrobiznesu XII (5):90–96

Kozera M, Parzonka M (2011) Wsparcie decyzji rozwojowych zasobami pozabilansowymi przedsiębiorstw rolniczych. J Agribus Rural Dev 3(21):35–46

Kulawik J (ed) (2008) Analiza efektywności ekonomicznej i finansowej przedsiębiorstw rolnych powstałych na bazie majątku WRSP. Wyd. IERiGŻ-PIB, Warsaw

Kulawik J, Józwiak W (eds) (2007) Analiza efektywności gospodarowania i funkcjonowania przedsiębiorstw rolniczych powstałych na bazie majątku Skarbu Państwa. Wyd. IERiGŻ-PIB, Warsaw

Lev B (2003) Intangibles at a crossroads. Controlling 15(3/4):121–127

Muntean B (2005) Knowledge management and innovation applied in agriculture. Bull Univ Agric Sci Vet Med Ser Horticult 62:158–162, Special issue

Petty R, Guthrie J (2000) Intellectual capital literature review: measurement, reporting and management. J Intellect Cap 1(2):155–176

Piekarz H, Stabryła A (1989) Analiza efektywności organizacyjnej jako narzędzie wspomagania procesu zarządzania. Zeszyty Naukowe Wydziału Ekonomiki Produkcji Uniwersytetu Gdańskiego 12:178–189

Pietrzak M (2003) Najlepiej wyceniać z kartą. Przegląd metod i narzędzi pomiaru kapitału ludzkiego. Personel i zarządzanie 10(151):16–22

Pulic A (2000) MVA and VAIC analysis of randomly selected companies from FTSE 250. Austrian Intellectual Capital Research Center, Graz. http://measuring-ip.at/Papers/ham99txt.htm. Accessed 30 May 2014

Sierpinska M, Jachna T (2004) Ocena przedsiębiorstwa według standardów światowych. Wyd. Nauk. PWN, Warsaw

Stahle P, Stahle S (2011) Value added intellectual co-efficient (VAIC): a critical analysis. J Intellect Cap 12(4):531–551

Stewart TA (2007) The wealth of knowledge: intellectual capital and the twenty-first century organization. Crown Business, London

Sullivan PH (2000) Value-driven intellectual capital. Wiley, New York

Szymańska E (2007) Analiza przedsiębiorstw agrobiznesu: (techniczno-ekonomiczna, finansowa i strategiczna). Wydawnictwo Wieś Jutra, Warsaw

Tan PH, Plowman D, Hancock P (2008) The evolving research on intellectual capital. J Intellect Cap 9(4):585–608

Wang MS (2011) Intellectual capital and firm performance. Annual conference on innovations in business and management. The Center for Innovations in Business and Management Practice, London

Williams MS (2001) Is intellectual capital performance and disclosure practices related? J Intellect Cap 2(3):192–203

Tripartite Collaborative Model Value Creation Experience of iEnterprise with Corporate and Nongovernmental Organization

Ilex K.K. Lam

Abstract This chapter details a study of the current state of the development of cross-sector collaboration among social enterprises, nongovernmental organizations (NGOs) and the corporate sector. It establishes a conceptual framework of a Tripartite Collaborative Model (TCM) with Social Exchange Theory, Inter-organizational Collaboration Theories and Stakeholder Theory with Value Creation to depict the logic of cross-sector collaboration among the predefined partners, namely, a work integration social enterprise (WISE), a created shared value (CSV) enterprise, and a sustainable NGO for value creation.

Under the framework of the TCM, iEnterprise, a privately owned WISE, established a call center in Hong Kong to create employment opportunities for people with disabilities and those from underprivileged communities while maintaining financial sustainability. The tripartite partnership of iEnterprise was developed with a "value added" outsourcing contract from a CSV corporate and a "win-win" servicing agreement with a sustainable NGO.

The successful value-creation experience of iEnterprise was analyzed and evaluated as a case study for the TCM. The set of performance indicators of iEnterprise was compared with other examples of WISEs from the government subsidy model and the cross-border franchising model in order to contrast the advantages and disadvantages of a TCM.

The findings confirmed the possibility of building a form of tripartite social enterprise under the collaborative framework of a TCM characterized by a low capital requirement and resulting in mission fulfillment together with financial sustainability, strategic operational efficiency and effective workfare creation on capital employed.

I.K.K. Lam, D.B.A., M.B.A., FHKIoD (✉)
iEnterprise Foundation, Emperor Center 1507, 288 Hennessy Road, Wanchai, Hong Kong

Hong Kong Rehabilitation Power, Unit 102, 1/F, The Waterfront, 1 Austin Road West, Tsim Sha Tsui, Kowloon, Hong Kong

Fullness Social Enterprise Society, Shop 2, G/F Youth Outreach Bldg., 2 Holy Cross Path, Sai Wan Ho, Hong Kong
e-mail: ilex.ienterprise@gmail.com

T. Dudycz et al. (eds.), *The Essence and Measurement of Organizational Efficiency*, Springer Proceedings in Business and Economics, DOI 10.1007/978-3-319-21139-8_9

Keywords Cross-Sector Collaboration • Work Integration Social Enterprise • Creating Shared Value • Outsourcing • People with Disabilities

1 Introduction

The social enterprise (SE) sector has made considerable economic impacts on societies. In the United Kingdom, the sector was estimated to have over £160 billion in terms of annual turnover and contributed £55 billion to the economy gross value added in 2013 (UK Cabinet Office 2013). In the United States, SEs are estimated to have generated revenues of about US$500 billion, about 3.5 % of total US GDP (Skoll World Forum 2013). Lam (2013) concurred the view of Surie and Ashley (2008) that social entrepreneurship and commercial entrepreneurship will no longer be dichotomous but would converge to the same entrepreneurship with dual value proposition of different mix of financial objective and social mission resulting from the proliferation of collaborations between for-profit and non-profit organizations. The British Council predicted that there would no longer be a recognizable 'social enterprise sector' by 2020 in Europe as the concepts and ideals of social enterprise would spread rapidly into all corners of society, becoming mainstream which will lead to cross-border collaboration among government, charities and for-profit businesses (Hilhost 2014).

There is no shortage of theoretical research and studies into management practice on bilateral collaborations within the commercial sector and NGO/social enterprise sector. However, research into tripartite partnerships with dual-value objectives in these sectors is limited. Given the importance of the social dimension evolving in the commercial sector and the demand for financial sustainability in the NGO and social enterprise sectors, this chapter reviews the current state of evolution of collaboration among corporates, and the NGO and social enterprise sectors, and attempts to establish a conceptual framework of a Tripartite Collaborative Model in which three distinctive partners—corporate, NGO and social enterprise—co-create economic and social values. The value-creation experience of iEnterprise under the framework of a TCM is compared with examples of the government subsidy model (GSM) and the cross-border franchising model (CBFM) in Hong Kong to contrast the advantages and disadvantages of TCM. This chapter then concludes with the theoretical and managerial contributions of this study, and several areas for future research.

1.1 The Rise of Cross-Sector Collaboration for Value Creation

The incorporation of social dimensions into corporate goals signifies an important milestone in current economic systems. Corporate social responsibility (CSR) has evolved from ethical notation to corporate philanthropy, then to strategic philanthropy (Porter and Kramer 2002), strengthening the link between CSR and competitive advantage (Porter and Kramer 2006) in the sense that corporate leaders should use the fundamentals of corporate strategy to find those philanthropic areas that not only benefit society, but also benefit the firm. Consequently, organizations should be able to find social needs that align with their particular expertise. Socially responsible investing (SRI) is another side of the coin, driving for the practice of CSR and enabling investors to have an impact on the practices and policies of firms through market mechanisms. In other words, this kind of investment can make a difference by not investing in or selling the stock of certain firms that are engaged in practices that the investors find objectionable. To develop more advanced and powerful forms of CSR, corporate social entrepreneurship (CSE) was promoted to accelerate companies' organizational transformation into more powerful generators of societal betterment by leveraging on the resources within and outside the organization (Austin et al. 2007). In addition, Porter and Kramer (2011) enlightened the concept of creating shared value (CSV) to advance the economic and social betterment and enhance competitiveness simultaneously by means of reconfiguring the company policies and operating practices. In essence, for-profit enterprises can serve the society by creating 'shared value' and using their core businesses to generate economic value through social progress.

A nongovernmental organization (NGO) is a citizen-based association that operates independently of government, usually to deliver resources or serve some social or political purpose. NGOs have become increasingly important in addressing humanitarian issues related to welfare and developmental aid. NGOs are being confronted with the competitive nature of acquiring funds and the need to demonstrate to funders that they have particular competencies, while continuing to adhere to their traditional welfare or development values.

Emerson (2006) generalized the value drivers of social entrepreneurship as the pursuit of social impacts, social innovation, the mobilization of commercial revenues; and the adoption of managerial methods for organizations regardless of for-profit or not-or-profit organization, private or public. Savitz and Weber (2006) emphasized the double, or even triple, bottom line, and the creation of mixed or hybrid added value ("blended value") with closely linked economic and social dimensions. Santos (2009) theorized social entrepreneurship and its economic roles as the development of sustainable solution to solve neglected social problems due to inefficiencies in our economic systems such as market failure, oversight of government policy or insufficient deliverables of NGOs.

NGOs have been encouraged by governments and charitable foundations to reduce their reliance on subsidies and donations by generating income through commercial practice (Pharoah et al. 2004). As part of this process, many social enterprises sought to build relationships with corporations in order to improve their viability as businesses (DTI 2005). Corporates, NGOs and social enterprises are no longer separately performing in different regimes but have started converging into different forms of business partnerships in terms of social value creation (Austin et al. 2007) Corporate–social enterprise collaboration has been developing widely with local and international partners. For instance, Grameen Danone Foods was a joint venture between Grameen Bank, the community development lender, and Groupe Danone, a leading French food company, in which the partners committed to the same social mission to develop a milk-processing plant and produce nutritionally enhanced yoghurt at affordable prices to help poor children escape the ravages of malnutrition in Bangladesh. Grameen Danone can be considered as the world's first creative multinational business with a social mission running as a for-profit organization (Yunus and Weber 2007).

1.2 Experience of Cross-Sector Collaboration in Hong Kong

In 2001, the Hong Kong Government launched the 'Enhancing Employment of People with Disabilities through Small Enterprise' (3E's) Project, which laid the foundation for social enterprise development. The total number of projects operated by SEs in Hong Kong reached 457 in 2014, an increase of more than 70 % from 6 years ago, and a 13 % increase on 2012. The majority of them are in catering and food production (20.4 %), lifestyle (18 %) and care and medical services (17.7 %). There was also a surge in businesses in recycling, and education and training, recording a 64 % and 42 % increase respectively. According to a survey conducted by the, social enterprises recorded a profit, loss or breakeven of 35 %, 32.5 % and 32.5 % respectively. In 2013, 26 SEs closed down due to keen competition, rising rental costs, and insufficient financial resources (SEBC News April 2014). In fact, most SE projects in Hong Kong are operated by charitable organizations and NGOs, and only 20 % through private investment. This invites criticism that the main challenges to the SE industry stem from its adhesion to NGO traditions and culture in welfare value creation and relatively weak business know-how and commercial discipline (Tang et al. 2008). In general, Hong Kong lacks a culture of knowledge sharing and collaboration, and "a siloed" mindset in the ecosystem, where for-profit and not-for-profit sectors rarely collaborate due to their different visions (Alto and Wong 2013). Therefore, it is essential for an entrepreneurial spirit to be incorporated into NGO culture to create a balance between social and economic goals.

For the future development of social enterprise in Hong Kong, a Bauhinia Foundation Research Center study (2013) reiterated the importance of changing mindsets and adopting a new business model with an innovative and entrepreneurial spirit for better social enterprise development. It also emphasized that social enterprises should not rely on funding from the government or other affiliated organizations but should explore alternative channels and operate as self-financing businesses in the long run (BFRC Weekly Analyses: Nov. 6, 2014). Alto and Wong (2013) suggested that improving cross-sector collaboration between the corporate and non-profit sectors held the key for the further development of social enterprises in these two sectors. The essential step is to identify the mechanisms to foster cross-sector dialogue and facilitate cross-sector collaboration (Chan and Yuen 2011; Au 2014).

2 Research Questions

With focuses on the value exchange and interaction in tripartite partnerships among corporates, NGOs and social enterprises, and its theoretical foundation and managerial implication, this study attempts to answer the following questions:

1. What are the characteristics of individual tripartite partners proposed for cross-sector collaboration?
2. What is the process of value exchange and value co-creation of the proposed tripartite approach?
3. What are the advantages and disadvantages of the proposed tripartite approach compared to other collaborative approaches in terms of value co-creation?
4. What are the theoretical and managerial implications of using the proposed tripartite approach?

3 Research Methodology

Through the literature review on the current evolution of collaboration between the corporate, NGO and social enterprise sectors, a conceptual framework of a Tripartite Collaborative Model (TCM) has been established to achieve the common goal of creating social and economic value. The dual value creation experience of iEnterprise with other partners was analyzed as a case study for TCM. The adopted case study approach is considered the most relevant due to the exploratory nature of the research in which identification and assessment of unexpected pattern can be revealed properly (Yin 1984). In fact, a case study approach is by far the most common in the social enterprise research arena and widely perceived as the most appropriate for studying the new phenomenon (Hoogendoorn et al. 2010). The iEnterprise experience of the TCM was monitored from the inception of the business idea, business model development, business negotiation of the tripartite partnership and the completion of the initial stage of the outsourcing contract. The examples of other collaborative models, the government subsidy model (GSM) and the cross-border franchising model (CBFM) are compared to contrast the advantages and disadvantages of TCM.

4 Conceptual Framework of Tripartite Collaborative Model

Corporate–social enterprise collaboration has been developing widely between local and international partners. There are numerous studies on business models for corporate–NGO collaboration for value co-creation (Powell et al. 1996; Reid et al. 2001). The research and attention had put on tripartite partnership but tilted towards the collaboration between government, NGOs and corporates, e.g. (HK Policy Research Institute 2005). There is a lack of research articulating the theoretical and practical aspects of the collaborative dynamics and practice of value co-creation among these organizations. The following section provides the theoretical foundation and formation of the conceptual framework for the Tripartite Collaborative Model.

4.1 Characteristics of Tripartite Partners

Given the dual mission of achieving financial goals jointly with social value creation, three independent organizations were defined for the conceptual framework of the Tripartite Collaborative Model. They are the work integration social enterprise (WISE), the created shared value (CSV) enterprise and the sustainable NGO.

Tripartite Partner: Work Integration Social Enterprises (WISE)
A work integration social enterprise is generally defined as a social enterprise aimed at integrating vulnerable people and groups into the labor market through economic activity under a sustainable operation. Most WISEs were founded by civil society actors: social workers, community activists, or trade unionists, in a context of persistent unemployment where the social actors lacked adequate public policy measures to tackle these problems. Consequently, initiatives emerged emphasizing the limitations of public intervention on behalf of those excluded from the labor market: the long-term unemployed, and those lacking qualifications or with social problems (Nyssens et al. 2012). The privately owned WISE with a dual mission was adopted for the Tripartite Collaborative Model with the focus on employment creation for people with disabilities and from the underprivileged community. It was independently established by a group of skills-based knowledge volunteers to solve a neglected social problem and achieve financial sustainability.

Tripartite Partner: CSV Enterprise
As advocated by Porter and Kramer (2011), a creating shared value enterprise (CSV Enterprise) is specifically defined as a commercial enterprise aimed at creating economic value with social value creation, which may have transformed from adopting a traditional set of corporate social responsible initiatives to creating shared value with a companywide strategy. Traditional corporate social

responsibility programs focus mostly on reputation and have only a limited connection to the business, making them hard to justify and maintain over the long run. However, the process of creating share value is linked to the improvement of company's competiveness, profitability to create economic values in the course of fulfilling social mission. There are several distinct ways to create economic value by creating societal value including redefining productivity in the value chain, reconceiving products and markets and building supportive industry clusters at the company's locations.

Outsourcing is one of the most common ways for commercial enterprises to enhance productivity along their own value chain thanks to the strategic benefit in obtaining external resources to replace internal resources with the accomplishment of the same goal. In general, the improvement of productivity from outsourcing for a CSV enterprise can be obtained by freeing internal resources for other purposes, reducing and controlling operating cost, improving host company focus, gaining access to world-class capabilities, complementarity of internal resources and transferring risks to a partner company (Griffiths 2010).

Sustainable NGO

A sustainable NGO is defined in the Tripartite Collaborative Model as a NGO partner aiming at creating sustainable societal value with enhanced business and management skills for financial sustainability. It distinguishes itself from a conventional NGO by the lesser extent of dependence on financial subsidy from government or donations.

It is widely noted that many NGOs in developing countries are increasingly creating business ventures with commercial enterprises by sharing the competencies, infrastructure and knowledge needed to operate in their target market to achieve their social objectives. This opens up collaborative opportunities and business practices between the NGO and commercial sectors (Brugmann and Prahalad 2007).

4.2 *Theoretical Foundation of the Tripartite Collaborative Model*

Out of a rich selection of topical literature, three relevant theoretical inter-organizational collaboration approaches have been adopted in developing the Tripartite Collaborative Model for social enterprises, corporates and NGOs. These are resource-based theory, network theory, and institutional theory. In addition, social exchange theory (SET) is used to construct the conceptual framework for TCM.

For resource-based theory, collaboration enables the partnerships to benefit mutually by developing difficult-to-imitate organizational capabilities through the transmission or sharing of resources (Hamel et al. 1989) and enjoying collaborative advantage, a critical source of competitive advantage in a different form, and re-conceptualizing their relationships with competitors.

Network theory postulates that the extent to which an organization can build an effective collaboration is a function of different factors. Its network position determines the boundary of the collaboration. Its network status serves and infers the outcome of future interactions (Gulati 1998). Its embedded relationships enable collaboration to be governed on the basis of relational rather than contractual mechanisms, which play a critical role in allowing organizations to access new knowledge (Nohria and Gulati 1994).

Institutional theory provides insights into collaboration according to different schools of thought. The institutional theorists working with new institutional economic traditions have stressed that bilateral exchanges for mutual benefits (Chi and Roehl 1997) and therefore effective collaboration may involve the development of incentives, which mitigate opportunism (Holmstrom 1982). Neo-institutional theorists in organization studies argued that collaboration has the potential to transform institutional structures such as social rules and belief systems within the individual partner organizations.

The collaborations between social enterprise, NGOs and commercial enterprise draw on ideas primarily from resource-based theory in obtaining collaborative advantage to build distinctive capabilities to address social problems whilst the network position, network status and embedded relationship of network theory provide insights into the realm and outcome of the collaboration. Institutional theory highlights the potential transformation of rules and beliefs within individual partners such as the importance of social responsibility to the corporate culture of commercial enterprise, sustainability in delivering the social mission of social enterprise, and the effectiveness of the resources utilization of an NGO.

Social exchange theory (SET) is among the most influential conceptual paradigms for understanding workplace behavior. Although different views of social exchange have emerged, theorists agree that social exchange involves a series of interactions that generate obligations (Emerson 1976). Within SET, these interactions are usually seen as interdependent and contingent on the actions of another person (Blau 1964). SET also emphasizes that these interdependent transactions have the potential to generate high-quality relationships. When each partner holds resources (whether economic, political or social) that are deemed valuable by the other partner, the norm of reciprocity is established. Collaboration is based on mutually beneficial patterns of co-operation where participants have better potential to access resources, choices between alternative courses of action or reaction, and anticipated outcomes.

Tripartite collaborations between social enterprise, commercial enterprise and NGOs, like all collaborations, involve both economic and social exchange. The exchange may involve benefits to either party which are either extrinsic and hold economic value, such as information and knowledge, or intrinsic and without overt economic value, such as support, business network or relationships (Blau 1964). In addition, intangible elements of knowledge, skills, and expertise may be exchanged

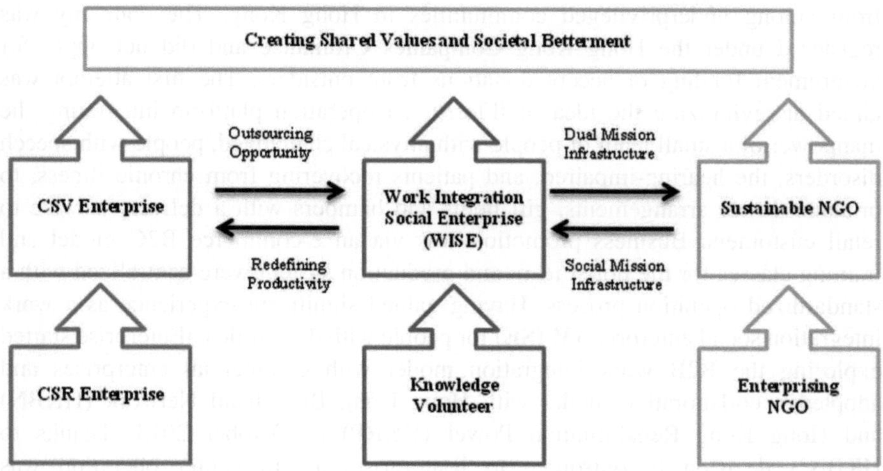

Fig. 1 The conceptual framework of the tripartite collaborative model

(Muthusamy and White 2005). Under the theoretical construct of SET, the Tripartite Collaborative Model is shaped with the following process:

- Specific value that each collaboration partner attributes to the inputs of their partners
- Competing practices and priorities intrinsic to the social enterprise, corporate and NGO
- Expected benefits of the collaboration to each partner
- Alignment of bilateral and common goals among collaboration partners

More specifically, the WISE contributes its values on business infrastructure with a dual-values mission to the sustainable NGO partner and redefines productivity with the CSV enterprise. The CSV enterprise delivers outsourcing opportunities to the WISE while the NGO reciprocates its social mission infrastructure and knowledge to the WISE. The three collaborative partners are aligned with and benefit from the same common goal of creating shared values and societal betterment together. The conceptual framework of the Tripartite Collaborative Model is depicted in Fig. 1.

5 Findings: iEnterprise with Tripartite Collaborative Model

5.1 Work Integration Social Enterprise: iEnterprise

iEnterprise was founded in 2012 by private capital and knowledge volunteers to develop business models to create employment for people with disabilities, and from among underprivileged communities in Hong Kong. The company was registered under the Hong Kong Companies Ordinance and did not apply for government funding or accept donations from outsiders. The first attempt was aimed at revitalizing the idea of iFlorist, an operation platform integrating the manpower of a small team of people with physical challenged, people with speech disorders, the hearing-impaired, and patients recovering from chronic illness, to produce flower arrangements, gift items and hampers with a delivery service to retail customers. Business promotion was via an e-commerce B2C model and training classes for the florist team and production system were centralized with a standardized operation process. Having gained significant experience as a work integration social enterprise (**WISE**) for people with disabilities, iEnterprise started exploring the B2B work integration model with commercial enterprises and adopted a collaborative model with Hong Kong Broadband Network (HKBN) and Hong Kong Rehabilitation Power (HKRP) in October 2013. Thanks to HKBN's decision to outsource to iEnterprise, a call center operation was established to support the 1083 telephone enquiry service for HKBN's Hong Kong subscribers. In February 2014, the call center commenced with 13 employees (five patients recovered from chronic disease, four physically handicapped, three early-retired women and one person recovering from mental illness) together with two founders supporting as knowledge volunteers. The picture of the iEnterprise call center team, its profile, the business development and negotiation process, and key parameters of the business proposal are shown in Diagrams 1, 2, and 3.

5.2 CSV Enterprise: Hong Kong Broadband Network

Hong Kong Broadband Network Limited (HKBN) is a leading broadband service provider, offering a diversified portfolio of products in fiber broadband and Wi-Fi access, communication and entertainment to over 1.4 million subscribers in Hong Kong. In May 2012, HKBN underwent a management buy-out and became majority-owned by funds advised by CVC Capital Partners and 87 co-owners. HKBN's commitment to corporate social responsibility is revealed in its publicly stated core purpose to "Make our Hong Kong a better place to live". The management team began transforming the corporate culture by developing its team of 2500 employees towards competitive advantage with the following core values (TREE):

- "**T**rustworthy"—be honest and genuine, keeping promises without compromising,
- "**R**esponsive"—be visionary and receptive, responding aptly and promptly,
- "**E**ntrepreneurial"—be responsible and unyielding, striving for excellence, and
- "**E**ngaging"—be devoted and considerate, attracting others to follow suit.

HKBN was also one of the pioneers of the development of a corporate knowledge volunteer team encouraging their middle and senior management to share experiences and expertise with social enterprises and social marketing projects. The management team of HKBN was constantly exploring opportunities for creating shared value (CSV) and leading this commercial enterprise to progress from a CSR to a **CSV enterprise**.

5.3 *Sustainable NGO: Hong Kong Rehabilitation Power*

Hong Kong Rehabilitation Power (HKRP) was founded in 1995 and became a non-profit and charitable rehabilitation organization providing direct services, training programs and employment in social enterprises to its members. The vision of HKRP is to promote social integration of people with and without disabilities and advocate an inclusive society with equal opportunities. Their mission statement is "To empower individuals with disabilities to achieve economic self-sufficiency, independent living, inclusion and integration into all aspects of society". Its training and employment has been connected to training programs for people with disabilities to uplift the employability of its members. In addition, different types of social enterprises were established in an attempt to provide immediate employment opportunities to those who had completed HKRP training courses. The social enterprise division of HKRP set up training programs for telemarketing and customer service programs for people with disabilities and attracted the interest and support of several commercial enterprises in Hong Kong.

HKRP received corporate philanthropy and government subvention to expand its development of call center operations, telemarketing and customer services several years ago. Unfortunately, the trend of cost reduction by outsourcing customer services operations to offshore partners reduced substantially the job opportunities offered by HKRP patrons to HKRP members especially those who had received training in telemarketing and customer services. As a result, the call center equipment and facilities became idle and qualified members were unemployed and involuntarily switched to other interests. In general, the Board of Directors realized not only the importance of entrepreneurial culture for HKRP but also the collaboration with partners to build its organization to become a **sustainable NGO**.

5.4 *Business Model of iEnterprise Call Center*

The description of the iEnterprise business model in the following section focuses on the logic of value exchange and value co-creation among the tripartite partners depicted in Fig. 1.

Value Exchange from "Value Added" Outsourcing Opportunity

To reduce costs, HKBN moved its call center and customer service operation out of Hong Kong several years ago, following the trend of serving Hong Kong customers from offshore customer service centers. To put the slogan "Make our Hong Kong a better place to live" into practice, the management began exploring ways of creating shared value from their business operations for the societal betterment of Hong Kong, apart from their CSR and knowledge volunteer initiatives. HKBN explored the feasibility of recruiting people with disabilities to work in its business operation in Hong Kong but was deterred by the difficulties, such as the requirement of a barrier-free environment, to accommodate this initiative. In terms of collaboration with NGOs for outsourcing the 1083 telephone enquiry service, progress was undermined by challenges related to the lack of a quality assurance system and compatible business culture to safeguard the success of the collaboration. With a strong business background and knowledge volunteers as founding members, iEnterprise was requested to submit a business proposal and outsourcing agreement to support HKBN customers with a telephone enquiry service, in which a new call center operation aiming to hire 13–15 people with disabilities and underprivileged people would be set up by iEnterprise in Hong Kong. In essence, the incoming telephone enquiries service would be shifted to the iEnterprise call center in Hong Kong for daily operation from 9 am to 6 pm and Monday to Friday. The memorandum of understanding was mutually agreed as follows:

- This project serves as an experiment for both parties, which should be organized with least risk exposure and least marginal cost.
- The trial period is fixed for 6 months and contract renewal will be subject to performance evaluation.
- The second-hand equipment and telephone devices are lent by HKBN to iEnterprise in order to reduce start-up project capital for a call center.
- The collaborative partnership between iEnterprise and HKRP was agreeable by HKBN.
- Future collaboration will be explored to enable employees with disabilities to work from home.
- The success of this outsourcing model should exemplify the corporate–social enterprise collaboration to the commercial sector in Hong Kong in order to promote social inclusion and the merit of creating shared value in the commercial sector.

Value Exchange from Redefining Productivity

- **Productivity**: The cost reduction, if any, in the short term may not be significant because of the production cost advantage of an offshore customer service operation. Since high labor turnover and inflation in their offshore operation was foreseeable, the collaboration with iEnterprise provided not only the first step for HKBN to develop a human resources strategy to analyze the impact of collaborative advantage between the iEnterprise call center team and its offshore team, but also transformed a CSR platform to CSV culture. In addition, enhanced productivity was expected as a result of manpower deployment to higher value-added customer service.

- **Corporate Image**: Exemplifying HKBN's corporate slogan "Make our Hong Kong a better place to live" by outsourcing specific operations to increase the productivity of people with disabilities and those from the underprivileged community in Hong Kong helps HKBN enrich its corporate image and facilitate its name recognition and market penetration strategy.
- **Customer Satisfaction**: Given all the customers of HKBN are based in Hong Kong, the 1083 telephone enquiry service provided by the iEnterprise call center in Hong Kong improves customer satisfaction since call center staff are familiar with local dialect and intelligence.
- **Employee Wellbeing**: HKBN advocates the importance of talent development and treats its employees as business partners. Those who participate in this outsourcing project have experienced social inclusion and the practice of HKBN's corporate slogan. The morale of those employees who involve in this project was enlightened by the fulfillment of social mission.

Value Exchange from Dual-Mission Infrastructure
iEnterprise has initiated the business network and outsourcing opportunity which in turn provided an unique employment opportunity to the members of HKRP. In addition, the HKRP management and project team could leverage on the experience and entrepreneurial skill of the knowledge volunteers from the iEnterprise team. As a typical WISE, iEnterprise aligned both financial sustainability and social mission with the support from HKRP to empower people with disabilities through identifying employment opportunities. A service agreement was developed so that the iEnterprise call center operation benefited from the most favorable terms by leveraging on HKRP's infrastructure, including office facilities and staff administrative support. The dual mission of iEnterprise bridges the potential gap and cognitive dissonance[1] between a profit-oriented corporate culture and the social welfare culture of an NGO.

Value Exchange from Socializing Infrastructure
With over 16 years of experience in serving people with disabilities, HKRB has accumulated a pool of members and service recipients who are people with disabilities or are patients recovered from chronic illness. Some members have attended training in telemarketing and customer services and suited to working in a call center. In addition, the infrastructure for the training can be customized to match the technical requirements and quality standards of HKBN. Both the 'hardware' of HKRP, such as a barrier-free office and call center facilities, and its 'software', like the administrative system for training, the employment recruitment platform and professional counseling services, combined as favorable conditions for partnering with iEnterprise for the call center operation. More importantly, HKRP was able to offer employment opportunities to its members and earned

[1] Cognitive dissonance is the state of having inconsistent thoughts, beliefs, or attitudes, especially as relating to behavioral decisions and attitude change.

income from service fees from the operation of the iEnterprise Call Center and hence the improvement of the productivity of their resources. Besides, this collaboration also enriched HKRP's entrepreneurial culture and its credentials to attract stakeholders.

6 Result: Value Co-creation

All partners and participants appreciated the successful results of the 6-month operation and tripartite agreements were renewed. The details of the value creation arising from this tripartite collaborative model are summarized as follows:

1. **Value Creation for HKBN:**
   - **Enhanced Productivity**: HKBN reported that productivity was improved by over 10 % on customer services by its offshore team after the 1083 telephone enquiry service was outsourced to iEnterprise because the equivalent offshore service team was deployed to other value-added operations and therefore improved overall productivity.
   - **Improved Customer Satisfaction**: Customer satisfaction was enhanced after the 1083 telephone enquiries were handled by Hong Kong operators thanks to local operators' better understanding of local idioms and accent. This reduced the average call duration and improved service quality.
   - **Better Public Recognition**: The CSR initiative of HKBN received the Gold Award of the Hong Kong Call Center Association as the "Best Contact Center in CSR Hong Kong 2014" even though the call center operation in Hong Kong had only been outsourced to iEnterprise for less than a year.
2. **Value Creation for HKRP**:
   - **Employability of People with Disabilities and from the Underprivileged Community**: This collaborative project created 13 job opportunities for employment over 6 months. In 2012–2013, HKRP provided vocational training with job attachment for 36 members through a job-attachment and employer subsidy program. After training, only 12 members were offered jobs and only seven members' employment periods lasted for more than 6 months. The details of the employment period and job nature after vocational training of HKRP are shown in Diagram 4.
   - **Stakeholders Revenue Ratio (SRR)**: The ratio between total key stakeholder revenue and business revenue is defined as the Stakeholders Revenue Ratio (SRR). High SRR means a high ratio of revenue created was distributed to target stakeholders, i.e. the higher the SRR, the better the fulfillment of the social mission for WISE. The members of HKRP who work in the iEnterprise Call Center and HKRP itself are the key stakeholders who benefited from workfare and service fees of 89 % and 7 % of business revenue of the call center operation respectively. Hence, the SRR of HKRP is 96 %. If

iEnterprise rents another office and sets up its administration team internally, the operational expenses will inevitably be higher. If HKRB had not teamed up with iEnterprise, it would have received no office administration fee and continued to suffer from the waste of idle resource. In this case, the SRR of HKRP was reduced to 89 %. Clearly, the collaboration between iEnterprise and HKRP created synergy in achieving social and economic goals for both parties.

- **Enterprising Spirit**: The collaboration between iEnterprise and HKRP cultivated an internal culture and working environment with a balance of social mission fulfillment and enterprising spirit highlighting the importance of efficiency and productivity. Although the impact of the enterprising spirit cannot be fully measurable after 6 months, the collaboration with iEnterprise has benefited HKRP in terms of attracting knowledge volunteers and strengthening the credibility of HKRP from the sight of its stakeholders.
- **Support from Knowledge Volunteers and Networking**: After learning of the potential of this tripartite collaborative arrangement, knowledge volunteers offered their support and networks for the creation of employment for people with disabilities and shared knowledge and expertise with the HKRP management team. In addition, the set up of tripartite collaboration in HKRP arouse potential outsourcing opportunities from other corporates.

3. **Value Creation for iEnterprise**:

- **Sustainable Operation with Minimum Capital Requirement**: As a work integration social enterprise (WISE), this Tripartite Collaborative Model integrates resources from partners and ensures a sustainable "win-win" outcome for all stakeholders to create employment and promote social inclusion effectively. Thanks to the support of all stakeholders contributing resources, social capital and knowledge, the start-up financial capital was minimized down to HK$40,000. The operation was already slightly profitable after 6 months. The cost breakdown in terms of revenue generated is shown in Fig. 2.
- **Surplus on Capital Employed (SOC)**: The operation reached breakeven in the third month and became profitable with a surplus of HK$2000 after 6 months. The yearly profit target was raised from HK$4000 to HK$6000 given the favorable terms for the next 12 months.[2] The target surplus on capital employed before tax is 15 % per annum, which will be retained for further development.
- **Yearly Workfare Created on Capital Employed (YWCC)**: The iEnterprise call center hired 13–15 people with disabilities and from among the underprivileged to work flexible hours and generate revenue of over HK$400,000 per year. Given the capital employed was HK$40,000, the yearly workfare on

[2] iEnterprise and HKBN have revised the agreement with new terms for another phase of collaboration since Sept. 2014

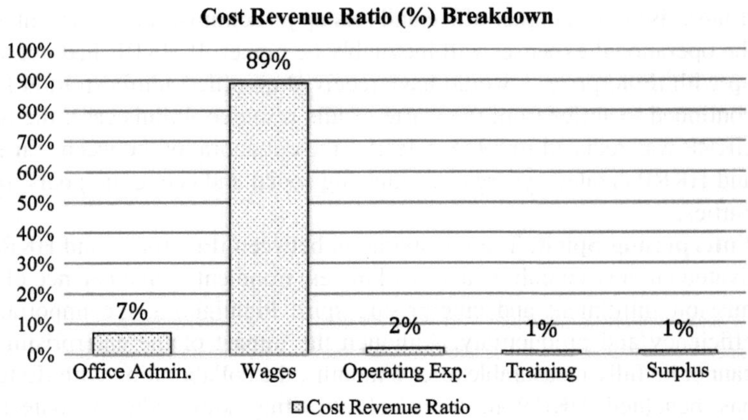

Fig. 2 The breakdown of cost revenue ratio (%) from Feb. to Dec. 2014 (source: iEnterprise)

capital employed (YWCC) was over ten times per year. In other words, one dollar of capital generated ten dollars of workfare per year.

- **Workfare Revenue Ratio (WRR)**: The total wage payment to employees was 89 % of the yearly revenue generated.
- **Stakeholders Revenue Ratio (SRR)**: The wages of the employees of the iEnterprise call center (89 %), service fee to HKRP (7 %) and surplus retained for iEnterprise (1 %) are the key stakeholders' interest arising from the business revenue of the call center. Hence, the SRR of iEnterprise Call Center is 97 %.
- **Tripartite Management System**: HKBN has confirmed that the service quality standard of the iEnterprise call center for the 1083 telephone enquiry service met its customer service standards. The lessons learned and experience accumulated provided a unique platform for collaborating with people with disabilities and the underprivileged, NGOs and commercial enterprise.

4. **Value Creation for Employees**

The Employee Self Evaluation and Job Expectation Survey were conducted before employment commenced and 6 months after the operation. The employees were asked to rank from 1, the lowest, to 5, the highest, for individual levels of confidence, competence and happiness at that stage. The job expectation survey also revealed the priority of their interest and expectation in working with iEnterprise in financial and social aspects such as improving financial capability, extending social network, working without discrimination and revealing individual capabilities. There was significant improvement in the overall wellbeing of the employees especially in financial capabilities and self-image after 6 months. The details of the survey is shown in Fig. 3 and summarized as follows:

- **Improved Self-Image**: The team of 13 employees manifested a well-balanced score in confidence, competence and happiness before the project

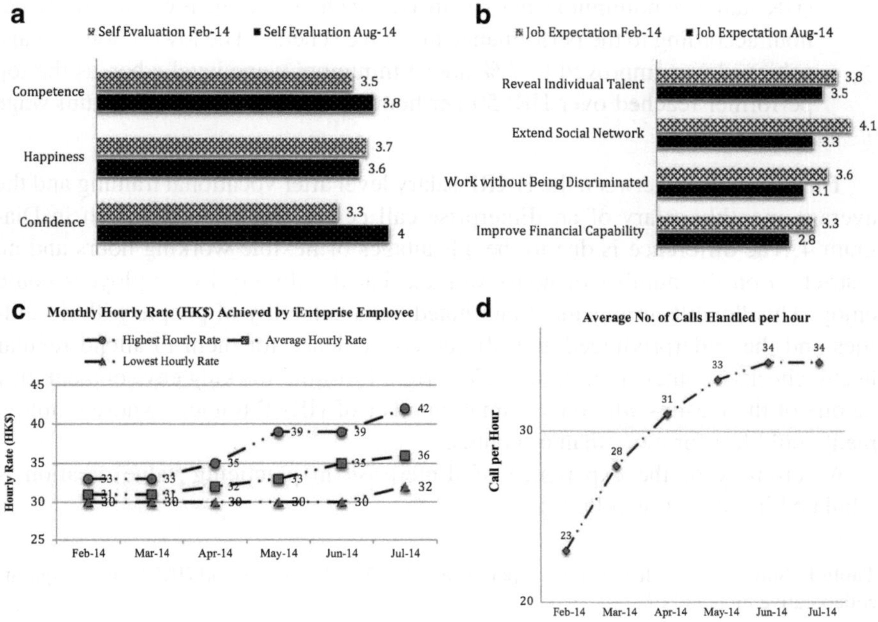

Fig. 3 (**a**) Employee self evaluation survey. (**b**) Employee job expectation survey. (**c**) Monthly hourly rate achieved iEnterprise employee from Feb to July 2014. (**d**) Average number of call handled per hour by iEnterprise employee (source: iEnterprise)

commenced. All attributes were ranked more than 3. The competence scored higher than confidence levels. It can be interpreted that respondents believed in their competence but lacked of confidence because other people might not trust their capabilities. Happiness was ranked the highest score among the attributes indicating the positive attitudes and self-motivating character of this group of employees with disabilities. The confidence and competence levels also improved significantly from an average score of 3.3–4, to 3.5–3.8 respectively after 6 months. Experience in overcoming challenges, meeting job targets and the benefits of financial and social rewards contributed to this upliftment of self-image.

- **Improved Wellbeing due to Job Satisfaction**: The Job Expectation Survey revealed the top priority as "Extend social network" following by "Work without discrimination" and "Reveal individual talent". "Improve financial capabilities" scored lowest, showing that unemployed people with disabilities and the underprivileged ranked equal opportunities in society over financial gain. The group's overall job expectation scores were lowered after 6 months due to the partial fulfillment of job expectations.
- **Improved Financial Capability**: The monthly aggregated productivity could gradually outperform the performance benchmark by 13 % after 6 months of operation. The average hourly wage improved from HK$30

(HK statutory minimum wage) to an average hourly wage level of HK$42 per hour according to the performance incentive scheme. The lowest hourly wage achieved was improved to 7 % above minimum wage level whereas the top performer reached over HK$50 per hour (over 40 % above minimum wage level).

The comparison between the HKRP salary level after vocational training and the average monthly salary of an iEnterprise call center employee is shown in Diagram 4. The difference is due to the advantages of flexible working hours and no restriction on the number of hours worked that the iEnterprise employees could enjoy. This flexible arrangement facilitated the availability of people with disabilities and the underprivileged and offered convenience for them to attend regular health checks or other commitments. The rigid full-time working environment may be one of the reasons why only a small number of HKRP trainees whose employment could last for more than 6 months.

A summary of the experience of iEnterprise in practicing value creation is tabulated in Table 1 as follows:

Table 1 Summary of value creation experience of HKBN, iEnterprise and HKRP under tripartite collaborative model (TCM)

Tripartite collaborative model (TCM)	Created shared value (CSV) enterprise	Work integration social enterprise (WISE)	Sustainable NGO
	Hong Kong Broadband (HKBN)	iEnterprise (iE)	HK Rehabilitation Power (HKRP)
Common Goal to Solve Social Problems	Practice corporate social responsibility Create societal betterment through business decisions	Promote social inclusion Equal employment opportunity	Promote social inclusion Empower people with disabilities
Mission Statement	Making HK a Better Place to Live	Creating Employment for People with Disabilities and the Underprivileged Community	Empowering the disabled to develop
Theory of Collaboration	Creating shared value Social exchange theory Theory of outsourcing	Resources-based theory Network theory Institution theory Social exchange theory	Resources-based theory Network theory Institution theory
Operating Mode	Outsourcing partnership	Work integration social enterprise	Collaborative partnership
Critical Exchange Value	Redefining productivity Outsourcing agreement with iEnterprise	Dual-mission enterprising infrastructure Collaborative Agreement with HKRP	Social mission infrastructure Collaborative Agreement with iEnterprise

(continued)

Table 1 (continued)

	Value creation	Value creation	Value creation
Economic Value Created	Enhanced productivity Improved customer satisfaction for 1083 telephone enquiry	Sustainable Operation Minimized initial capital Established social capital	Revenue on idle resources Synergies on existing infrastructure
Social Value Created	Better public image	Created 13–15 jobs	Job opportunities for members Improved business culture
Employee Wellbeing	Better morale due to enhanced caring culture	Financial wellbeing Stable and favorable working environment Stronger confidence Better competence Extended social network	Better network for social capital Improved enterprising spirit Enhanced credibility for stakeholders' support
Performance Measurement	Outperform productivity benchmark by 10 % Corporate citizenship award/CSR award	Surplus on Capital Employed (SOC) = 15 %p.a. Yearly Workfare Created on Capital Employed (YWCC) = 10 times per year Workfare Revenue Ratio (WRR) = 89 % Stakeholders Revenue Ratio (SRR) = 97 %	Stakeholders Revenue Ratio (SRR) = 96 % Social enterprise performance award

7 Discussions

7.1 Theoretical Considerations on Potential Conflicts in Practice

Social exchange theory views interactions from an exchange perspective in which social costs and benefits are 'traded' in relationships governed by normative rules and agreements. Di Domenico et al. (2009) pinpointed that different goal priorities of partners, ownership structures, stakeholders' preference, governance mechanisms and lines of accountability may lead to a series of tensions, which may cause conflicts and disintegration of collaborations.

However, stakeholder theorists within the additional value creation paradigm argued that introducing value creation for all stakeholders broadens the framework of management, bringing it closer to a more realistic optimum balance of economic and social benefit created, generating new cooperative value-creation capabilities, and overcoming some conflicts (Argandoña 2011).

The experience of iEnterprise was favorable in the sense that there was no significant conflict whatsoever among partners thanks to the 'win-win' collaborative relationship through value exchange and value creation. Intuitively, a potential conflict between HKBN and iEnterprise could have arisen in the course of fulfilling the conflicting goals of social responsibility against cost rationalization. However, both HKBN and iEnterprise had redefined productivity and value proposition related to value creation to key stakeholders such as customer satisfaction, employee morale and retention, resources deployment for other value-added activities and enhanced public image. Similarly, HKRP would have rejected offering favorable terms to iEnterprise at the time of negotiation. iEnterprise has succeeded in persuading HKRP to appreciate the reputational benefits and synergy arising from more successful employment cases beneficial to its members and turning idle resources productive through this partnership.

Yunus generalized the lessons learned from his experience in running a social business, which were internalized as collaboration principles in this Tripartite Collaborative Model to avoid conflicts and reduce business risk as follows (Yunus et al. 2010):

- Specify mission statement clearly to all stakeholders at the outset to avoid conflicts
- Recruit like-minded fellows with the same social mission
- Find complementary partners to leverage expertise and resources
- Challenge conventional thinking and basic assumptions to create new strategies
- Undertake continuous strategic experimentation to minimize risk and maximize the firm's rate of learning

7.2 *Evaluation of Tripartite Collaborative Models*

In order to evaluate the performance of TCM, the government subsidy model represented by the 3E's Project and the cross-border franchising model represented by DiDHK were chosen given the same mission of employment creation for people with disabilities.

Government Subsidy Model (GSM): 3E's Project

The 'Enhancing Employment of People with Disabilities through Small Enterprise' (3E's) Project was characterized as a model of government subsidy. In 2001, the 3E's Project was launched by the Social Welfare Department of the Hong Kong Government to provide grants for NGOs to set up small enterprises to enhance the employment opportunities of people with disabilities. The progress of the 3E's Project was reported[3] as follows:

- There were 385 employees with disabilities in 3E's Projects, around 10 % below the job opportunities target.

[3] As of September 2013.

- The average grant per people with disability job for the 81 approved projects varied widely from $12,500 to $368,800.[4] This grant per people with disability job ratio was affected by the nature of the projects and business models adopted.[5]
- The funding needed for creating a job for a person with disabilities had increased 3.4 times from HK$54,000 in the fiscal year 2002/03 to HK$241,000 in 2012/13.
- The average number of jobs for people with disabilities created by each project dropped from 11.4 in 2002/03 to 5.8 in 2012/13.
- There are 45 social enterprises operating beyond the funding period, in which 16 social enterprises (36 %) were still running in deficit. This indicated that many funded projects operating beyond the funding period had not yet achieved a self-financing status but were still subsidized by their sponsoring bodies.
- One dollar of grant generated 7.2 dollars of workfare for the employee with disability over 9.3 years. The failure rate of 3E projects was low at 16 % while the sustainable projects contributed ongoing workfare to people with disability, reducing reliance and financial burden on welfare subsidy (Kee 2013).

Cross Border Franchising Model (CBFM): Dialogue Experience (Formerly Dialogue in the Dark, Hong Kong)

Dialogue in the Dark (DiD) was a social enterprise started in Germany in 1988 to "provide jobs for blind people and change people's minds on the disabled". The organization gradually spread globally. Inspired by its impact, a group of social entrepreneurs was licensed a franchise to found Dialogue in the Dark, Hong Kong (DiDHK) in 2008. DiDHK trained the visually impaired as tour guides of a specially constructed "pitch-black" exhibition which allowed sighted participants to experience a world without light. Through role reversal, the visually impaired showed their capabilities of navigating in the dark and the sighted could sample the life of the visually impaired, helping enhance people's empathy towards the visually impaired.

The achievement of DiDHK was highlighted as follows:

- Without any government subsidy, DiDHK hired more visually impaired individuals than any other private company and experienced successful development with widespread popularity in HK (DiD HBS Business Case 2012).
- DiDHK's performance is measured through both economic and social value creation in terms of financial sustainability, employment of visually impaired staff, recipients' benefits, volunteer force, community awareness and the success of outplacement.

[4] The project in which average grant of HK$12,500 for PwD per job created was a cleaning and servicing company which was granted with only HK$21,000. The one where average grant of HK $368,800 per job created was a restaurant which received the grant of HK$1,385,000.

[5] Response of SWD to Audit Commission Report 62, item 35, Section 4, Chapter 4, p. 122 (Chinese version).

Table 2 Comparison of tripartite collaborative model (TCM), government subsidy model (GSM) and cross border franchising model (CBFM)

Collaborative model	Government subsidy model (GSM)	Cross border franchising model (CBFM)	Tripartite collaborative model (TCM)
Project/Social Enterprise	3E Project[a]	DiDHK[b]	iEnterprise
Start-Up Capital/Beneficiary			
Grant/Capital Employed	HK$700,000 (Average)[c]	HK$6,500,000[d]	**HK$40,000**
Average Number of Employees	7	**22**	13
Financial Sustainability			
Surplus on Capital Employed	0 %[e]	**17 %**	15 %
Years of Establishment	**9.3 Year**[f]	4 Years	0.75 Year
Mission Fulfillment			
Average Number of Employees with Disabilities or Underprivileged	7	**22**	13
Capital Employed per Job Created	HK$100,000	HK$295,000[g]	**HK$3000**
Average Monthly Salary per Employee with Disabilities	HK$6245[h]	**HK$9300**[i]	HK$2431[j]
Average Yearly Salary per Employee with Disabilities	HK$74,940	**HK$111,600**	HK$29,172
Yearly Workfare Created Per Project	HK$0.5 M[k]	**HK$4.06M**[l]	HK$0.4M
Strategic Operating Efficiency			
Workfare/Revenue Ratio (WRR)	0.60	0.29	**0.89**
Stakeholders Revenue Ratio (SRR)	0.60	0.61	**0.96**
Yearly Workfare Created on Capital/Grant Employed (YWCC)	0.77[m]	0.62[n]	**10.00**
10-Year Workfare Created on Capital/Grant Employed (YWCC)	7.7	6.2	**100**
Strategic Workfare Creation			
Years of Establishment	**9.3 Year**[o]	4 Years	0.75 Year
Average Number of Job Created	7	**22**	13
Accumulated Workfare Created Since Inception	HK$ 5.0M	**HK$ 16.M**[p]	HK$0.3M
Yearly Workfare Created	0.53M	**4.0M**	0.4M

(continued)

Table 2 (continued)

Collaborative model	Government subsidy model (GSM)	Cross border franchising model (CBFM)	Tripartite collaborative model (TCM)
Average Number of Job Created Assuming HK$6.5M was Funded to the Project	65	22	**2112**
Accumulated Workfare Creation Assuming HK$6.5M is Given to the Project	HK$4.6M	HK$4.0M	**HK$65M**

[a]Data collected from the Audit Commission Report Hong Kong, "Promoting the Development of Social Enterprises" 4 April 2014
[b]Sales Data collected from DID HBS Case, "Dialogue in the Dark, Hong Kong: A Role Model for Social Enterprises in the Making", Richard Ivey School of Business Foundation, 2012 and Dialogue in the Dark, Hong Kong Social Performance Measurement Project 2013
[c]$52,364,580 was granted to 75 social enterprises
[d]Total capital investment since inception
[e]The estimate of surplus is close to zero if not negative
[f]Median life span
[g]Capital Employed/no. of job created/: HK$6.5M/22
[h]There were 541 people with disability employed generating yearly workfare of $40,542,540 implying an average monthly income of $6245
[i]Average Monthly Salary per Employee in 2013 = HK$2.45M/12 months/22 employees = HK $9300
[j]Median Salary in the period of Feb. to Aug. 2014
[k]Workfare created per year = HK$6245 × 12 × 7 = 0.5 M
[l]VI Workfare plus outplacement = HK$2.45 M + HK$1.61 M = HK$4.06 M
[m]Total yearly workfare = $6425 × 12 × 7 = 539,700; capital employed = HK$700,000; YWCC = 0.77
[n]Workfare for visually impaired staff and Outplacement/Capital = 4.06 M/6.5 M = 0.62
[o]Median life span
[p]The total sum of visually impaired staff workfare and outplacement from 2010 to 2013 = 4.06 M × 4 = 16.2 M
Note: The most remarkable values among the collaborative models are given in bold

- From a 10-year investment horizon, from 2010 to 2019, the total return on investment was estimated to be 1:14.7, i.e. every one dollar invested by the social enterprise's investors had HK$14.70 worth of financial and social returns generated in this 10-year horizon.

The comparison of these three models, TCM, GSM and CBF is tabulated in Table 2 and summarized as follows:

- **Start-up Capital Requirement**: TCM/iEnterprise demonstrated its advantage of the least capital requirement and in turn gave rise to the lowest capital employed per employee with disability among these models of comparison. Clearly, the lower the start-up capital requirement, the lower was the entry hurdle encountered by social entrepreneurs or knowledge volunteers to spearhead a new project. The greater number of jobs created to the beneficiary, together with the low capital requirement, singled out the advantage of TCM.
- **Financial Sustainability**: Although the priority is sustainability but not profitability, a profitable operation was required to serve as a barometer of enterprise

performance and sustainability for future development. The average life of a 3E's Project was 9.3 years, revealing its survivability partially due to the subsidy and support by the government and individual parent organization . The operation of CBF/DiDHK became profitable a few years after inception whereas iEnterprise became profitable just only 6 months after its inception. However, any change of the outsourcing contract due to new policy or management change of HKBN would lead to business upheaval at iEnterprise. If the minimum wage in Hong Kong continues to rise to a level that neither HKBN or iEnterprise can afford, the TCM/iEnterprise Call Center operation will cease unless a new CSV enterprise partner is found.

- **Mission Fulfillment**: The social mission of these models was primarily the same, i.e. creating jobs for people with disabilities. The greater the number of jobs created from a particular collaboration model, the higher is the degree of mission fulfillment. In terms of the number of jobs created and workfare created for employees with disabilities, CBF/DiDHK performed the best among these three models. However, the high ratio of Capital Employed Per Job Created indicated the potential entry barrier for Cross Border Franchising Model. The average monthly income of iEnterprise employee was the least due to the characteristic of flexible working hours adopted to meet employees' personal style.
- **Strategic Operating Efficiency**: TCM/iEnterprise demonstrates the highest ratio of sharing the revenue with their stakeholders (96 %). The merit of the TCM model was the cost structure incurring almost no fixed cost whereas the variable fee for administration and facilities (7 %) also benefited HKRP as one of the key stakeholders. In addition, the trust between the partners and the nature of this 'one-on-one' institutional relationship minimized the costs for client acquisition and maintenance that required in other models. The Strategic Operating Efficiency of GSM/3E's Projects is estimated at around 60 % of revenue, assuming the rest of the cost of operation came from office rent and production costs. In DiDHK, the total workfare created was 29 % of the revenue because the supporting workers who were not visually impaired were also recruited. Its Stakeholders Revenue Ratio was 61 % in which the contribution to profit and outplacement were 13 % and 19 % respectively. One dollar of investment in DiDHK generated 0.60 dollar of workfare for the visually impaired employee. It was reported that one dollar investment in DiDHK was expected to generate total value of HK$14.70 including both financial profit and social value from 2010 to 2019. However, the workfare created within this period is HK$6.20, about 42 % of the total value because other significant social value created through education for social inclusion was regarded as non-workfare arena. In this context, iEnterprise exhibited the highest potential of workfare creation efficiency with one dollar creating over HK$10 and HK$100 workfare in 1 year and 10 years horizon respectively.
- **Strategic Workfare Creation**: CBFM/DiDHK was ranked the top in terms of accumulated workfare created since inception. However, it became the least when the workfare was compared taking into account of individual capital employed. iEnterprise had superior performance in terms of a low capital requirement and a high workfare created per capital employed. As per the latest

record, the capital employed in DiDHK and iEnterprise is HK$6.5 million and HK$0.04 million respectively. The ratio of jobs and workfare created for DiDHK and iEnterprise is 22 jobs/HK$4 million and 13 jobs/HK$0.4 million respectively. For the sake of comparison, if the same amount of HK$6.5 million was executed with TCM, TCM would contribute workfare of over HK$65 million and the number of jobs created would climb to over 2000 employees.[6]

The subsidy element of GSM, extending the average life span of the projects sponsored, was regarded as the main advantage of this model but this was achieved at the expense of self-sustainability of individual social enterprises. The beauty of the CBFM was demonstrated by its job-creation and fulfillment of social inclusion but the potential hurdle was the relatively high capital requirement for a social entrepreneur to start with. The outstanding features of TCM, with the example of iEnterprise, were low capital start-up, low fixed costs, high strategic operating efficiency due to the high rate of revenue sharing to stakeholders and the system of flexible working hours accommodating to the specific needs of people with disabilities and from among the underprivileged community. Its disadvantages arose from the fact that relatively low-income jobs were created and the business risk resulting from a 'one-on-one' institutional relationship in this B2B model.

7.3 *The Role of Social Capital in Tripartite Collaborative Model: Synergy Versus Positive Externality*

According to Robert Putnam (2000), social capital refers to the collective value of all social networks and the inclinations that arise from these networks to do things for each other. The TCM highlighted the importance of social capital contributed by the collaborative partners, employees and the local community.

For HKRP, the implication of social capital is involved in building up social relations, formal and informal social networks, shared values, obligations, expectations, group membership, trust, reciprocity, empowerment, good business practices and civic engagement.

In the commercial sector, social capital has been used at various times to explain superior managerial performance, the growth of entrepreneurial firms, improved performance of functionally diverse groups, the value derived from strategic alliances (Koka and Prescott 2002) and enhanced supply chain relations.

For HKBN, social capital can be drawn from the development of its "soft power" to build its unique reputation and genuine social mission to be a responsible corporate citizen. This "soft power" was instrumental to strengthen the bonding among stakeholders of HKBN including employees, clients, suppliers and shareholders (Tse 2009).

---

[6] Assuming the repeatability of this model, no problems in identifying outsourcing projects and sufficient labor supply.

For the founders of iEnterprise and some other aspiring social entrepreneurs, typically those launching second careers, the social capital built over years among industry peers, acquaintances, and key influencers become a superlative asset, perhaps more valuable than other forms of capital. Not only is the network itself extended, but also a rich set of economic resources mobilizing them in new and creative ways.

In the tripartite partnership among iEnterprise, HKBN and HKRP, the social capital was bonded within individual organizations and bridged among collaborative partners. Although it is difficult to access and measure the magnitude of social capital generated, bonding social capital was experienced by attracting the support of knowledge volunteers and active participation from individual employees of the partners. The bridging of social capital was created through the synergy enjoyed by the partners in terms of saving start-up cost/capital, sharing resources and enhancing productivity of certain idle resources in HKBN and HKRP, e.g. computer and telephone systems.

More specifically, the role of social capital in the iEnterprise Tripartite Partnership was revealed by the synergy created during the start-up phase of the iEnterprise call center as follows:

- Facilities and Administration Synergy: The iEnterprise call center leveraged on the spare capacity of HKRP's infrastructure and facilities and their administrative support with favorable terms. The service fee were linked to monthly revenue. The cost saving for iEnterprise was estimated around 5 % of annual revenue, i.e. HK$20,000.
- Manpower from Knowledge Volunteers: Without the support of volunteers during the start-up, the total cost would have increased by 10 % of the annual revenue, i.e. HK$40,000.
- Operating Expenses Subsidy: HKBN supported iEnterprise with second-hand computers and telephone equipment, which reduced the overall start-up capital expenditure and operating expenses by approximately 3 % of annual revenue, HK$12,000.
- Training and Quality Assurance Program: iEnterprise managed the recruitment and training of employees with support from the HKBN and HKRP training teams. The training cost reduction was estimated as 2 % of annual revenue, HK $8000.
- Total start-up capital saved was HK$80,000
    - (i) Social capital on volunteerism[7]—human Resource: HK$ 40,000
    - (ii) Social capital on relational asset—training: HK$8000
    - (iii) Social capital on resource synergy—facilities and equipment: HK$32,000

[7] According to United Nations, Volunteerism benefits both society at large and the individual volunteer by strengthening trust, solidarity and reciprocity among citizens, and by purposefully creating opportunities for participation.

Table 3 The components of financial and social capital

Capital employed with financial and social capital	HK$	Total capital ratio (%)
Social Capital-Volunteerism	40,000	33
Social Capital-Relational Asset	8000	7
Social Capital-Resource Synergy	32,000	27
Financial Capital (Start-up Capital)	40,000	33
Total Financial Resources	72,000	60
Total Capital Resources (Financial + Social)	120,000	100

- If there was no social capital contributed by the partners, the start-up capital of the iEnterprise call center required at "market rate" would have increased by 200 % from HK$40,000 to HK$120,000. The first year result would have been 19 % deficit instead of 1 % surplus in terms of expected annual revenue. The proportion of financial and social capital components is listed in Table 3 and the breakdown of cost/revenue (%) with and without social capital is shown in Fig. 4.

7.4 *Positive Externality*

When third parties benefit from an activity in which they are not directly involved, the benefit is called a positive externality. In this tripartite partnership of TCM, the external benefit spillover from individual partners cannot be measured numerically but only illustrated by the impact of value creation, bonding and bridging of social capital within and among individual partners in the long run as follows:

(A) Positive Externality to Social Inclusion:

- Public awareness of the importance of social inclusion and equal opportunity
- Improved public attitudes towards the capability of people with disabilities and the underprivileged community
- Potential reflux of employment opportunities to Hong Kong beneficial for poverty alleviation
- Potential impact on the effectiveness of government welfare policy and the saving of government welfare expenditure for social inclusion

(B) Positive Externality to WISE:

- Improving legitimacy of WISE through dual objectives of societal betterment and financial sustainability
- Widening the scope of knowledge volunteerism to change maker/social entrepreneur with individual social capital under the collaborative framework of TCM

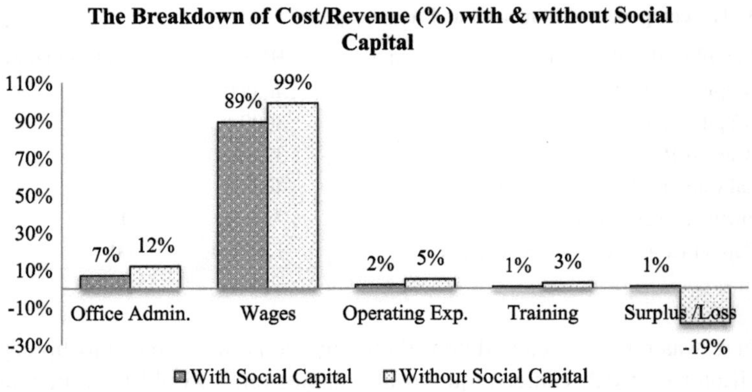

Fig. 4 The breakdown of cost/revenue ratio (%) breakdown with and without social capital from Feb. to Dec. 2014 (source: iEnterprise)

– Promoting the prototype of work integration social enterprise (WISE) with cross-sector collaboration between for-profit organizations and NGOs

(C) Positive Externality to Corporates: Synergy and Productivity

– Example of creating shared value with outsourcing practice in the Commercial Sector
– Example of corporates collaborative partnership with social enterprise
– Internalization of "CSV Enterprise" and the development of corporate social entrepreneurs
– Example of the improvement of "soft power" to enhance employee morale and customer satisfaction
– Example of brand building to improved public image and recognition

(D) Positive Externality to NGOs: Employability and Employment Opportunity

– Alternatives to improve employability of people with disabilities and the underprivileged community
– Example of social enterprise and NGO collaborative partnership
– Improved the well-being of employees with disabilities and their families
– Impact of enterprising NGO and the development of social innovation

The pictorial description of the positive externality of TCM is shown in Fig. 5.

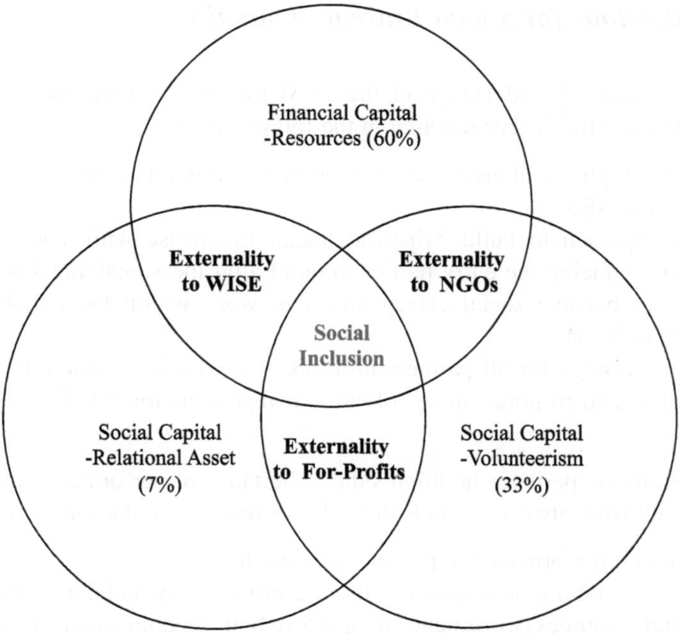

Total Capital (Financial and Social) Employed	HK$	Total Capital Ratio
Social Capital-Volunteerism	40000	33%
Social Capital-Relational Asset	8000	7%
Financial Capital- Resources	72000	60%

Fig. 5 The positive externality of tripartite collaborative model (source: iEnterprise)

8 Contributions and Limitation

8.1 Implication for Theoretical Development

This chapter reveals the contributions of TCM to social entrepreneurship particularly in the following areas:

- Tripartite Collaborative Model (TCM) combines the paradigms of Social Exchange Theory and Inter-organization Collaboration Theories to form a new conceptual framework for tripartite partnership for social and economic values creation.
- This chapter invites the exploration and verification of a theoretical and conceptual framework of TCM with the advantage of the mobility and measurability of social capital and positive externality.
- Further research can develop the management principles with stakeholders theory and value creation in order to reduce tension and avoid conflicts among tripartite partners.

8.2 *Implications for Social Entrepreneurship*

This chapter reveals the advantage of the TCM for social entrepreneurship and highlights the need for further research in the following areas:

- Low risk but high social and economic return for corporates, NGOs and social enterprises (WISE)
- A unique approach to build Tripartite Social Enterprise with a low capital requirement reducing the entry barrier to build a business enabling knowledge volunteers to become social entrepreneurs to work within the collaborative framework of TCM
- "Win-Win" strategy for all partners in terms of economic productivity, social value creation and corporate image of individual partners for to tackle neglected problems

The iEnterprise experience highlights the importance of performance measurement in the following areas and sheds the light for research in the following areas:

- Mission-driven performance to prevent mission drift
- Financial sustainability to improve corporate survivability and development
- Total capital resources performance to optimize both economic and social return on financial and social capital investment
- Strategic operation efficiency to safeguard the extent of mission fulfillment and
- Social capital and positive externality to account total financial and social impact of the project

8.3 *Implications for the Development of the TCM Ecosystem and Tripartite Social Enterprise*

The development of the Tripartite Collaborative Model is mainly based on the alignment of both social and economic missions among individual partners to generate employment opportunities for people with disabilities and from among the underprivileged community. With dual-mission infrastructure, the WISE integrates the outsourcing operation from CSV enterprise and leverages on the social mission infrastructure, such as availability of target beneficiary and social capital from the sustainable NGO. The WISE reciprocates economic and social value to the outsourcing CSV enterprise and manages the outsourcing operation according to the expected quality standard. The revenue side of the WISE can be fixed in advance through negotiation between the WISE and the CSV enterprise while the cost expenditure can also be fixed according to the expected salary level of the employees, manpower planning and incentive schemes, if any. The uncertainty primarily stems from managing the deliverables in the operation and the change of the specific social mission of the CSV enterprise. In other words, the business risk of the WISE is relatively low once the terms of the tripartite partnership is fixed. This TCM provides a practical institutional platform for social entrepreneurs and knowledge volunteers, in particular those who prefer to take less risk at the beginning of a social entrepreneurship. Further research on TCM Ecosystem development will be instrumental in creating employment and improving the employability of the target beneficiary with the following focus:

- Macro analysis to identify "value-added" outsourcing opportunity from different industry and quest for CSV enterprises
- Micro analysis to identify the skills set or deliverables available from the target beneficiaries and create specific talent pools
- Social capital analysis to capture the network and resources available as synergy for partnerships and the availability of sustainable NGOs
- Knowledge volunteer analysis to align the variety of managerial skills for tripartite partnerships and incubate the formation of Tripartite Social Enterprise
- Funding platform analysis to channel social investment with optimum funding size, and mapping the expectation on dual-value objectives among tripartite partners

8.4 Implication for Policy Makers

Among the 360,000 people with disabilities in Hong Kong, only 13 % are economically active, which is much lower than the rate of more than 60 % economically active people in Hong Kong according to HK Government Statistics (2012–2013). TCM provides a new dimension to create employment for people with disabilities. Through outsourcing, iEnterprise acquired the job opportunities from HKBN's offshore service center for a Hong Kong operation. Policy makers should facilitate the development of the TCM together with the proper ecosystem to channel job opportunities from overseas markets or the return of employment opportunities back to Hong Kong from the offshore centers. In addition, the TCM has contributed to the determinants of key performance indicators such as capital requirement, mission fulfillment, strategic operation efficiency and workfare creation productivity, to evaluate the efficiency and impact of individual projects. More importantly, the TCM serves as one of the effective bridges for cross-sector collaboration between NGO and commercial sector to promote societal betterment.

8.5 Limitations

The limited operational history of iEnterprise representing a tripartite partnership provides little information on the potential causes of problems affecting partnerships and their solutions. Given that TCM focuses on productivity and social inclusion through job creation, its scalability and repeatability for other social impacts needs to be further explored. However, the experience of iEnterprise with TCM serves to highlight the merits of this tripartite approach but not its versatility.

9 Conclusion

This chapter reviews the evolution of the social dimensions of the commercial sector and the growing demand of 'enterprising' NGOs for the sake of financial sustainability. The Tripartite Collaborative Model (TCM) depicts a conceptual framework to integrate specific corporates, NGOs and social enterprises to fulfill the same dual mission: social responsibility and financial sustainability. The case study on iEnterprise verified the merit of the TCM in which the work integration social enterprise (WISE), the CSV enterprise and the sustainable NGO partnered to share knowledge and expertise, resources and business opportunities and exercised social capital collectively to create jobs for people with disabilities and from among the underprivileged community. Each partner enjoyed a "win-win" outcome in terms of economic and social value creation, beneficial to individual organizations and societal betterment. The iEnterprise experience highlights the possibility of building a form of Tripartite Social Enterprise characterized with low capital requirement together with high workfare creation, remarkable strategic operational efficiency and successful mission fulfillment jointly achieved under the collaborative framework of TCM. This cross-sector collaboration approach can be further researched to mobilize the social capital of like-minded fellows, knowledge volunteers, social entrepreneurs, social investors, commercial leaders, NGOs and policy makers to tackle neglected social problems. This chapter contributes not only to the theoretical and managerial aspects of cross-sector collaborations but also shed the light to future research for the development of the TCM ecosystem to achieve societal betterment.

Appendix

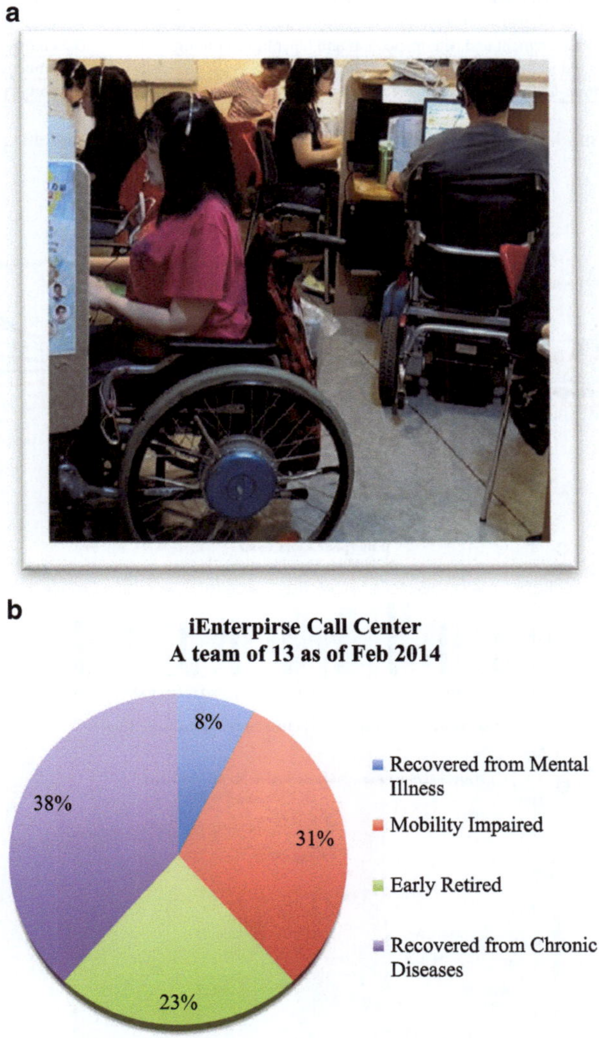

Diagram 1 (**a**) iEnterprise Call Center Team. (**b**) The team profile iEnterprise Call Center as of February 2014 (source: iEnterprise)

Idea Generated and Informal Discussion	October 21, 2013
Signing of Non-Disclosure Agreement	October 28, 2013
Historical Data Analysis and Feasibility Study	November 15, 2013
Business Proposal Submitted by iEnterprise	November 22, 2013
Shortlisted NGOs and Decision on partnering with HKRP	November 29, 2013
Interview of Shortlisted Candidates for Further Training	December 9, 2013
Set Up Requirement and Site Inspection and Operators Training	December 13, 2013
Testing and Rehearsal of Call Center Operation	December 21, 2013
iEnterprise Call Center Commencement	February 8, 2014

Diagram 2 The key milestone of iEnterprise Call Center development process (source: iEnterprise)

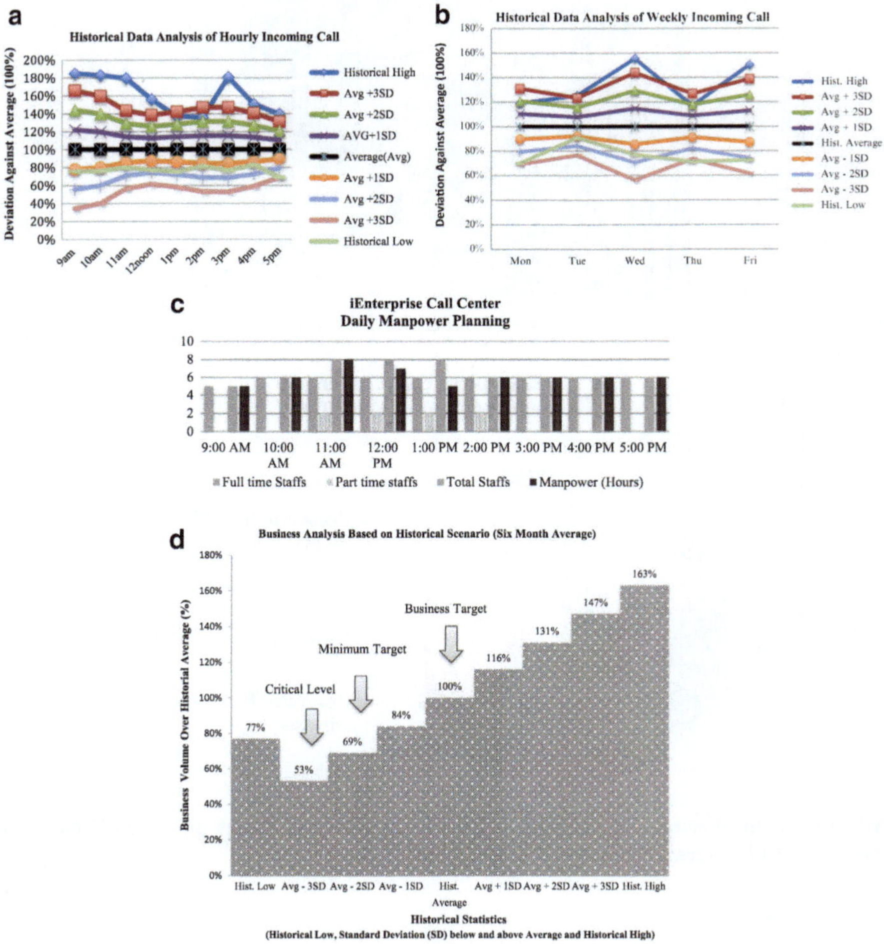

Diagram 3 (**a**) Feasibility study—historical data analysis of hourly incoming call for manpower planning. (**b**) Feasibility study—historical data analysis of weekly incoming call for manpower planning. (**c**) Manpower planning on daily basis. (**d**) Business volume analysis based on historical statistics (source: iEnterprise)

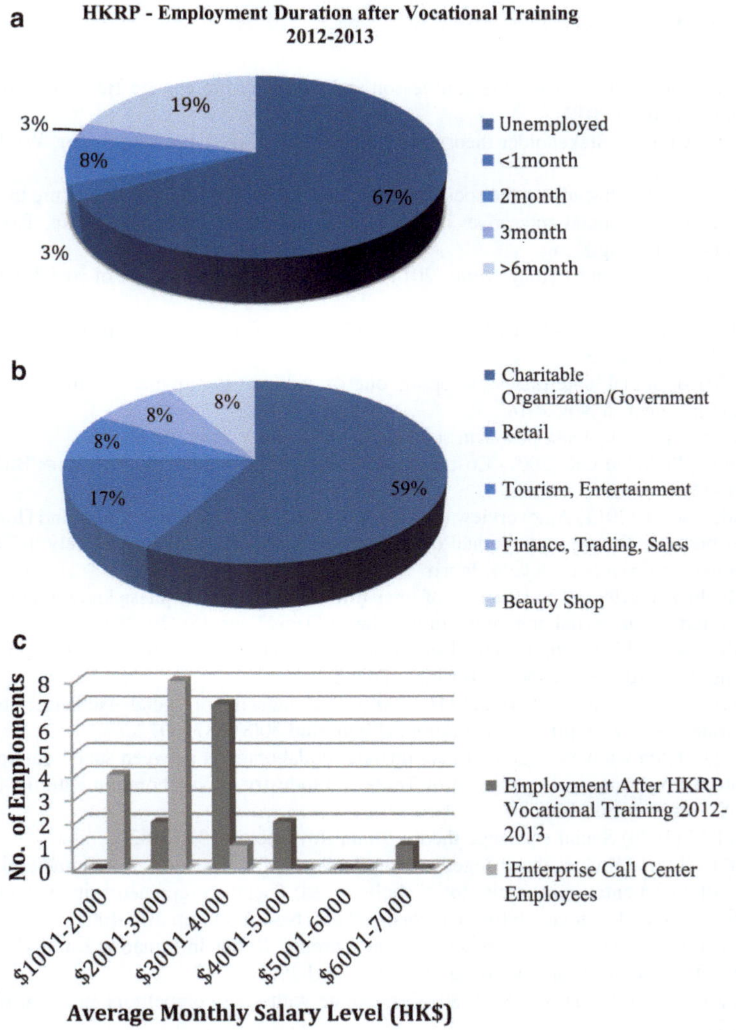

Diagram 4 (**a**) Employment duration after HKRP vocational training 2012–2013. (**b**) HKRP—nature of employment after vocational training 2012–2013. (**c**) HKRP—salary level of employment after HKRP vocational training (2012–2013) and iEnterprise employees (source: HKRP Annual Report 2013–2014, iEnterprise)

References

Alto P, Wong PM (2013) Mind the gap: lesson and findings from engage HK. Asia Community Ventures, August 2013

Argandoña A (2011) Stakeholder theory and value creation. IESE working paper, WP-922 May 2011

Au K (2014) Research study on the social enterprise sector in Hong Kong—to capture the existing landscape of the social enterprises in Hong Kong. Center for Entrepreneurship, The Chinese University of Hong Kong

Audit Commission Report Hong Kong (2014) Promoting the development of social enterprises. 4 Apr 2014

Austin JE, Gutierrez R, Ogliastri E, Reficco E (2007) Capitalizing on convergence. Stanf Soc Innov Rev 5(1):24–31

BFRC (2014) Social enterprises: stepping out of welfare stereotype. Bauhinia Foundation Research Center. 6 Nov 2014

Blau P (1964) Exchange and power in social life. Wiley, New York, pp 88–91

Brugmann J, Prahalad CK (2007) Co-creating business's new social compact. Harv Bus Rev 85 (2):80–90

Chan KM, Yuen T (2011) An overview of social enterprise development in China and Hong Kong. Paper prepared for the international conference on possibilities of Civil Society in East Asia, Ritsumeikan University, Kyoto, Japan

Chi T, Roehl TW (1997) The structure of inter-firm exchanges in business know-how: evidence from international collaborative ventures. Manag Decis Econ 18:279–294

DID HBS Case (2012) Dialogue in the Dark, Hong Kong: a role model for social enterprises in the making. Richard Ivey School of Business Foundation

Di Domenico ML, Tracey P, Haugh H (2009) The dialectic of social exchange: theorizing corporate–social enterprise collaboration. Organ Stud 30(8):887–907

DTI (2005) Match winners: a guide to commercial collaborations between social enterprise and private sector business. Department of Trade and Industry in collaboration with the Community Action Network, London

Emerson RM (1976) Social exchange theory. Annu Rev Sociol 2:335–362

Emerson J (2006) Moving ahead together: implications of a blended value framework for the future of social entrepreneurship. In: Nicholls A (ed) Social entrepreneurship, new models of sustainable social change. Oxford University Press, New York, pp 391–406

Griffiths D (2010) The theory and practice of outsourcing. Kudos Information Limited

Gulati R (1998) Alliances and networks. Strat Manag J 19:293–317

Hamel G, Yves LD, Prahalad CK (1989) Collaborate with your competitors and win. Harv Bus Rev 67:133–139

Hilhost R (2014) What will social enterprise look like in Europe by 2020? British Council, EU Region, January 2014

Holmstrom B (1982) Moral hazard in teams. Bell J Econ 13:324–342

Hong Kong Policy Research Institute (2005) A study on tripartite partnership: benchmarking study from an international perspective, 2005

Hoogendoorn B, Pennings E, Thurik R (2010) What do we know about social entrepreneurship. an analysis of empirical research. Int Rev Enterpren 8(2):71–112

Kee CH (2013) Social return on investment (SROI) of enhancing employment of people with disabilities through small enterprise project (3E). FSES Newsletter Issue 4, August 2013

Koka BR, Prescott JE (2002) Strategic alliances as social capital: a multidimensional view. Strat Manag J 23:795–816

Lam I (2013) Social enterprise: mission analysis and practice of value creation. Dissertation of Doctor of Business Administration, United Business Institute (UBI), Belgium, May 2013

Muthusamy SK, White M (2005) Learning and knowledge transfer in strategic alliances: a social exchange view. Organ Stud 26(3):415–441

Nohria N, Gulati R (1994) Organizations and environment. In: Smelser N, Swedberg R (eds) Handbook of economic sociology. Princeton University Press, Princeton, NJ, pp 529–555
Nyssens M, Defourny J, Gardin L, Laville JL (2012) Work integration social enterprises and public policy: an analysis of the European situation. EMES Research Network
Pharoah C, Scott D, Fisher A (2004) Social enterprise in the balance. Charities Aid Foundation, Glasgow
Porter ME, Kramer MR (2002) The competitive advantage of corporate philanthropy. Harv Bus Rev 80(12):56–68
Porter ME, Kramer MR (2006) Strategy and society: the link between competitive advantage and corporate social responsibility. Harv Bus Rev 84(12):78–92
Porter ME, Kramer MR (2011) The big idea: creating shared value. Harv Bus Rev 89:1–17
Powell WW, Kenneth WK, Laurel SD (1996) Interorganizational collaboration and the locus of innovation: networks of learning in biotechnology. Admin Sci Q 41:116–145
Putnam R (2000) Bowling alone: the collapse and revival of American community. Simon and Schuster, New York
Reid D, Bussiere D, Greenaway K (2001) Alliance formation issues for knowledge-based enterprises. Int J Manag Rev 3:79–100
Santos FM (2009) A positive theory of social entrepreneurship. Faculty and research working paper, INSEAD
Savitz A, Weber K (2006) The triple bottom line: how today's best-run companies are achieving economic, social and environmental success and how you can too. Jossey-Bass, Hoboken, NJ
Skoll World Forum (2013) What is the impact economy anyway? Forbes, 5 Aug 2013
Surie G, Ashley A (2008) Integrating pragmatism and ethics in entrepreneurial leadership for sustainable value creation. J Bus Ethics 81(1):235–246
Tang KL, Fung HL, Au KYF, Lee JKC, Ko LSF (2008) Social enterprise in Hong Kong: toward a conceptual model. Final report submitted to Central Policy Unit of the Government of the Hong Kong Special Administration Region of the People's Republic of China, April 2008
Tse E (2009) Corporate social responsibility and social capital: finding the business value. Booz and Company
UK Cabinet Office (2013) Social enterprise: market trend—based on a BIS small business survey 2012. A report by BMG Research 2013
Yin RK (1984) Case study research: design and methods. Sage, Beverly Hills, CA
Yunus M, Weber K (2007) Creating a world without poverty: social business and the future of capitalism. Public Affairs, New York
Yunus M, Moingeon B, Lehmann-Ortega L (2010) Building social business models: lessons from the Grameen experience. Long Range Plann 43:308–325

Is the IPO Anomaly in Poland Only Apparent or Real?

Joanna Lizińska and Leszek Czapiewski

Abstract Market anomalies have absorbed many academics and investors. Uncovering puzzling results is still an attractive research task. Anomalies are perceived as empirical findings inconsistent with accepted asset pricing models. Many of them were found illusory, and appeared to be not robust to the methodology, sample or period choice. Some anomalies weakened substantially, reversed themselves, disappeared or even reappeared after some time. There have been anomalies that have fascinated economists from all over the world. One of these was the short-term underpricing and long-term underperformance phenomenon observed after initial public offerings (IPOs). Are IPOs really offering investors an unfailing opportunity to earn money at the moment of going public, resulting in a huge amount of money being left on the table by the issuing firms? Is investing in IPO firms in the long run an easy way to lose money? Are the short- and long-term abnormal returns robust enough to become recognised as statistically and economically significant? The research aimed to answer the questions using a broad set of benchmarks and empirical approaches. The study comprised of all of the non-financial firms that made their initial public offering on the Warsaw Stock Exchange between 1995 and 2013.

Keywords Initial public offerings • IPO • Warsaw Stock Exchange • Benchmark • Underpricing • Underperformance

1 Introduction

Uncovering market anomalies and challenging the efficient market hypothesis (Fama 1970) has been a quite attractive issue for researchers. The issue was also an area of huge interest to market participants, eager to find an unfailing way to earn money. Soft- and hardware capabilities, together with numerous databases make it possible to calculate almost everything for the whole world.

Anomalies can be defined as empirical findings inconsistent with the predictions of accepted asset pricing models. The discussion around anomalies covered

J. Lizińska (✉) • L. Czapiewski
Poznan University of Economics, Poznan, Poland
e-mail: joanna.lizinska@ue.poznan.pl; leszek.czapiewski@ue.poznan.pl

T. Dudycz et al. (eds.), *The Essence and Measurement of Organizational Efficiency*, Springer Proceedings in Business and Economics, DOI 10.1007/978-3-319-21139-8_10

overlapping issues such as the efficient market hypothesis, market rationality, complete knowledge of the economic structure, stock price determination models or behavioural evidence of investor decisions.

The most famous anomalies that have been uncovered so far were connected with equity public offerings (Ritter 1991, or Loughran and Ritter 1995), earnings announcements (such as in Foster et al. 1984), seasonal regularities (e.g. Cross 1973; Lakonishok and Smidt 1988) or referred to small capitalization firms (Fama and French 1992), book-to-market levels (Basu 1977), or accruals (Sloan 1996), just to mention some of the more prominent examples. The triggering price behaviour after initial public offerings (IPOs) was observed both for the short as well as over the long run. It was so puzzling and persistent that it was re-challenged many times for the US exchanges. For a long time, it has also fascinated economists who have tried to check its relevance for capital markets all over the world. Previous studies have generally shown positive abnormal returns on the first day after going public, which was called IPO underpricing. Most of the previous research documented negative abnormal returns in the long-run, up to three and sometimes even 5 years after issuing. This second phenomenon was called IPO underperformance. However, there are opinions that these anomalous results were just a consequence of method deficiencies. Fama still advocates the efficient market hypothesis (1998, 2010). He questioned the relevancy of anomaly-detecting methods, especially over the long run.

There have been relatively few studies that have examined this issue in emerging markets, which are supposed to have different risk and return characteristics than developed markets. Empirical evidence of IPO underpricing for the Polish stock market is not so wide as for developed markets.

Although the reasons for short-term IPO underpricing are still puzzling, there has generally been agreement that the first day close price is on average significantly higher than the offer price. Recent years have been times of sudden changes on capital markets. The years up to 2007 were mostly a bull market period. Then, huge market turbulences appeared with sudden falls in equity prices. After 2009, market indexes started to rise along with an increase in optimistic investor behaviour. But the question arises: are investors still as optimistic in pricing Polish IPOs during the first day of trading following the huge market declines in recent years?

Most studies concluded that IPOs underperform in the long run. However, there is no general agreement that abnormal long-run returns are significantly different from zero. Besides, it has become apparent that results are very sensitive to the reference portfolio choice (Brav and Gompers 1997; Stehle et al. 2000; Schuster 2001; Drobetz et al. 2005). Many methods of abnormal performance detection have appeared in the long-term event study literature, but there has been no general and unified approach to estimation methods. The most widely applied market return did not seem to be a good benchmark for IPO securities' returns, due to the higher risk characteristics of IPO companies (Loughran and Ritter 2000). Is anomalous price behaviour still observed in Poland, even after employing a broader set of empirical methods?

The present research aimed to observe the IPO short- and long-term returns on the Warsaw Stock Exchange using a variety of different methods. Nine benchmarks were employed in order to estimate underpricing and 3- and 5-year long-term buy-and-hold and cumulative abnormal returns, along with parametric and non-parametric tests. This was to lend more robustness to the results. The fresh evidence for Polish equity issuance is presented with a sample covering IPOs from 1995 to 2013. As far as the authors are aware it is the first study for the Polish market estimating IPO performance up to the fifth year following the day of going public. The research also contributes to the debate on the importance of the benchmark construction.

This chapter was partly supported by the Polish Ministry of Science and Higher Education as a research project (UMO-2011/01/B/HS4/02361).

The rest of the chapter is structured in the following way. In the next section the existing literature and results of prior studies on the existence of both short- and long-term IPO anomalies are commented on. Section 3 describes the dataset, methodology and presents descriptive statistics. In Sect. 4 estimates of short- and long-term abnormal returns are discussed. Section 5 states the conclusions.

2 Previous Literature

Abnormal returns following initial public offerings have been broadly discussed with evidence from all over the world (Ritter 2003, among many others). The issue was also present in research done for the Warsaw Stock Exchange.

The early studies on the short-term price behaviour for Polish IPOs revealed median abnormal WIG-adjusted underpricing of 16.0 % for 1991–1999 (Aussenegg 2000), 28.1 % for 1991–1998 (Lyn and Zychowicz 2003), and 14.4 % during 1991–1999 (Jelic and Briston 2003). Later studies also confirmed positive median WIG-adjusted initial returns: 6.5 % for the period of 1998–2008 (Jewartowski and Lizińska 2012), 15.7 % (mean) for 2005–2009 (Cornanic and Novak 2013), for 2004–2009 it was estimated to be 6.9 % (Czapiewski and Lizińska 2014), and 34.1 % for 1991–2000 in comparison to 13.5 % for the later period of 2001–2011 (Czapiewski et al. 2013).

There were also some studies concerning the long-term performance of Polish initial public offerings. The first results were published by Aussenegg (2000) for the 1991–1999 period, revealing median WIG-adjusted 3-year buy-and-hold returns equal to –61.1 %. An interesting result was the positive mean BHAR of 11.5. Lyn and Zychowicz, for the years from 1991 to 1998 (2003) did not find significant evidence of underperformance for the third year after going public. Jelic and Briston (2003) examined IPOs for the period from 1991 to 1999 and documented mean cumulative abnormal return of –37.8 % and mean abnormal buy-and-hold return for the 3-year period of –26.5 %. Jewartowski and Lizińska (2012) worked with a sample of WSE offerings from 1998 to 2008 and reported median 3-year buy-and-hold abnormal returns of −44.5. Czapiewski and Lizińska (2014) for the sample of 2004–2009 revealed median buy-and-hold abnormal returns at the third IPO anniversary at the level of −24.9 %.

It would be very hard, if not impossible in the limited space of a single article to present the results of all the studies on short- and long-term price behaviour of IPO firms covering all markets worldwide. It has become one of the most widely discussed anomalies, interesting both for researchers and investors. The evidence on underpricing is mostly concluded with revealing positive initial abnormal returns. However, the results have been strongly dominated by market index-adjusting.

The worldwide evidence on long run post-IPO performance can be seen as controversial, as different research projects have often reported contrasting results. This is not rare even within the same stock exchange. For example, contradictory results were reported for the Australian Stock Exchange. Lee et al. (1996) observed severe underperformance in the long run whereas Da Silva Rosa et al. (2003) found no evidence of underperformance in the subsequent years. For Spanish IPOs, Farinos (2001) revealed no underperformance up to the third year after the IPO. Ansotegui and Fabregat (1999) reported that IPO firms listed in Spain did experience negative 3-year returns after the IPO date using the market index and an industrial index as benchmarks.

Some studies showed that conclusions of the long-term event study analysis for IPO were very benchmark-sensitive (Brav and Gompers 1997; Stehle et al. 2000; Schuster 2001; Drobetz et al. 2005). Market indexes have been the most commonly chosen benchmarks. However, this could result in underperformance underestimation as stressed by Loughran and Ritter (2000). There were also arguments that benchmarks should be designed to also include firm characteristics such as size or book-to-market ratio (Brav and Gompers 1997). Stehle et al. (2000) showed that such benchmarks appeared to give more reliable results for long-term event analysis. Ritter (1991) and Loughran and Ritter (1995) analysed US IPOs and reported negative returns up to the fifth year after the offering. In a more recent study, Gompers and Lerner (2003) found that long-term IPO performance was very sensitive to the method of normal return estimation. They found some evidence for negative long-term returns for value-weighted event-time buy-and-hold abnormal returns. However, they also revealed that underperformance disappeared after application of equally-weighted event-time cumulated and buy-and-hold abnormal returns.

3 Data Sources, Methodology and Descriptive Statistics

The research was conducted for equity securities quoted on the Warsaw Stock Exchange (WSE) in Poland. The source of data was Ceduła, Notoria Serwis, the official site of the WSE (http://www.gpw.pl) and www.gpwinfostrefa.pl. In the first step, it was essential to prepare the authors' own database covering daily close prices and financial statements. The existing sources did not have satisfactory data quality. In consequence, the database for the research also included delisted firms and close prices with the necessary adjustments (dividends, splits and preemptive rights).

The original sample consisted of 405 non-financial IPOs offered from 1995 to 2013 on the Polish main stock market, the Warsaw Stock Exchange (WSE). The sample included only such initial offerings that were connected with a new common stock issuance, without prior trading history on alternative markets. As the long-run returns were estimated up to the 5-year event window, the sample was limited to cover the period of 1995–2008 with 345 IPOs to make the estimation possible for all of the IPOs. Here, the sample period ended in 2008 and the quoting data ended in 2013. The necessary data were not always complete, so some reductions were made in the later research steps.

Table 1 provides a few main IPO firm characteristics. It contains the average level of leverage expressed by total debt divided by total assets for the period before the IPO date (D/A), return on assets expressed by net income divided by total assets for the period before the IPO date (ROA) and market value of equity for the first day in the aftermarket (MV).

The performance was examined using different time periods. First, it was observed in the first day in the aftermarket. The returns were calculated with daily close prices. The raw initial return for security i was calculated by:

$$IR_{i,t} = \frac{IP_i}{PO_i} - 1 \tag{1}$$

where IP_i was the first aftermarket price for IPO i and PO_i was the offer price for IPO i.

Then, initial adjusted returns were obtained by subtracting the benchmark returns from stock returns:

Table 1 Descriptive statistics for Polish IPOs

	D/A	ROA	MV
Panel A: 1995–2013			
Mean	43.18 %	6.32 %	819.5 mln
Median	45.37 %	4.63 %	104.4 mln
Kurtosis	−0.13	2.56	8.39
Skewness	−1.13	20.25	79.98
N	343	395	405
Panel B: 1995–2008			
Mean	42.36 %	6.19 %	576.4 mln
Median	45.37 %	4.70 %	98.6 mln
Kurtosis	−0.08	2.74	8.81
Skewness	−1.24	22.70	84.92
N	287	335	345

$$IAR_{i,t} = IR_{i,t} - IR_{i,t}^{B}, \tag{2}$$

where $IR_{i,t}^{B}$ was the daily return on the benchmark portfolio in the IPO.

Next, buy-and-hold abnormal returns (BHARs) were calculated to observe the long-term IPO price behaviour up to the fifth year after the offering.

The buy-and-hold return for IPO i for selected event windows was defined as:

$$BHR_{i,T}^{1} = \prod_{t=1}^{T} (1 + R_{i,t}) - 1 \tag{3}$$

where $R_{i,t}$ was the daily return in trading day t, and T was the aftermarket trading session number with 1 assigned to the first day after going public. It was assumed that a year was equivalent to 252 trading days. The buy-and-hold return for the corresponding reference portfolio for IPO $i(BHR_{i,T}^{B})$ was defined as:

$$BHR_{i,T}^{1,B} = \prod_{t=1}^{T} \left(1 + R_{i,t}^{B}\right) - 1 \tag{4}$$

where $R_{i,t}^{B}$ was the daily return on the benchmark portfolio in trading day t for IPO i.

The buy-and-hold abnormal return for each IPO i and the given benchmark and the selected event window ($BHAR_{i,T}^{1,B}$) was given by:

$$BHAR_{i,T}^{1,B} = BHR_{i,T}^{1} - BHR_{i,T}^{1,B} \tag{5}$$

The cumulative abnormal return (CAR) was employed as an alternative performance measure. The general formula for abnormal market adjusted return ($AR_{i,t}$) for each IPO i for t session was expressed as:

$$AR_{i,t} = R_{i,t} - R_{i,t}^{B} \tag{6}$$

The abnormal returns ($AR_{i,t}$) were cumulated to get cumulative abnormal returns ($CAR_{i,T}$) for different event windows up to the 5 year.

Detecting long-run abnormal stock returns is usually disputable. Barber and Lyon (1997) reported that many of the commonly used methods of calculating long-run returns in event studies suffer from flaws or biases. They recommended using buy-and-hold abnormal returns. On the other hand, Mitchell and Stafford (2000) and Brav (2000) concluded that the buy-and-hold approach would be more sensitive to the cross-sectional dependence problem among firms. The buy-and-hold approach has usually been recommended to simulate a real investing situation with buying securities at the IPO date, holding it for a specified period of time and selling it afterwards.

IPO returns are supposed to be very volatile during the first period after going public. There are some studies where the first period in the aftermarket was excluded from the analysis. Here, the first starting point for the long-term event window was the first day close price, as described above. It resulted in an abnormal buy-and-hold ($BHAR_{i,T}^{1,B}$) and cumulative ($CAR_{i,T}^{1,B}$) return estimation. Two alternative ways of detecting long-term IPO underperformance, were applied. The second starting point for the event window was the closing price after the first quarter in the market (63 trading days). The assumption here was: let us give investors time to gather information about the new firms and then observe the relative IPO performance. Long-term IPO performance was measured here from the fourth trading month (where 1 month was defined as 21 trading days) to avoid possible noise. In consequence, buy-and-hold ($BHAR_{i,T}^{64,B}$) and cumulative ($CAR_{i,T}^{64,B}$) returns were obtained. The third starting point for observing the price behaviour was based on the assumption that IPOs tend to cluster in time, to benefit from highly optimistic investor valuations. Then, the sentiment-influenced around-issue closing price is not supposed to be a good comparison for the future price in long-term event studies. In consequence, the future close price was compared with the offer price (PO_i). Hence, buy-and-hold ($BHAR_{i,T}^{offer,B}$) and cumulative ($CAR_{i,T}^{offer,B}$) returns were achieved.

Several previous studies have shown that long-term performance measures are very benchmark-sensitive (Brav and Gompers 1997; Stehle et al. 2000; Schuster 2001; Drobetz et al. 2005). Existing market indexes were the most commonly chosen benchmark for estimating abnormal price behaviour, as it is quite an easy and convenient way to adjust raw returns. The problem that arises is whether the market index is able to check the risk level correctly. The market-adjusted returns could also be a consequence of systematic return patterns of a group of companies, unrelated to the fact of going public (Ahern 2009). Many previous papers concluded that IPO firms tended to underperform the market in the long run. However, such a reference portfolio also contains issuing firms. Loughran and Ritter (2000) pointed out that this might result in underestimating the level of underperformance. On the other hand, eliminating IPO firms without time limits once and for all was questionable because of the limited number of firms on the WSE. A kind of a trade-off was employed, and each IPO firm was eliminated from possible reference portfolios during the first year after its IPO date.

Some authors argued that benchmark portfolios should be designed on the basis of characteristics of the firms, such as size or book-to-market ratio (Brav and Gompers 1997 or Brav 2000). Stehle et al. (2000) showed that such benchmarks appeared to give more reliable results for long-term event analysis. This research included the application of nine reference portfolios to observe the IPO anomaly in a broad context. The first benchmark was the existing market index for the Warsaw Stock Exchange, mainly the WIG index. Eight alternatives were adopted to measure IPO firm performance against similar firms. Such a benchmark could be as well one control firm as a portfolio of securities (Ang and Zhang 2002). The research was conducted for the sample of WSE listed companies, where it could be very difficult to find one very similar neighbour to adjust the performance properly in the case of some IPOs. For this reason, portfolio-matching was adopted here. That makes it possible to then match the portfolios according to only one feature or according to many dimensions simultaneously. The second approach is expected to result in a better matching, but it can sometimes cause problems with the size of benchmark portfolios, especially for smaller exchanges. Single and multidimensional matching was adopted in the research. The number of characteristics is usually limited to no more than two or three. As it is usually applied on small or even medium exchanges, the construction of benchmarks was designed on the basis of two characteristics of the firms: company size and book-to-market ratio. Size was measured as the market value of common equity on the IPO day. Size portfolios were obtained by a classification of firms listed on the Warsaw Stock Exchange according to the market value of equity for all WSE firms on the IPO day in order to obtain size quartiles. Book-to-market ratio was calculated using capitalisation of the IPO firm during the first day of trading and book value of equity from the last year before the IPO. Then, each IPO was assigned to the relevant quartile and its benchmark was constituted by firms belonging to the same size quartile. Next, book-to-market portfolios were obtained by a classification of all firms listed on the Warsaw Stock Exchange according to book-to-market on the IPO day of a particular offering in order to obtain book-to-market quartiles. Then, each IPO was assigned to the relevant quartile and its benchmark was constituted by firms belonging to the same book-to-market quartile. A similar procedure was used for the formation of two-dimensional portfolios. The WSE was divided by company size into quartiles, and simultaneously into four groups using book-to-market ratios for the most recent data of a particular IPO. Following this, 4×4 groups were created and each IPO was compared to the results of one of 16 portfolios.

The return on the benchmark portfolio on trading day t designed for IPO $i(R_{i,t}^{B})$ was estimated as the mean of estimated returns for similar companies. The reference portfolio performance was aggregated into an overall measure on an equal- or value-weighted basis.

According the above procedures for the formation of portfolios, the relevant benchmarks were:

WIG	The existing main WSE index
ALL_ew	The equally-weighted mean return for all WSE companies
ALL_vw	The value-weighted mean return for all WSE companies; value weighting was done daily
MV_ew	The equally-weighted mean return for the WSE companies in the size quartile; the breakpoints for those portfolios were calculated for each IPO on the basis of the market capitalisation from the IPO date
MV_vw	The value-weighted mean return for the WSE companies in the size quartile; the breakpoints for those portfolios were calculated for each IPO on the basis of the market capitalisation from the IPO date; value weighting was done daily

BM_ew	The equally-weighted mean return for the WSE companies in the book-to-market quartile; the breakpoints for those portfolios were calculated for each IPO on the basis of the book-to-market ratio from the IPO date
BM_vw	The value-weighted mean return for the WSE companies in the book-to-market quartile; the breakpoints for those portfolios were calculated for each IPO on the basis of the book-to-market ratio from the IPO date; value weighting was done daily
MV&BM_ew	The equally-weighted mean return for the WSE companies according to the size quartile and book-to-market; the breakpoints for those portfolios were calculated for each IPO on the basis of the market capitalisation and book-to-market ratio from the IPO date; the portfolios were formed by first forming size quartiles for the WSE firms and then, book-to-market quartile breakpoints were formed; each company was allocated to one of those 16 portfolios
MV&BM_vw	The value-weighted mean return for the WSE companies according to size quartile and book-to-market; the breakpoints for those portfolios were calculated for each IPO on the basis of the market capitalization and book-to-market ratio from the IPO date; the portfolios were formed by first forming size quartiles for the WSE firms and then, book-to-market quartile breakpoints were formed; each company was allocated to one of those 16 portfolios; value weighting was done daily.

To minimise the potentially detrimental effect of extreme outliers, Winsorising was applied. Outliers were found with the use of the interquartile range (*IQR*). The lower bound was set as $Q_1 - 1.5 \cdot IQR$ and the upper bound as $Q_3 + 1.5 \cdot IQR$.

The Shapiro-Wilk test was used to test the distribution normality of abnormal returns. A conventional parametric test has often been supposed to confirm long-run abnormal performance where none was present (Kothari and Warner 1997; Barber and Lyon 1997). Hence, both a parametric and non-parametric test was employed, namely the Student t-test and the Wilcoxon signed-rank test.

In consequence, the short-term IPO performance was observed on the basis of daily returns with nine benchmarks. The long-term IPO anomaly was challenged with two general approaches (BHARs, CARs), nine reference portfolios (WIG, ALL_ev, ALL_vw, MV_ev, MV_vw, BM_ew, BM_vw, MV&BM_ew and MV&BM_vw), three reference prices (the 1st day close price, the 64th day close price and the offer price) with observations up to the third and the fifth IPO anniversary. As a result of the research design, a variety of different methods was tested to observe the IPO anomaly.

4 Results

This section presents the results of the analysis of short-tem underpricing and long-term underperformance for the Warsaw Stock Exchange in Poland.

First, the short-term performance of IPO firms was considered. It was checked for two samples. The first sample was used for both the short- and long-term research with 345 initial public offerings and covered the period from 1995 to 2013. The sample period for long-term studies started in 1995 and ended in 2008 in order to make the 5-year performance analysis possible for all of the IPOs, with the price data ending in 2013. In order to examine the short-term performance on the most recent data, the full sample of 405 IPOs from 1995 to 2013 was also investigated. The abnormal initial returns were also Winsorized. The results are shown in Table 2.

It can be seen that independently of the benchmark used, the initial adjusted returns were positive. Although there were some differences between results for alternative benchmarks, these were rather small. The minimum mean achieved for 1995–2013 was 13.58 for value-weighted two-dimensional size and book-to-market matching (MV&BM_vw), and the maximum was 13.84 for value-weighted book-to-market matching (BM_vw). The minimum median totalled 9.53 with equally-weighted book-to-market matching (BM_ew) and the maximum was 10.14 with equal-weighted size matching (MW_ew). The underpricing level was slightly lower in terms of means and medians for the more recent sample (1995–2013) in comparison to the sample covering the years from 1995 to 2008. This was similar to the conclusions of previous studies for the Warsaw Stock Exchange. The Shapiro-Wilk test revealed the non-normality of the distribution of abnormal initial returns. The returns were statistically significant at the 1 % level, both with the parametric and the non-parametric test.

After studying the short-term IPO anomaly, buy-and-hold and cumulative abnormal returns were examined. As described earlier in the chapter, nine benchmarks were used. The BHARs in the third and fifth year after the IPO date, when the security was bought during the first day of trading, are shown in Table 3. The results for the cumulative approach are in Table 4.

Independently of the benchmark used, the results reveal the existence of negative abnormal returns in the third and fifth year after going public for investments, starting on the first and 63rd day in the aftermarket. More severe underperformance was documented for benchmarks with value-weighting than equal-weighting. This is in line with Loughran and Ritter's results (1995). Adjusting portfolios by characteristic-based reference revealed worse long-term returns in comparison to a simple market-adjusting with WIG index. This is in accordance with Loughran and Ritter's suggestion (2000) that adjusting by index results in underestimation of the underperformance as the index also contains the issuing firms.

As the distribution of abnormal returns was non-normal, the emphasis was placed on medians. Long-term investor experience captured by compounding daily returns and by cumulating abnormal returns showed that the most negative

Table 2 Short-term IPO performance according to first-day abnormal returns

		ALL		MV		BM		MV&BM	
	WIG	ew	vw	ew	vw	ew	vw	ew	vw
Panel A: 1995–2008									
Mean [%]	14.95	14.85	14.97	14.84	14.88	14.76	15.02	14.76	14.72
Median [%]	11.69	11.46	11.31	11.35	11.43	11.22	11.20	11.39	11.50
% negative	72	73	72	73	73	72	72	73	73
Skewness	0.41	0.39	0.42	0.39	0.39	0.37	0.41	0.37	0.37
Kurtosis	−0.33	−0.39	−0.30	−0.40	−0.39	−0.43	−0.31	−0.38	−0.40
p-val (S-W)	0.0000***	0.0000***	0.0000***	0.0000***	0.0000***	0.0000***	0.0000***	0.0000***	0.0000***
p-val (t-Stud)	0.0000***	0.0000***	0.0000***	0.0000***	0.0000***	0.0000***	0.0000***	0.0000***	0.0000***
p-val (WSR)	0.0000***	0.0000***	0.0000***	0.0000***	0.0000***	0.0000***	0.0000***	0.0000***	0.0000***
N	326	326	326	326	326	325	325	319	319
Panel B: 1995–2013									
Mean	13.78	13.70	13.79	13.69	13.72	13.62	13.84	13.63	13.58
Median	9.99	9.99	9.87	10.14	9.93	9.53	10.01	10.04	10.12
% negative	73	73	73	73	73	73	73	74	73
Skewness	0.50	0.48	0.51	0.48	0.48	0.46	0.50	0.46	0.46
Kurtosis	−0.03	−0.11	−0.00	−0.12	−0.10	−0.16	−0.02	−0.10	−0.13
p-val (S-W)	0.0000***	0.0000***	0.0000***	0.0000***	0.0000***	0.0000***	0.0000***	0.0000***	0.0000***
p-val (t-Stud)	0.0000***	0.0000***	0.0000***	0.0000***	0.0000***	0.0000***	0.0000***	0.0000***	0.0000***
p-val (WSR)	0.0000***	0.0000***	0.0000***	0.0000***	0.0000***	0.0000***	0.0000***	0.0000***	0.0000***
N	384	384	384	384	384	383	383	377	377

Notes: Significance at the 1 % (***) level. Tests: Shapiro-Wilk test (S-W), Student t test (t-Stud), Wilcoxon signed rank test (WSR). Benchmarks: WIG index, mean equity return (ALL), size portfolio (MV), book-to-market portfolio (BM), size and book-to-market portfolio (MV&BM) with equal weighting (ew) and value weighting (vw)

Table 3 Long-term IPO performance according to buy-and-hold abnormal returns

1995–2008 IPOs	3-year returns		5-year returns	
Panel A	WIG		WIG	
Mean [%]	−20.46		−33.42	
Median [%]	−34.41		−48.80	
% negative	70		75	
Skewness	0.61		0.65	
Kurtosis	0.06		0.19	
p-val (S-W)	0.0000***		0.0000***	
p-val (t-Stud)	0.0000***		0.0000***	
p-val (WSR)	0.0000***		0.0000***	
N	334		297	
Panel B	ALL_ew	ALL_vw	ALL_ew	ALL_vw
Mean [%]	−41.57	−82.69	−68.05	−131.83
Median [%]	−47.79	−88.74	−54.66	−128.90
% negative	76	85	79	89
Skewness	0.12	0.34	−0.14	0.13
Kurtosis	−0.06	0.20	−0.01	0.15
p-val (S-W)	0.0000***	0.0000***	0.0000***	0.0000***
p-val (t-Stud)	0.0000***	0.0000***	0.0000***	0.0000***
p-val (WSR)	0.0000***	0.0000***	0.0000***	0.0000***
N	334	334	297	297
Panel C	MV_ew	MV_vw	MV_ew	MV_vw
Mean [%]	−46.69	−148.96	−57.93	−268.62
Median [%]	−43.47	−107.91	−47.16	−162.38
% negative	75	89	78	94
Skewness	−0.03	−0.48	−0.09	−0.88
Kurtosis	−0.37	−0.48	−0.02	0.14
p-val (S-W)	0.0000***	0.0000***	0.0000***	0.0000***
p-val (t-Stud)	0.0000***	0.0000***	0.0000***	0.0000***
p-val (WSR)	0.0000***	0.0000***	0.0000***	0.0000***
N	334	334	297	297
Panel D	BM_ew	BM_vw	BM_ew	BM_vw
Mean [%]	−57.04	−73.84	−74.79	−114.79
Median [%]	−52.42	−76.69	−67.34	−108.40
% negative	77	83	79	89
Skewness	−0.09	0.12	−0.13	0.02
Kurtosis	−0.17	0.12	−0.13	0.26
p-val (S-W)	0.0000***	0.0000***	0.0000***	0.0000***
p-val (t-Stud)	0.0000***	0.0000***	0.0000***	0.0000***
p-val (WSR)	0.0000***	0.0000***	0.0000***	0.0000***
N	333	333	296	296
Panel E	MV&BM_ew	MV&BM_vw	MV&BM_ew	MV&BM_vw
Mean [%]	−36.30	−99.19	−41.72	−158.13
Median [%]	−33.69	−73.73	−30.47	−100.29

(continued)

Table 3 (continued)

Panel E	MV&BM_ew	MV&BM_vw	MV&BM_ew	MV&BM_vw
% negative	69	84	70	87
Skewness	−0.08	−0.41	−0.23	−0.61
Kurtosis	−0.24	−0.33	−0.06	−0.11
p-val (S-W)	0.0000***	0.0000***	0.0000***	0.0000***
p-val (t-Stud)	0.0000***	0.0000***	0.0000***	0.0000***
p-val (WSR)	0.0000***	0.0000***	0.0000***	0.0000***
N	327	327	290	290

Notes: Significance at the 1 % (***) level. Tests: Shapiro-Wilk test (S-W), Student t test (t-Stud), Wilcoxon signed rank test (WSR). Benchmarks: WIG index, mean equity return (ALL), size portfolio (MV), book-to-market portfolio (BM), size and book-to-market portfolio (MV&BM) with equal weighting (ew) and value weighting (vw)

results were achieved after accounting for size effect with value-weighting. All of the BHARs and CARs for the third and fifth IPO anniversary were statistically significant. The magnitude of underperformance also proved that it was economically significant. The levels of abnormal performance for WIG-adjusted and characteristic-based portfolios are illustrated on Fig. 1. An interesting finding was that the cumulative abnormal returns were partly positive at the third and fifth IPO anniversary for three benchmarks (WIG, MV&BM_ew and MW_ew adjusting).

Brav and Gompers (1997) and Fama (1998) concluded that the long-term underperformance of initial public offerings was not an IPO-specific phenomenon, but rather the effect of a broader anomaly observed for small firms. In other words, the IPO anomaly may merely be a result of a more systematic pattern of returns on capital markets. Given that IPO firms tend to be smaller firms, the long-run underperformance after offerings may be perceived as a size anomaly instead of an IPO anomaly. However, the introduction of alternative benchmarks did not confirm the nonexistence of the IPO anomaly on the Polish exchange for the sample period of 1998–2013. Even after accounting for size and book-to-market characteristics, the research revealed significant underperformance. Additionally, the division into small and large companies was introduced. The sample of IPOs on the Warsaw Stock Exchange from 1995 to 2008 was divided into three groups according to the market value of equity on the IPO day with the bounds at the 0.33rd and 0.66th percentile. Then, the underperformance of IPOs with the lowest and highest capitalisation levels was observed (SmallCap and BigCap, respectively). The differences between both groups were tested with the use of the Mann-Whitney test. The results are detailed in Table 5 and illustrated on Fig. 2.

Previous studies generally concluded that small firms tended to perform worse in the long-term (Ritter 1991; Page and Reyneke 1997). However, some studies found the opposite (Jelic et al. 2001; Corhay et al. 2002; Ahmad-Zaluki et al. 2007).

Table 4 Long-term IPO performance according to cumulative abnormal returns

1995–2008 IPOs	3-year returns		5-year returns	
Panel A	WIG		WIG	
Mean [%]	−10.11		−11.20	
Median [%]	−14.57		−9.64	
% negative	58		53	
Skewness	0.12		−0.08	
Kurtosis	0.13		0.07	
p-val (S-W)	0.0298**		0.0027***	
p-val (t-Stud)	0.0205**		0.0479**	
p-val (WSR)	0.0113**		0.0642*	
N	334		297	
Panel B	ALL_ew	ALL_vw	ALL_ew	ALL_vw
Mean [%]	−20.61	−53.52	−20.98	−71.87
Median [%]	−21.54	−58.08	−20.46	−67.84
% negative	62	76	57	79
Skewness	0.10	0.21	−0.10	−0.03
Kurtosis	0.22	0.27	0.25	−0.02
p-val (S-W)	0.0062***	0.0073***	0.0807*	0.0016***
p-val (t-Stud)	0.0000***	0.0000***	0.0004***	0.0000***
p-val (WSR)	0.0000***	0.0000***	0.0007***	0.0000***
N	334	334	297	297
Panel C	MV_ew	MV_vw	MV_ew	MV_vw
Mean [%]	−22.84	−80.17	−19.23	−106.17
Median [%]	−25.93	−79.33	−17.93	−97.69
% negative	63	81	59	84
Skewness	0.14	0.03	−0.03	−0.09
Kurtosis	0.11	0.03	0.15	−0.03
p-val (S-W)	0.0503*	0.2298	0.1939	0.1182
p-val (t-Stud)	0.0000***	0.0000***	0.0010***	0.0000***
p-val (WSR)	0.0000***	0.0000***	0.0016***	0.0000***
N	334	334	297	297
Panel D	BM_ew	BM_vw	BM_ew	BM_vw
Mean [%]	−30.41	−49.00	−34.07	−66.70
Median [%]	−30.71	−49.71	−30.31	−62.55
% negative	65	75	64	76
Skewness	0.13	0.09	−0.05	−0.08
Kurtosis	0.03	0.02	0.02	0.06
p-val (S-W)	0.0470**	0.0348**	0.2966	0.0327**
p-val (t-Stud)	0.0000***	0.0000***	0.0000***	0.0000***
p-val (WSR)	0.0000***	0.0000***	0.0000***	0.0000***
N	333	333	296	296
Panel E	MV&BM_ew	MV&BM_vw	MV&BM_ew	MV&BM_vw
Mean [%]	−23.40	−67.16	−21.28	−90.19
Median [%]	−18.23	−60.35	−14.97	−77.00

(continued)

Table 4 (continued)

Panel E	MV&BM_ew	MV&BM_vw	MV&BM_ew	MV&BM_vw
% negative	57	77	55	75
Skewness	−0.26	−0.30	−0.34	−0.45
Kurtosis	0.14	0.10	0.19	0.35
p-val (S-W)	0.0001***	0.0001***	0.0000***	0.0000***
p-val (t-Stud)	0.0000***	0.0000***	0.0036***	0.0000***
p-val (WSR)	0.0001***	0.0000***	0.0207**	0.0000***
N	327	327	290	290

Notes: Significance at the 1 % (***), 5 % (**) and 10 % (*) level. Tests: Shapiro-Wilk test (S-W), Student t test (t-Stud), Wilcoxon signed rank test (WSR). Benchmarks: WIG index, mean equity return (ALL), size portfolio (MV), book-to-market portfolio (BM), size and book-to-market portfolio (MV&BM) with equal weighting (ew) and value weighting (vw)

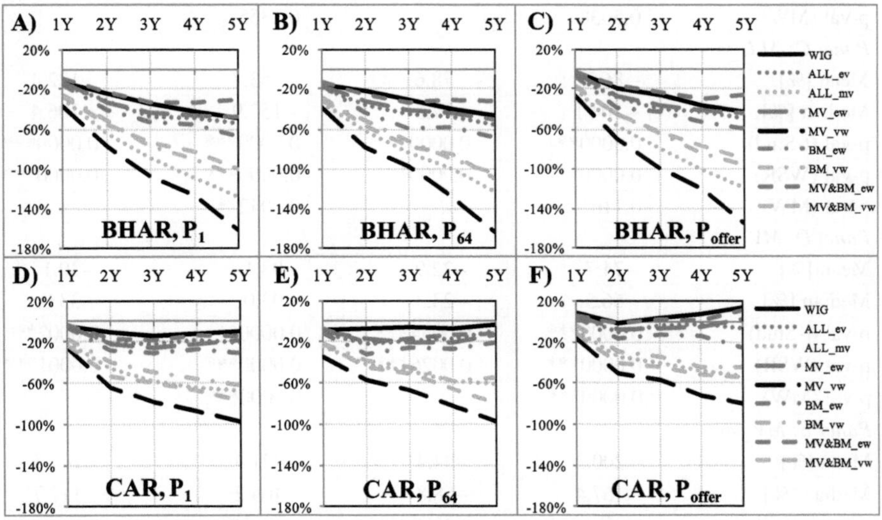

Fig. 1 Median long-term performance of IPOs

The long-term underperformance for the Warsaw Stock Exchange was definitely more severe in the group of smaller IPOs. But it did not disappear for offerings from bigger companies. Even here, the average 3- and 5-year abnormal cumulated and compounded returns were significant and strongly negative.

Table 5 Buy-and-hold abnormal returns for small and big capitalization firms

	3-year returns		5-year returns	
1995–2008 IPOs	SmallCap	BigCap	SmallCap	BigCap
Panel A: WIG				
Mean [%]	−24.4	−16.7	−46.3	−25.1
Median [%]	−46.4	−26.6	−62.6	−42.2
p-val (t-Stud)	0.0008***	0.0210**	0.0000***	0.0002***
p-val (WSR)	0.0006***	0.0046***	0.0000***	0.0002***
p-val (MW)	0.0951*		0.0043***	
Panel B: ALL_ew				
Mean [%]	−40.2	−42.8	−74.1	−69.4
Median [%]	−53.7	−42.4	−63.0	−49.7
p-val (t-Stud)	0.0000***	0.0000***	0.0000***	0.0000***
p-val (WSR)	0.0000***	0.0000***	0.0000***	0.0000***
p-val (MW)	0.5638		0.2355	
Panel C: ALL_vw				
Mean [%]	−86.7	−78.6	−153.7	−122.4
Median [%]	−104.1	−77.3	−157.9	−106.4
p-val (t-Stud)	0.0000***	0.0000***	0.0000***	0.0000***
p-val (WSR)	0.0000***	0.0000***	0.0000***	0.0000***
p-val (MW)	0.1161		0.0042***	
Panel D: MV_ew				
Mean [%]	−74.7	−22.9	−98.1	−30.1
Median [%]	−66.5	−23.3	−93.0	−33.0
p-val (t-Stud)	0.0000***	0.0034***	0.0000***	0.0002***
p-val (WSR)	0.0000***	0.0026***	0.0000***	0.0001***
p-val (MW)	0.0000***		0.0000***	
Panel E: MV_vw				
Mean [%]	−200.2	−94.4	−421.4	−141.5
Median [%]	−167.4	−68.8	−404.2	−112.7
p-val (t-Stud)	0.0000***	0.0000***	0.0000***	0.0000***
p-val (WSR)	0.0000***	0.0000***	0.0000***	0.0000***
p-val (MW)	0.0000***		0.0000***	
Panel F: BM_ew				
Mean [%]	−46.2	−68.5	−71.6	−79.0
Median [%]	−51.0	−54.9	−71.0	−72.8
p-val (t-Stud)	0.0000***	0.0000***	0.0000***	0.0000***
p-val (WSR)	0.0000***	0.0000***	0.0000***	0.0000***
p-val (MW)	0.1717		0.9615	
Panel G: BM_vw				
Mean [%]	−79.6	−69.2	−133.2	−100.0
Median [%]	−89.0	−66.2	−142.4	−85.9
p-val (t-Stud)	0.0000***	0.0000***	0.0000***	0.0000***
p-val (WSR)	0.0000***	0.0000***	0.0000***	0.0000***
p-val (MW)	0.0583*		0.0032***	

(continued)

Table 5 (continued)

	3-year returns		5-year returns	
1995–2008 IPOs	SmallCap	BigCap	SmallCap	BigCap
Panel H: MV&BM_ew				
Mean [%]	−51.6	−23.5	−64.4	−27.0
Median [%]	−41.2	−22.8	−39.3	−26.7
p-val (t-Stud)	0.0000***	0.0035***	0.0000***	0.0023***
p-val (WSR)	0.0000***	0.0020***	0.0000***	0.0009***
p-val (MW)	0.0141**		0.0771*	
Panel I: MV&BM_vw				
Mean [%]	−122.7	−71.3	−207.7	−102.9
Median [%]	−90.4	−56.7	−116.6	−85.2
p-val (t-Stud)	0.0000***	0.0000***	0.0000***	0.0000***
p-val (WSR)	0.0000***	0.0000***	0.0000***	0.0000***
p-val (MW)	0.0013***		0.0213**	

Notes: Significance at the 1 % (***), 5 % (**) and 10 % (*) level. Tests: Shapiro-Wilk test (S-W), Student t test (t-Stud), Wilcoxon signed rank test (WSR), Mann-Whithey test (MW). Benchmarks: WIG index, mean equity return (ALL), size portfolio (MV), book-to-market portfolio (BM), size and book-to-market portfolio (MV&BM) with equal weighting (ew) and value weighting (vw)

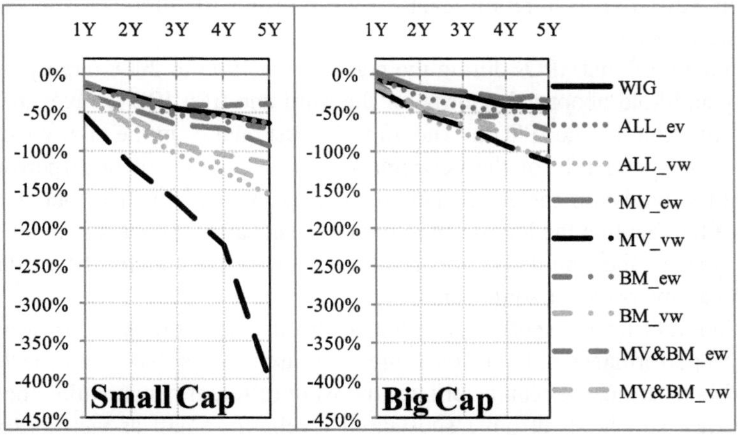

Fig. 2 Long-term IPO performance for small and big firms

5 Conclusion

This study is a part of the discussion on the existence of the IPO anomaly. It employed a wide set of benchmarks and methods in the process of abnormal performance analysis. The chapter focused on short- and long-term abnormal performance for a sample of IPOs on the main market of the Warsaw Stock Exchange in Poland. The present study differs from previous studies in several aspects. First, it contributes to the literature by updating the results for the IPO anomaly for Poland. Abnormal performance was examined using a recent sample of IPOs, also covering the recent crisis years. The main sample covered the period from 1995 to 2008. The second sample period from 1995 to 2013 was used for detecting short-term underpricing.

The conclusions are also important in terms of enriching the discussion with the application of alternative reference portfolios. Here, size, book-to-market and two-dimensional benchmarks were introduced along with equal- and value-weighting. In most of the studies for emerging markets or smaller exchanges the abnormal returns were dominated by index-adjusting. As proved by other studies, such a general market comparison is not supposed to be an ideal benchmark in the IPO case.

The research also provides evidence of the 5-year abnormal performance of initial public offerings in Poland, whereas previous studies only examined 3-year returns.

The benchmarks used to check for the size and book-to-market ratio did not show big differences in short-term returns. Independently of the benchmark used, the initial adjusted returns on the first trading day were positive. Although there were some differences in return levels between results for alternative benchmarks, they were rather small.

The data on Polish IPOs during the period from 1995 to 2008 largely confirms that buy-and-hold abnormal returns for the third and fifth IPO anniversary in the case of investing on the IPO day and after the first quarter in the aftermarket were negative, independently of the benchmark used. The level of underperformance depended strongly on the method used to measure performance, but it did not influence the fact that the long-term returns were negative. However, an interesting finding was that the cumulative abnormal returns were positive for the third and the fifth IPO anniversary for some benchmarks.

Smaller IPO firms experienced more severe underperformance. However, the long-term performance of large companies was also not positive. Even checking for size and book-to-market characteristics by using different benchmarks, the underperformance still holds at quite substantial levels, for small as well as for large businesses. Such results suggest, at least for the Polish initial public offerings during the sample period of 1995–2008, that anomalous IPO returns cannot purely be a manifestation of more systematic return patterns in the capital market. However, we leave the question about the existence of the IPO anomaly open, as such negative and such long-lasting performance after equity offerings is still quite puzzling.

References

Ahern KR (2009) Sample selection and event study estimation. J Empir Finance 16(3):466–482

Ahmad-Zaluki NA, Campbell K, Goodacre A (2007) The long run share price performance of Malaysian initial public offerings (IPOs). J Bus Finance Account 34(1-2):78–110

Ang JS, Zhang S (2002) Choosing benchmarks and test statistics for long horizon event study. http://papers.ssrn.com/sol3/papers.cfm?abstract_id=303803 (26.04.2014)

Ansotegui C, Fabregat J (1999) Initial public offerings on the Spanish Stock Exchange. Working Paper (ESADE)

Aussenegg W (2000) Privatization versus private sector initial public offerings in Poland. Multinatl Finance J 4(1–2):69–99

Barber BM, Lyon JD (1997) Detecting long-run abnormal stock returns: the empirical power and specification of test statistics. J Financ Econ 43(3):341–372

Basu S (1977) Investment performance of common stocks in relation to their price-earnings ratios. J Finance 32(3):663–682

Brav A (2000) Interference in long-horizon event studies: a Bayerish approach with applications to initial public offerings. J Finance 55:979–2016

Brav A, Gompers PA (1997) Myth or reality? The long-run underperformance of initial public offerings: evidence from venture and nonventure capital-backed companies. J Finance 52(5): 1791–1821

Corhay A, Teo S, Tourani-Rad A (2002) The long run performance of Malaysian initial public offerings (IPOs): value and growth effects. Manag Finance 28(2):52–65

Cornanic A, Novak J (2013) Signaling by underpricing the initial public offerings of primary listings in an emerging market. http://ssrn.com/abstract=2273470 (26.04.2014)

Cross F (1973) The behavior of stock prices on Fridays and Mondays. Financ Analyst J 29(6): 67–69

Czapiewski L, Lizińska J (2014) Performance of Polish IPO firms: size and profitability effect. Gospodarka Narodowa 1:53–70

Czapiewski L, Jewartowski T, Kałdoński M, Mizerka J (2013) Determinanty natychmiastowych stóp zwrotu za akcji spółek Skarbu Państwa dokonujących pierwotnych ofert publicznych. www.researchgate.net (20.11.2013)

Da Silva Rosa R, Velayuthen G, Walter T (2003) The sharemarket performance of Australian venture capital-backed and non-venture capital-backed IPOs. Pac Basin Finance J 11(2): 197–218

Drobetz W, Kammermann M, Wälchli U (2005) Long-term performance of initial public offerings: the evidence for Switzerland. Schmalenbach Bus Rev 57:253–275

Fama EF (1970) Efficient capital markets: a review of theory and empirical work. J Finance 25(2): 383–417

Fama EF (1998) Market efficiency, long-term returns, and behavioral finance. J Financ Econ 49(3):283–306

Fama EF (2010) Rational irrationality. Interview with Eugene Fama (by John Cassidy). The New Yorker, 13. http://www.newyorker.com/rational-irrationality/interview-with-eugene-fama (28.08.2014)

Fama EF, French K (1992) The cross-section of expected stock returns. J Finance 47(2):427–465

Farinos JE (2001) Rendimientos anormales de las OPV en Espana. Investigaciones Economicas 25(2):417–437

Foster G, Olsen C, Shevlin T (1984) Earnings releases, anomalies, and the behavior of security returns. Account Rev 59(4):574–603

Gompers PA, Lerner J (2003) The really long-run performance of initial public offerings: the Pre-Nasdaq evidence. J Finance 58(4):1355–1392

Jelic R, Briston R (2003) Privatisation initial public offerings: the Polish experience. Eur Financ Manag 9(4):457–484

Jelic R, Saadouni B, Briston R (2001) Performance of Malaysian IPOs: underwriters reputation and management earnings forecasts. Pac Basin Finance J 9(5):457–486
Jewartowski T, Lizińska J (2012) Short-and long-term performance of Polish IPOs. Emerg Market Finance Trade 48(2):59–75
Kothari SP, Warner JB (1997) Measuring long-horizon security price performance. J Financ Econ 43(3):301–339
Lakonishok J, Smidt S (1988) Are seasonal anomalies real? A ninety-year perspective. Rev Financ Stud 1(4):403–425
Lee P, Taylor S, Walter T (1996) Australian IPO pricing in the short and long run. J Bank Finance 20(7):1189–1210
Loughran T, Ritter JR (1995) The new issues puzzle. J Finance 50(1):23–51
Loughran T, Ritter JR (2000) Uniformly least powerful tests of market efficiency. J Financ Econ 55:361–389
Lyn EO, Zychowicz EJ (2003) The performance of new equity offerings in Hungary and Poland. Global Finance J 14(2):181–195
Mitchell ML, Stafford E (2000) Managerial decisions and long-term stock price performance. J Bus 73(3):287–329
Page MJ, Reyneke I (1997) The timing and subsequent performance of initial public offerings (IPOs) on the Johannesburg Stock Exchange. J Bus Finance Account 24(9&10):1401–1420
Ritter JR (1991) The long-run performance of initial public offerings. J Finance 46(1):3–27
Ritter JR (2003) Differences between European and American IPO markets. Eur Financ Manag 9(4):421–434
Schuster JA (2001) The cross-section of European IPO returns. Working paper. http://eprints.lse.ac.uk/24859/1/dp460.pdf?origin=publication_detail (26.04.2014)
Sloan R (1996) Do stock prices fully reflect information in accruals and cash flows about future earnings? Account Rev 71(3):289–316
Stehle R, Ehrhardt O, Przyborowsky R (2000) Long-run stock performance of German initial public offerings and seasoned equity issues. Eur Financ Manag 6(2):173–196

The Relevance of Context for Goodwill Impairment Decisions Within Hall's Framework

Radu-Daniel Loghin

Abstract Goodwill provides the proverbial canary in the coal mine for financial reporting since any hint of impairment allows financial users to determine conditions of worsening economic conditions, thus enabling a company to thrive within its stakeholder environment. Goodwill impairment decisions require benchmarks, assumptions about growth rates and other subjective elements left to the management's discretion. All these variables are intertwined with the companies' cultural framework. This paper tries to investigate the determinants and quality of goodwill impairment decisions within two separate accounting cultures under Hall's classification of low-context/high-context considering high-context emerging European markets such as Poland and Romania as well as low-context emerging African markets such as South Africa and Zimbabwe in two models, one investigating goodwill impairment decisions with the other focusing on the relevance of goodwill numbers. The findings suggest that cultural context is connected through various proxy variables to goodwill impairment decisions, thus shedding light on a set of novel variables for consideration.

Keywords Cultural context • Goodwill impairment • Value relevance

1 Introduction

Efficiency represents the accomplishment of or ability to accomplish a goal or set of objectives with a minimum expenditure of resources. We cannot define a single criterion for efficiency since the means for attaining the goals are as varied as the goals themselves. From an accounting perspective, goals are defined by the holders of equity and debt as the resources dispensed for the achievement of said objectives. Those are represented by the company's assets. Those assets are acquired from the holders of debt and equity at a certain cost to the enterprise and as such have a certain value attached to them. This value is subject to impairment charges when the items stop fulfilling the needs of the equity and debt holders. Impairment

R.-D. Loghin (✉)
University of Economic Studies, Academia de Studii Economice, Bucureşti, România
e-mail: Radu.loghin@lognet.ro

T. Dudycz et al. (eds.), *The Essence and Measurement of Organizational Efficiency*, Springer Proceedings in Business and Economics, DOI 10.1007/978-3-319-21139-8_11

charges are a means to communicate the reduction of efficiency on a per-item basis and thus allow stakeholders to take appropriate actions suitable for their needs.

Not all assets are fully covered by financial statements and appropriate disclosures. While tangible assets and the reasons of their impairment can be deemed as appropriate by all parties regardless of context, decisions pertaining to the impairment of intangible assets still lack a formal consensus among practitioners. Such a discrepancy can be traced back to the cultural context which shapes the understanding of the benefits incurred by the acquisition of other reporting entities. Since the original court ruling in Broad vs. Jollyffe in 1620, the meaning of goodwill has shifted from that of merely a non-competition covenant obtained from an able competitor to a broader meaning which embodies various understandings such as super profits, reputation, firm values and commercial credit.

Like any modern management decision, goodwill impairment driven by shorter product life cycles, increasingly higher variety of products and services, rapid changes in technology, low predictability of customer preferences and a larger number of markets and distribution channels (Roman et al. 2014) as well as mastery of modern innovations like business intelligence systems (Loghin and Dinu 2014). By these virtues, the management of a company must provide a superior understanding to its shareholders and stakeholders of the internal workings of their companies without jeopardizing the confidentiality of the actual trends of the company which shed a light on data which would enable the competitors to find secretive information about the inner workings of the company.

On these grounds, goodwill appears to be a low-context Anglo-Saxon accounting issue. However, the focus for accounting research is shifting from the low-context environment to high-context reporting landscapes. Since the term goodwill itself forms a linguistic barrier for accounting researchers who hail from countries with high context cultures such as those in South-Eastern Europe, most of the studies have been conducted within a low-context environment. Olante (2013) sheds light on the reliability of accounting goodwill numbers by examining whether goodwill impairment losses arise from overpayment for the target at the time of the acquisition, rather than from a subsequent deterioration of goodwill values for a sample of 929 US acquisitions finding that certain types of acquisitions have characteristics that make impairment inevitable. Xu et al. (2011) find that goodwill impairment charges are negatively viewed by investors, on average, but financial health moderates the relation with the implication that the goodwill impairment charge conveys value relevant information. Hamberg and Beisland (2014) examine the value relevance effects of changes in goodwill accounting in a low-context European setting using Swedish data to illustrate that under the impairment-only option, stock returns do not correlate with the goodwill impairment. Baboukardos and Rimmel (2014) find that in a high-context culture such as Greece, where the application of fair value accounting has been seen as more problematic, fair value accounting generates relevant accounting numbers but only for those companies that comply highly with IFRS disclosure requirements. These disclosure requirements belong to a low-context culture with a detailed level of disclosure.

This study frames the issue of goodwill impairment within the cultural context as defined by Hall's cultural framework (1976) building new dimensions to account for the various differences between the four accounting jurisdictions sampled for the empiric design.

2 Framing the Issue of Goodwill Accounting in a Cultural Context

In order to understand the relevance of reported goodwill and its determinants we must first look at goodwill as a legal right upheld by the bylaws and statutes of most economically-developed countries. From the earliest times merchants have banded together in cartels to protect their interests or demanded special privileges from the rulers of certain provinces or even obtained valuable know-how in establishing trading posts. These disparate strategies or behaviors enabled some to prosper while others failed. Merchants opened shops, way stations and warehouses in strategic places enabling them to draw customers from afar or secure a place in the local market. Other merchants held customer records with them while peddling goods from trading hub to trading hub without appropriate storage and distribution facilities.

In some places cultural attitudes and practices enabled the survival of merchants who held certain sets of qualities be it location, reputation, the sounding of the firm or the customer list. In a later period these types of behavior ware cemented by means of linguistic assignment to the set of intangible assets which cannot be identified separately on the balance sheet as goodwill, firm value, reputation, protection and other such disparate concepts, some being more measurable than others. Loghin (2014a) describes the meanings and implications of each concept. It was first the concept of super profit derived from the works of Karl Marx in 1894 (Marx 1980) which drew the link between efficiency and goodwill at an early stage. Later, with an analytical Western thinking shaping over accounting research this concept became less popular with the shaping of Kaner's (1937) new theory of goodwill which endorsed a holistic approach to goodwill with the recognition of the role played by different uncharted intangible assets as value holders for the company.

While the framing of the accounting debate divides the profession between those who accept the impairment treatment of goodwill and those who do not, an older argument divides the accounting profession according to the cultural dimensions of each jurisdiction. This makeup of traits is based on research performed by Gray (1988) in which the various accounting practices are reduced to a fixed number of dimensions. Gray's dimensions are inspired by Hofstede's work in the 1980s (1980), and assume that an accounting culture is reducible to the arbitrary set of values shared among its professionals. The various value systems or attitudes of accountants may be expected to be related to and derived from societal values with special reference to work related values. Accounting 'values' will in turn impact on accounting systems (Gray 1988) with performance disclosures affecting the outstanding goodwill itself and the company's reputation.

As a consequence of embracing a multicultural perspective on the development of accounting in different jurisdictions one has to draw upon previous work, which separates jurisdictions into those which can be comprehended without a high-level of acquaintance with the framework called low-context cultures and those which cannot be comprehended without a first-hand experience of the meanings drawn from official reports and letters called high-context cultures. A legal perspective on this distinction can be found in Loghin (2014b) which illustrates that jurisdictions which have a lower level of context as defined by their use of native precedents into the court system are also more flexible when it comes to endorsement of low-context international standards, being encouraged by their status to adopt International Financial Reporting Standards (IFRS) earlier than their more rigid and contextual counterparts.

In Caterham vs. Birkin in South Africa a legal understanding of goodwill, as the subject of proprietary rights, is defined. Goodwill has no independent existence apart from the business to which it is attached (Loghin, 2014b) It is local in character and divisible if the business is carried on in several countries a separate goodwill attaches to it in each. This concept of goodwill permeates the low-context Anglo-Saxon accounting framework, and can draws some criticism from the standpoint of an entity operating within the confines of a high-context accounting culture. For a start the definition completely ignores the key feature of high-context accounting, which is a holistic approach to the disclosures. In high-context cultures, reports can be communicated with verbal support from the accountant to the owners whereby additional information framing the context of the decisions is outlined and thus the information presented is thereby more relevant to some segments while irrelevant to others, especially outsider investors who probe the market for opportunities.

Ding et al. (2008) propose four stages for goodwill accounting development based upon the balance sheet theory.

1. A pure static phase which corresponds to a creditor protection mindset. This framework endorses immediate expensing or rapid amortizations (over 5 years) for investors who do not trust the covenant between them and the sellers of goodwill.
2. A weakened static phase which applies a write-off against equity.
3. A dynamic phase with a going concern where the goodwill is still assumed to have a finite life which implies the recognition of an asset, with application of amortization over a long period.
4. The actuarial phase which corresponds to the going concern assumption but without notion of consumption of economic benefits leading to recognition of an asset, with impairment testing based on discounted (actuarial) cash flows.

Thus during the development of goodwill accounting practices within high-context jurisdictions such as Vietnam there are stages relating to the development of incentives for accounting treatments generated by the steady expansion of an autonomous merchant middle class. In fact, the term employed in Vietnam for the designation of goodwill (*loi the thuong mai* or commercial advantage) pays homage to that of commercial fund (fond commercial) found in French accounting literature with an opposite accounting treatment.

Accounting research has thus far missed the opportunity to test the differences between various emerging markets which hail from cultural strains. In most studies the authors usually emphasize developed markets as the sources for the samples and most developed markets are low-context markets. This provides ample opportunity for an empirical research.

3 Study Design, Sample and Methodology

For the purpose of achieving the goals of the research a sample was drawn from the companies listed at Harare Stock Exchange, Johannesburg Stock Exchange, Bucharest Stock Exchange and Warsaw Stock Exchange. The arguments in favor of the sample were that it covers both African and European Stock markets and it covers the high-context/low-context requirement for homogeneity.

The main characteristic of the jurisdictions selected for the panel was the degree of international isolation fostered during the Cold War when the French General Chart of Accounts was published. Zimbabwe and South Africa, while capitalist societies during the period were not recognized by key players due to ethnic issues namely the Apartheid and the Rhodesian Bush War and Romania and Poland ware isolated politically from major developed markets by their socialist-oriented governments.

This isolation began to wane with the fall of the Iron Curtain, the end of Apartheid in South Africa and the formation of a new political coalition in Zimbabwe which included native stakeholders. These events happened in the 90s and thus provide a fresh insight into the workings of high-context/low-context cultures equalizing with their peers.

Zimbabwe was selected since it has the second oldest stock exchange in Sub-Saharan Africa and was among the first to fully endorse International Financial Reporting Standards back at the end of the twentieth century. It also provided a glimpse into the performance of equities reported under the International Financial Reporting Standards. South Africa was selected for its rich and novel interpretations of goodwill accounting including some cases which discourage practitioners from overstating goodwill. Both jurisdictions share a common border and business interests dating from the Cold War period.

Other reasons for the inclusion of such equities and their international recognition as emerging markets are reported upon by Loghin (2014a, b) into the legal framework study. Worthy of mention is the fact that both jurisdictions had until the adoption or convergence to International Financial Accounting Standards (IFRS) rejected native developments and guidelines set by their native accounting professionals.

Table 1 Number of purchases with a higher stake than 50 % in the jurisdictions sampled

Jurisdiction	Total purchases	Purchases >50 % stake	Before IFRS 3	IFRS 3	IFRS 3 revised
Poland	7122	1431	362	501	568
Romania	506	238	70	88	80
Zimbabwe	134	46	23	14	9
South Africa	5781	2336	1467	387	482

Romania was selected together with Poland since both countries shared a common border until the outbreak of the Second World War and both started recognizing goodwill on the balance sheet during 1993–1994. The mechanism for standardization was also similar and was government driven. While in Zimbabwe and South Africa the structure set for accounting regulations was in the form of standards, in the case of Romania and Poland the structure for accounting regulations was provided for in the form of regulations.

As we can observe in Table 1 the total number of purchases increased after the adoption of IFRS 3 "Business Combinations" revised, the number of purchases has increased in all jurisdictions considering that before the IFRS 3 "Business Combinations" there was a long span of time for the implementation of alternative stanards.

Since the focus of the study is the impact of practices relating to goodwill accounting, the number of entities involved in the study was selected on the basis of a few vital criteria. The first one is that companies had to be listed in the countries selected for the purpose of the study with a primary quote on the stock exchange, meaning the company either had to be native or form the subsidiary of a larger fiscal group listed separately. The companies were drawn from the Thomson Reuters DataStream database for the last period associated with the financial years 2013 and 2014 since there are international groups which publish their financial statements following different 12-month periods than the solar calendar year.

By the selection process the number of companies was deemed to stand at 2237 equities. Further criteria for the inclusion was the existence of goodwill in the reporting period or the previous (with writing off of goodwill to zero in the current period included), the latest financial reporting period reported and mapped in XBRL, the removal of suspended entities and the availability of the financial reports at the time of the data collection period.

By applying these rules a sample of 119 equities was selected without a few eligible companies from the sample for a reduction in bias based on an equivalent number of companies operating within high-context and low context cultures. It can be argued that the European subsample reflects a high-context cultural framework as opposed to the African subsample, which in connection with Brittish colonial rule has been exposed to a low-context cultural framework.

The focus of the research is to fulfill a series of objectives. All these objectives are outlined by the rules defined in International Accounting Standard (IAS)

Table 2 The policies of discount rates according to Hall's distinction for the sample

	Range for multiple discount rates	Min	Max	Non-disclosure	Single discount rate
Average	5.67 %	11 %	16.40 %	32 %	38 %
LC	6.27 %	12 %	18 %	27 %	33 %
HC	4.36 %	7.90 %	12.26 %	39 %	42 %
Count	36	36	36	38	45

36 "Impairment of Assets" and IFRS 3 "Business Combinations". The sources of data ware Thomson Reuters Eikon as well as financial records of the companies manually collected for the purpose of the paper and the processing software used to integrate the disparate sources of data was MS Office Excel 2007 suite.

The first hypothesis of the study involves the disclosure and range of for the discount rates used for the calculation of the market value of purchased goodwill by analyzing the content of the financial reports. While the companies can avoid this disclosure requirement by using obfuscating language within the reports for the sale of privacy, such are the requirements imposed by the International Accounting Standards Bureau (IASB) for a perceived increase in accounting quality (Table 2).

The hypotheses regarding this side of goodwill reporting is the following:

H1: There is a correlation between the disclosure of discount rates and Hall's classification

H01: There is no correlation between the disclosure of discount rates and Hall's classification

Since all reporting entities selected for the sample provide their financial statements in comparative IFRS financial statements the impact of the institutional disclosure environment is mitigated. A Mann-Whitney test performed on the maximum disclosure rates is significant at 0.01 % for the disclosed maximum discount rate.

The second test relates to the impact of cultural context on the value relevance of net goodwill numbers reported in the financial statements of the company. The model is based on the Ohlson model as tuned by Loghin and Seria's (2014) paper with the Boolean variable accounting for the level of context.

The hypotheses put forth regarding the quality of goodwill reporting are the following:

H2: There is an influence of Hall's classification on the relevance of goodwill numbers

H02: There is no influence of Hall's classification on the relevance of goodwill numbers

The variables selected for the purpose of this second hypothesis set are closing price of equity at the date of reporting the financial results, the total equity of the company minus net goodwill, net income and net goodwill. Since the samples of low-context (58 equities after the elimination of two equities with abnormal earnings) and high-context (59 equities) are balanced, we can test the hypothesis by comparing the performance of two models (one for the low-context (lc) and another for the high-context (hc) parts of the sample). The lag between the date of the financial statements and the day of the end period is on average greater than 4 months so the reported earnings were considered relevant if they correlated with the closing price of the equity the day after the financial statements were published so all stakeholders and shareholders could take time to build models, test their predictions against the actual results as well as other means of inspecting the reliability of the financial statements.

The null hypothesis would be rejected if the statistical performance of the two models is similar (with the range of R squared lower than 5 %, and with significant p-values for all variables involved.

According to IFRS 3 "Business Combinations", goodwill is measured as the difference between:

- The aggregate of (i) the value of the consideration transferred at fair value, (ii) the amount of any non-controlling interest (NCI), and (iii) in a business combination achieved in stages, the acquisition-date fair value of the acquirer's previously-held equity interest in the acquire, and
- The net of the acquisition-date amounts of the identifiable assets acquired and the liabilities assumed (measured in accordance with IFRS 3) [IFRS 3.32].

Thus a prime proxy for the necessity of goodwill impairment would be the drop in market capitalization below the book value of equity for the consolidated entity. These international accounting standards endorsed by many jurisdictions as mandatory for public listed companies on their stock exchanges hold the requirements for publishing goodwill amounts in the balance sheet. As such we can consider the difference between the market value of equity at the end of the fiscal year minus total equity to form a proxy for the necessity to hold goodwill impairment tests for the whole group of companies. In an early stage this proxy reveals the following data. Out of 117 companies only 19 % had reasons to test their goodwill impairment and reach the second level of the test based upon the stock market performance of their equities, while more than a third impaired their goodwill based upon the underlying assumptions put forth by the management.

Thus, we discover a weak negative link between the requirement for a second test but almost no direct correlation between the depreciation decision and the actual requirement for such a test, as well as a faint correlation between context and the depreciation decision.

For a better understanding of the impairment decision a model is built to account for the impairment decision, a dependent variable acting as a dummy variable (1 if impairment decisions were undertaken an 0 if an impairment decision was not undertaken during the period).

The variables selected for the impairment decision process ware as follows:

- The age of the company (expressed as the natural logarithm of the time between the incorporation of the company and the financial period end date). Older companies would have more experience in dealing with financial crisis and absorb the shocks of recession better than newer start-up companies since the latter would lack the established goodwill to preserve its customer base available. Older companies would also have a more established tradition and context than newer ones. This would determine lower levels of goodwill impairment than newer ones for the same sector.

- The synchronicity with Gross Domestic Product (GDP) growth trends, the dummy variable 1 if the growth of the company's market capitalization has the same sign as that of the countries' GDP growth and 0 if it does not. A company which is more synchronous with its environment might mask the need for an impairment test of goodwill, while one which is asynchronous would be more likely to test its goodwill for depreciation for the sake of prudence.
- Segment allocation of goodwill which is a dummy variable equal to 1 if the company allocates goodwill to operating segments in a separate note or not. A company which allocates goodwill across segments would have more assumptions to make in terms of the growth rate than one which allocates only to the level of cash-generating assets. No predicted sign for this variable.
- The variance of return on assets (ΔROA). This variable would provide a strong signal that a goodwill impairment test would have to be conducted at the distinct level of CGU.
- The net ratio of intangible assets per total assets (expressed as the ratio of intangible assets to total assets in t). This ratio would imply that the company possesses a large amount of licenses, copyrights and other intangible values which combined with a network effect would enhance the efficiency of a company.
- The ratio of book value of the equity to the market value of the capital at the end of the financial period or BV/MV ratio.
- The revenue per share ration which is predicted to be negatively correlated with the impairment decision since investors expects a growth of their revenue as an effect of a merger.
- The beta coefficient of the company's equity on the primary stock market. A company with a Beta coefficient greater than 1 would imply a company integrated within its local context, while a company with a beta less than 1 would imply the opposite.
- The size of the company expressed as the natural logarithm of the company's total assets.

The method employed for the purpose of this objective is the regression analysis considering the following hypotheses for the model:

H3: Older, more established companies would be less likely to impair their goodwill.

H4: A company more embedded within its economic framework would be less likely to impair its goodwill.

H5: Older, more established companies would be more likely to impair their goodwill.

H6: A company more embedded within its economic framework would be more likely to impair its goodwill.
H7: There is no link between cultural context and goodwill impairment in the new IFRS environment

4 Results

Following the first empirical test under Dancey and Reidy's (2004) criterion we must draw a weak link between the level of cultural context and the disclosures regarding the discount rates employed for the determination of the amount of goodwill impairment. While the quality of the impairment process may not affected by this lack of transparency, such details do encourage the growth of foreign investment within a company. This bears no relationship with the audit report though. Only one company which disclosed its discount rate and assumptions got a qualified audit report and that belonged to a low-context accounting culture. The lack of a disclosure pertaining to the discount rate used for the study implies the reliance on unobservable inputs when determining assumptions regarding the development of the market.

Comparing the performance of Ohlson's model as endorsed by Loghin and Seria (2014) the findings are somewhat surprising considering the expectation that low-context accounting systems would provide better earnings for the shareholders of the companies (Table 3).

From the value relevance model we observe that goodwill numbers are more relevant in a low-context environment where the rates selected for the impairment tests are readily available. There are some issues with the adjustment of the data series but most adjustments performed using the outstanding number of shares has to assume that the investors themselves perform the required mental computations when it comes to finding a means of comparing two different companies. The further assumption made by the researchers is that large companies would tend to divide their capital into smaller shares to facilitate trading but there are more complexities. Some entities may increase or decrease their equity between the end date and reporting date.

There are definitely more complexities to the adjustment factor than achieving a comparison between small and large companies. Most equities involved in the purchase of goodwill are themselves entities large enough to afford a purchase of an entity without losing control to that entities' ownership (Table 4).

Table 3 Statistical data for the relevance model

	Adjusted R^2	Intercept	Goodwill (t/coeff.)	NE (t/coeff.)	NI (t/coeff.)
LC	0.81	Negative	8.08/12.56	5.2/1.39	2.2/2.8
HC	0.84	Positive	0.73/0.54	2.46/0.31	8.2/7.01
Significance			LC significant	Both	Both

Table 4 The ANOVA statistical performance for the impairment decision model

	Coeff.	Standard error	t-Stat	P-value	Lower 95 %	Upper 95 %	Lower 95.0 %	Upper 95.0 %
Intercept	−1.52	0.61	−2.47	0.015	−2.74	−0.30	−2.75	−0.30
BV/MV	−0.01	0.06	−0.14	0.891	−0.13	0.120	−0.14	0.120
Beta	0.16	0.12	1.38	0.170	−0.07	0.408	−0.07	0.408
Age	0.19	0.04	2.41	0.017	0.020	0.216	0.02	0.216
% intangible	1.27	0.75	1.68	0.096	−0.23	2.779	−0.23	2.779
Segments	−0.01	0.09	−0.14	0.888	−0.19	0.169	−0.19	0.169
ΔROA	−0.01	0.01	−0.29	0.769	−0.02	0.012	−0.02	0.018
Synchronicity	0.18	0.12	0.93	0.353	−0.13	0.37	−0.13	0.367
Size	0.06	0.03	2.11	0.036	0.003	0.12	0.01	0.122
Revenue/share	−0.44	0.24	−1.82	0.070	−0.92	0.04	−0.92	0.038

The model is explains 13 % of all impairments performed in the four jurisdictions. While this result may seem discouraging, variables drawn from its development might allow the emergence of better models which merge with other empiric results. While the variables which account for creative accounting practices ware omitted from the study as well as variables pertaining to corporate governance, the variables accounting for efficiency as well as one relating to cultural context (age of the company).

The age of the company is significant within the 5 % significance bracket. Other significant variables found ware the intangible assets ratio, which are drivers of the world economy in the new low-context dominant world. The segments allocation of goodwill has a weak correlation with the impairment decision. An entity which is synchronous with its economic environment is not relevant for the goodwill decision, thus the decision is drawn primarily from the local context of the entity and not the general economic environment. This decision is surprising since the biggest segment of companies was formed of those who chose to not disclose their discount rate or adopted a single discount rate for the impairment of goodwill. The potentially-viable variable determining further insight is the beta coefficient for the equity, which might consider alternative interpretations.

A first for the study was that all companies which recorded goodwill ware considered with provisions for a two statistical observations which had disrupted reporting and records. The sample was neutral on the issue of personal and business goodwill, involving industries which rely on a mixture of personal and business goodwill.

Older companies, which are more entrenched in the low-context accounting setting as defined by the Anglo-Saxon legal environment are more likely to impair their goodwill, implying a tighter connection between the business cycle and the underlying goodwill accumulated by these companies.

Thus hypothesis 5, that which implies that older companies are more likely to impair their goodwill is partially confirmed. A model with a higher R^2 is required to fully confirm the hypothesis. All other hypotheses are invalidated by their corresponding p-values.

5 Conclusions

Overall, most of the hypotheses have been confirmed. While low-context accounting systems award a higher significance for the reported goodwill and encourage an impairment of goodwill, accounting measures provided by high-context accounting cultures provide a relevant mix of financial data different from that of low-context cultures which emphasize the role of earnings in deterring the performance of a company and thus the impairment of its goodwill.

Accounting forms a part of human language, and is subject to the same rigors as any form of communication. As such, accounting shall follow all the norms of communication. These norms are dictated by the socio-cultural framework of the jurisdiction, which are set teleological by the members of that jurisdiction.

By enforcing uniform regulations across cultures, those regulations lose their context and the very worldview which enabled their appearance. Accounting globalization can be achieved following two different strategies, pertaining to high context or low context communications. Either all jurisdictions agree on the same accounting principles and interpretations by endorsing a single set of accounting standards, as with IFRS or they preserve their accounting principles and interpretations, while providing a common platform for financial reporting. As the taxonomy reveals, language has a decisive role to play in cognition and attitudes towards accounting standard setting, with jurisdictions endorsing goodwill achieving the highest level of compliance with the IFRS framework, or acting to be part of the framework, or trying to play a role in its development.

Acknowledgement This work was cofinanced from the European Social Fund through Sectoral Operational Programme Human Resources Development 2007–2013, project number POSDRU/159/1.5/S/134197 "Performance and excellence in doctoral and postdoctoral research in Romanian economics science domain"

References

Baboukardos D, Rimmel G (2014) Goodwill under IFRS: relevance and disclosures in an unfavorable environment. Account Forum 38(1):1–17. doi:10.1016/j.accfor.2013.11.001

Dancey C, Reidy J (2004) Statistics without maths for psychology: using SPSS for windows. Prentice Hall, London

Ding Y, Richard J, Stolowy H (2008) Towards an understanding of the phases of goodwill accounting in four western capitalist countries: from stakeholder model to shareholder model. Acc Organ Soc 33(7):718–755

Gray SJ (1988) Towards a theory of cultural influence on the development of accounting systems internationally. In: Abacus, available on-line at ACIS http://www.acis.pamplin.vt.edu/faculty/tegarden/5034/handouts/Gray-Abacus-1988.pdf. Accessed 1 Mar 2014

Hall ET (1976) Beyond culture. Anchor Books, New York

Hamberg M, Beisland LA (2014) Changes in the value relevance of goodwill accounting following the adoption of IFRS 3. J Int Account Audit Tax 23(2):59–73. doi:10.1016/j.intaccaudtax.2014.07.002

Hofstede G (1980) Culture's consequences. Sage, Thousand Oaks, CA

Kaner H (1937) A new theory of goodwill. Sir Isaac Pitman, London

Loghin RD (2014a) A pragmatic approach to accounting standard setting for business combinations. In: Proceedings of the 9th international conference accounting and management information systems AMIS 2014, The Bucharest University of Economic Studies, 11–12 June 2014

Loghin RD (2014b) Emerging common law decisions in goodwill accounting regulation. SEA Practl Appl Sci 4:275–288, http://EconPapers.repec.org/RePEc:cmj:seapas:y:2014:i:4:p:275-288

Loghin RD, Dinu F (2014) The impact of business intelligence recognition on goodwill reporting. Procedia Econ Finance 15:1779–1786. doi:10.1016/S2212-5671(14)00859-4

Loghin RD, Seria C (2014) The relevance of goodwill reporting in an Islamic context. Pract Appl Sci 5:385–392, http://EconPapers.repec.org/RePEc:cmj:seapas:y:2014:i:5:p:385-392

Marx K (1980) Das Kapital, 4th edn. University of Utah, Salt Lake City

Olante ME (2013) Overpaid acquisitions and goodwill impairment losses—evidence from the US. Adv Account 29(2):243–254. doi:10.1016/j.adiac.2013.09.010
Roman C, Roman A-G, Meier E, Mocanu M (2014) Research on the evolution of controlling tasks and their delimitation from audit tasks. Theorl Appl Econ 21(12):13–26
Xu W, Anandarajan A, Curatola A (2011) The value relevance of goodwill impairment. Res Account Regul 23(2):145–148. doi:10.1016/j.racreg.2011.06.007

Efficiency Evaluation Criteria of Tour Guides' Communication Activities

Gabriel Łasiński and Małgorzata Maria Bogdan

Abstract Tour guide profession is connected with fulfilling various social roles and hence it demands having developed communication competences. This paper situates communication activities of tour guide in praxeological-systemic model of presentation and takes up concepts of effectiveness of those activities.

Next to the substantive contents of excursions, a selection of appropriate means of communication determines the success of excursions conducted by a given tour guide. Authors suggest usage (by tour guides) persuasive communication which allows to accomplish established results of communication activities to greater extent. Simultaneously authors attempt to create efficiency evaluation criteria of tour guide communication with a tour group.

As a result of studies, based on the observation of feedback given by tour groups, basic effective evaluation criteria of tour guides' communication activities were distinguished. They were divided into: proxemic behavior, verbal interactions, visual behavior, unequivocally positive assessments and unequivocally negative assessments. Each criteria were further analyzed in this paper.

According to the authors prevalence of awareness and understanding of specified feedback can improve the quality of guiding services.

Keywords Efficiency • Efficiency evaluation • Efficiency evaluation criteria • Tour guiding • Communication • Tourism

1 Introduction

Nowadays, the profession of a city and a provincial tour guide in Poland can be practised by everyone, although until 2013 an adequate license assigned by the marshal of province was required. According to the transcripts of the Act on Tourism Services "tasks of the tour guide are guiding tourists or visitors, giving professional and actual information about country, visited spots, areas and venues, caring for tourists or visitors to the extent arising from a contract, and while

G. Łasiński • M.M. Bogdan (✉)
Department of Communication and Management in Sport, Wrocław University School of Physical Education, Wrocław, Poland
e-mail: malgorzata.m.bogdan@gmail.com

T. Dudycz et al. (eds.), *The Essence and Measurement of Organizational Efficiency*, Springer Proceedings in Business and Economics, DOI 10.1007/978-3-319-21139-8_12

conducting tourists in the mountains caring for their safety especially during mountain trips which require appropriate techniques and professional equipment." (Art. 20 Paragraph 2, Act of August 29th, 1997 on tourist services, unified text: Journal of Laws of 2004, No. 133, item 884) Simultaneously an obligation to hold a license applies only to mountain guides. (Art. 21, Act of August 29th 1997 on tourist services, unified text: Journal of Laws of 2004, No. 133, item 884) In the face of no obligation to hold a license by the city and the provincial tour guide, it may raise serious doubts about whether the information given by them are professional and actual and whether the way of their communication is optimal.

There should be emphasized the specifics of a tourism sector, which essence are production and consumption of impressions that occur at the same time and during a geographical displacement. "Production and consumption at the storyscape are interwoven. The interaction of producers and consumers at historic sites is a praxis of poesis through which cultural meaning is created. In this sense, consumption of culture become its production and is achieved through performance." (Chronis 2005, p. 402)

International scientific literature on the tourism service is extensive. However, it comprises topics mainly connected with a tourist' subjective evaluation of tour guides' or tour leaders' service. Issues connected with how to present and interpret a tourist space are rarely mentioned and papers, based on research conducted during sightseeing excursions (e.g. Lugosi and Bray 2008), are exceptional. This was the main reason why the authors took up the topics of the quality of tour guides' communication. The study is intended to achieve a higher level of an identification of communication' process.

A concern for an efficient communication in professions connected with tourist services became an inspiration for a broader research project which one aspect will be presented in this paper. A goal of this paper is specifying and characterization of evaluation criteria of tour guides' communicational behaviors in terms of a praxeological presentation model.

2 Tour Guides' Social Roles

Literature defines different social roles that are attributed to the tour guides. Among them: information-giver and source of knowledge (Cohen 1985; Holloway 1981; Hughes 1991; Lin et al. 2014; Reisinger and Steiner 2006), entertainment-giver (Lin et al. 2014; Reisinger and Steiner 2006), leader (Cohen 1985; Geva and Goldman 1991; Howard et al. 2001; Lin et al. 2014; Reisinger and Steiner 2006), teacher (Fine and Speer 1985; Holloway 1981; Mancini 2001; Pearce 1982), culture broker (Bunten 2011; Holloway 1981; Katz 1985; Lin et al. 2014; McKean 1976; Reisinger and Steiner 2006), interpreter and translator of the strangeness (Almagor 1985; Cohen 1985; Holloway 1981; Katz 1985; Ryan and Dewar 1995; Bogdan and Łasiński 2015). The guide is entrusted with the purest of public relations missions:

to encapsulate the essence of a place and to be a window onto a site, region, or country (Pond 1993).

Each of mentioned roles is strongly associated with communicational tasks posed to the guides. Furthermore, according to the cited Act, the essence of a tour guide's job is guiding, giving information and care what makes the job associated like no other with a permanent interpersonal communication. In this sense the striving to increase an efficiency of tour guides' work will be striving to improve their communication activities.

Regardless of a communication model, based on which the communication activity shall be considered, communication process consists of: content of a message and a way of a message transmission, which connect participants of the process. Thus the efficiency of tour guides' communication activities can be considered at the substantive level—the content of a message or at the methodological level—the way of communication. As far as the substantive content is an interest of semioticians, the authors focus on the efficiency of the way of communication.

3 Application of the Praxeological-Systemic Model of Presentation in Tour Guide's Communication Activities

In the praxeological-systemic point of view there were isolated four basic forms of social behaviors: autopresentation, presentation, inside group interactions and between group interactions (Łasiński and Wiejak 2004).

Sightseeing tour combines many different forms of interpersonal communication, which create a specific character of the presentation. Referring to the earlier presented social roles of tour guides, the following aspects can be attributed to their presentation:

- Educational
- Tutorial
- Social event
- Entertainment
- Adventure et al.

A model presentation, submitted as a structural scheme, includes:

- Presenters' objectives and resources
- Surroundings of the presentation
- Techniques, tactics and strategies used by the presenter to influence the audience
- Results associated with a level of recipients' conviction to:
  - Make a decision/refrain from making a decision (purchase, sale, change of attitude)

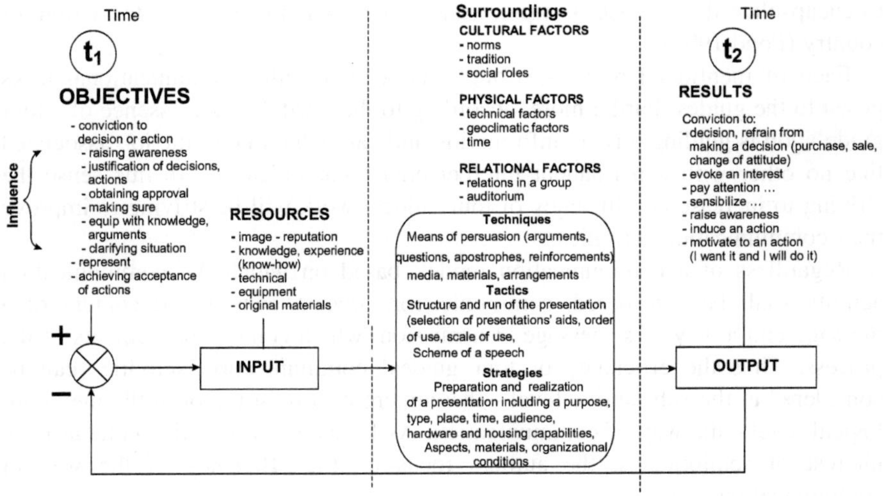

Fig. 1 Praxeological model of presentation (*Source*: Łasiński and Wiejak 2004)

– Evoke an interest
– Pay attention
– Sensibilize
– Raise the awareness
– Induce an action
– Motivate to an action (Fig. 1)

In the praxeological point of view the efficiency may exist as i.a.:

- Efficacy, understood as a compliance of a result with an objective,
- Effectiveness, understood as positively evaluated results of work,
- Economy, understood as benefit-cost ratio (Łasiński 2003).

With regard to the communication activities of tour guides' during excursions the most apt measure of the efficiency will be the effectiveness.

A transformation of the input presenter's resource into the output results proceeds by applying the specific strategies, tactics and techniques. The communication process in the tour guide's profession follows the constant and clearly defined strategy:

- The main and necessary actors of the communication process are the tour guide and the participants of a tour,
- The guide with the visitors move together along the route,
- Surroundings of the tour is filled with objects, events and people, and is an illustration of a content of the tour guide's narrative,
- Typical conditions of the tour are open spaces, and less frequently—closed spaces,

- Conditions are not always propitious for guiding according to a tour program.

The guide chooses tactics and techniques freely to match the content, situation and recipients. The optimization of tactics and techniques may improve the effectivity of the tour guide's communication activities.

The interpersonal communication in presentation is realized in a convergent manner in all channels of communication:

- Verbal channel—language
- Paraverbal channel—vocal channel
- non-Verbal channel—body language

Apart from the listed channels, external media, that support an illustration of a verbal expression, must be taken into account. All of the channels create a hierarchical levels which become an interpretative context for the lower situated (Skibiński 2012). A verbal information is a content of a message and the higher levels are the way of transmission, that will be analyzed further (Fig. 2).

A selection of certain means of communication situates the communication activity of a tour guide at some point of a continuum extending between an informative and a persuasive type of communication (Fig. 3).

Table 1 shows the characteristics of both types of communication.

An application of merely the informative content in the presentation results that it is just a simple message. Only the usage of the persuasion allows the presenter to focus the communication on striving to the established results of the presentation (Fig. 1).

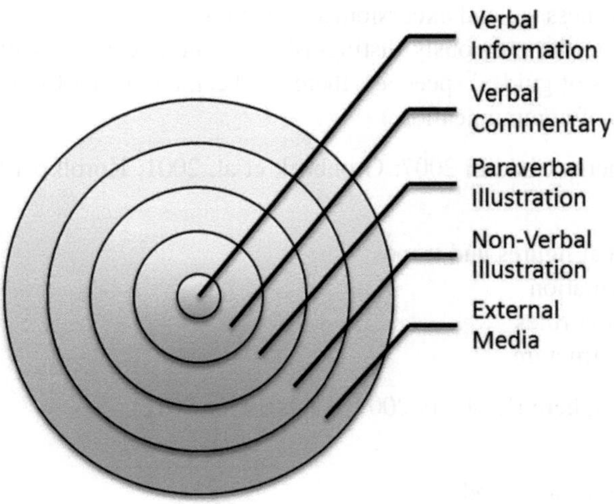

Fig. 2 Interpretational levels in an interpersonal communication

Fig. 3 Continuum of types of communication

Table 1 Characteristics of an informative and a persuasive communication (own work for Filipiak 2003)

Type of communication	Characteristics of communication
Informative	• Description • Narrative • Definition • Demonstration
Persuasive	• Bidirectional and symmetric transmission • Use of verbal and non-verbal symbols • Striving for consolidation, change or shaping attitudes and behaviors

4 Research Methodology

In the framework of a broader research project in 2011 and 2012 a qualitative study was conducted that comprised: an observation of communication interactions during Wrocław city tours and a rhetorical analysis of presentations of 19 tour guides who led the tours.

The data collection consisted of making audiovisual recording during the city tours and direct, non-participant observation.[1] In the next step the obtained material has been played back many times, transcribed into computer text and further analyzed. The registered narrative has been analyzed in details in the light of adopted rhetorical criteria. Simultaneously there were analyzed relations between a content of a message and excursionists' reactions.

According to the previously distinguished communication channels, as a basis for the analyzis of guides' speeches, there has been adopted a following classification of means of communication:

1. Verbal sphere (Cialdini 2007; Gronbeck et al. 2001; Korolko 1990; Szymanek 2001)
   - Rhetorical figures and tropes
   - Argumentation
   - Persuasion rules
   - Speech structure
2. Paraverbal sphere (Leathers 2007; Tarasiewicz 2012)
   - Timbre
   - Volume of the sound
   - Pitch of the voice
   - Rate of the speech

[1] A type of an observation was classified as direct and non-participant because the researcher was present during the interactions but she didn't take part in the process, only accompanied the situations.

- Articulation
- Pronunciation
- Silence
- Intonation
- Dialect and accent
- Pause

3. Non-verbal sphere (Leathers 2007)
   - Facial expression
   - Visual behavior
   - Body communication/gestures, posture
   - Proxemic behavior
   - Touch
   - Physical appearance

4. External media
   - Teaching aids that increase an attractivity of the speech (e.g., pictures, source texts)
   - Teaching aids that increase an efficiency of the speech (e.g., microphone, laser pointer)

It must be stressed that not all of these means of communication can be modified by the sender, e.g., the timbre is an individual feature of each man and it cannot be changed. However, the auditorium hears the timbre and evaluates it as pleasant or unpleasant and therefore it is a factor that affects the reception of the message.

For the guide performing the speech, the source of evaluation of his way of presentation and guiding, including the means of communication, is the behavior of tour groups. In view of the established aim of this paper there will not be presented the results concerning the rhetorical analyzis of the tour guides' presentations but only the analyzis of the tour groups' behaviors as an evaluation criteria of the effectiveness of tour guide's communication activities.

According to the structural model (Fig. 1) feedback (=information from the recipient to the sender) provides the assessment of actions undertaken by the message sender. It provides an assessment of a compliance of the results with the input objectives and allows to optimize the future guide's behaviors. The aspirated goals of the tour guide's presentation during the excursion are not measurable elements, such as conviction to an action or decision but the elements that are internalized by the participants of a tour, e.g., evoking an interest, sensibilization, attracting attention, raising awareness.

5 Interpretation of Results

The tour group's behaviors are less readable than the behaviors of the guide, who organizes and manages the communication process during an excursion. The tour group is a complex communication recipient that is composed of people who adopt the transmitted message in an individual way.

As a result of observations of tour groups' behaviors there were distinguished behaviors' categories that can be used as indicators of an extent to which they succeed in generating an intended listeners' attitude:

1. Proxemix behaviors.
2. Verbal interactions.
3. Visual behaviors of tour participants.
4. Unequivocally positive assessments.
5. Unequivocally negative assessments.

An interpretation of each behaviors illustrates the Table 2.

It is hard to attribute to the guide's activity a measurable assessment of its efficiency. It must be stressed that the subject of an evaluation are the narrative with all presentation aids chosen by the guide. Assuming that the effectiveness of presenter's communication activity is connected with reactions induced among the audience, the criteria given in Table 2 will help to systematize the assessment of these activities and, as intended, to optimize the subsequent actions during that and the next excursions.

6 Conclusions and Recommendations

Showing an interaction process during the sightseeing tours with an usage of the praxeological-systemic model of presentation highlights the elements of relationships between a guide, as the presenter, excursionists as the auditorium and the surroundings.

Due to the fact, that the goal of this paper was the specifying and the characterization of an evaluation of tour guides' communicational behaviors there were distinguished several indicators, that suggest beneficial or non beneficial behavior. The indicators are the criteria of an evaluation of tour guides' communication activities. An awareness of the indicators may allow the presenter to modify properly his behaviors by entering more beneficial behaviors and avoiding non beneficial behaviors. Thereby he obtains: gaining attention, concentration and interest of an audience.

The established intention of the research was realized. As a result the universal classification of an evaluation' indicators of tour guides' communication activities was created.

Table 2 An interpretation of tour groups' participants' behaviors

Behavior category	Behavior indicator	Behavior assessment
Proxemic behaviour	• Dispersed group of people	– Non beneficial; makes it difficult for the group to focus on the narrative
	• Group stands around the guide	– More beneficial than the previous one; people behind the guide are less capable of receiving the speech than the others
	• Group stands in front of the guide (possibly in semicircle)	– Beneficial; all participants are seeing the guide
Verbal interactions	• Silence	– May suggest that the group listens intently—beneficial – May suggest boredom and weariness—non beneficial (a type of the eye contact is pivotal to understanding the type of the silence)
	• Active verbal interactions	– Spontaneous—usually very beneficial (except for negative comments); may suggest that the group is curious or intrigued and that the presentation is well-oriented – Induced—beneficial if they are matched to the level of knowledge of the audience
Visual behaviors	• Eye contact with the speaker	– Beneficial
	• Following the object of a story	– Beneficial
	• Dull eyes	– Non beneficial
Unequivocally positive assessments	• Praises directed at the speaker	– Definitely beneficial
	• Adequate responses to the message—e.g., joke → laughter, bloody story → fright etc.	– Definitely beneficial
	• Applause	– Definitely beneficial
Unequivocally negative assessments	• Criticism against the speaker	– Definitely non beneficial
	• Adequate responses to the message—e.g., joke → no reaction, bloody story → no interest etc.	– Definitely non beneficial
	• The group is taking away the dominance the guide should have—e.g., shift towards other attractions or taking the lead by teachers who are reprimanding talking children etc.	– Definitely non beneficial

It is to be noticed that there have not been done any research works, that has been undertaking an issue of an evaluation of tour guides' communication behaviors'. In the face of the fact that exercising the guide's profession does not require any license, with an eye to increasing the quality of services there should be developed further detailed solutions regarding expected results in this profession.

The presented classification is a novel and can be used universally not only by tour guides and other tour services' workers but also by representants of other professions connected with public speaking (e.g., teachers, spokesmen, politicians, managers, clerics).

References

Act of August 29th, 1997 on tourist services, unified text. J Laws of 2004, No. 133, item 884

Almagor U (1985) A tourist's "vision quest" in an African game reserve. Ann Tour Res 12:31–47

Bogdan M, Łasiński G (2015) Retoryka w pracy rezydentów biur podróży. In: Załęska M (ed) Retoryka w komunikacji specjalistycznej. Polskie Towarzystwo Retoryczne, Warszawa

Bunten AC (2011) The paradox of gaze and resistance in native American cultural tourism: an Alaskan case study. In: Skinner J, Theodossopoulos D (eds) Great expectation: imagination and anticipation in tourism. Berghahn Books, New York, pp 61–81

Chronis A (2005) Constructing heritage at the Gettysburg storyscape. Ann Tour Res 32:386–406

Cialdini RB (2007) Wywieranie wpływu na ludzi. Teoria i praktyka. Gdańskie Wydawnictwo Psychologiczne, Gdańsk

Cohen E (1985) The tourist guide: the origins, structure and dynamics of a role. Ann Tour Res 12:5–29

Filipiak M (2003) Homo Communicans wprowadzenie do teorii masowego komunikowania. Wydawnictwo Uniwersytetu Marii Curie-Skłodowskiej, Lublin

Fine EC, Speer JH (1985) Tour guide performances as site secularization. Ann Tour Res 12:73–95

Geva A, Goldman A (1991) Satisfaction measurement in guided tours. Ann Tour Res 18:177–185

Gronbeck BE, German K, Ehninger D, Monroe AH (2001) Zasady komunikacji werbalnej. Zysk i S-ka Wydawnictwo, Poznań

Holloway J (1981) The guided tour: a sociological approach. Ann Tour Res 8:377–402

Howard J, Thwaites R, Smith B (2001) Investigating the roles of the indigenous tour guide. J Tour Stud 12:32–39

Hughes K (1991) Tourist satisfaction: a guided "cultural" tour in North Queensland. Aust Psychol 26:166–171

Katz S (1985) The Israeli teacher-guide: the emergence and perpetuation of a role. Ann Tour Res 12:49–72

Korolko M (1990) Sztuka retoryki. Przewodnik encyklopedyczny. Wiedza Powszechna, Warszawa

Łasiński G (2003) Sprawność zarządzania organizacją sportową. Studia i Mografie nr 70 AWF, Wrocław

Łasiński G, Wiejak K (2004) Identyfikacja procesów komunikowania w wybranych formach zachowań społecznych (ujęcie prakseologiczno-systemowe). Prace Naukowe Akademii Ekonomicznej im. Oskara Langego we Wrocławiu 1044:60–72

Leathers DG (2007) Komunikacja niewerbalna. Wydawnictwo Naukowe PWN, Warszawa

Lin Y-H, Ting Y-S, Hsu Y-L, Wu C-C (2014) Tourists' perceptions of tour guides in visiting Taiwan. Int J Organ Innov 6:192–202

Lugosi P, Bray J (2008) Tour guiding, organisational culture and learning: lessons from an entrepreneurial company. Int J Tour Res 10:467–479

Mancini M (2001) Conducting tours. Delmar Thomson Learning, Albany

McKean P (1976) Tourism, culture change and culture conservation. In: Banks DJ (ed) Ethnic identity in modern Southeast Asia. Mouton, The Hague, pp 237–247

Pearce PL (1982) The social psychology of tourist behavior. International series in experimental social psychology, vol 3. Pergamon, Oxford

Pond K (1993) The professional guide: dynamics of tour guiding. Van Nostrand Reinhold, New York

Reisinger Y, Steiner C (2006) Reconceptualising interpretation: the role of tour guides in authentic tourism. Curr Issues Serv 9:481–498

Ryan C, Dewar K (1995) Evaluating the communication process between interpreter and visitor. Tour Manag 16:295–303

Skibiński A (2012) Gregory Bateson i kontekstowa teoria komunikacji. Różnica, która czyni różnicę, i wzorzec, który łączy. In: Kulczycki E, Wendland M (eds) Komunikologia. Wydawnictwo Naukowe IF UAM, Poznań, pp 69–88

Szymanek K (2001) Sztuka argumentacji. Słownik terminologiczny. Wydawnictwo Naukowe PWN, Warszawa

Tarasiewicz B (2012) Mówię i śpiewam świadomie. Podręcznik do nauki emisji głosu. Towarzystwo Autorów i Wydawców Prac Naukowych Universitas, Kraków

Controlling in the Banking Industry: The Case of Romania

Mihaela Mocanu and Victoria Stanciu

Abstract Most companies are interested in increasing their efficiency. Controlling offers those some of the instruments needed for this purpose. A particular industry where controlling is vital is the banking industry. The paper's objective is to investigate controlling in the banking industry of Romania. More specifically, the author intended to analyze how controlling in banks has evolved in Romania over the past few years. The research design is empirical in nature. As proxy for the evolution of controlling in banks, the researcher uses the development of job announcements for the position of controller in the Romanian banking industry. The announcements are classified according to: language of the job announcement; geographical area of the employer; the controller's tasks; the controller's professional requirements; education and qualification; practical experience; personal attributes; age; salary etc. The results of the research consist in the current profile of a controller in a Romanian bank and in an overview of its evolution over time. The research fills in an important gap in the Romanian academic literature, which lacks studies on the topic of controlling, on one hand, and on the banking industry, on the other hand.

Keywords Controlling • Banking • Controller profile • Romania

1 Introduction

Nowadays, the management decision process is becoming increasingly complex, being characterized by shorter product life cycles, increasingly higher variety of products and services, rapid changes in technology, low predictability of customer preferences and a larger number of markets and distribution channels (Roman and Mocanu 2011; Ghinea and Ghinea 2015; Ţibulcă 2015). On this background, there is a stringent need for a superior management support system which can provide the required information and which can reconcile the planning, the control and the information supply for the company's welfare. Such tasks are carried out by controlling (Mocanu 2014). Despite the importance of controlling, it has been

M. Mocanu (✉) • V. Stanciu
University of Economic Studies, Bucharest, Romania
e-mail: mihaela.mocanu@cig.ase.ro; victoria.stanciu@cig.ase.ro

T. Dudycz et al. (eds.), *The Essence and Measurement of Organizational Efficiency*, Springer Proceedings in Business and Economics, DOI 10.1007/978-3-319-21139-8_13

given less attention in the Romanian academic literature. There are just a few doctoral theses (Sin (Cazacu) 2009; Oargă 2006a; Găman 2011) and a few empirical papers (Oargă 2006a, 2009), written on the topic of controlling. Researchers do however acknowledge the relevance and significance of controlling as managerial support function (Tulvinschi 2010). At international level, controlling is mostly given the proper consideration in the German-speaking area. The present paper fills in this gap in the literature. The objective of the research is to investigate controlling in the banking industry of Romania. The choice of the banking sector is first of all due to its importance for the economy. The foundation of a highly developed and capital-intensive economy is considered to be a sound banking industry. All economic areas can be significantly affected by disorders in the banking industry, as Hartmann-Wendels (2010) states. In no other sector are the interdependencies and the potential consequences of the individual corporate collapses as far-reaching and unforeseeable as in the financial sector (Ţurlea et al. 2010). The paper is structured as follows. First of all, the research design is presented. Secondly, a short review of the relevant literature is carried out by the author, in order to create the context of the result. Third of all, the results of the research are detailed. Last but not least, the fourth section debates the results and draws the conclusions of the study.

2 Research Design

The research design is empirical in nature. The research searched the archive of four job portals: www.bestjobs.ro, www.ejobs.ro, www.hipo.ro, and www.myjob.ro. These are the most known and accessed job portals in Romania. Their archive expands over the period 2011–2014, for www.bestjobs.ro and www.myjob.ro, 2005–2014 for www.ejobs.ro, and 2006–2014 for www.hipo.ro. Of interest for the research were only the jobs in the controlling department of banks, therefore, the keywords after which the search took place were: "controller" & "bank", "controlling" & "bank", "controlling" & "banca" (the Romanian word for "bank") and "controller" & "banca". Only the title of the job announcement, which contains the position and the employer, has been searched for these keywords.

The main hypotheses of this empirical research are the following:

H1: A controller should have at least 3 years of relevant experience.
H2: A candidate for a controller position should have a university degree in a subfield of economics.
H3: Good knowledge of financial reporting belongs to the controller's profile.
H4: Communication skills are considered to be essential for an employee in the controlling department.
H5: English skills are a must for a controller.

3 Literature Review

Controlling in companies nowadays is without any doubt extremely important. However, the academic literature on controlling in Romania is scarce. First of all, this lack of awareness on the importance of controlling is also shown by the small number of doctoral research on controlling. Only three theses have been identified on this topic: "From the monopolist controlling towards competitive controlling" (Bucharest, 2009)—thesis written by Sin (Cazacu) Violeta under the supervision of professor Dumitrana Mihaela; "Bank controlling, integrated concept of performance-oriented management" (Bucharest, 2011)—thesis written by Mihaela Mioara Găman under the supervision of professor Turlea Eugeniu; "Controlling—A Management Instrument. Controlling in Romania"—thesis published in 2006 by Valentina Oargă in Timisoara (Oargă 2006a).

Second of all, there is confusion about the term "controlling". Some papers such as Szabone Bohus (2010) or Cucui and Obreja (2009) use the word wrongly, instead of "control". The object of the current research is financial controlling, but there is a variety of other types of controlling, depending on the area of research. For instance, there are papers about project controlling (Buşe et al. 2008), marketing controlling (Pop and Pelău 2005; Pelau 2007) or quality controlling (Mateides and Pohančanik 2007; Krištofik 2007).

Last but not least, relevant papers are Oargă (2006b), Tulvinschi (2010), and Oargă (2009). The significance of controlling is argued by Oargă (2006b), whereas the author underlines the challenges faced by managers nowadays (uncertainty, competition, new technology etc.) and the support offered by controlling in dealing with such challenges. Tulvinschi (2010) considers that controlling is a must for enhancing business performance and for preserving the competitive advantage, as managerial support in strategic and operational decision making. Thus, the paper brings arguments in favor of the importance of controlling and also offers a clear explanation on the difference between controlling and control. According to Oargă (2009), controlling is currently practiced in over 90 % of German organizations, in more than 70 % of Austrian ones and in over a third of Hungarian ones. Accurate data are not available for Romania, but it is likely that less than 10 % of organizations use this management tool in their activity.

There are also empirical papers on controlling in Romania. Of particular interest is Oargă (2009), which is one of the few empirical researches on controlling in Romania. The research method used was the in-depth interviewing of Alexander & Son Timisoara's controller, in June 2009, over the course of five meetings. In this context, another relevant paper is Oargă (2006b), which is also practice-oriented. The research consists in a proposal for implementing controlling in a Romanian retail company.

In a modern approach, the research of Dascălu et al. (2007) aims to enlarge the conceptual framework of controlling, to identify several human resources controlling specific aspects and to ensure a set of indicators for human capital assessment and socio-controlling. On the contrary, a traditional perspective on controlling is given by Dumitrescu (2012). The author is in favor of "management by systems", according to which the economic entity is composed of several subsystems having determined actions and relationships between them, exchanges resources with its environment and is disturbed by internal and external factors.

In conclusion, few are the papers written in Romania on controlling in the financial field. Even fewer are the empirical ones. The present research aims at filling in this literature gap by adding valuable knowledge on the controlling function and on profile of the controller as professional in Romania.

4 Results

Following this data collection, a number of 63 job announcements resulted, out of which 54 different. This can be explained by the fact that some of the announcements were posted on more than one portal or they were re-posted at certain time intervals on the same website. These announcements have been published by 17 different banks, out of which 16 disclosed their name and just 1 recruited anonymously, through an agency. All the jobs were for the capital of Romania, Bucharest. The language of 69 % of the jobs was English, while the rest of 31 % of the announcements were in the national language—Romanian.

When posting a job, an employer has to choose the required experience level for that job, in order to ease up the search process for the candidate. There are mainly four possible levels: entry (0–3 years of experience), middle (3–5 years), senior (over 5 years) and executive. 12 out of 54 jobs are entry-level, 10 out 54 are middle-level, and 8 are senior-level, while for two no information is available. The other 22 jobs left are mixed: 7 are mentioned as both entry- and middle-level, 10 jobs are middle and senior-level, while 3 are senior and executive. In case of one job, the entry-level and the senior-level are mentioned, and in case of another one, all three levels (entry, middle, and senior) are present.

In case of five job announcements, nothing about the degree requirements was mentioned. However, according to all of the remaining 49 jobs, a university degree was mandatory. Interesting is the type of major required from the job applicants. 74 % of the employers wish to hire a graduate in economics. 18.5 % accept either a major in economic sciences or a major in technical sciences. 44 % mentioned a very precise major such as accounting, finance, or even computers and cybernetics. Nine job announcements (16 %) require a university degree, without mentioning anything about the major.

In case of 11 jobs, a further qualification besides the university degree is desired. Such qualifications are the following: ACCA (the Association of Chartered Certified Accountants), CFA (Chartered Financial Analyst), CIMA (Chartered Institute of Management Accountants), MBA (Master of Business Administration), CNMV (Comisia Natională a Valorilor Mobiliare—National Securities Commission). In 8 out of 11 cases, such a qualification is only a plus, and not a must.

More than 93 % of the job announcements include among the requirements English language skills. 65 % of these jobs require specifically advanced English skills. 7 % say nothing about language skills, but as they are written in English, the requirement is in our opinion, somehow intrinsic. Some announcements mention other languages as being a plus if known by the candidate, respectively Hungarian, French and German. Two jobs explicitly request for business English skills.

Solid computer skills are also part of the controller profile. A majority of 87 % of the jobs require computer skills. The most desired software package to be used by the controller is Microsoft Office (63 %), whereas from this package Excel (50 %), followed by Access (30 %) are considered by employers to be most important. The use of SAP is a plus in case of 13 % of the job offers. Less than a third of the announcement also mention other computer skills, such as: skills in the use of IBM Cognos Powerplay, Hyperion, GPM, Reuters Xtra, or the use of real estate database systems, Business Intelligence tools, and other (unspecified) reporting software.

Regarding the technical knowledge/skills, 10 % of the jobs require "controlling know-how", in general. However, about a third of the job announcements are more specific, requesting International Financial Reporting Standards knowledge. The same is also true for knowledge of the Romanian Accounting Standards (RAS), which is mandatory for a third of the jobs. The ability to convert financial statements from RAS to IFRS is also included in this category of skills. Additionally, as the sample investigated in the present research consists only in jobs posted by banks, another requirement is that the candidates are familiar with the legislation typical for the banking sector. Around a fifth of the announcements (more specifically, 28 %) mention this.

Strong analytical skills are without any doubt part of the controller profile in Romanian banks, being mentioned in more than half (namely 69 %) of the announcements. The ability to make proper decisions in a timely manner is appreciated by 12 % of the employers in the sample. Strong organizational skills are valued by 63 % of the banks. They expect that the controller is able to work under pressure and has the capacity to plan, organize, prioritize, and control workloads in order to meet tight deadlines.

As expected, soft skills are not forgotten when looking for the ideal candidate in a controlling position. Only 17 % of the job announcements do not include soft skills. Highly appreciated are the communication skills, both written and verbal, as well as the team spirit. The following wording is used for soft skills considered to be essential in controlling: "strong interpersonal skills", "effective communication", "positive attitude", "ability to promote communications and teamwork that result in a cohesive and collegial work team", "ability to foster a cooperative work environment", "negotiation skills", "conflict solving abilities", "sociable person", "conviction power" etc. Still, the top skills are communication skills (54 % of the jobs) and the ability to work in a team (59 % of the positions).

Surprisingly, there are job postings that explicitly mention the expectation of employers regarding the character of their future employees. Integrity and responsibility, besides the sense of duty, the professionalism, the reliability, are highly valued. Integrity is clearly included in 9 (17 %) job announcements, while responsibility—in slightly more than a fifth (in 15 announcements). Some actually mention the code of ethics of the employees, or the statement regarding the zero tolerance to fraud and illegal acts. However, more than half (65 %) do not include any reference on the candidate's character.

According to the author's expectations, no job announcement mentions anything about sex, salary or age.

5 Discussions and Conclusions

All in all, the majority of the hypotheses have been confirmed. Regarding hypothesis H1, according to which a controller should have at least 3 years of relevant experience, it was shown that 40 out of 54 jobs, namely 74 % are not entry-level, but require an experience of over 3 years.

Secondly, the author postulated that a candidate for a controller position should have a university degree in a subfield of economics. This hypothesis was also validated. 49 jobs mention the requirement of a university degree and two thirds (namely 74 %) of the employers specifically want an economist.

The third hypothesis which states that good knowledge of financial reporting belongs to the controller's profile was also confirmed by the empirical research. However, the percentage of banks that explicitly include this in the job announcements is rather law. Only a third of the jobs need IFRS knowledge and a third of the total number of announcements require RAS knowledge, whereas 20 % require both.

According to the international trend in controlling and, most specifically, in the accounting profession, soft skills are not to be ignored. The author postulated that communication skills are considered to be essential for an employee in the controlling department. Indeed, more than half (54 %) of the jobs posted mention good and even excellent communication skills, both written and verbal.

Fifth, the research was also shown that English skills are a must for a controller. More than 93 % of sample jobs mention English skills among the job requirements English. The remaining 7 % have no note on language skills, but as they are written in English, the requirement is implied.

Acknowledgement This work was cofinanced from the European Social Fund through Sectoral Operational Programme Human Resources Development 2007–2013, project number POSDRU/159/1.5/S/142115 "Performance and excellence in doctoral and postdoctoral research in Romanian economics science domain".

References

Buşe F, Simionescu A, Buşe GF (2008) The fundamentation of taking decisions and coordinating for controlling in projects management. Rev Manag Econ Eng 7(2):25–31

Cucui G, Obreja C (2009) Controlling, an indispensable activity for performance management. Sect Sic Econ 29:32–37

Dascălu C, Dumitrana M, Caraiani C (2007) Controlul de gestiune si gestiunea resurselor umane. J Account Manag Inf Syst 19:42–58

Dumitrescu A (2012) Improving public sector performance by strengthening the relationship between audit and accounting. Theor Appl Econ 19(11):85–90

Găman MM (2011) Controlling bancar, concept integrat de conducere orientată spre obţinerea de performanţă. Dissertation, Bucharest University of Economic Studies

Ghinea VM, Ghinea M (2015) Organizational culture dynamics. Preamble. Quality—access to success 16(144):69–72

Hartmann-Wendels T (2010) Regulierung von Leasing- und Factoringunternehmen. Zeitschrift für Bankrecht und Bankwirtschaft 2:99

Krištofik P (2007) Cost aspects of total quality management. Studia Universitatis, "Vasile Goldis" Arad. Seria Stiinte Economice I(17):77–86

Mateides A, Pohančanik P (2007) Some aspects of quality controlling. Studia Universitatis, "Vasile Goldis" Arad. Econ Sci I(17):187–194

Mocanu M (2014) Towards a definition of controlling. Studies and scientific researches. Econ Ed 20:62–66

Oargă V (2006a) Controlling—a management instrument. Controlling in Romania. Augusta & Artpress Publishing House, Timişoara

Oargă V (2006b) Proposal of controlling implementation in a Romanian company. Theor Appl Econ 10(505):61–66

Oargă V (2009) Controlling as a unit of production planning and control. Romanian case studies. Rom Econ J 34(4):61–84

Pelau C (2007) Structuri organizatorice la nivel de intreprindere pentru implementarea marketing-controllingului. Manag Mark 1:133–142

Pop NA, Pelău C (2005) Elemente de controlling în marketingul relaţional—metode de evaluare a clienţilor. Rev Manag Econ Eng 4(3):43–52

Roman C, Mocanu M (2011) Current challenges generated by the "management approach" (II). Financ Audit 7:27–32

Sin (Cazacu) V (2009) De la controlling-ul monopolist la cel concurenţial. Dissertation, Bucharest University of Economic Studies

Szabone Bohus M (2010) The reliability of accounting information. Studia Universitatis, "Vasile Goldis" Arad. Econ Sci I:48–52

Tulvinschi M (2010) Relevant costs for decision in an effective controlling system. Theor Appl Econ 5(546):49–58

Ţurlea E, Mocanu M, Radu C (2010) Corporate governance in the banking industry. J Account Manag Inf Syst 3(9):379–402

Ţibulcă IL (2015) How do fiscal policy decisions influence business confidence? Case study: the manufacturing sector. J East Eur Res Bus Econ 2015:1–8

The Use of Fuzzy Logic in the Enterprises Business Efficiency Assessment

Tomasz L. Nawrocki

Abstract The article presents a model proposal for enterprises business efficiency assessment based on fuzzy logic. The main concept of proposed solution is based on one of so called the model system of inequalities variants, embracing changes in the scope of total assets and basic results categories of income statement. The main reason for developing this model was to fulfil the gap in the scope of synthetic measure of enterprises business efficiency, taking into account variety of sources shaping the final net result.

Keywords Enterprises efficiency • Model system of inequalities • Fuzzy logic • Financial results

1 Introduction

Business efficiency of enterprises is one of the main problems undertaken by economics and management studies. It has a timeless character and is always important (Jonek-Kowalska 2012) because it provides entrepreneurs with the possibility to survive, what is the key condition to realize other objectives such as growth, development, maximizing owners benefits or building market value. In the literature one can find different definitions and interpretations for efficiency term (Kozuń-Cieślak 2013), but generally it is considered from two perspectives: economic and organizational. The first of them is the result of V. Pareto theory of efficient resources allocation development (Samuelson and Nordhaus 1995), which comes down the efficiency to the relation effects-expenditures needed in order to be achieved. Efficiency, defined in this way is widely used in economics, enterprises economics and accounting and such a view point is adopted later in the discussion. The second approach to efficiency, which is considered on the basis of organization and management theory, is related to the praxeological approach. Efficiency, in this case, is treated as a broad category relating to positive results and attributes of the

T.L. Nawrocki, Ph.D. Eng. (✉)
Faculty of Organization and Management, Institute of Economics and Informatics, Silesian University of Technology, ul. Roosevelta 26-28, 41-800, Zabrze, Poland
e-mail: tomasz.nawrocki@polsl.pl

T. Dudycz et al. (eds.), *The Essence and Measurement of Organizational Efficiency*, Springer Proceedings in Business and Economics, DOI 10.1007/978-3-319-21139-8_14

organization (Pszczołowski 1977), which may be assessed using a variety of criteria, not only financial.

The complexity of objective category for the company and the consequent variety of criteria to evaluate its efficiency, make that similarly to the efficiency alone the issue of its measurement and evaluation has multi-faceted and ambiguous character. For this reason the measurement of enterprises efficiency is one of the most dynamically developing scientific concepts in the recent decades (Skrzypek 2002). Commonly used methods for measuring efficiency are based mainly on three approaches: *indicative* (constructing relations between different financial values; e.g. ROA—*Return on Assets*, ROE—*Return on Equity*), *parametric* (based on known in microeconomic theory production function, which defines technical relation between expenditures and production; methods: SFA—*Stochastic Frontier Approach*, TFA—*Thick Frontier Approach*, DFA—*Distribution Free Approach*), *nonparametric* (using linear programming procedure while disregarding the impact of random factor on the efficiency of objects and potential measurement errors, as well as the analysis of the relation between expenditures and final effects, methods: DEA—*Data Envelopment Analysis*, FDH—*Free Disposal Hull*) (Szymańska 2010).

In this article, the discussion on the measurement of enterprises efficiency focuses on the indicative approach, which due to the ease and wide application has gained great popularity in both business practice and scientific research. In this approach we can basically highlight three groups of indicators: *accounting* (treating efficiency as the relation between incomes and costs and obtained by the enterprise result values to other economic values), *financial* (based on the financial flows as a key assessment parameter) and *market* (concentrating on the company's shareholders point of view), identifying for each of these indicators absolute or relative (relational) measures (Jaki 2012; Copeland et al. 1990; Michalak 2012). Moreover, enterprises efficiency can also be viewed from the different time perspective. In such case on one hand we deal with *dynamic efficiency*, which regards the ability to growth and development in the long term perspective, and *static efficiency*, which focuses on avoiding wastage of possessed resources and their optimal allocation (Kozuń-Cieślak 2013).

Regarding the above outlined issues related to the problems of measuring and evaluating the enterprises efficiency, in the indicative approach we should also pay attention to some of its shortcomings and limitations. Although, this approach offers a wide range of different types of enterprises efficiency measures, it is difficult to clearly identify their importance from the point of view of an overall (synthetic) assessment—on one hand, we cannot consider all measures as equally important, on the other hand we cannot identify which one is the least and the most important. In addition, one of the main drawbacks of this approach is the risk of distortion of the enterprises efficiency measurement as a result of one-off events (e.g. revaluation of assets, profits or losses from the investments) which quite often can distort different result categories, which are the most frequent base for calculating efficiency results, especially including profitability. Because of the above, the main objective of this paper is to elaborate and empirically verify, based on the fuzzy logic and indicator approach, model of enterprise business efficiency assessment which will allow to obtain synthetic result of this issue, while limiting the impact of one-off events. Additionally, with respect to the division of the efficiency into static and dynamic, it has been assumed in the model, that the final result will be decided by both, the level of respective indicators as well as their changes in time according to model system of inequalities, what should ensure greater objectivity of such obtained assessment.

2 Economic Efficiency and Management Rationality

Economic efficiency is a way of measuring the efficiency and usefulness of a given economic activity, expressed by comparing the values of obtained effects (production, sales, value added, profit) to the expenditure factors used to obtain them (employment, assets, raw materials, capital). Within this approach the efficiency is often understood as the economic effectiveness of an organization meaning the skilful use of determined resources within the given time, the number of products and services ensuring the satisfaction of customer needs where the effectiveness must be characterized by usefulness and quickness of operation. Presenting effectiveness as a quantity category by relation between effects and expenditures means, that effectiveness of enterprise activities, understood as the ability to create the desired effects, is an important factor and the necessary condition for the achievement and increasing efficiency. If the actions undertaken by the enterprise are not effective that means that they do not provide expected results, thus are inefficient. At the same time effectiveness alone is not the only factor deciding about efficiency of enterprises operation because even with high operations effectiveness their efficiency may run at a low level or can turn out to be inefficient way of conducting business on the market. It can be said, that the effectiveness of operation is translated into effects and the efficiency of operations depends on the effects, which are closely linked to the incurred expenditures in order to obtain them (Skrzypek 2012).

The concept of efficiency is closely linked to the concept of rational management, which in its theory takes into account two formulas: productivity and savings. Productivity formula assumes achieving maximum results at constant specific expenditures. Savings formula assumes obtaining certain effects, while aiming at minimizing the costs (Matwiejczuk 2006).

Basically enterprise business operation, under certain conditions, may have double character—the extensive management or intensive management. In the first case, the growth of business effects (revenues, profits) is achieved by increasing engagement of resources (tangible assets, employees), both in terms of quantity/value and time. The second of the identified types of management is based on achieving the growth in business operation per unit of engaged resources as a result of releasing internal reserves, in particular through effective technical and organizational progress. This increase is associated with higher labor productivity with expenditure-saving character, better utilization of economic resources and the increase in profitability (Bednarski 2001). Based on the characteristics of the two above-mentioned types of management it is not difficult to conclude, that the requirements of rational economic activity are better met by intensive management. Thus, companies should strive to improve their economic results by maximizing the impact of intensive factors and limiting the impact of extensive factors. At the same time, extensive management can be considered as reasonable only in case when the enterprise reaches certain barrier in the scope of intensive development opportunities, where further growth can be obtained only by expanding present operation scale (Bednarski 1979).

In this context it is worth to present one of the easiest and very useful possibilities to assess the quality of enterprise resource management, which can be run using a comparative analysis based on the quantitative indicators model system of inequalities (Bednarski 2001). This approach is the basis for the proposed later in this article concept of enterprises efficiency assessment fuzzy model.

In most general terms, in this method it is essential to achieve inequality dynamics of such quantitative indicators as equity and net profit:

$$i_E < i_{NP}, \tag{1}$$

where:

i_{EC}—growth index of equity,
i_{NP}—growth index of net profit (loss).

If this inequality is valid, a company conducting business activity efficiently engages own and outside capital, thus achieving higher profitability per unit of engaged equity. This situation indicates simultaneously, that the company complies with the principle of striving for optimal combination of production factors and the principle of profitable activity. These principles highlight, that the business operation of the enterprise should strive to achieve the best effects as a result of using production factors. As the final result of the enterprises operation is their net financial result, which is the basic source of their future development, it is justified to point out, that this category should be maximized. However, in this case it is not about simple growth of net profit compared to the net profit from the previous period, but it is about the relation of these quantities in relation to the equity used in both abovementioned periods by the enterprise. Due to the profitability of engaged equity we can state if the operational business was run efficiently and contributed to the increase of enterprise value or if it does not.

As the equity owned by the enterprise may be allocated in assets (fixed and current assets) and personal assets (number of employees in the enterprise), and the result of engaging equity in these resources is not only net profit but also, perhaps most of all, production and revenues from sales, the above mentioned inequality can be developed to the following form:

$$i_{Em} < i_A < i_{SR} < i_{NP}, \tag{2}$$

where:

i_{Em}—growth index of employment,
i_A—growth index of assets,
i_{SR}—growth index of sales revenues,
i_{NP}—growth index of net profit (loss).

If the specified model system of quantitative indicators dynamics is calculated for the comparable period, the higher assets dynamism than employment ($i_E < i_A$) shows that enterprise has growing fixed and tangible assets which are at the disposal of enterprise employees giving the opportunity to expand its business activity. Further analyzing this inequality model, higher dynamism of revenues from sales than assets ($i_A < i_{SR}$) shows the higher productivity of engaged assets and further efficient technical as well as organizational improvements. Higher net profit dynamism than revenues ($i_{SR} < i_{NP}$) shows the higher profitability of the enterprise's sales.

If in a given period the enterprise shows dynamism indexes of employment, assets and production in line with the presented system of inequalities, it can be said that it implements intensive management option and uses opportunities, which are given by technical and organizational progress.

In addition, developing the above model system of inequalities, we can assess the relation between relative changes of sales revenues and financial results at different levels of income statement:

$$i_{SR} < i_{GPS} < i_{NPS} < i_{PO} < i_{GP} < i_{NP}, \tag{3}$$

where:

i_{SR}—growth index of sales revenues,
i_{GPS}—growth index of gross profit (loss) on sales,
i_{PS}—growth index of net profit (loss) on sales,
i_{PO}—growth index of profit (loss) from operational activity,
i_{GP}—growth index of gross profit (loss),
i_{NP}—growth index of net profit (loss).

Through this analysis one can find out if the final financial result of the enterprise is actually determined by its core business, or rather by the operations related to the other operational activity or financial activity, which are often one-off events.

In business practice, it is very difficult to keep all of the above mentioned relations between indicators. However, the more real systems of inequalities are similar to those postulated, the better should be assessed the economic and financial situation of audited entity and its efficiency.

Considered in the context of the above inequalities systems quantitative indicators can also provide a basis for the construction of various relation indicators, informing about achieving a level of efficiency in the various fields of activity in a given enterprise:

$$\mathrm{PA} = \mathrm{SR}/\mathrm{A} - \text{productivity of assets components} \quad (4)$$

$$\mathrm{GPM} = \mathrm{GPS}/\mathrm{SR} - \text{gross profit margin on sales} \quad (5)$$

$$\mathrm{NPM} = \mathrm{NPS}/\mathrm{SR} - \text{net profit margin on sales} \quad (6)$$

$$\mathrm{OPS} = \mathrm{PO}/\mathrm{SR} - \text{operational profitability of sales} \quad (7)$$

$$\mathrm{GSP} = \mathrm{GP}/\mathrm{SR} - \text{gross sales profitability} \quad (8)$$

$$\mathrm{NSP} = \mathrm{NP}/\mathrm{SR} - \text{net sales profitability} \quad (9)$$

Of course, in case of each of the above relations it is more favorable if they have higher values, but only the fulfillment of previously identified model systems of quantitative indicators inequalities guarantees the evidence of their progression.

3 The Concept of Enterprises Business Efficiency Assessment Fuzzy Model

3.1 *Reasons for Model Development*

Although presented in the previous section possibilities to assess the efficiency of enterprises based on an indicative approach are relatively easy in practical application and provide quite extensive understanding of the issue, one can also point out some of its shortcomings. In particular we should pay attention to the issue regarding the lack of synthetic measure, which would provide a resultant for the considered model systems of inequalities or quality relations. Differences in the dynamics of individual indicators and financial relations even with not particularly large number of analyzed enterprises is usually significant, thus, considering many indicators, significantly hinders to rank entities from the most effective to the least effective. In addition, we must remember about the generally negative dependency which occurs between the dynamics of respective quality (relation) indicators changes and their value level. In case of high profitability or productivity indicators their further significant improvement in the future periods might not be possible because of reaching by the enterprise certain efficiency barrier within the given model of business. Low profitability and productivity indicators may be subject to significant improvement by gradually eliminating rooted within the enterprise imperfections, which are less onerous to correct. A separate, equally important issue in the context of the indicator approach to assess the efficiency of enterprises operations is the quality of financial result, in particular those reported in the later result levels of income statement. The point here is to what extent these results are shaped by the core business of the enterprise, and to what extent by one-off events. In the analysis of the enterprises financial condition a great importance is attached to the indicators based on such categories as operating result (EBIT) and net profit, while these values may be (and often are) subject to a significant distortion. These distortions typically involve other operating activities (e.g. updating the value of assets components), financial operation (e.g. results on completed investments) or taking into account tax burdens for the given period (changes in deferred tax). Thus, focusing on the quantities uncritically reported in the enterprises financial statements we can relatively easy make the omission mistake, which will skew the result of the efficiency assessment and may lead to a wrong decision.

The above imperfections in indicative approach, combined with the possibilities offered by the fuzzy sets theory are the reasons to elaborate basic assumptions of enterprise efficiency assessment fuzzy model, which is presented and practically verified in the further part of this article.

The model has the following characteristics, which partially reduce the shortcomings outlined above:

- Combination of analytical and synthetic evaluation of enterprises business efficiency, achieved through the use of partial criteria, then aggregated to more general assessments
- Combination of quantitative and descriptive approach to the efficiency assessment, manifested in the quantitative dimension used to measure the efficiency indicators and descriptive way to determine their diversity (the use of descriptive characteristics of the individual criteria: low/medium/high; negative/neutral/positive)
- The use in evaluation process data contained in public sources of information—companies financial statements
- Taking into account in the enterprise efficiency assessment both: levels of used measures and their change in time (connecting static and dynamic approach for measuring efficiency)
- Cleaning efficiency assessments (final and intermediate) from the impact of one-off events, which translates into their higher quality and greater objectivity

3.2 Basic Assumptions and Criteria for Assessing the Enterprises Business Efficiency in the Proposed Model

As noted earlier, the basis for the development of this enterprise business efficiency assessment model was a model system of quantitative indicators inequalities—one of the possibilities within the indicative approach to efficiency assessment.

Application of fuzzy sets for detailed calculations for assessing enterprises efficiency entails the construction of the fuzzy model, based on expert knowledge. Information necessary to achieve this goal must be obtained through the interview questionnaire, or in case, where the model developer has the knowledge in the subject of analysis, one can develop his own model. In this case, the second option was chosen.

As the basic source of information in evaluating the enterprises business efficiency was accepted public information disclosed by the enterprises in their financial reports, especially in the income statement.

The detailed criteria for assessing the efficiency for the elaborated model were selected, taking into account two model systems of quantitative indicators inequalities and resulting from them financial relations as well as the need to purify respective resulting categories from one-off events. As a result, on the way to a final enterprises efficiency assessment, there were isolated intermediate assessments, regarding another resulting areas in income statement, starting from efficiency on core business level, through efficiency on the basic activity, operational, gross result and on net profit level ending.

In assessing the efficiency of core business productivity of assets and gross margin on sales were taken into account. Within these two areas there were identified two assessment categories—the value level of these measures on a given moment and their percentage change in relation to the base period. In case of further efficiency assessments there were taken into account efficiency assessment from an earlier level and sales profitability regarding analyzed result level in income statement, which is a resultant of a given efficiency measure and its percentage change. And so, in case of the next efficiency of basic activity assessment, it was included on one hand efficiency at core business level and on the other hand assessment regarding net margin on sales, which is the result of the value level of this margin and its percentage change relative to the base period.

Similarly there was foreseen obtaining efficiency ratings on further resulting levels, but due to the possible impact of one-off events, in relation to percentage changes of respective profitability measures there was also assumed additional adjustment with the impact of other operations (efficiency at operational level and gross profit) or deferred tax (efficiency at the net profit). The adjustment takes into account both the value of this result as well as the value change in comparison to the base period, referring these quantities to the absolute value (module) of the resultant category presented at previous result level in income statement (for the result from remaining operations the point of reference was the net profit (loss) on sale; for the result on financial operations the point of reference was the operational profit (loss) and for the deferred tax gross profit (loss). This procedure allows an objective assessment of one-off events impact for respective efficiency measures, regardless of their differences in value, resulting from the size of enterprise's activities or the dynamics of change.

The overall structure of the proposed enterprise business efficiency assessment model is shown in Fig. 1. It should be noted, that further efficiency assessments in proposed solution, are growing, cumulatively, which results directly from the model construction. Thus, the assessments do not apply only to a particular segment of the enterprise's activity (the exception is only the first efficiency assessment relating strictly to the area of core business), but combine it with the observations obtained for the previous areas. Because of that, the most desirable situation is the

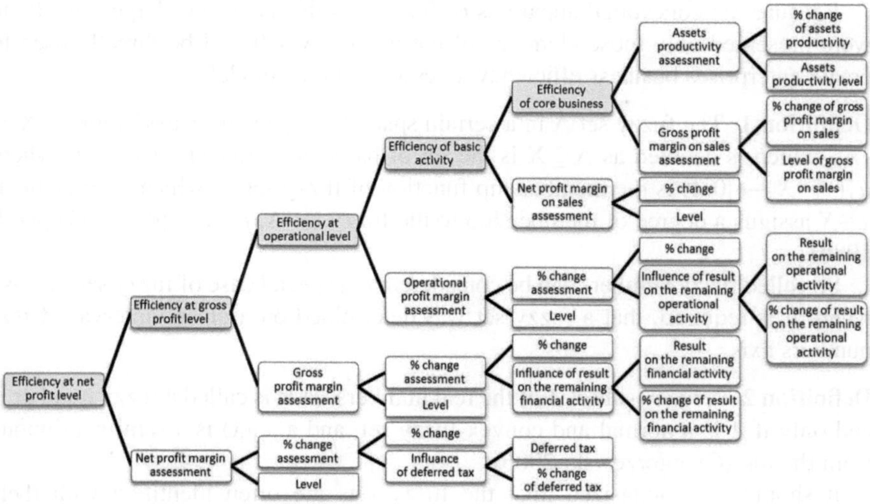

Fig. 1 The overall structure of the proposed enterprises business efficiency assessment model

one when demonstrated at the very beginning high assessment of efficiency in the core business area is maintained at the next assessment levels, all the way to the final assessment.

3.3 The Basic Concepts of Fuzzy Sets Theory

Presentation of the enterprises business efficiency assessment fuzzy model building process requires discussing the basis of the fuzzy sets theory.

The stimulus for the research development on the theory and practical application of approximate inference methods, including fuzzy sets, were difficulties with the use of classical set theory to describe complex or poorly defined concepts. The first person to point that out was Lotfi A. Zadeh, the creator of fuzzy sets theory (Zadeh 1965).

In the classical set theory the transition from full membership of the element to its total non-membership is a leap (either the element belongs to the set or it does not) and therefore presenting vague concepts with this type of sets raises a number of problems. In fuzzy sets theory it is assumed, however, that an element may partly belong to a given set, and at the same time to its complement, and therefore there does not apply the law of the excluded center. In the fuzzy sets transition from membership to a set to non-membership to a set is progressive (this progressive change is expressed by the so-called membership function), thus this concept allows to define vague notions and imprecise quantities.

Because the conceptual apparatus of fuzzy sets theory is very large, thus there were presented only those elements of the theory, which will be directly used to create enterprises business efficiency assessment fuzzy model.

Definition 1 The fuzzy set A in a certain space (the space of consideration), X = {x}, which is denoted as A ⊆ X is the set of pairs: $A = \{(\mu_A(x), x)\}$, $x \in X$, where $\mu_A(x) : X \rightarrow [0, 1]$ is the membership function of fuzzy set A, which each element $x \in X$ assigns a degree of membership to the fuzzy set A, $\mu_A(x) \in [0, 1]$ (Kacprzyk 1986).

So called fuzzy numbers can be considered as a special case of fuzzy sets in case where it is required, that a fuzzy set was determined on a closed interval of real numbers axis.

Definition 2 A fuzzy subset A of the real numbers set R is called a fuzzy number if and only if A is a normal and convex fuzzy set, and a $\mu_A(x)$ is a semi-continuous from the top (Grzegorzewski 2006).

It should be emphasized, that the fuzzy sets are often identified with their membership functions, which have their direct graphic interpretation (Piegat 2003). The choice of these functions depends primarily on the amount of information about the system being modeled, as well as the quality of the model tuning methods, that are available for modeling person. Among all types of membership functions the greatest simplicity and versatility of application can be found in polygonal functions (triangular or trapezoidal), because they require a small amount of information and their values at intermediate points can be determined by using a simple linear interpolation method.

Another important concept of fuzzy logic is a linguistic variable.

Definition 3 The definition of linguistic variable is fully characterized by the quintuple: (H, T, U, G, M), where X is the name of the variable, T is the set of terms of X, U is the universe of discourse, G is a syntactic rule for generating the name of the terms, and M is a semantic rule for associating each term with its meaning, that is, a fuzzy set defined on U (Łachwa 2001).

Although the mathematical formalism of linguistic variable is relatively complicated, its intuitive sense is simple—linguistic variable is the one which values are not numbers, but sentences in a specific language, equated in semantic sense with specific fuzzy sets. For example, linguistic variable called "profitability of equity" may take as values fuzzy sets representing following features: high, medium, low, so quality, rather than quantity features.

The basic mean which allows to present dependencies between adopted linguistic variables are fuzzy conditional sentences (Bartkiewicz 2000):

$$\text{IF } x \text{ is } A \text{ THEN } y \text{ is } B, \tag{10}$$

where the expression "x is A" is called the "predecessor", which contains a set of conditions (rules), and the expression "y is B" means "successor" or conclusion.

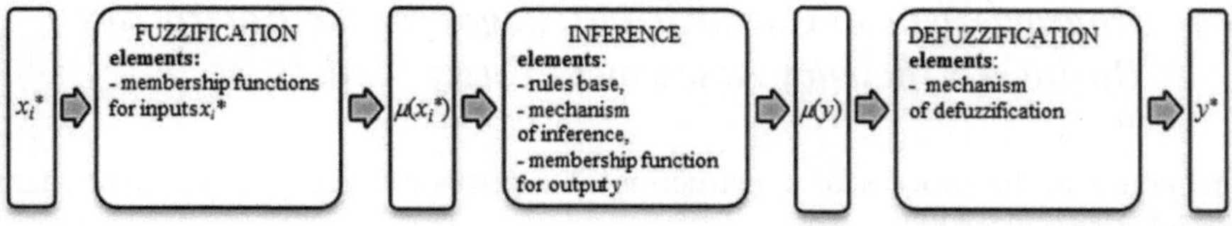

Fig. 2 General scheme of fuzzy model

Predecessor of the rule can also have the character of complex sentence, where generally it is accepted, that it is a conjunction of a certain fuzzy sentences (Bartkiewicz 2000):

$$\text{IF } x_1 \text{ is } A_1 \text{ AND} \ldots \text{AND } x_m \text{ is } A_m \text{ THEN } y \text{ is } B. \tag{11}$$

Typically, the relation between the same variables is described not by a single rule, but by so called rules bank (base) of form (Bartkiewicz 2000):

$$\begin{aligned} &\mathrm{R}_1 : \text{IF } x_1 \text{ is } A_1^1 \text{ AND} \ldots \text{AND } x_m \text{ is } A_m^1 \text{ THEN } y \text{ is } B^1 \\ &\mathrm{R}_\mathrm{m} : \text{IF } x_1 \text{ is } A_1^K \text{ AND} \ldots \text{AND } x_m \text{ is } A_m^K \text{ THEN } y \text{ is } B^K \end{aligned} \tag{12}$$

Rules bank is treated in a fuzzy inference process as a whole—a subsystem, which cumulative effects are subjected to further processing. In inference process for data inputs are activated all the rules contained in the bank, and the results of their actions are then merged into the resulting fuzzy set, which is the value of the y variable. The given rules bank may describe the relation between the input and output of the entire system, or it may be part of a more complex hierarchical structure.

The equivalent models of real systems in fuzzy logic are so called fuzzy models. The most important and most widely used in practice type of fuzzy model is Mamdani model, which is a set of rules, each of which defines one fuzzy point of space (Piegat 2003). A typical fuzzy model consists of three modules: fuzzification, inference and defuzzification (Fig. 2).

To the inputs of fuzzy model the source data x_i^* is introduced. In FUZZIFICATION module fuzzification operation is carried out—the membership degrees of each input data to respective fuzzy sets are calculated. Then, in the INFERENCE module, basing on the input membership degrees $\mu(x_i^*)$ and previously developed rules bank, so called resulting membership function $\mu(y)$ of the model output is calculated. Since this function has usually diffused form, what makes interpretation of the final results difficult, in many cases it is necessary to change it into exact value y^*. This operation is carried out within DEFUZZIFICATION module.

3.4 Characteristic of Construction Stages for the Enterprises Business Efficiency Assessment Fuzzy Model

Procedure in the process of constructing enterprises efficiency assessment fuzzy model is presented below.

Stage 1 Gathering input data for the model.

According with the adopted assumptions, the basic criteria for assessing business efficiency in proposed solution, are based entirely on public data, which may be obtained by analyzing the content of financial statements.

Stage 2 Determination for the needs of "fuzzification" module the form of fuzzy sets for respective input variables, determination for these variables so called basic terms set and the division of their value spaces.

Because of similarities in the expression in natural language assessments of individual variables, for the purpose of this fuzzy model it is proposed to adopt for input variables two dictionaries of linguistic values and division of these variables values spaces into three fuzzy sets with the names:{low, medium, high} or {negative, neutral, positive}. In case of output variables value space, in order to facilitate the assignment of ratings depending on the situation diversity, it is proposed to divide it into five fuzzy sets named: {low, low-medium, medium, medium-high, high}.

Moreover, because of the ease of use and great versatility, it is recommended to adopt the triangular shape of the membership function for each fuzzy set for both input variables $\mu(x)$ and output $\mu(y)$—Fig. 3.

It should be noted that the variables of fuzzy model can be divided into two groups. The first group consists of input variables, the values of which result directly from the enterprises financial statements and depending on the nature of a given variable are in the range from 0 (or $-\infty$) to $+\infty$. The second group consists of variables, which are the result of fuzzy inference and they take values between 0 and 1. Therefore, in case of the first group of variables, values describing the individual fuzzy sets (a, b, c), should be determined based on consultation with experts or if the model constructor has the knowledge, arbitrarily. In this case, it was decided for the second of these options, assuming even distribution of variable

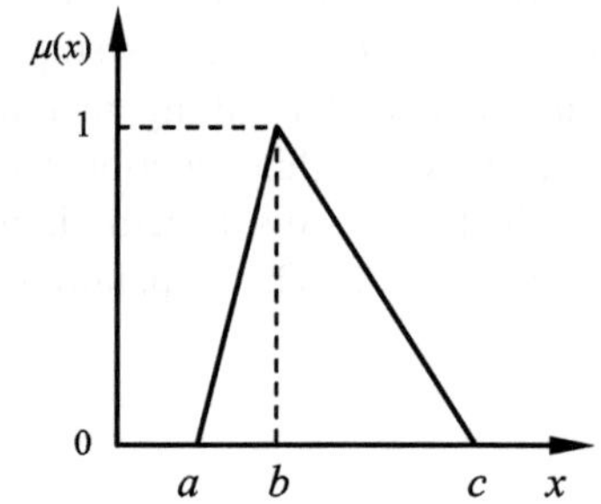

Fig. 3 Triangular fuzzy set

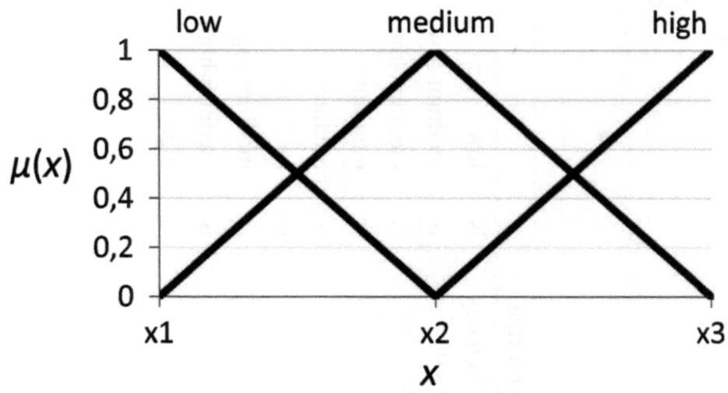

Fig. 4 The general form of the input variables membership function to distinguished fuzzy sets

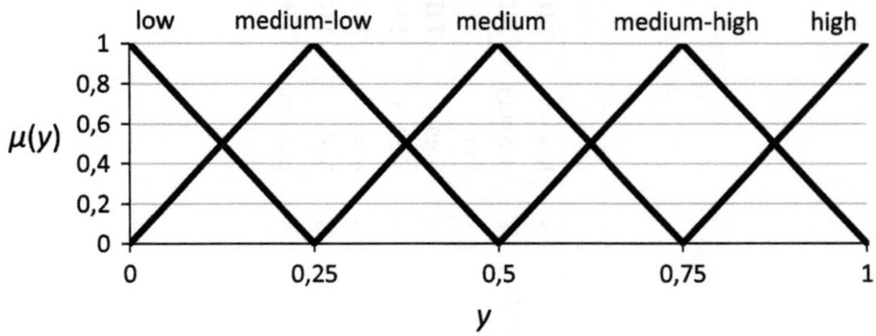

Fig. 5 The output variables membership function to distinguished fuzzy sets

value space using triangular fuzzy sets, but in relation to the input variables their descriptive values ($x1$, $x2$, $x3$) are determined based on the distribution of each variable in the context of the industry and in case of percentage change variables based on the situation shown by model systems of inequalities (Figs. 4 and 5).

The final fuzzification of input variables to the model was performed using simple linear interpolation method (Bartkiewicz 2000).

Stage 3 Creating for the needs of "inference" module relevant rules bases, determining the mechanism of inference and defining output membership function of the model.

Specific rules bases in the proposed solution were developed independently based on collected, over several years, experience in the course of research. As a part of the model one can distinguished 17 bases of rules IF-THEN (each base consists of 9 rules). Due to large space, that would take all of 17 bases, below it was presented sample rules base for assessing the core business efficiency (Table 1).

In order to carry fuzzy inference, to implement conjunction conditions in individual rules (calculating veracity degrees of predecessors), it is proposed to apply the operation PROD given in the formula (Piegat 2003):

Table 1 Rules base for assessing core business efficiency

Rule	Predecessor of a rule								Consequent of a rule			
R1	**IF**	Assessment in the area of assets productivity	is	low	**AND**	Assessment in the area of gross profit margin on sales	is	low	**THEN**	Efficiency of core business	is	low
R4	**IF**		is	low	**AND**		is	medium	**THEN**		is	medium-low
R2	**IF**		is	medium	**AND**		is	low	**THEN**		is	medium-low
R7	**IF**		is	low	**AND**		is	high	**THEN**		is	medium
R3	**IF**		is	medium	**AND**		is	medium	**THEN**		is	medium
R5	**IF**		is	high	**AND**		is	low	**THEN**		is	medium
R6	**IF**		is	medium	**AND**		is	high	**THEN**		is	medium-high
R8	**IF**		is	high	**AND**		is	medium	**THEN**		is	medium-high
R9	**IF**		is	high	**AND**		is	high	**THEN**		is	high

$$h = \mu_{A1 \cap A2 \cap A3}(x_1, x_2, x_3) = \mu_{A1}(x_1) \times \mu_{A2}(x_2) \times \mu_{A3}(x_3). \tag{13}$$

In comparison to other t-norm operators (e.g. MIN operator), the PROD operator responds to the changes in all inputs x_i model with low computation burden.

On the other hand, to find the resulting fuzzy sets for respective rules (i.e. reducing the accuracy of the successor rules using the veracity of its predecessor) and merging rules action in one output set it is recommended to perform in accordance with SUM-MIN scheme (Piegat 2003):

$$\mu_{B*}(y) = \mathrm{MIN}(\mu_B(y), h), \tag{14}$$

$$\mu(y) = \mathrm{SUMA}(\mu_{B*1}(y), \ldots, \mu_{B*K}(y)) = \sum \mu_{B*K}(y). \tag{15}$$

The basic advantage of using SUM-MIN scheme in inference process is taken into account when calculating the resulting $\mu(y)$ function of all component functions $\mu_{Bi*}(y)$ from the respective rules and not, as is in case of the MAX-MIN scheme only this function, where the degree of membership for a given y output value is the biggest.

Stage 4 Determining for the needs of "defuzzification" module a method of converting the outputs of the model from the fuzzy values to the accurate (non-fuzzy) figures.

With respect to the proposed previously triangular membership functions for fuzzy sets in respective variables, defuzzification can be performed for example, by means of sum center method. In this case, the resulting value of the fuzzy model output (y^*) is expressed with the formula (Piegat 2003):

$$y^* = \frac{\sum_{i=1}^{l} y_i \sum_{K=1}^{m} \mu_{B*K}(y_i)}{\sum_{i=1}^{l} \sum_{K=1}^{m} \mu_{B*K}(y_i)}, \tag{16}$$

where:

l—number of elements of the discrete basic set Y,
m—number of rules of fuzzy model.

After the quantization of input and output space variables, the development of knowledge bases and the definition of fuzzy inference mechanism and defuzzification method, we receive ready to be used fuzzy model for enterprise business efficiency assessment.

It should be also noted, that the various assessments in the considered model take values from 0 to 1, where 0 is seen as the least favorable value and 1 as the most advantageous.

4 Empirical Verification of the Proposed Fuzzy Model

4.1 The Detailed Assumptions of the Research

In order to verify the proposed model there was carried out the business efficiency assessment for six companies from the retail industry involved in managing clothing brands, which shares are listed on the Warsaw Stock Exchange—LPP SA Capital Group SA (LPP), Monnari Trade SA (Monnari), Gino Rossi Capital Group SA (Gino Rossi), CCC Group SA (CCC), Prima Moda SA (Prima Moda) and Vistula Group SA (Vistula).

Efficiency assessment was run for the period from 2010 until 2013 included, and the data needed for calculating respective criteria of this assessment were obtained from published by the companies in the considered period annual reports.

Due to the fact of possible calculation problems in regards to percentage change criterion of respective profitability indicators it was assumed that:

- In case when in the reference period and in the studied period profitability indicator was negative, its percentage change (irrespectively from its direction) was treated as zero
- In case when in the reference period profitability indicator was negative and in the studied period was positive, its percentage change was somewhat arbitrarily assumed as 1000 %, to show the significant character of the progression (the exact result in this case is impossible to be calculated from mathematical point of view)
- In remaining cases the percentage change of profitability indicator was calculated without additional assumptions according to standard relative change formula.

All calculations within respective rules bases of the proposed model were conducted on the basis of self-elaborated formulas structure in MS Excel.

4.2 Research Results

In the framework of the entire proposed model for enterprises business efficiency assessment there can be obtained 17 results (each result corresponds to one rules base), however from the relevance point of view this scope can be reduced to five—corresponding to respective efficiency criteria on different generality level of enterprise business which were distinguished within the model structure (Fig. 1). Changes in the scope of these efficiency categories in years 2010–2013 were presented in Fig. 6. Earlier in Fig. 7 were presented in graphic form main input quantities of the model which were the basis for calculations.

Taking into consideration situation among the studied companies in the scope of respective efficiency measures used within the discussed model in years 2010–2013

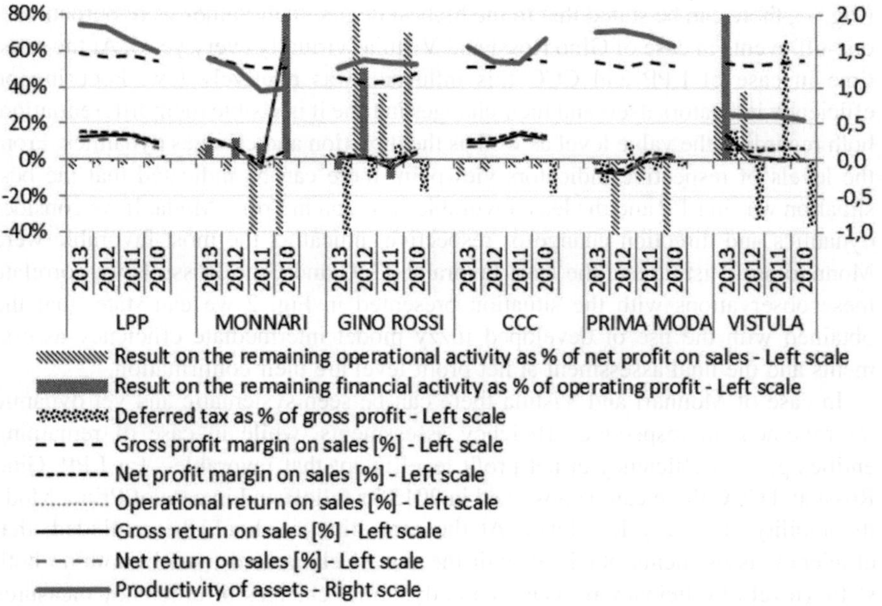

Fig. 6 Main efficiency assessments for researched companies obtained from the fuzzy model

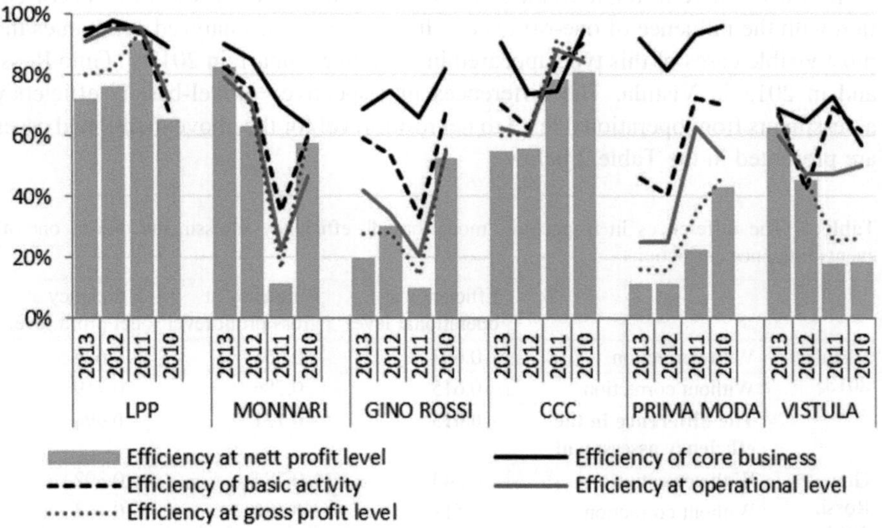

Fig. 7 Main input quantities of the model—efficiency indicators and results on the remaining operational and financial activity plus deferred tax—for researched companies

(Fig. 7), there can be stated that to the highest degree their values were burden with one-off events in case of Gino Rossi and Vistula (virtually every year). At the same time in case of LPP and CCC this influence was relatively low. Focusing on efficiency indicators itself and their changes in time it is visible their differentiation, both regarding the value level as well as the direction and changes dynamics. From the levels of respective indicators viewpoint there can be indicated that the best situation was in LPP and the least favorable situation in Prima Moda. If we consider dynamics and direction change of respective indicators the most favorable were Monnari and Vistula and the least favorable CCC and Gino Rossi. If we correlate these observations with the situation presented in Fig. 2 we can state, that the obtained with the use of developed fuzzy model intermediate efficiency assessments and the final assessment at net profit level are their confirmation.

In case of Monnari and Vistula there can be seen systematic and yet dynamic improvement in respective efficiency assessments, while in case of remaining entities general efficiency at net profit level is not that favorable—for LPP, Gino Rossi and CCC there can be observed in 2013 its falloff and in case of Prima Moda its stability at a very low level. At the same time it should be reminded, that efficiency assessments obtained with the use of elaborated model combine both static (level of efficiency measures) and dynamic (changes of efficiency measures in time) approach, thus is visible in Fig. 7 stability of some profitability indicators readings in case of LPP translated into the falloff of final "model-based" efficiency assessments of this entity.

It is worth here to relate to the issue of obtained efficiency assessments correction with the influence of one-off events. In relation to the analyzed companies the most visible cases of this type appeared in 2010 in Monnari, in 2012 in Gino Rossi and in 2013 in Vistula. The differences in respective "model-based" efficiency assessments from operational level to net result level for the above mentioned cases are presented in the Table 2 below.

Table 2 The differences in respective "model-based" efficiency assessments due to one-off events influence corrections

		Efficiency at operational level	Efficiency at gross profit level	Efficiency at net profit level
Vistula, 2013	With correction	0.603	0.665	0.624
	Without correction	0.615	0.786	0.719
	The difference in the efficiency assessment	**−0.013**	**−0.121**	**−0.094**
Gino Rossi, 2012	With correction	0.343	0.284	0.302
	Without correction	0.511	0.482	0.463
	The difference in the efficiency assessment	**−0.168**	**−0.198**	**−0.161**
Monnari, 2010	With correction	0.465	0.594	0.575
	Without correction	0.472	0.722	0.691
	The difference in the efficiency assessment	**−0.007**	**−0.128**	**−0.116**

Presented in the table differences of efficiency assessments can be considered as the confirmation of the elaborated model effectiveness in the scope of limiting influence of one-off events on generated intermediate and final results. In all discussed cases significant positive results influence on the remaining operational or financial activity was properly corrected in case of model assessments, what translated into their significant reduction in comparison to the reported state.

5 Summary

The model presented in this article should be treated as initial proposal of a tool, which enables to assess in a complex way enterprises business efficiency, which in final stage will be expressed by a number in the interval from 0 to 1. At the same time it does not deny the possibility to orientate in the management effects of the enterprise in relation to narrower areas of its operation, i.e. core business efficiency, basic activity, operational or at gross result level. The proposed tool can be used with success to compare efficiency of entities operations within different sectors of economy, what in correlation with the used numerous efficiency measures, which are distinctive to indicative approach, is much easier and with correction of one-off events influence, ensures more objective final results. At the same time it should be noted, that despite obvious advantages of the proposed model, which were obtained by using to its construction fuzzy sets theory, it requires further testing and improvements. Diversity of situations which can be stated during enterprise financial analysis is such significant, that the improvement process of research tools can be de facto considered as continuous.

References

Bartkiewicz W (2000) Zbiory rozmyte. In: Zieliñki JS (ed) Inteligentne systemy w zarządzaniu. PWN, Warszawa, pp 72–140

Bednarski L (1979) Analiza ekonomiczna. PWE, Warszawa

Bednarski L (2001) Analiza finansowa w przedsiębiorstwie. PWE, Warszawa

Copeland TE, Koller T, Murrin J (1990) Valuation: measuring and managing the value of companies, 1st edn. Wiley, New York

Grzegorzewski P (2006) Wspomaganie decyzji w warunkach niepewności. Metody statystyczne dla nieprecyzyjnych danych. EXIT, Warszawa

Jaki A (2012) Mechanizmy procesu zarządzania wartością przedsiębiorstwa. Wydaw. UE w Krakowie, Kraków

Jonek-Kowalska I (2012) Racjonalizacja kosztów jako sposób poprawy efektywności działania w spółce restrukturyzacji kopalń. In: Dudycz T, Osbert-Pociecha G, Brycz B (eds) Efektywność—rozważania nad istotą i pomiarem, vol 261. Wydaw. UE we Wrocławiu, Wrocław, pp 103–115

Kacprzyk J (1986) Zbiory rozmyte w analizie systemowej. PWN, Warszawa

Kozuń-Cieślak G (2013) Efektywność—rozważania nad istotą i topologią. Studia i Prace Kwartalnik KES SGH, No 4. Wydaw. SGH, Warszawa, pp 13–42
Łachwa A (2001) Rozmyty świat zbiorów, liczb, relacji, faktów, reguł i decyzji. EXIT, Warszawa
Matwiejczuk R (2006) Zarządzanie marketingowo-logistyczne. Wartość i efektywność. C.H. Beck, Warszawa
Michalak A (2012) Efektywność jako kryterium wyboru modeli finansowania inwestycji rozwojowych w górnictwie. In: Dudycz T, Osbert-Pociecha G, Brycz B (eds) Efektywność—rozważania nad istotą i pomiarem, vol 262. Wydaw. UE we Wrocławiu, Wrocław, pp 241–260
Piegat A (2003) Modelowanie i sterowanie rozmyte. EXIT, Warszawa
Pszczołowski T (1977) Celowość, skuteczność, efektywność. Prakseologia 3(63):5–13
Samuelson PA, Nordhaus WD (1995) Ekonomia, t. 1. PWN, Warszawa
Skrzypek E (2002) Jakość i efektywność. Wydaw. UMCS w Lublinie, Lublin
Skrzypek E (2012) Efektywność ekonomiczna jako ważny czynnik sukcesu organizacji. In: Dudycz T, Osbert-Pociecha G, Brycz B (eds) Efektywność—rozważania nad istotą i pomiarem, vol 262. Wydaw. UE we Wrocławiu, Wrocław, pp 313–325
Szymańska E (2010) Efektywność przedsiębiorstw—definiowanie i pomiar. Rocz Nauk Rol G 97(2):152–164
Zadeh LA (1965) Fuzzy sets. Inf Control 8:338–353

Institutional Conditions for Improving the Efficiency of the Health Care System in Poland

Jarosław Plichta

Abstract The health care system in Poland requires thorough institutional changes. Problems occurring therein cannot be tracked down merely to a lack of funds. Institutional analysis based on the achievements in various fields can reveal a number of reasons for inefficiency of the system by referring to transaction costs, agency costs and costs associated with the transfer of property rights. This applies not only to relationships and contracts between the patient and the doctor, but also between all the actors involved in the process of redistribution and service. System optimization and reducing inefficiencies should be applied to contract analysis and is based on the comparative approach to indicate the best possible solution in terms of efficiency. It is important to adopt a holistic approach, draw on the achievements of different scientific disciplines, and expand the economic analysis of qualitative factors that relate to the sociological phenomena of human behavior and psychology. The identified institutional shortcomings of the current health care system cannot be remedied without applying complementary solutions that shall reduce the formation of the so-called externalities. Today, it is difficult to talk about the health services market, since many of these services are contracted without taking into account the criterion of quality and the results achieved. The existing health care system's asymmetry of information reveals a number of opportunistic behaviors and phenomena characteristic of the agency problem. An attempt to identify and assess the magnitude of transaction costs and agency costs seems to be a challenge. However, it seems to be, in addition to the governance structure and managerial competencies, the main source of inefficiency in health care in Poland.

Keywords Transaction costs • Health care system • Agency problem

J. Plichta (✉)
Cracow University of Economics, Kraków, Poland
e-mail: plichtaj@uek.krakow.pl

T. Dudycz et al. (eds.), *The Essence and Measurement of Organizational Efficiency*,
Springer Proceedings in Business and Economics, DOI 10.1007/978-3-319-21139-8_15

1 Introduction

The health care system in Poland is redistributive, and due to budgetary constraints, it enforces pro-efficiency and rationalization measures on individual entities providing health care services. In this approach, which does not differ much from the command system, no fundamental solutions based on problem analysis have been found nor are sought to increase efficiency in the entire process of contracting and implementation of these services. It seems that the institutional approach leaves room for a wider than usual analysis of processes and conditions of phenomena taking place in the health care system. The article will discuss theoretical and practical topics relating to the achievements of the mainstream disciplines, mainly the new institutional economics, such as: transaction cost theory, agency theory and the theory of property rights, which are based on analysis of selected contracts underlying the relationship building between participants in the market exchange processes of health care services (Table 1).

An important role in these processes is played by behavioral factors, limited rationality and information asymmetry common in services markets, not only the health care market. It seems that the micro-economic approach can bring a lot to the discussion on the efficiency of the health system in Poland, supplementing the dominant macro-economic approach that has so far been contaminated by political influences, and the public discourse dominant belief about the unique nature of the processes taking place in the area to which an analysis based on economic efficiency cannot be applied (Plichta 2013).

Table 1 Theoretical foundation for institutional approach in health care system

Theoretical background	Examples of problems	Representative
Property rights	Health as private good/asset. Who should invest and take care of it? (individual or society) How should the money be distributed? Who should decide about individuals' health status?	Harold Demsetz, Armen Alchian
Opportunistic attitudes and behaviors	What are the costs of opportunism and asymmetry of information between the entities in transaction process of health care	Olivier E. Williamson
Influence of institutional environment	What is the role and influence of formal and informal institutions imbedded in culture and social processes?	Douglas C. North
Comparative analysis in research	How can we research the costs? What is the benefit of applying comparative analysis in health care system?	Kenneth Arrow
Institutional and technological efficiency	Could we use efficiency as the main goal of evaluating health care system? How should we measure and combine production and transaction costs?	Jerry R. Green, Eytan Sheshinski

Source: Own work

2 Reasons for Institutional Approach to the Health Care Services Market in Poland

The health care system and its operation is a major social, economic and political issue in every country. Individual health has been an important measure of quality of life and a nation's level of socioeconomic development. Health care system is one of the key elements of the wider health generating process. Although the huge expenses, both public and private, made for this end continue to rise, there is no consensus among researchers and practitioners as to the relationship between the magnitude of expenditure and improvement in health and quality of life (Folland et al. 2011) In addition to the undoubtedly important topic of financing and redistribution of funds for health care, There is also the rarely considered issue of efficiency of the entire "industry" related to the production of health, as interrelated processes, e.g. medical therapy, surgery using specialized equipment or individual behaviors and decisions that have positive or negative consequences for our health, e.g. sports. Following this thought, we find systems out there which seek financing for the production of health as an individual issue (e.g. China) or as a social issue mainly financed from the state budget, e.g. Sweden (Moks 2010).

This last example does not preclude the need for reforms to improve the effectiveness of managing the funds spent by, among others, primary health care privatization and the purchaser-provider splits. Certainly it is not only the financial capacity of the country that underlies the adoption of a particular model of financing, but there is a large influence of institutional conditions, the adopted rules, practices, attitudes and behaviors of members of society and their mutual relations.

The contributing factors certainly include the cultural level, including organizational culture and technology culture that provide for a more efficient use of financial resources and more effective implementation of public health goals. Due to emerging negative externalities such as misallocation of benefits among the members of society e.g. by moving people from a queuing system to a system of private funding outside the health care system, the system in Poland should undoubtedly change. In Poland, there exists the problem of bribes or hidden costs. The results of research "The diagnostic of society 2013" led by the team of J. Czapiński and T. Panek show that this "hidden" expenditures per capita were 287 zloty (ca. 70 EURO) in 2013 (Czapiński and Panek 2014). According to the latest data from the Central Statistical Office, the main reason for discontinuing appointments with a specialist was the long waiting time before the appointment (49.8 % of households), and in case of seeing a dentist, lack of money (48.4 % of households) Fig. 1.

This area needs a broad and multifaceted analysis of processes and institutional conditions that underlie the inefficiency of the system.

Past publications and research related to health in Poland and throughout the world shows a growing interest in the institutional approach (Nojszewska 2011; Folland et al. 2011). The historical and evolutionary approach (North 1981, 1989) is

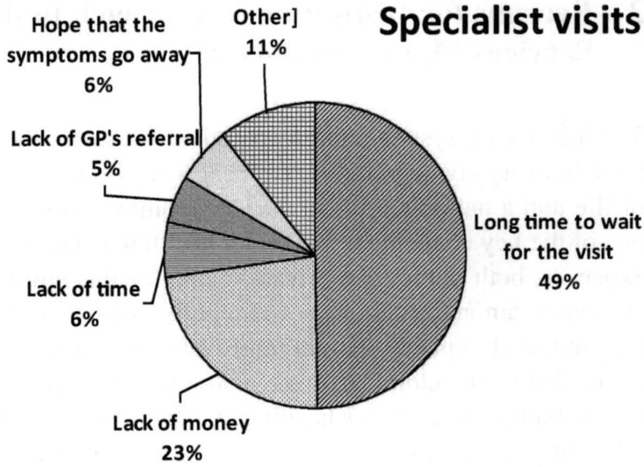

Fig. 1 Reasons for choosing not to see a specialist physician including a dentist despite an existing need in 2013 (*Source*: Own work based on: Health care in households in 2013, General Statistical Office 2014, p. 4)

a significant contribution to the analysis of institutional structures and processes, pointing to the continuity of institutional processes and the problem of the so-called "path dependence", which in Poland serves as a brake to excessively radical changes. It seems that especially in Poland, this dependence of the health sector from the historical context prevents often substantive discussion on the basis of economics or even management on the institutional level. It should be noted that the processes in the area of health care should be considered as part of the social processes and thus economic processes which are a form of creation of social relations.

The problem of exchange, as the key to the analysis of social and economic phenomena, is a crucial theme in sociological theory, in principle, in most approaches. Starting from the functional theory, through evolutionary theories to exchange theories, the issue of description and analysis of human behavior and the creation of more and more complex social structures, or, more broadly, institutions, is associated with the exchange of different kinds of values and providing an institutional framework and effective exchange structures for this reason, including exchange networks (Turner 2008). The process of creating ever more complex forms of exchange and their durability derive essentially from the properties of the objects of the transaction and the characteristics of the subjects of the exchange. It takes place in the institutional environment, most often understood as a set of rules and structures to ensure the proper way of production and exchange processes in line with the objectives of the participants in these processes. The rather simplistic, mechanistic modeling assumptions adopted in neoclassical economics resulted in a revival of economic views indicating a much broader context of their social, political and, above all, cultural nature in the twentieth century.

The solutions for many economic problems associated with the acquisition, processing and distribution of scarce resources were sought in the achievements of other disciplines, such as sociology, psychology or anthropology, without giving up the achievements in mathematics, biology and physics. It seems that today, more and more the importance is attached to holistic approaches (Wojtyna 2009) and postmodern ones focusing on a multidisciplinary perspective for solving problems, which today is always more or less global. As part of a broad, multifaceted and still evolving institutional trend, one can point to a number of approaches that go beyond the assumptions of neoclassical economics, while not giving up its achievements, e.g. the concepts O.E. Williamson (1998). These include the transaction cost theory, the agency theory and the theory of property rights. Without characterizing each one of them, we can point to a number of elements common to these approaches, to affect the evaluation of the points of view of the effectiveness of exchange processes. These include:

- Adopting analysis of a single transaction as the basis
- The assumption of limited rationality of the entities participating in the exchange
- Importance of characteristics (specifics) of the transaction objects (products, services, property rights, material, financial, human, and information resources)
- The existence of the phenomenon of asymmetric information (resulting in part from the above assumptions)
- The important role of property rights, their transfer and various forms of delegation
- Dominant position of information processes in relation to technological processes in the evaluation of the effectiveness and impact on the structure of the coordination of economic processes
- Intentional nature of the exchange process also reflected in opportunistic attitudes and behaviors
- Consideration of the impact of institutional conditions, the so-called institutional environment, in the analysis
- Application of the comparative analysis in research

Indication on these basic assumptions in the context of the analysis of processes in the area of health care makes it possible to draw attention to the hitherto neglected phenomenon, and on the other hand, to go beyond the perception of the economy by many representatives of the health sector through the lens of a negative view of the free competition and privatization. From an institutional point of view, the health system has significant flaws, which could include:

- Anti-incentive nature of the solutions used in the relationship between the participants in the process. No incentives in the form of e.g. co-motivation result in a low proportion of the population who invest in their own health
- No system of incentives (rewards and punishments) in the form of, for example, increasing or decreasing the amount of health insurance contributions depending on individual behavior
- Linking health insurance contributions to income, and not the diagnosis and evaluation of health status and prospects of each patient. The contributions are now essentially a tax on salaries
- Weakness of the exchange processes due to eliminating the stimulus in the form of disclosing the prices of received medical services. The issue of funding is another problem

- Low level of health knowledge and health awareness of the citizens
- The system is focused mainly on treatment of symptoms, not causes
- Common asymmetry of information due to the lack of sufficient comprehensive information on health and medication accessible to the patient from doctors and providers at different stages of the process and the quality of these services
- Lack of an integrated information system providing comprehensive medical knowledge about the patient and the treatment process and the costs related thereto
- Errors in diagnosis and treatment and the ineffectiveness of the treatment process

These characteristics reveal the strong role of institutional factors affecting the structure, processes, and consequently the efficiency of the health care system.

3 Mechanisms and Characteristics of Transactions in the Health System

Health is a private good. Its life-long maintenance is an effort comparable with the need to restore the loss of value of property. It is a resource conditioning the realization of one's goals in life. This task, however, cannot be achieved fully on one's own, so in the context of a given society, the members look for ways to protect it, partly on their own and partly with other entities. This basic factor triggers a process of exchange and encourages its participants to create optimal conditions for themselves. Transactions related to the exchange of healthcare services and products in the form of e.g. the purchase of medicines are of the most systematic character. The frequency of transactions is one of the dimensions of transactions in the transaction cost theory and affects the degree of internalization of resources and processes, and thus the structure of their coordination (market vs. company). The result is a division of social roles forcing specialization and, through e.g. the economies of scale or the effect of experience, higher efficiency achieved by doctors.

Medical knowledge will be an essential component of value in the medical services as a specific resource, which is due to the high risk of so-called sunk costs and cannot be acquired by each participant in the exchange. Frequency of transactions, the characteristics and specificity of resources, which is medical knowledge or ability to use specialized equipment and tools, is a prerequisite for the formation of inefficient transactional processes. The reason for this is the fact that an investment in specific information, technological and organizational resources used in health care promote opportunistic attitudes and behaviors involving e.g. prescribing certain drugs under the influence of incentives from pharmaceuticals' manufacturers, application of procedures that are not bringing the patient any benefit (the placebo effect), promoting products of unproven properties, not providing services or assigning them for other patients to perform etc. Transactional processes in the health care market are related to the properties (attributes) of both entities and objects of the transactions. An example of the hidden characteristics of objects of the transaction was studied by Ackerlof, who showed a link between hidden characteristics, or ones difficult to assess by the purchaser, in the case of automobiles, and choices made in this market. Thus appearing negative selection (adverse selection) directs car buyers' demand not to cars of the highest quality but the ones with lower quality at an average price (Plichta 2010). This causes rewarding of the so-called "lemons" and eliminating good products from the market.

- Lack of quality criteria for the evaluation of medical services
- Therefore, no possibility of assessing the quality of services by the buyer and the payer
- The use of the price criterion in the absence of quality criteria and no possibility of verification which causes the increase of low-quality services at lower and lower prices (market for lemons)

This is a problem affecting the efficiency, which is demonstrated by the fact that over the years, the society has created a variety of formal and informal institutions aimed at correcting undesirable behaviors in this area, e.g. the Hippocratic Oath, the Code of Medical Ethics, Medical Court or the Civil Code and the Penal Code.

As can be seen from the above examples, inefficiency may emerge not only in the physician-patient relationship, but also in the relationship between the physician and the health care facility. In relations of exchange in the health system, therefore, the agency problem is disclosed, resulting from asymmetric information existing between the Principal and the Agent. The process of collecting health insurance and its redistribution enforces an entire system of co-dependencies between Principals and Agents—from patients (employees), through health care professionals, health care institutions, the National Health Fund, the Government, Social Security and employers—the payers) and the employee (the patient). See Fig. 2.

It is also characteristic that the actors involved in the whole process of doing a transaction act simultaneously in a dual role of both the Principal and the Agent. The physician acts, towards the patient, as the Principal, "contracting" for them a determined behavior towards achieving good health. Inability to exercise running control of the process creates a situation of asymmetric information. This can lead to behaviors contrary to the intentions of the doctor. This phenomenon is difficult to estimate, but physicians believe that in the course of multiple treatments, especially lengthy and demanding ones, the inappropriate behavior of patients has big impact on the outcome of treatment, e.g. in the field of oncology. This is manifested by abandoning treatment or starting an alternative one, or searching for other ways of treatment, e.g. in extreme cases offered by persons who do not have the knowledge and expertise in this field, e.g. folk healers. Consequently, in case of relapse of the disease, patients return to the initial treatment and hide the fact that they had taken various substances and used alternative treatments, which can lead to a situation where treatment does not bring effects anymore. On the other hand, the patient is the Principal, contracting the process of organization of the health care system to

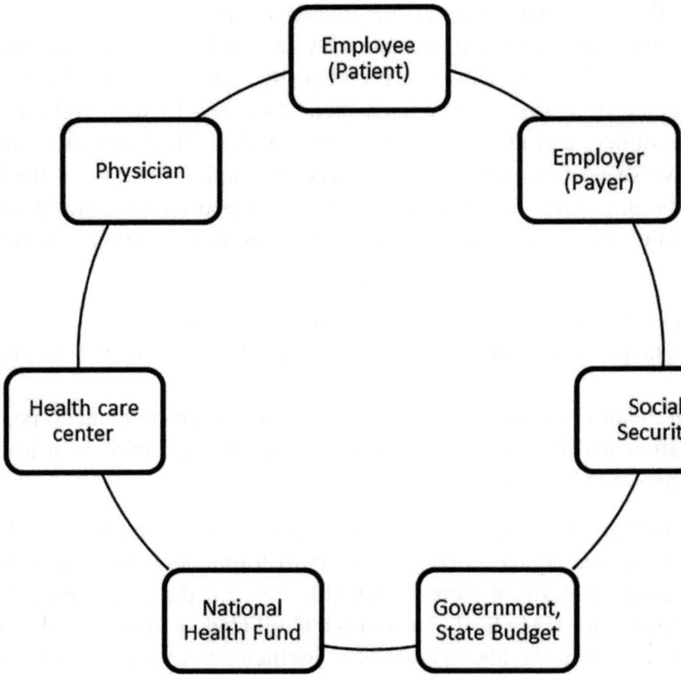

Fig. 2 Simplified diagram of the type of Principal-Agent relationships in the process of contracting health care in Poland (*Source*: Own work)

the public institutions. Inefficiency can occur in all relationships taking place in the health care system, in transactions between actors involved in the process. For example, one can point to the following relationships: patient-physician, physician-health care facility, health care facility-National Health Fund, etc. It should be also mentioned that a very important role in the whole process is played by the employer-employee relationship and the employer-Social Security relationship, where the collection of health insurance has the nature of a tax from labor resources.

Contracts between the actors in health care are commonly relational. The contract includes such a relationship of the parties that even under conditions of high uncertainty; it is characterized by long-term continuity. Significantly, the mutual advantage of the agreement allows informal conditions dominate over formal ones. The common interest, individuals ways of self-defense and defense from a trusted partner are warrants of the relationship. The term "relational" is to serve the difficult task of an overall description of the organizational forms that will solve the problems of coordination and motivation. The relational contract is therefore creating organizational forms of transactions involving a process of simple market exchange, through a sequence of transitional forms to the hierarchical system of the company. The essential difference between the neoclassical and the relational (implicational) contract lies in the fact that the former involves such rules of the game (input and output), which allow to play the game with the changing environment, until the legal form of the contract is achieved. In the relational contract, the rules of the game are formed throughout the course of cooperation, and their implicational characteristics are not verifiable (Stankiewicz 2012).

Referring to public choice theory, this approach to individual by units of public institutions faces a number of problems affecting its effectiveness. In the agency relationship at every stage of this complex process, there is the threat of abuse (moral hazard) or self-interest pursuing behavior at the expense of the Principal (hidden action) (Hough 2013).

An example is the behavior of road users, which, as of 2013 caused the cost of 34.2 zloty billion per year, and the costs of treatment of accident victims in the same year were estimated by the National Health Fund at 3 billion zloty.[1] The main cause of accidents is speeding. In addition, a greater sense of security by having health insurance increases the threat of abuse. This example of functioning in an environment of reduced control applies to contracting and treatment in the present system in Poland. The awareness of the fact that "everybody has health insurance" and the obligation to purchase insurance reduce the concern of many people in their medical condition, e.g. through an unhealthy lifestyle, poor nutrition, unhealthy leisure styles etc. This anti-incentive state of matters invites abuse in this area, which, in extreme cases, leads to the adoption of free riding attitudes and living at the expense of others, e.g. by simulating diseases and taking fictitious sick leaves (Table 2).

Table 2 Causes of agency costs in Principal-Agent relations in health care in Poland

Agent type	Examples of situations and actions causing agency costs
Regulating institution	No transparency in the legislation process, lobbying from pharmaceutical companies
Executing institution	Unclear tender procedures and preparing of executive acts, non-transparent system of employment
National Health Fund	Limited information access to the principals of operation of the Fund, unclear criteria and changing method of allocation of scarce resources (e.g. Contracted amounts or financing various treatment procedures)
Community Health Center/Physician	Limited knowledge of treatment and its quality (*hidden action and hidden characteristics*), no integrated system of identification and ways of treatment, place of treatment, patient history and used or purchased drugs
Patients	Lifestyle, use of medical drugs and supplements without the knowledge of the physician, hiding information about behaviors affecting health (e.g. use of prohibited substances)

Source: Own work

[1] Raport Koszty Wypadków Drogowych w Polsce w 2013 r. (2015). Instytut Badawczy Dróg i Mostów. https://www.ibdim.edu.pl. Accessed 23 Feb 2015.

4 Directions of Research on the Effectiveness of Health Care Processes

In 2013, Poles spent a record 35 billion zloty on private health services, including 23 billion zlotys on drugs—including non-prescription ones—and on dietary supplements. Today, 2.5 million people have an additional health insurance, including almost 800,000 paying for it out of their own resources, while the remaining group is insured by their employers within company medical benefits. According to the plans of the National Health Fund, it will spend nearly 70 billion zloty on health care in 2015.

The current health care system is founded on social solidarity which, through regulation of the benefits and their availability, eliminates those who cannot wait for an appointment, treatment or surgery, from the system. Thereby, it transfers the costs to expenditures from private funds, leaving in the system low-income individuals, the elderly and those whose scope of necessary care is in no way possible to be financed from private sources. This reinforces the growing discontent of those who pay a lot into the system and receive very little or no benefits from their services. It is certainly one of the reasons for low willingness to pay health care contributions or to increase them by the professionally active part of the society.

For many years, it has been postulated to differentiate the approaches to health care in Poland. This has been the direction of the still ongoing reforms in all the countries that had previously relied mainly on private insurance (e.g. USA) or had an insurance system funded by the State budget (e.g. Sweden, the Netherlands). Reasons of such activities are several. In each of the extreme solutions, various kinds of negative externalities have been revealed over time. These are most often results in the form of exclusion of a section of the society from health care or its insufficient quality, leading to lowering of the quality of life for all citizens over time. In turn, imposing the obligation of financing health care on the society without different types of incentives to stimulate this can result in moral hazard and free riding behaviors, which will increase the costs of the system's operation and in the sense of injustice in people who pay for the effects of such attitudes and behaviors. The results usually involve increasing health insurance and the rising costs of the entire system. Due to the need to reduce the impact of externalities and introduce various self-regulatory mechanisms to the health care system at the level of individual contracts realized between the participants in this process, mixed solution proposals seem to be the most desirable ones from this point of view. Underlying this notion are some institutional prerequisites. Firstly, some factors affecting health are random (independent) of the person. There is, therefore, a serious problem in the risk assessment by individual entities. Typically, a subjective risk assessment differs from statistical calculations, which has been shown, by Tverski and Kahneman in the theory of perspectives. There is therefore a need to assign this task to specialists or insurance companies based on their activity on an actuarial risk analysis. Secondly, the assessment of one's health is often subjective due to various psychological or cultural reasons. As a result, each person has a different structure of preferences for spending on health maintenance. Individual decisions and actions in this area, however, have an impact on other members of the society, appearing in the form of so-called externalities. They may be positive or negative. An example of a negative effect may be absenteeism and its consequences for employers and colleagues. A positive externality may manifest itself in the form of pro-health behaviors, which find followers in the immediate environment of the individual. Pilot study by the author conducted on a group of more than 160 people, mostly aged 18–25, shows that over 70 % are aware that the poor state of individual health has a negative impact on other persons in the immediate environment e.g. the family and friends. The results regarding the treatment of one's health as a private matter of each individual are interesting, as the respondents claim that in this area nobody should impose any particular course of action. Only less than 40 % of the above respondents said they agree or strongly agree with this statement. This may indicate a limited trust in individual choices and conduct of people in this area, or may express expectations of support from the state or society (Table 3).

The presented preliminary results of author's own pilot study have produced a picture of the attitudes indicating the importance of health in the structure of values and the need to protect individual health and to invest in it. However, it also reveals an extremely low level of awareness of the factors affecting health and its protection. This is indicated by a similar level of firm responses in terms of the three main

Table 3 Attitudes towards individual health and its protection on the basis of own research

Statement on the attitudes towards one's own health and its protection	"Agree" and "Totally agree" responses in %
Health is a commodity, which you need to take care of and invest in, e.g. through proper diet, sports, etc.	53.05
Health is a private matter of every human being and nobody should impose any practices in this area	40.24
Taking care of your health involves costs and expenses related to health care that are more important than spending on other purposes	57.93
Taking care of your health comes at a cost, but the costs associated with health care expenses are just the same as all the other life costs (i.e. they are not more important than spending on other purposes)	19.75
Good health status depends not on individual behavior, but on random events, fate, etc.	11.18
Good health depends on genes, therefore human behavior, e.g. disease prevention does not matter	14.20
Good health does not depend on you, but on the behavior and actions of other people (e.g. stress, overworking, etc.)	22.22
Health is dependent largely on your lifestyle and individual decisions taken in this regard	15.43
The poor state of my health has a negative impact on other persons in my immediate environment, e.g. family and friends	70.81

Source: Own work

groups of factors, namely: genes, the natural and social environment, and individual behaviors and lifestyle. Especially the last factor is noteworthy, where the low score can indicate not only a poor level of knowledge, but also attitudes and behaviors characteristic of moral hazard (lack of accountability), where a healthy lifestyle, e.g. physical activity, is not closely associated with the awareness of one's individual self-care. The results of the question concerning opportunism are very interesting. Majority of the questioned said that they very seldom hid private information about their health from physicians. However, when asked about the reason of withholding information by patients they answered that:

- In 70 % is it shame
- In 54 % is it lack of knowledge about reasons of illness
- In 68 % is it lack of trust in physicians
- In 34 % is it expectation of "good" diagnosis
- In 36 % is it expectation of prescription to buy or get the drugs
- In 54 % is it aversion to discuss one's own health status
- In 29 % is it fear of using patient information (e.g. habits)

This reason could lead to wrong diagnosis, inadequate and expensive care process. Illustration of selected aspects of attitudes and behaviors points to the need for research on the identification and analysis of the mechanisms and factors influencing the decision-making in the participants in the health care system. The shortcomings of the current health care system in Poland indicated at the beginning of the article may be partly solved by the diagnosis of contracts in the whole process, choosing the best solutions, and taking into account the institutional environment. Directions of research in this area may concern:

- Cultural determinants of behavior and attitudes towards health
- Analysis of the historical transformations of health care institutions in Poland
- A deep analysis of property rights not only within the problem of governance structure but also in the entire transaction process
- The application of the experience of the management studies, especially of process management and management of tangible and intangible assets in the health system
- Working to develop a research methodology in the area of health care
- Economic research based on multifaceted analysis of effectiveness
- Social and psychological research as a basis for creating the institutional framework and social communication in the field of health care

5 Conclusions

The presented chosen approaches and discussion relating to the various concepts in the context of the New Institutional Economics pay attention to aspects that have been scarcely present in the discussion on the changes in the health care system in

Poland. Analysis of world literature in this field indicates the development of this approach and its impact on changes in many countries. As in other processes of social exchange, the approach to health as a resource should be based on the most accurate economic, sociological or psychological diagnosis. This holistic approach is increasingly found in many publications, and it seems that it will be developed in Poland as well. Changes in the health care system in Poland should take account of the institutional approach, which reveals a number of contractual processes having a definite impact on efficiency. Conditions conducive to the asymmetry of information or investments in specific assets reveal a number of negative behaviors and phenomena. In order to meet demand for improved efficiency and changes in the system, extensive research should be developed in this area to provide reliable information which is the basis of optimal decision making. Issues presented in the article are merely a pretext for a broader analysis in this regard.

References

Czapiński J, Panek T (eds) (2014) The diagnosis of society 2013. Ministerstwo Pracy i Polityki Społecznej and Centrum Rozwoju Zasobów Ludzkich, Warszawa

Folland S, Goodman AC, Stano M (2011) Ekonomia zdrowia i opieki zdrowotnej. Wolters Kluwer Business, Warszawa

Health care in households in 2013, General Statistical Office 2014, Warszawa

Hough D (2013) Irrationality in health care: what behavioral economics reveals about what we do and why. Stanford University Press, Stanford

Moks M (2010) Szwedzki system ochrony zdrowia—wybrane kierunki jego reformowania. Oeconomica Copernicana 1:151–164

Nojszewska E (2011) System ochrony zdrowia w Polsce. Wolters Kluwer Polska, Warszawa

North DC (1981) Structure and change in economic history. Norton, New York

North DC (1989) Institutions and economic growth: an historical introduction. World Dev 17 (9):1319–1332

Plichta J (2010) Problem "Market for Lemons" na rynku usług: zarys problemu. In: Zeszyty naukowe—Zarządzanie produktem: kreowanie produktu, vol 153. Uniwersytet Ekonomiczny w Poznaniu, Poznań, pp 119–127

Plichta J (2013) Institutional conditions for restructuring of the medical services market in Poland. In: Borowiecki R, Jaki A, Rojek T (eds) Contemporary economies in the face of new challenges: economic, social and legal aspects. Foundation of the Cracow University of Economics, Kraków, pp 449–457

Raport Koszty Wypadków Drogowych w Polsce w 2013 r (2015) Instytut Badawczy Dróg i Mostów. https://www.ibdim.edu.pl. Accessed 23 Feb 2015

Stankiewicz W (2012) Ekonomika instytucjonalna. Zarys wykładu, Warszawa, p 111

Turner JH (2008) Struktura teorii socjologicznej. PWN, Warszawa

Wiliamson OE (1998) Ekonomiczne instytucje kapitalizmu. PWN, Warszawa, p 29

Wojtyna A (2009) Współczesna ekonomia—kontynuacja czy poszukiwanie nowego paradygmatu. In: Fiedor B, Hockuba Z (eds) Nauki Ekonomiczne wobec wyzwań współczesności. PTE, Warszawa, pp 25–49

Method of Simplified Evaluation of the Commercial Potential of R&D Projects

Edward Stawasz and Daniel Stos

Abstract The paper reviews selected approaches and methods for assessing R&D projects useful for effective innovation management. It presents a method of simplified assessment based on the concept of the threshold (minimum) value of economic effects, i.e. the value covering capitalised project expenditures constituting the basis for estimating the rate of economic efficiency for variants of the implementation of R&D projects. The lower the rate of economic effects based on their threshold value, the more efficient the R&D project is. The usefulness of the proposed method is assessed based on the example of a research unit conducting activities in the area of advanced research and development of technical solutions and their deployment in the field of electro-technical equipment and systems. The presented method of evaluation of R&D projects can be used in the initial assessment of the project, at the phase of preparation of the project concept when the research unit seeks to choose variants of implementation, as well as at various stages of project implementation (at R&D project checkpoints) when the research unit seeks to effectively manage the research process, deciding whether to continue or curtail research activities.

Keywords R&D project • Commercial potential • Types and methods of evaluation

1 Introduction

The implementation of research and development (R&D) projects requires good management as well as incurring substantial capital expenditures. In the initial stages of work on the project, capital expenditures may be limited, however, as the work progresses through the subsequent phases, expenditures grow significantly, reaching the highest value at the level of industrial deployment. It is rare that all the phases of an R&D project should be carried out in the framework of a single entity with a uniform ownership structure. Even in the early stages of the project there is sometimes a need for technology transfer between entities. This transfer can be

---

E. Stawasz (✉) • D. Stos
University of Lodz, Lodz, Poland
e-mail: stawasz@uni.lodz.pl; danstos@poczta.fm

T. Dudycz et al. (eds.), *The Essence and Measurement of Organizational Efficiency*, Springer Proceedings in Business and Economics, DOI 10.1007/978-3-319-21139-8_16

accomplished in different ways but each of them requires, to a smaller or larger extent an estimate of the value of the project at the stage in which the transfer is made (Stawasz and Stos 2011).

One can find in the literature many interesting concepts on the management of R&D projects (e.g.: the concepts of selection of innovative ideas or a staged evaluation process of R&D projects), as well as methods of measurement and evaluation of the commercial potential of R&D projects (this paper reviews six groups of basic methods). The most popular methods of assessing the effectiveness of projects include traditional financial and economic techniques based on the calculation of the basic economic and financial parameters of projects, in particular the ratio of economic outputs to inputs (e.g.: the use of discounted cash flow calculation, applied also in the more developed analyses conducted by means of the decision tree method). These methods are complicated and expensive, require numerous market, technical and legal analyses, hence they are used primarily in the so-called in-depth evaluation of the commercial potential of R&D projects or innovative solutions.

The aim of the paper is to present a method of simplified evaluation of the commercial potential of R&D projects which can be used for the preliminary assessment of the project, even in the zero phase when the research unit seeks to select project variants and effectively manage the research process at the designated checkpoints of the R&D project. This method concerns the concept of the threshold value of economic effects, understood as the capitalised value of R&D expenditure increased by the estimated internal deployment expenditures, including the assessment of the probability of technical and economic success.

In the later section of the paper, an attempt is made to verify the proposed method on the example of a research unit conducting activities in the area of advanced research and development of technical solutions and their deployment in the field of electro-technical equipment and systems. The R&D project evaluation is always based on an assessment of the commercial potential. This potential can be estimated using a variety of analytical and synthetic indicators, the estimate however must result in an assessment of the value of this potential.

2 Selected Concepts and Methods to Assess the Commercial Potential of R&D Projects

Research institutions and companies focused on the efficient management of R&D projects concentrate on the search for projects with a high technical, market and economic potential (Wang et al. 2010). The principal issue in this area is the generation and evaluation of a significant number of ideas/concepts in order to select in the evaluation process only the most attractive. One of the main issues is the efficient elimination of unattractive projects that do not prognosticate desirable results for the institution implementing them. This process is problematic as there is a contradiction here. On the one hand, the implementation of ineffective ideas takes time and money, on the other hand, a detailed analysis of the project is also expensive and absorbing (expert opinions, market research, etc.) (Christensen et al. 2008; Thomke 2001).

Many interesting methods for measuring and assessing the innovation potential found in the outcomes of R&D projects can be find in the literature. Concepts of selection of innovative ideas are used very often used, e.g. the concept of "idea funnel" [Harvard Business Essentials 2005], the *R-W-W* (real, win, worth it) *screen* (Day 2007), Cooper's *Stage—Gate Process System* (Cooper 2005), the method of evaluating the *degree of implementation maturity* (Mazurkiewicz et al. 2013), the method of evaluation of commercial potential of a new technology with *Fuzzy logic* (Bandarian 2007) or the *innovation process model* of Tidd et al. (2005), due to their scope of verification of the probability of success of an innovative product concept. The essence of these approaches is based on conducting only a general selection of ideas at the beginning of the project, then as the work progresses, evaluation criteria become increasingly detailed. Gradually, unattractive projects are "sifted out" and only the ones fit for the market in one way or another are left. Every subsequent phase of the project costs increasingly more than the previous one, which means that the assessment process assumes a growing commitment of time and resources, depending on the completion of assessment of subsequent phases in terms of the conformity of the idea with the strategy and objectives of the project and in terms of whether the idea meets certain technical, market and financial criteria, which may tested or its production can be initiated (Stawasz and Stos 2011).

The staged process of the evaluation of R&D projects has its advantages and disadvantages, since it is relatively simple and transparent, allowing its widespread use. The process allows the rejection step by step less profitable concepts until only the most promising ones remain. This reduces the loss on the part of the research institution or a company in the event of major defects in the project (market or technical), by stopping its implementation at a relatively early stage. On the other hand, a detailed analysis and evaluation of the project can be costly and absorbing (expert opinions, market research, etc.), especially for smaller entities (Chaston 2010). Another disadvantage of the staged approach is the possibility of manipulation, i.e. such modification of assumptions of the project by the evaluation team that the "ailing" project should meet the expectations of the institution's management (Christensen et al. 2008).

In the assessment of the commercial potential of R&D projects, one can distinguish six groups of methods and techniques used for the evaluation and selection of the best R&D projects in order to control the allocation of resources involved (Heidenberger and Stummer 1999):

1. Benefit Measurement Methods.
2. Mathematical Programming Approaches.
3. Decision and Game Theory.
4. Simulation Models.

5. Heuristics.
6. Cognitive Emulation.

Benefit measurement methods relate to the procedures for selecting the most profitable projects based on a given budget. The projects that are preferred in the selection process are the ones that should achieve the greatest benefits. These methods include: traditional financial and economic techniques, a scoring approach (related to the use of a limited set of decision variables), comparative models (assuming the implementation of procedures for a direct comparison of a given solution to another, or to a set of other similar solutions), as well as techniques of group decisions (related to the collection and use of opinions provided by experts in their field of specialisation). The Delphi methods are a group of widely applied techniques of this type (Stawasz et al. 2013).

Methods associated with mathematical programming form a significant group of project evaluation methods. These include: linear programming models and non-linear programming models. One of the methods of linear programming is Data Envelopment Analysis (DEA), useful in analyses related to the commercialisation of technologies (Bana e Costa and Thore 2002; Berg 2010). It belongs to a group of non-parametric techniques for measuring the effectiveness of business performance which do not require knowledge of the functional relationship between inputs and outputs (Valderrama and Groot 2002).

Methods based on the decision and the game theory are divided into approaches based on the decision tree and those approaches based on the game theory. Both approaches consider future events or responses of the environment of companies and other entities that are uncertain with regard to their existence and scope. The differences between the two approaches relate to, among others, the fact that the decision theory assumes that changes in the environment are independent variables in relation to the actions of a given entity/company, while the game theory involves an analysis of reasonably acting competitors (which implies a response to the actions of a given company). In the framework of models relating to the decision theory, the main role is played by decision trees—allowing a detailed estimation of risks and benefits associated with the project. They are useful in the situation when the probability of success can be assessed in the different phases of the project (Tritle et al. 2000; Rostek 2014). The difficulty lies however in the fact that the preparation of analysis with the use of the decision tree for projects in the very early stages of development requires well-trained staff and commitment of significant resources.

Models using elements of the decision theory and financial techniques are also applicable in estimating the value of R&D projects. Simplified methods in this group include the First Chicago method, which can be applied in the case of projects based on R&D activities. Its various forms are applied in analyses used by venture capital/private equity investors (Achleitner and Lutz 2005). The method entails evaluating the results of the three project scenarios: the most likely, the best and the worst. In addition, the probability of the failure of the project due to the lack of research and development success is also considered. Each scenario has its own probability of occurrence. It can be said that the method in question is based on an analysis of the consequences of events under certain assumptions, it is more of an analytical tool for risk management and the efficiency of the projects under consideration than a tool to analyse their quality.

Financial analysis instruments are also applied in the more developed analyses carried out by means of the decision tree method. They relate to situations such as, among others, the completion of the research process and the time of making the decision-making time on the possible commercialisation of a given solution.

Another type of method is simulation models. These reflect the real situation with greater accuracy than optimisation models and are used in situations when carrying out experiments under real conditions is impractical for various reasons (time, costs, etc.).

Methods relating to cognitive emulation are used to build a model of the actual decision-making process occurring within the organisation. The models are constructed based on previous experience related to events occurring in comparable circumstances (Tritle et al. 2000). This fact results in certain restrictions associated with the use of this method, which is more suitable to support tactical decisions, with very limited applicability in relation to individual and unique situations such as R&D projects.

3 Assumptions of the Method of Simplified Evaluation of the Commercial Potential of Innovative Technical Solutions

The stage-gate assessment model (including stages and stage gates) used for innovative project management can be seen as the basis of methodology to assess the commercial potential of R&D projects. The project stages are determined from the point of view of research and technique. Stage-gates are checkpoints for the specified phases of the project designated to assess the end results of a given phase and make a decision whether to continue work on the project. The end result of each phase of an R&D project includes specific outcomes. These are concepts and ideas of varying degrees of detail and documentation—components, prototypes, trial and final versions. The evaluation of the commercial potential of R&D projects can be carried out before the commencement of the research and after each phase of the R&D process, i.e.: the concept phase, the R&D phase, the prototyping and verification phase, as well as the deployment phase.

In the context of the stage-gate process, one can point to the significant specificity of the early stages of the development of technology. In particular, in terms of high risk projects, often connected with technologies that have the potential to replace the widely used solutions on the market. In this situation, instead of a traditional approach, it is advisable to use technology-oriented stage-gates in the early stages of the technological process (Mazzarol 2011).

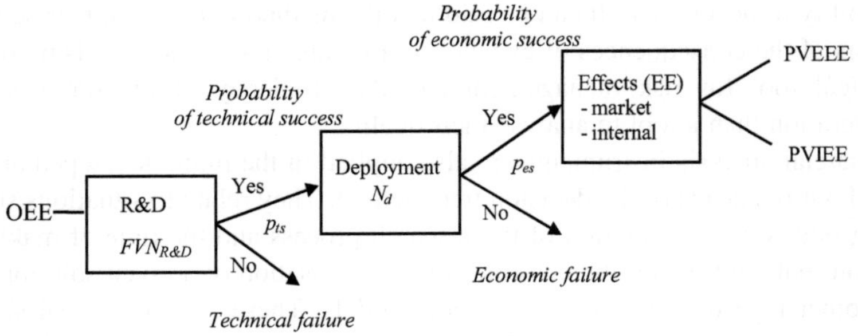

Fig. 1 Stages of the R&D commercial project potential assessment. OEE—estimated economic value of the project at the time of commercialisation; pts—probability of technical success; pes—probability of economic success; FVNR&D—capitalised R&D expenditures at the time of commercialisation; Nd—deployment expenditures; EE—total sum of economic effects; PVEEE—discounted at the time of commercialisation net value of external economic effects of the project; PVIEE—discounted at the time of commercialisation net value of internal economic effects of the project

The diagram of the stages (and phases) of an R&D project and its economic effects is shown in Fig. 1. It includes stages of R&D and deployment activities. The resulting economic effects of the application of new solutions can be divided into internal and external ones.

The starting point for the evaluation of the commercial potential of an R&D project is the ability to assess the probability of obtaining a new solution (the technical success of R&D activities)—which is a prerequisite for making its economic assessment relating to quantifiable economic effects from the economic application of the resulting solutions in such categories as income and profits, costs and expenses, efficiency and productivity, quality and reliability, price, etc. Depending on the phase in which the assessment is carried out, it always takes into account the level of capitalised expenditures (taking into consideration changes in value over time) needed to carry out the subsequent phases of implementation and the level of deployment expenditures. Deviations from the assumptions for the various phases affect the economic effects of the project and the valuation of the results of deviations is an important element in the assessment.

The procedure for evaluating the commercial potential of R&D projects may include a preliminary assessment (general) and a detailed (in-depth) assessment. The preliminary assessment should be carried out for the zero phase (i.e. before deciding on the implementation of a given R&D project) and for the initial phases (i.e. the concept phase, the R&D phase, the prototyping and verification phases). In contrast, the in-depth evaluation can be performed for each phase. It is advisable, however, for it to be carried out in the later phases of the project, i.e. in the phase of deployment and commercialisation, in order to determine the real possibility of implementing the solution through a detailed analysis of the factors affecting economic success (Stawasz et al. 2013).

Using one of the most popular methods of assessing the effectiveness of projects, it can be assumed that the estimated economic value of the R&D project is equal to the difference between the sum of discounted at the time of commercialisation values of economic effects of the R&D project, i.e. the discounted net value of the external economic effects of the project and/or the discounted net value of the internal economic effects of the project and the sum of the capitalised expenditures incurred during the R&D and deployment phases, i.e.:

$$OEE = (PVEEE + PVIEE) - (FVN_{R\&D} + N_d) \tag{1}$$

The R&D project is economically viable, if $OEE > 0$.

R&D expenditures include expenditures on subsequent phases and activities of project implementation, and should be estimated using an interest rate as a basis for estimating the price of purchase of innovative solutions by the commercial user. For social projects, a minimum interest rate (e.g. 4 %) can be assumed, whereas for business projects this rate should additionally include a risk premium. R&D expenditures have phase-specific standards in the course of the project (defined in the zero phase) and the adherence to these standards should be evaluated in terms of economic effects.

Deployment expenditures include all the expenditures for the economic application of the solution. In the analysis, they are set at the minimum level necessary for the technical implementation of production under normal industrial conditions or under the guidance of industry innovators/inventors, in the case of innovative solutions—the estimate is carried out by experts.

R&D expenditures and deployment expenditures comprise *initial expenditures* on an innovative solution and can provide a basis for estimating the threshold effects ensuring a return on investment.

The discount rate (r) of the effects of the user of the innovation is calculated according to the formula $r = 1 - p_{st}p_{se}$, where p_{st} means the probability of technical success and p_{se}—the probability of economic success.

In the assessment of the commercial potential of R&D projects, when there is possible to reliably the estimate the economic effects, the project is economically viable, if the total sum of discounted economic effects is not lower than the sum of capitalised initial expenditures:

$$(PVEEE + PVIEE) \geq (FVN_{R\&D} + N_d) \tag{2}$$

Only above value $(FVN_{R\&D} + N_d)$ is there economic value added for the use of R&D outcomes by the investor.

The earlier the time of the assessment of its economic effects, the more difficult it is to assess reliably the market and financial parameters required to make this evaluation. Nowadays however, there is a growing need to conduct such assessments even in the zero phase when a research unit seeks to select variants of research projects to implement, while having to cary out many projects simultaneously with limited resources.

The presented-below proposed methodology of the so-called simplified evaluation of the commercial potential presented below is based on the concept of their threshold effects understood as the quotient of the capitalised value of R&D expenditures (through their capitalisation at the time of commercialisation of research products) increased by estimated internal deployment expenditures on the product of the probability of technical and economic success. The simplification consists in replacing forecasts of future economic benefits (revenues, cost reduction) and external expenditures on deployment with subjective assessments of the probability of technical and economic success of the implementation of the project in specific identified areas of risk. Deployment expenditures are limited to internal expenses incurred by the research unit in the phase of commercialisation of outcomes of the R&D project.

Through the application of the concept of the future value in the capitalisation of R&D expenditures, the threshold value of economic effects, i.e. the value which covers the capitalised initial expenditures of the research project, decreases as the period between the time of incurring the expenditures and the time of commercialisation of research projects shortens.

For the evaluation of R&D projects, two measures related to the concept of threshold effects may be used: an absolute measure (the future threshold value of economic effects—FTEE) and a relative measure (the rate of economic efficiency—EER). The use of the absolute measure in the zero phase allows the comparison of the economic efficiency of individual variants of the implementation of the given R&D project as well as the monitoring of changes in the assessment of effectiveness in further stages of the project, while the use of the relative measure allows the comparison of the economic efficiency of simultaneously implemented projects with varying levels of R&D expenditures and internal deployment expenditures. The reduction in the value of these indicators in the subsequent phases of implementation of the project justifies a positive evaluation of the project. The method of calculating both measures is presented below:

$$FTEE = (FVN_{R\&D} + FVR_c + N_d)/(p_{st}p_{se}) \tag{3}$$

where:

$FTEE$—future threshold value of economic effects (at the time of commercialisation of the project)

$FE_{R\&D}$—future value (at the time of commercialisation of the project) of R&D expenditures,

$FVPc$—future value (at the time of commercialisation) value of revenues from commercialisation of research products created in the phases of the R&D project implementation

N_d—value of internal deployment expenditures,

p_{st}—probability of the technical success of the project,

p_{es}—probability of economic success of the project.

Whereas—the rate of economic efficiency (EER):

$$EER = (FTEE - N_{R\&D})/N_{R\&D} \quad (4)$$

where:

FTEE—future threshold value of economic effects (at the time of commercialisation of the project)
$N_{R\&D}$—value of R&D expenditures,

Both discussed measures of evaluating the commercial potential of R&D projects allow the assessment of variants of an R&D project and effective management of an innovative project at the designated project checkpoints. The threshold value of the economic effects as an absolute measure can be used in the planning and management of a single project, while the rate of economic efficiency as a relative measure can be used in the selection of project variants or in the process of managing of a portfolio of R&D projects.

4 Simplified Evaluation of the Commercial Potential of the Selected R&D Project

The presentation of the usefulness of the proposed method to estimate the commercial (economic) potential of R&D projects in the form of the measurement of the future threshold value of economic effects (FTEE) and the rate of economic efficiency (EER), was carried out based on the example of a research unit conducting activities in the area of advanced research and development of technical solutions and their deployment in the field of electro-technical equipment and systems. A preliminary calculation of project expenditures is as follows:

1. The project will be implemented in four R&D phases:
   (a) The concept preparation phase,
   (b) The basic research phase,
   (c) The research and development phase,
   (d) The prototyping and deployment testing phase.
2. The following part of the project is the phase of commercialisation, including deployment activities related to the testing and demonstration of the way the product works, as well as the search for market applications of the technology.

3. Total project expenditures of which:	5400.000 PLN,
(a) on R&D activities	4600.000 PLN,
(b) on deployment activities related to commercialisation	800.000 PLN.

4. The expenditures will be financed from both public and private funds, including the unit's own internal funds as well as external funds (e.g.: venture capital, a lender, etc.) of a variable funding structure, in which the share of public funds gradually decreases with the transition to the subsequent phases of the R&D project, while the share of private funding increases; the commercialisation phase is financed entirely through private funding; the initial concept phase is funded from the R&D unit's own sources.
5. The probability of the technical success of the project was evaluated by the expert research method at the level of 0.9 and of its economic success at the level of 0.8.

The initial budget for the project was prepared as follows (see Table 1):

On the basis of the preliminary assessment of the commercial potential of the project, the main risk factors of the project's implementation were estimated. Divided into technical factors (related to R&D and deployment) and economic factors (related to economic, production and market parameters), which allowed the estimation of the cost of capital in terms of different sources of financing for the project at its various phases (see Tables 2 and 3).

The risk factors related to the implementation of the project and its commercialisation were included in the cost of private capital, and the social cost of public capital was assumed at the lowest level—the rate of return on the lowest risk investment, i.e. without the project risk premium—currently, for example, bonds at 4 %. For the earliest periods, the risk rates typical of the highest risk projects, from 25 to 12 %, were assumed. The value of deployment expenditures was estimated for the date of the planned commercialisation of the project (the end of the zero period).

In order to estimate the future value of the indicators, it was assumed that expenditures on the various phases of the research will be incurred "in advance", and expenditures on its deployment incurred "in arrears". Thus, the time for incurring the first expenditures and the time for incurring the expenditures on commercialisation of the project divides the implementation of the project into five periods.

The value of internal deployment expenditures was estimated at the amount of 800.0 PLN for the date of the planned commercialisation of the project (the end of the zero period).

The capitalised value of expenditures on the research project taking into account the R&D and deployment potential is 7507.6 PLN, with the nominal value of R&D expenditures at the level of 5400.0 PLN. Assuming that the probability of technical success amounts to 0.9 and that of the economic success to 0.8, the threshold value of economic effects of the project ensuring the return on investment is therefore (see: Table 4)

Table 1 The volume and distribution of project expenditures

	Item	R&D period					Commercialisation period
			−4	−3	−2	−1	0
I.	Project expenditures	5400.0					
II.	The financing structure of project expenditures						
1.	Public funds (%)		0	90	40	20	0
2.	Private funds (%)		100	10	60	80	100
	Including:						
(a)	Internal (%)		100	100	60	60	20
(b)	External (%)		0	0	40	40	80
III	Distribution of R&D expenditures (%)		10	30	50	10	
IV	R&D expenditures		460.0	1380.0	2300.0	460.0	
1.	Public funds		0.0	1242.0	920.0	92.0	
2.	Private funds including:		460.0	138.0	1380.0	368.0	
(a)	Internal		460.0	138.0	828.0	220.8	
(b)	External		0.0	0.0	552.0	1470.2	

Table 2 The structure and distribution of the cost of the capital financing the project in the different phases of its implementation

	Item	R&D period				Commercialisation period
	Estimate of the capitalisation rate of expenditures	−4	−3	−2	−1	0
I	Cost of capital					
1.	Social (%)	4	4	4	4	4
2.	Commercial (%)	25.0	20.0	12.0	9.6	6.4
	Including					
(a)	Internal (%)	25	20	16	12	8
	External (%)	12	10	8	6	6
(b)	WACC—weighted average cost of capital (commercial rate) (%)	25.0	5.6	9.3	8.5	6.4

Table 3 Estimated future value indicators

	Item	R&D period				Commercialisation period
	Future value indicators	−4	−3	−2	−1	0
1.	Public funds	12,167.0	11,699.0	11,249.0	10,816.0	1.0
2.	Private capital (WACC)	30,518.0	12,435.0	13,050.0	11,768.0	1.0
	Including:					
(a)	Internal	30,518.0	20,736.0	15,609.0	12,544.0	1.0
(b)	External	17,623.0	14,641.0	12,597.0	11,236.0	1.0

• for a return on private expenditures	6833.6 PLN,

• for a return on total expenditures	10,427.2 PLN.

The threshold value of the project (FTEE) can therefore be used for the evaluation of the project variants that differ in terms of:

- The length of the period in which work is conducted in the different phases of the project (e.g. its increase or decrease).
- Distribution of expenditures over time.
- Distribution of sources of funding for expenditures.
- Assessment of the probability of technical and economic success.

It is possible, therefore, to draw the conclusion that the best variant of the project is the variant for which the FTEE is lower. If, for example, a variant of the same total R&D expenditures but over a shorter period of time (e.g. three periods) and with no private capital is considered for the above-described project, the analysis of this variant is as follows (see Table 5).

The presented calculations show that this variant is more efficient as the threshold value of economic effects is 9488.6 PLN (10,427.2 PLN in the previous variant), even though this variant is associated with a more expensive form of financing (without the participation of external private capital).

The FTEE as an absolute value is not useful, however for the comparison of variants of a given project that differ in terms of initial expenditures. The rate of economic efficiency may serve this purpose: in the described example the EER for total expenditures is 1.27 = (67,076.0−4600.0)/4600.0.

This variant of the research project in which the EER (the lower bound of the project equals zero, there is no upper bound) is lower is more cost-effective. When the possibility of implementing projects is limited, the portfolio of R&D projects implemented by a research unit should consist of projects with the lowest value of EER and the "k" number of projects for which:

Table 4 The threshold value of economic effects

	Item	Project implementation periods					
	Estimate of the capitalisation rate of expenditures	−4	−3	−2	−1	0	Total
A.	Capitalised project expenditures						
1.	Total	1403.8	1739.2	3022.7	541.9		6707.6
2.	Public	0.0	1453.0	1034.9	99.5		2587.4
3.	Internal	1403.8	286.2	1292.4	277.0		3259.4
4.	External	0.0	0.0	695.4	165.4		860.8
B.	Threshold value of economic effects (FTEE)						
I	R&D expenditures						
1.	Public						2587.4
2.	Private						4120.2
II	Total R&D expenditures						6707.6
III	Deployment expenditures					800.0	800.0
IV	Total expenditures						7507.6
V	Probability of technical success (p_{st})						0.9
VI	Probability of economic success (p_{se})						0.8
VII	Threshold value of economic effects (FTEE)						
	For the return on private expenditures						6833.6
	For the return on total expenditures						10,427.2

$$\sum_{i=1}^{k} E_{R\&D}(P_i) < E \qquad (5)$$

where:

$E_{R\&D}(P_i)$—nominal expenditures for i-th research project
E—total value of expenditures that a research unit can incur (including subcontracts to other research units).

Table 5 A variant of the research project: project implementation time reduced to three periods without external private funds

	Item		R&D period				Commercialisation period
A.	Estimate of the capitalisation rate of expenditures		−4	−3	−2	−1	0
I	The financing structure of project expenditures (%)						
1.	Public funds		0	90	40	20	0
2.	Private funds		100	10	60	80	100
	Including:						
(a)	Internal		100	100	100	100	20
(b)	External		0	0	0	0	80
II	Cost of capital						
1.	Social (%)		4	4	4	4	4
2.	Commercial (%)		25	20	16	12	6
	Including:						
(a)	Internal (%)		25	20	16	12	8
(b)	External (%)		0	0	0	0	0
	Distribution of project expenditures (%)		0	20	50	30	
B.	Project expenditures	4600.0	0.0	920.0	2300.0	1380.0	
1.	Public funds		0	828.0	920.0	276.0	
2.	Private funds		0	92.0	1380.0	1104.0	
	Including:						
(a)	Internal		0.0	92.0	1380.0	1104.0	
(b)	External		0.0	0.0	0.0	0.0	
C.	C. Future value indicators						
1.	1. Public funds		12,167.0	11,699.0	11,249.0	10,816.0	10,400.0
2.	2. Private funds						
	Including:						
(a)	Internal		30,518.0	20,736.0	15,609.0	12,544.0	10,800.0
(b)	External		10,000.0	10,000.0	10,000.0	10,000.0	10,000.0

D.	Capitalised project expenditures						Total
1.	Total		0.0	1159.5	3188.9	1683.4	6031.8
2.	Public		0.0	968.7	1034.9	298.5	2302.1
3.	Internal		0.0	190.8	2154.0	1384.9	3729.7
4.	External		0.0	0.0	0.0	0.0	0.0
E.	Threshold value of economic effects						
I	R&D expenditures						
1.	Public						2302.1
2.	Private						3729.7
II	Total R&D expenditures						6031.8
III	Deployment expenditures						800.0
IV	Total expenditures						6831.8
V	Probability of technical success						0.9
VI	Probability of economic success						0.8
F.	Threshold value of economic effects (FTEE)						
	For the return on private expenditures						6291.3
	For the return on total expenditures						9488.6

5 Summary and Conclusions

In general, it can be assumed that one of the better methods to assess the commercial potential of R&D projects can be a simplified evaluation based on the concept of the threshold value of the economic effects. The simplification consists in replacing forecasts of future economic benefits (revenues, cost reduction) and capital expenditures on deployment with subjective assessments of the probability of technical and economic success of the implementation of the project in specific identified areas of risk. This method can be used widely: both in the initial assessment of the project, even in its zero phase of the project, when a research unit seeks to select variants of projects and effectively manage the research process at the designated checkpoints in the R&D project.

It is worth noting that the threshold value of the economic effects of the R&D project estimated on the basis of the proposed method does not specify the expected benefits derived from the commercialisation of products of the given project, it is only a reference point for subsequent stages of evaluation. The advantage of the proposed method is that it requires no estimation of market and economic parameters associated with high risk, which are particularly difficult to assess in the early stages of R&D projects. Simplified evaluation, however, is no substitute for in-depth evaluation of the economic efficiency of R&D projects carried out in the phase when the decision concerning their implementation is made.

The analysed cases—used to determine the method based on the threshold value of economic effects of the R&D project and the rate of economic efficiency—allow one to reach the conclusion that this method can be used to evaluate different project variants that differ in terms of:

- The length of the period in which work is conducted in the different phases of the project (e.g. its increase or decrease).
- Distribution of expenditures over time.
- Distribution of sources of funding for expenditures.
- Assessment of the probability of technical and economic success.

References

Achleitner A-K, Lutz E (2005) First Chicago method: alternative approach to valuing innovative start-ups in the context of venture capital financing rounds. Betriebswirtsch Forsch Prax 57 (4):333–347

Bana e Costa C, Thore S (2002) The many dimensions of an R&D project: multi-criteria analysis. In: Thore S (ed) Technology commercialization: DEA and related analytical methods for evaluating the use and implementation of technical innovation. Kluwer, Boston

Bandarian R (2007) Evaluation of commercial potential of a new technology at the early stage of development with fuzzy logic. J Technol Manag Innov 2(4):73–85

Berg S (2010) Water utility benchmarking: measurement, methodologies, and performance incentives. IWA, London

Chaston I (2010) Entrepreneurial management in small firms. Sage, London
Christensen CM, Kaufman SP, Shih WC (2008) Innovation killers. Harv Bus Rev 86(1):98–105
Cooper RG (2005) Product leadership. Pathways to profitable innovation. Basic Books, New York
Day GS (2007) Is it real? Can we win? Is it worth doing? Managing risk and reward in an innovation portfolio. Harv Bus Rev 85(12):110–120
Harvard Business Essentials (2005) Zarządzanie kreatywnością i innowacją. MT Biznes, Warszawa
Heidenberger K, Stummer C (1999) Research development project selection and resources allocation: a review of quantitative modeling approaches. Int J Manag Rev 1(2):197–224
Mazurkiewicz A, Belina B, Giesko T, Karsznia W (2013) Operational system for the assessment of the implementation maturity level of technical innovations. Maint Probl 4:1–5
Mazzarol T (2011) Entrepreneurship and innovation. Tilde University Press, Prahran
Rostek K (2014) Modeling commercial potential of innovative projects. Int Rev Manag Bus Rev 3 (1):77–95
Stawasz E, Stos D (2011) Selected aspects of the valuation of innovative undertakings. Oper Res Decis 3–4:57–68
Stawasz E, Głodek P, Stos D, Stos-Roman A (2013) Metody analizy potencjału wdrożeniowego i komercyjnego innowacyjnego produktu technicznego lub procesu technologicznego. Uniwersytet Łódzki, Lodz
Thomke S (2001) Enlightened experimentation: the new imperative for innovation. Harv Bus Rev 79(2):67–75
Thore SA (ed) (2002) Technology commercialization: DEA and related analytical methods for evaluating the use and implementation of technical innovation. Kluwer, Boston
Tidd J, Bessant J, Pavitt K (2005) Managing innovation: integrating technological, market and organizational change, 3rd edn. Wiley, Hoboken
Tritle GL, Scriven EFV, Fusfeld AR (2000) Resolving uncertainty in R&D portfolios. Res Technol Manag 43(6):47–55
Valderrama TG, Groot TLCM (2002) Controlling the efficiency of university research in the Netherlands. In: Thore S (ed) Technology commercialization: DEA and related analytical methods for evaluating the use and implementation of technical innovation. Kluwer, Boston
Wang J, Lin W, Huang Y-H (2010) A performance-oriented risk management framework for innovative R&D projects. Technovation 11–12:601–611

On the Importance of Free Cash Flow Metrics Bias Resulting from Static Approach to Free Cash Flow Analysis

Aleksandra Szpulak

Abstract This paper discusses the accumulation of FCF for companies operating under different industry specific conditions resulting in a positive or negative difference between the length of the operating cycle and payables deferral period. On the basis of simulations on an easy spreadsheet financial model of company operations, it proves that: (1) in the case of a growing company operating under conditions of negative cash conversion cycle the FCF are systematically overestimated by a permanent increase in surplus cash generating from credit delivered by suppliers and employees and as such do not satisfy the definition of FCF, (2) indicates that FCF from operations suffer from timing and matching problems because they count accounting periods instead of operating cycles and therefore valuations based on such FCF are systematically overestimated every time the cash inflows from operating cycle occur earlier to the corresponding cash outflows and, reversely, are systematically underestimated every time the cash inflows from operating cycle occur later to the corresponding cash outflows. To overcome these problems, the on-going approach to free cash flows analysis that matches outflows and corresponding inflows is suggested. The application of a simple NPV to evaluate cash investments in the operating cycle (i.e. cash investments in operating working capital) based on net cash flows generated by operating cycle counts adequately for the industry specific differences in timing of operating cash flows and removes the relevant bias in FCF.

Keywords Operating working capital • Operating cycle • Free cash flow from operations • Accrual accounting • Net present value

1 Introduction

Over the last 20 years, researchers have observed the increasing role of cash flows to investors based on the perception that cash flows are less prone to manipulation, are more easily measured and more intuitive compared to accounting earnings.

A. Szpulak (✉)
Wroclaw University of Economics, Wrocław, Poland
e-mail: aleksandra.szpulak@ue.wroc.pl

T. Dudycz et al. (eds.), *The Essence and Measurement of Organizational Efficiency*,
Springer Proceedings in Business and Economics, DOI 10.1007/978-3-319-21139-8_17

Every year, more and more companies report FCF in their annual report. Unfortunately there is lack of market consensus for FCF metrics (Vernimmen 2005), some refer to pitfalls in measuring FCF (Estridge and Lougee 2007) others on attempts to manage reported cash from operations (Lee 2012). This paper elaborates on additional weaknesses of free cash flow metrics that disclose when simultaneously analyzing, similar in many respects, growing companies but operating under different industry conditions resulting in a different length of operating cycle and payment deferral period. Indicated bias origins in static approach to free cash flow analysis i.e. the operating cycle cutoff point is the arbitrary defined point and therefore the operations are left continuously unfinished.

Apart from the introduction, this paper consists of four sections. The first expounds on the dual perception of investments in operating working capital—once from the cash flow stand point i.e. cash investments in operating working capital (named cash investments in OWC, *CashOn*OWC) and the other from the accrual accounting perspective (commonly known as net operating working capital, NOWC). This part points the cash investments in OWC as a source of potential bias of FCF metrics. The second part elaborates on the bias, shows its consequences for companies operating under different industry conditions defined by the length of the cash conversion cycle, particularly consider negative and positive cycles. This section indicates the cause of the bias: it is a static approach to FCF analysis. Section 4 introduces the on-going approach to free cash flow analysis, which works on full operating cycles and treats each cycle as a separate cash investment in OWC. For valuation purposes, ordinary NPV is employed. The last section points the consequences of free cash flows bias for corporate financial management in the areas of: (1) investors' preferences comparing FCF to ordinary accounting earnings as a measure of company profitability; (2) application of DCF methods based on FCF for valuation; (3) short-term corporate financial management; (4) liquidity measurement and (5) the application of the on-going approach to free cash flow analysis suggested in this paper.

2 Cash Investments in Operating Working Capital

Net operating working capital (NOWC), as defined by many, reflects the amount of investor supplied capital employed in the operating current assets. NOWC as calculated from company balance sheet stands for the operating current assets minus the operating current liabilities. Operating current assets consist of inventories, accounts receivable and operating cash while the operating current liabilities consist of accounts payable and accruals:

$$NOWC = OCA - OCL = OC + AR + INV - AP - Ac = OC + WCR \quad (1)$$

where: OCA—operating current assets, OCL—operating current liabilities, INV—inventory, AR—accounts receivable, OC—operating cash, AP—accounts payable, Ac—accruals (mainly salaries and taxes), WCR—working capital requirements.

Does every company need to invest in the NOWC? Our intuitive answer to that question is positive, as probably no one has seen a company with zero NOWC, however in theory it is possible. Taking at first glance the cash flow perspective instead of accrual accounting zero investments means no cash outlays for OWC. Imagine a company that, for simplicity, once produces only one product, which consumes all delivered materials and simultaneously sells the final product so there are no inventories. The company gives trade credit of length T^{AR} to its customers and after that time records on its cash account operating cash inflow CF^{+} equal to revenues. The company also receives trade credit of length T^{AP} to pay all operating costs including materials and work reflected by operating cash outflow CF^{-}. Under certainty, cash investments in OWC result only from timing differences between the length of operating cycle and the payment deferral period, reflected in our simplified model by T^{AR} and T^{AP} respectively. In corporate finance such a difference ($T^{AR} - T^{AP}$) is known as the Cash Conversion Cycle (CCC) (Richards and Laughlin 1980) and stands for the length of time the investment in the operating cycle is recovered. If the operating cycle and payment deferral periods are equal ($T^{AR} = T^{AP}$). No investor supply cash is invested in the operating cycle and therefore cash investments in OWC equals 0. If the operating cycle exceeds the payment deferral period, company investors are forced to temporarily invest amount of CF^{-} in the operating cycle for the period CCC. If the payment deferral period exceeds the operating cycle, the company investors not only do not supply any cash to finance the operating cycle, but temporarily own the CF^{-} for the period CCC. It is a sort of invisible (from the cash flows perspective) credit, as ultimately after that period, the company must pay its bills in amount of CF^{-}. Now, imagine that the company operating under conditions of $T^{AR} = T^{AP}$ repeats such an operating cycle every day to produce quantity Q of its final product per day. Considering the story from the company's inception, cash investments in OWC are always zero regardless of the growth in the quantity Q produced. Under uncertainty, however, cash investments in OWC are in any case increased by safety stocks of such operating current assets as inventories and cash kept as a result of volatility in timing and magnitude of operating cash flows.

Recall the simplified model of company operations as described above and let us now return to the accrual accounting and consider investments in NOWC as calculated from Eq. 1 for each case. First, as a result of time difference between revenues and cash inflows and expenditures and cash outflows accounts receivable and accounts payable (together with accruals referring to work used in the operating cycle) disclosure on the company balance sheet starting from the first day of operating cycle. As both revenues and costs are recognized in accordance with accrual accounting earnings, appear as well on the right side of the balance sheet and the NOWC as a difference between revenues in form of accounts receivable and costs in form of accounts payable equals accounting earnings. When $T^{AR} = T^{AP}$ operating cash inflow and operating cash outflow appear on the same day and on this day the balance sheet cash equals accounting earnings. Under accrual accounting, if $T^{AR} = T^{AP}$ up to T^{AP} investors invest in the operating cycle profits that are accrued (i.e. cumulated and deferred) so generally the accounting earnings that will transform into cash in future, particularly at T^{AR}. Such NOWC and accounting earnings equality holds regardless of the length of CCC and only the structure of NOWC changes as the operating cycles proceed. Such changes in the NOWC structure are thoroughly described by Wędzki (2003).

In general, the difference between the accounting earnings and cash at hand equals the change in so-called accruals[1] (Dechow 1994). There are two types of accruals: long-term, resulting from changes in long term accounts (e.g. depreciation, provisions) and short-term, resulting from changes in the working capital. As our considerations limit to the investments in the operating cycle, long-term accruals are irrelevant and the cash at hand or cash from operations (CFO) equals:

$$CFO_t = E_t - \Delta WCR_t = E_t - WCR_t + WCR_{t-1} \tag{2}$$

where: CFO—cash from operations, E—accounting earnings as a difference between all recognized revenues and costs over the period t, WCR—working capital requirements, ΔWCR is a change in WCR or short—term accruals.

The idea behind Eq. 2 in light of our simplified model is obvious—as accounting earnings consist in part equal to WCR_t of revenues and costs that are not settled until the end of period t that part needs to be excluded to drive on cash at hand at the end of t. Consequently, there was a part equal to WCR_{t-1} of revenues and costs that was not settled until the end of the previous accounting period $t-1$ but is transformed into cash over the period t and therefore needs to be included to drive on cash at hand at the end of period t. Under conditions of $T^{AR} > T^{AP}$ accrued revenues exceed accrued costs while under $T^{AR} < T^{AP}$ accrued costs exceed accrued revenues. Figures 1 and 2 are the graphical presentations for the discussed relationships.

Cash investment in OWC refers to the area indicated by B in both situations as displayed on Figs. 1 and 2 respectively. However, under $T^{AR} > T^{AP}$ area B represents the amount of investor supplied capital invested in the operating cycle on a cash basis and under $T^{AR} < T^{AP}$ area B indicates the amount temporarily owned by company (a sort of invisible, credit delivered by suppliers and workers) as the corresponding revenues (area A) have been already settled. Ultimately, this amount of cash investments in OWC, as defined by area B, differs from traditional accrual accounting NOWC by profits included in the accounts receivable.

[1] These accruals differ from the accruals mentioned in Eq. 1 where accruals stands for position in balance sheet.

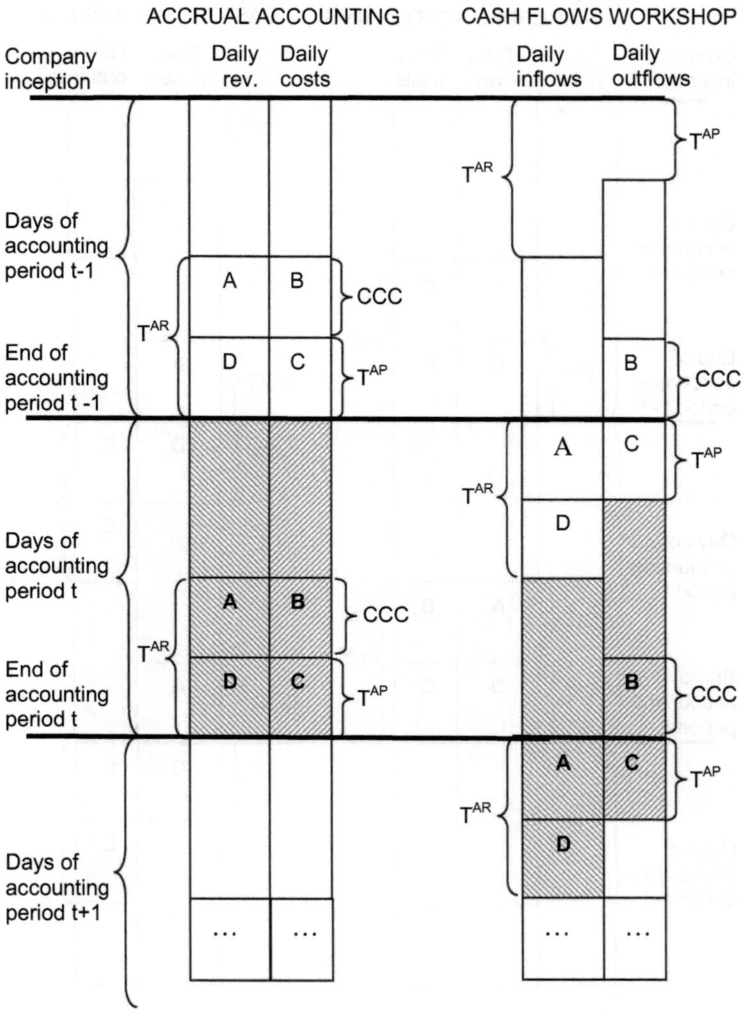

Fig. 1 Accrual accounting vs. cash flows workshop for companies operating in conditions of positive Cash Conversion Cycle, where: T^{AR}—trade credit period granted by the company; T^{AP}—trade credit period received by the company; CCC—cash conversion cycle. Under assumption of continuous operations, no inventories and constant demand (sales) the *vertical hinge* of *each box* stands for days of operations while the *horizontal hinge* stands for size of the variable listed at the *top of the box*. Area B indicates cash investments in OWC, area of A + D – C is the WCR (or short-term accruals), A and D refer to credit sales outstanding (accounts receivable) at the end of accounting period, C refers to accounts payable not settled at the end of the accounting period. Only in zero profit conditions *CashOn*OWC = NOWC, otherwise credit sales outstanding exceed costs not yet settled by the amount of profits. CFO is accounting earnings (revenues minus costs) less ΔWCR. CFO as a sum of all cash inflows and outflows as recorded over analyzed period includes *box* B. Inclusion of *box* B in CFO results in matching and timing problems of cash flows

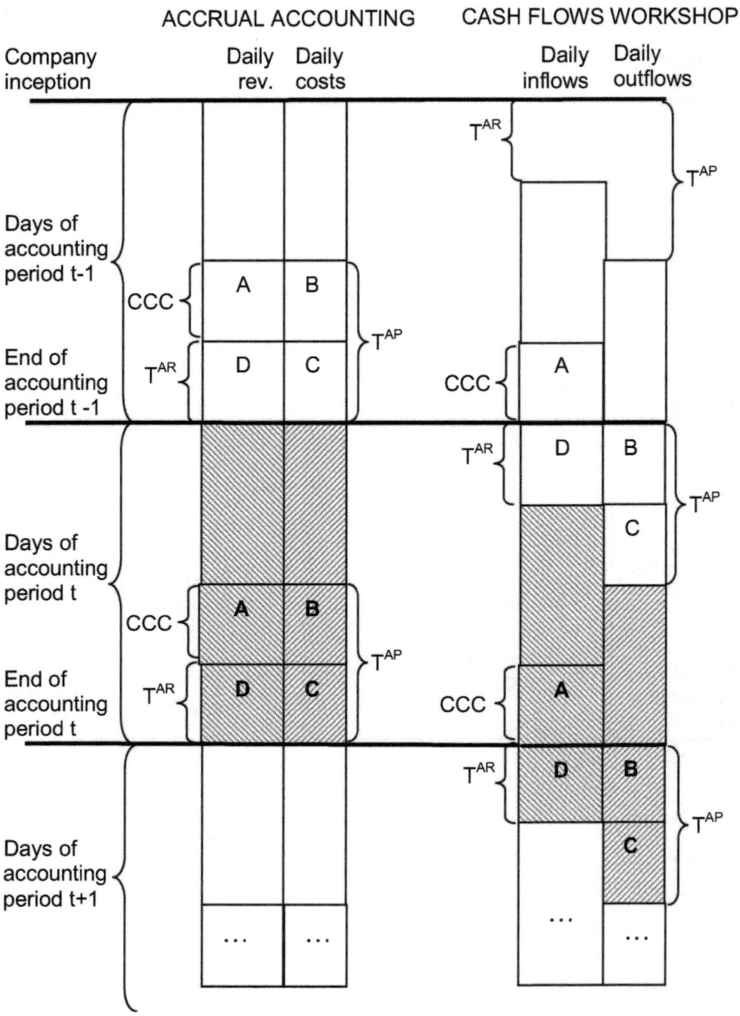

Fig. 2 Accrual accounting vs. cash flows workshop for companies operating in conditions of negative Cash Conversion Cycle, where: T^{AR}—trade credit period granted by company; T^{AP}—trade credit period received by the company; CCC—cash conversion cycle. Under assumption of continuous operations, no inventories and constant demand (sales) the *vertical hinge* of *each box* stands for days of operations while the *horizontal hinge* stands for size of variable listed at the *top of the box*. Area A indicates cash surplus as a sum of inflows, appearing prior to the corresponding outflows equal to area B. Area B stands for cash temporarily owned by the company over period CCC that serves for paying accounts payable equal to B. Therefore cash investments in OWC equals area B. WCR (short-term accruals) is the area of $D - B - C$, D equals to credit sales outstanding (accounts receivable) at the end of accounting period t, B and C are accounts payable not settled at the end of accounting period. Only in zero profit conditions *CashOn*OWC = NOWC, CFO are accounting earnings (revenues minus costs) less ΔWCR, inclusion of area A in CFO results in timing and matching problems of cash flows

In a more extended model, including the possibility of inventories, the amount AP that refers to inventories that was already paid adds to CFO by corresponding CF^- and creates investments in the future cash inflows.

Cash investments in OWC at any time t results from timing differences of cash flows (as reflected by area B) and its variability and equals to:

$$CashOnOWC_t = -\sum_1^t RCF_t^- - \sum_1^t CF_t^- + \sum_1^t NCF_t^+ \tag{3}$$

where: *CashOn*OWC—cash investments in OWC, CF^-—operating cash outflows, RCF^-—operating current assets safety stocks, NCF^+—operating net cash inflows, i.e. calculated on costs of goods sold basis, t—day of company operations no. (starting at 1, that stands for company inception):

$$\begin{aligned} RCF_t^- &= RM_t + RFG_t + ROC_t \\ NCF_t^+ &= S_{t-T^{AR}+1} \cdot c \end{aligned} \tag{4}$$

where: RM—materials safety stocks, RFG—finish goods safety stocks, ROC—operating cash safety stocks, S—sales in units, c—unit costs of goods sold, T^{AR}—trade credit period granted by the company.

CashOnOWC stands for cumulated sum of cash outlays as generated from company inception and engaged in on-going operations at the moment of analysis, i.e. engaged in operations that have been already started and not finished at the moment of analysis, e.g. the end accounting period. This amount appears only due to time differences between corresponding operating flows, i.e. outflows and inflows. *CashOnOWC* could be either positive or negative. Negative *CashOnOWC* stands for a sum of outflows a company has already made at the time of analysis in on-going operations, while positive *CashOnOWC* stand for a sum of outflows the company will have been making in on-going operations in consecutive future periods. The sign of *CashOnOWC* in general depends on industry and company specific conditions, i.e. negative *CashOnOWC* refers to positive CCC while positive *CashOnOWC* refers to negative CCC. Between the NOWC (Eq. 1) and *CashOnOWC* (Eq. 3) the following relationship exists[2]:

[2] Equation 5a can be easy proof in the following way. In Fig. 1 at the end of accounting period t $NOWC = A + D - C$. As $AR = A + D$ and $AP = C$, A is a part of AR and refers to revenues i.e. costs increased by earnings: $A = B + E(B)^{AR}$ and similarly $D = C + E(C)^{AR}$, such that $E^{AR} = E(B)^{AR} + E(C)^{AR}$. Having from balance sheet AR, AP and from income statement E to get B we need to adjust AR on E^{AR} and subtract C that is $A + D - E^{AR} - C = NOWC - E^{AR}$. In Fig. 2 it would be: $D - E^{AR} - B - C = NOWC - E^{AR}$. Cash flows workshop indicates on Fig. 1 that the net cash flows (as calculated from formula 5a) are negative while on Fig. 2 are positive, therefore to get signs of *CashOnOWC* consistent with cash flows workshop the appropriate correction ("−" before bracket) is done in formula 5a.

$$\begin{aligned} CashOnOWC_t &= -\left(NOWC_t - E_t^{AR}\right) \\ E_t^{AR} &= \sum_{t-T^{AR}+2}^{t} S_t \cdot e \end{aligned} \tag{5a}$$

where: E_t^{AR}—sum of accounting earnings included in accounts receivables as calculated on the basis of net sales, e—unit accounting earnings, i.e. unit price p_s less of unit costs of goods sold c.

The formula given in Eq. 5a allows us to estimate the amount of *CashOnOWC* on commonly available data from financial statements.

Besides the total amount of cash, investments in OWC currently held by the company, we can also investigate the additional cash investments in OWC made at the moment of analysis comparing to analogous previous moment. Incremental investment *ΔCashONOWC* equals:

$$\begin{aligned} &\Delta CashOnOWC_t = CashOnOWC_t - CashOnOWC_{t-1} = \\ &= -\left(\Delta NOWC_t - \Delta E_t^{AR}\right) \end{aligned} \tag{5b}$$

If a company operates under the condition of a positive CCC, *ΔCashONOWC* equals additional cash delivered by investors for on-going operations at the time of analysis comparing to the previous time. If a company operates under the condition of a negative CCC, *ΔCashONOWC* equals additional cash delivered by suppliers and workers and refers to increments in cash surplus the investors temporarily own at the time of analysis comparing to the previous time.

The problem discussed in the next section concerns the distribution of the areas A, B, C and D within EBIT, FCF and NCF generated by a growing company operating under different industry specific conditions.

3 FCF Metrics Bias Resulting From a Static Approach to Free Cash Flows Analysis

Accrual accounting, as a fundament of accounting earnings, let it be EBIT, is outstanding for matching revenues and corresponding costs. Under this rule, however, the time of payment is irrelevant and therefore all areas: A, B, C and D are included while calculating EBIT. As time of payment is irrelevant, the differences between the length of operating cycle and payment deferral period are not reflected in EBIT et al.

The core of all metric for FCF defines this sort of flows available for distributions to investors as $EBIT(1-T_c)-I_n$ where T_c–is a marginal cash tax rate and I_n are cash investments in future growth (investments above the amortization). Such investments reflects capital expenditures and changes in the operating working capital, therefore $I_n = capex + \Delta WCR$. Let us assume, for practical reasons, that $capex = 0$

and analyze the effect of the changes in WCR alone, consequently the variable of interest is FCF from operations. Employing the cash flows workshop to measure the FCF from operations we see from Figs. 1 and 2 that only area B is included in FCF under $T^{AR} > T^{AP}$ and only area A under $T^{AR} < T^{AP}$. This means that two companies with the same EBIT could produce different FCF thus giving misleading signals to investors. Under $T^{AR} > T^{AP}$ positive FCF means free cash available for distribution to investors at a given point in time but the same is not true for $T^{AR} < T^{AP}$ as FCF includes cash from invisible credit as delivered by suppliers and workers which are not parties of company investors.

The detailed analysis of the influence of the sector specific length of CCC on FCF considers the finite planning horizon T and includes the accumulation of FCF until that horizon starting from company inception. Similarly, as in the previous analysis, we think of a simplified model of company operations; however, the company is a growing one (growing at a constant rate *g*). Under the conditions of $T^{AR} > T^{AP}$ FCF are lower from base case FCF (generated under $T^{AR} = T^{AP}$) as always the $WCR_t > WCR_{t-1}$. Under the conditions of $T^{AR} < T^{AP}$ cash flows are higher than the base case FCF as always the $WCR_t < WCR_{t-1}$ (WC is negative for that conditions). The reason is that cash flows workshop for calculating FCF cuts the operating cycle off at the arbitrary defined period (the end of the accounting period) and does not take into consideration the fact that the operating cycle will continue in the future. FCF does not capture the corresponding flows—inflows for $T^{AR} > T^{AP}$ (area A) and outflows for $T^{AR} < T^{AP}$ (area B) and therefore suffers from timing and matching problems.

Contrary to FCF other flows—net cash flows NCF are cash flows from investment that match cash outflows with corresponding cash inflows. NCF are flows that consider the magnitude and timing of operating cash flows thus are superior to EBIT (which consider only magnitude of financial flows) and are superior to FCF which mismatch operating flows. To calculate NCF the area A needs to be included under $T^{AR} > T^{AP}$ and area B under $T^{AR} < T^{AP}$.

Figures 3, 4, and 5 are graphical presentations of the discussed relationships and compare the evolution of $EBIT(1-T_c)$, FCF and NCF from company inception to the end of planning horizon T. All companies in Figs. 3, 4, and 5 have the same EBIT. All graphs are the results of simulations based on a simple spreadsheet financial model of company operations.

The operating income after taxes $EBIT(1-T_c)$ is the same in all discussed cases, however it seems on the basis of FCF, that companies that operates under $T^{AR} < T^{AP}$ generate more free cash available for distribution than the rest of companies. The point is that FCF under $T^{AR} < T^{AP}$ (negative CCC in general) is supplied by invisible credit that needs to be paid. This, however, contradicts the idea of FCF because following (Daves et al. 2004, p. 17) company does not use FCF to purchase operating assets. Figure 6 compares evolution of FCF under different length of CCC and clearly display the bias included in FCF metrics.

The cutoff point in the operating cycle at the end of accounting period defines static approach to free cash flow analysis similarly to liquidity analysis based on traditional liquidity ratios. Such static approach is in contrast to on-going concern

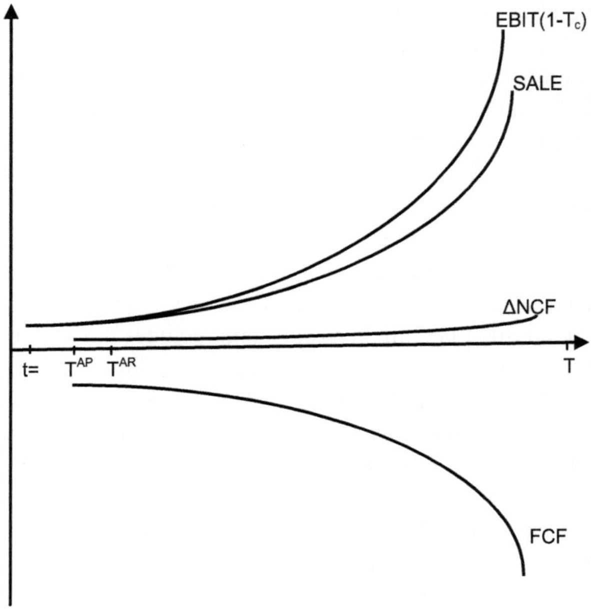

Fig. 3 The evolution of $EBIT(1-T_c)$, FCF and ΔNCF for growing company under $T^{AR} > T^{AP}$ ($EBIT(1-T_c) < \Delta WCR$). Under conditions of $T^{AR} > T^{AP}$ FCF counts for cash investments in OWC which for growing company increases in each subsequent period. As FCF cuts off future inflows from already made outflows, the result is negative FCF (while $EBIT < \Delta WCR$). At the same time ΔNCF takes these future inflows into consideration and therefore are positive and follow the sales growth pattern

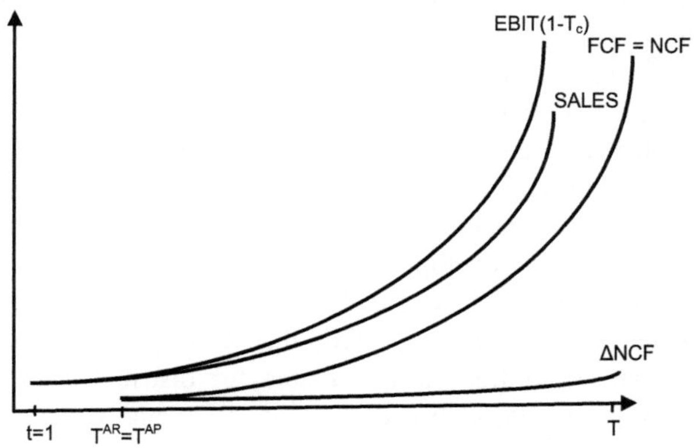

Fig. 4 The evolution of $EBIT(1-T_c)$, FCF and ΔNCF for growing company under $T^{AR} = T^{AP}$. Such company needs no cash investments in OWC, at the same time investments in OWC are "on paper" only unless the materials inventory investments are included. Nevertheless, this investment is done in only a few subsequent operating cycles, not for the whole upcoming accounting period and its growth. FCF follows $EBIT(1-T_C)$ and is shifted to the right of it

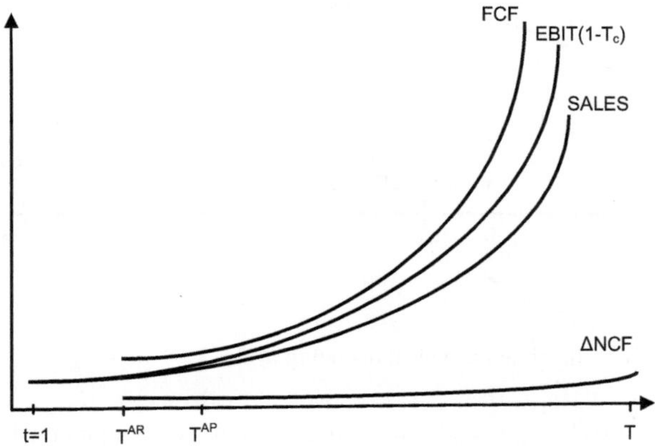

Fig. 5 The evolution of EBIT(1−T$_c$), FCF and ΔNCF for growing company under $T^{AR} < T^{AP}$ (ΔWCR < EBIT(1−T$_c$)). Under conditions of $T^{AR} < T^{AP}$ FCF counts for cash investments in OWC (invisible from cash flows perspective credit received from suppliers and workers) and therefore are at any time higher from EBIT as ΔWCR is always negative. As FCF cuts off future outflows from already recorded inflows, the result is positive FCF. At the same time NCF takes these future inflows into consideration and therefore are positive and follow the sales growth pattern

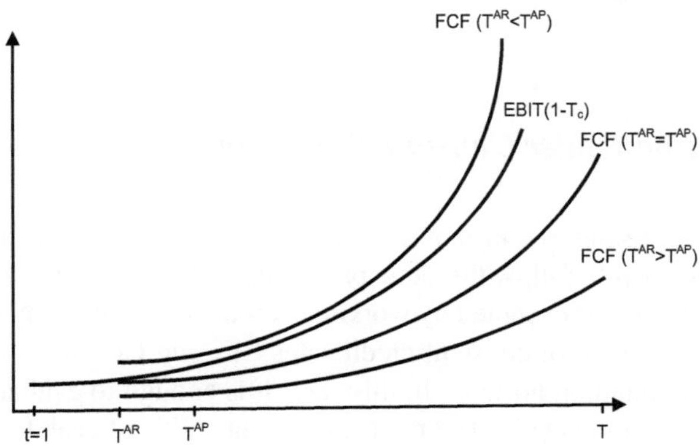

Fig. 6 The comparison of FCF under different sector conditions resulting in different lengths of CCC (ΔWCR < EBIT(1−T$_c$)). EBIT(1−T$_c$) is the same for all companies

that relies on full operating cycle—the approach to free cash flows analysis described below.

4 Ongoing Approach to Free Cash Flow Analysis

The financial model of company operations developed in this section is a general one and thus has rather pragmatic meaning for managers and students because it easily captures the core idea employed for valuation. The company operating cycle consists

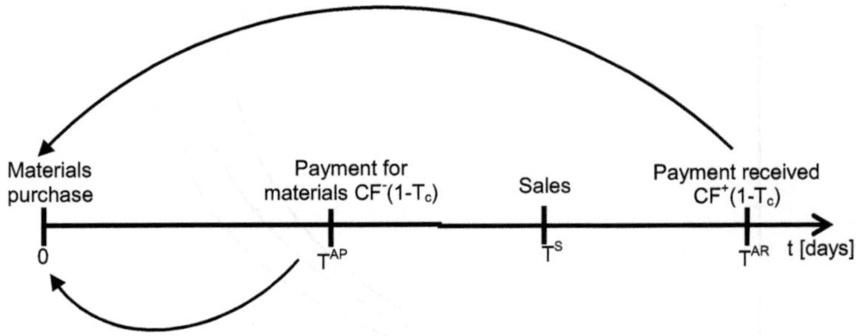

Fig. 7 The cash flows timeline for typical operating cycle

of purchasing—production—sales—collection and is spontaneously financed by accounts payable. Cash flows associated with this cycle are operating cash inflows CF^+ and operating cash outflows CF^- (see Fig. 7). As T^{AR} and T^{AP} do not coincide CF^- refers to cash investments in OWC. Both cash flows CF^+ and CF^- appears at the end of the trade credit periods T^{AR} and T^{AP} respectively as it is not economically justified to settle accounts earlier for customers or company. The model assumes the tax rate equals the marginal cash tax rate T_c and continuous flows resulting from sales means that such a timeline starts each day of company operations.

4.1 Valuation Under Constant Credit Sales

Assuming that the sales is constant over the whole planning horizon T cash flows for any operating cycle follow the same pattern described by timing and magnitude of cash flows. Timing is designed by working capital policy decision variables: T^{AR} and T^{AP} and as a result of constant credit sales CF^+ and CF^- magnitude does not change over the planning horizon. In this case, it is enough to evaluate investment in one typical operating cycle. The net present value NPV of cash flows associated with this typical operating cycle equals to:

$$NPV = -\frac{CF_{T^{AP}}{}^{-}(1-T_c)}{(1+r)^{T^{AP}}} + \frac{CF_{T^S+T^{AR}}{}^{+}(1-T_c)}{(1+r)^{T^S+T^{AR}}} \tag{7}$$

where: r—required rate of return, T^S—time of sales.

Introducing infinite horizon the value of such infinite net cash flow is a value of perpetuity:

$$V_0 = \frac{NPV}{r} \tag{8}$$

4.2 Valuation Under Discretionary Time Pattern of Credit Sales

As sales are rarely constant over the planning horizon T, in practice it is more realistic to assume that sales follow a time pattern: $CS(t)$. It can be a time pattern of any type including seasonal variations and, moreover, the sales pattern is free to change over time. Cash flows CF^{+} and CF^{-} are functions of sales and follow a sales time-series pattern, therefore cash flows are functions of time $CF^{+}(t)$ and $CF^{-}(t)$. The timing of cash flows results from T^{AP} and T^{AR}. Cash flows pattern properties generate from both: working capital policy parameters T^{AP} and T^{AR} and sales time pattern. As each operating cycle cash flows may differ due to sales time pattern and its changes, we need to include all cash flows generated from sales to evaluate cash investments in OWC over the whole planning horizon T. Introducing more convenience for analysis continuous discounting, first we calculate the NPV_t representing the net present value of cash flows for each operating cycle beginning at t:

$$NPV_t = -CF(t)^{-}(1 - T_c) \cdot e^{-rT^{AP}} + CF(t)^{+}(1 - T_c) \cdot e^{-r\left(T^{S}+T^{AR}\right)} \quad (9)$$

Secondly, we calculate the NPV of the whole project—cash investments in OWC made over the entire planning horizon T[3]:

$$NPV = \int_0^T \left| \left(-CF(t)^{-}(1 - T_c) \cdot e^{-rT^{AP}} + CF(t)^{+}(1 - T_c) \cdot e^{-r\left(T^{S}+T^{AR}\right)} \right) e^{-rt} \right| dt = \\ = \int_0^T \left| NPV_t \cdot e^{-rt} \right| dt \quad (10)$$

Introducing infinite horizon the value of such infinite net cash flows is a value of:

$$V_0 = \lim_{T \to \infty} \int_0^T \frac{NPV_t}{(1+r)^t} \quad (11)$$

[3] Valuation model developed in this section origins in the paper of (Sartoris and Hill 1983). Their model is a very general one to evaluate changes in working capital policy and, in fact, reduces to general valuation model.

5 Managerial Implications for Corporate Financial Management

5.1 *What Measures of a Company Performance Do Investors Prefer?*

There is quite a large debate in the literature on which measure of company performance is better—traditional accounting earnings or cash flows while predicting stock market returns. Apart from that, none, to the best of my knowledge, describes the variability of stock market returns at a reliable level, the results concerning the significance effects are mixed. Based on empirical investigation some argue that accounting earnings outperform cash flows (like Dechow 1994; Sloan 1996). Conclusions concerning FCF metrics bias resulting from static approach to free cash flows analysis as described in this paper ads additional argument against application of FCF. The problem is more severe for young companies (where cash investments in OWC are quite large comparing to gained EBIT), companies with quite large variability in the level of OWC (for that companies FCF tends to change direction from period to period) and companies with long CCC (where the amount of cash investments in OWC are quite large). Not surprisingly though, (Dechow 1994) observe the disadvantage of cash flows over accounting earnings in this listed situations. There will also be some situations in which the FCF metrics bias would not create a bias at all, e.g. constant sales (there are no additions to cash investments in OWC for such case) and CCC close to zero (there are no cash investments in OWC at all for CCC equals zero).

5.2 *Valuation Based on FCF*

Financial theorists assume that only cash flows matter when valuing an asset—these are investment outlays and corresponding inflows. However, what creates a value is not the change in the cash position but net additions (i.e. earnings) to wealth (Vernimmen 2005). FCF from operations exhibit the change in the company operating cash position not the wealth *per se* because considering the wealth we need to include future flows from currently held investments. Additionally, these end of period cash investments in OWC take into consideration only a few future subsequent operating cycles not the whole upcoming accounting period therefore we rather should calculate investments in WCR as $\Delta WCR = WCR_{t+1} - WCR_t$ not $\Delta WCR = WCR_t - WCR_{t-1}$.[4] Although financial theorists (Shrieves and Wachowicz 2001) prove that FCF and NPV give adequate results and both are

[4] Only linear trend in EBIT requires constant additions to cash investments in OWC and for this special case these additions are the same over future and current year.

just a variation of the DCF valuation method, this is only the truth when the end of horizon FCF includes repayment of the whole cash investment in OWC. Under conditions of $T^{AR} > T^{AP}$ these would be very large positive flows and under conditions of $T^{AR} < T^{AP}$ these would be very large negative flows. Both offset the preliminary bias in FCF, thus discounted NCF, and discounted by the same cost of capital FCF produce the same result. Considering the infinite horizon however FCF does not include such repayment of the whole cash investments in OWC therefore FCF are biased. It is reasonable to conclude that valuation based on FCF produce biased results: undervalued for $T^{AR} > T^{AP}$ (positive CCC in general) and overvalued for $T^{AR} < T^{AP}$ (negative CCC in general).

5.3 Short-Term Financial Management as Abandoned Source of Wealth

Under the theory of a growing company (Copeland et al. 2005, p. 498), it seems that what creates growth are future new investments and what creates value is the rate of return on that investment higher than the required one. The rate of return gained by the company comes from both: *capex* and cash investments in OWC. The former is known as capital budgeting and the latter as short-term financial management or working capital management. It is not an easy task, however, to find a paper referring to efficiency of working capital management, especially merging working capital management efficiency evaluation with the wealth maximization framework. A few exceptions to list are: (Sartoris and Hill 1983; Kim and Chung 1990; Arcelus and Srinivasan 1993; Rutkowski 2000; Wędzki 2003; Szpulak 2014). It is more like a stereotype that managing working capital concerns managing financial liquidity and conjunction with efficiency is delivered only by the minimization of costs of operating current assets stocks. Contrary, Eqs. 7, 9, and 10 define this straightforward relationship between efficiency of working capital management and wealth maximization criterion. Describing the inflows and outflows occurring at the date of trade credit periods, both granted and received, as functions of sales in units and such additional parameters like: discount rate, prices sale, materials, labor and inventory carrying and shipping, the delay of salaries payments, penalty charges for late payments, rate on overdue payment from collection agency and time the company decides on selling overdue balances, limits of materials consumption, ordering cycle, delivery batch and delivery cycle and operating assets safety stocks to mention only the most common enables managers to decide on optimal working capital policy in line with wealth maximization. Working on cash flows at the same time enables the control of financial liquidity.

5.4 Measuring Financial Liquidity

There is a very special business situation that could be a potential source of financial abuse: Let us imagine a growing company with negative CCC. In light of the analysis of FCF from operations made in this paper, increments of cash investments in OWC increase with every operating cycle, *ceteris paribus*, leaving a company with increasing sources of surplus cash. This is due to increments in the invisible credit as delivered by suppliers and workers. Free use of such a temporary cash surplus—particularly financing *capex* or, worse, distribution of it in form of dividends may result in company bankruptcy as soon as the sales stops increasing or declines. In general, for companies with negative CCC cash investments in OWC as measured by Eq. 3 should be covered with non-operating current assets net of non-operating current liabilities: (non-operating current assets sums up to short-term investments, assuming they are liquid i.e. may be used at any time without much lost in the value):

$$\frac{NLB_t}{-\left(WCR_t - E_t^{AR}\right)}, \qquad WCR < 0 \tag{12}$$

where: NLB—net liquid balance as a difference between non-operating current assets and non-operating current liabilities, WCR—net operating working capital (Eq. 1), E^{AR}—sum of accounting earnings included in accounts receivable (Eq. 5a).

Ratio close to 0 indicates very high financial risk and high probability of bankruptcy particularly in the event of declining market conditions.

5.5 What Needs to Be Done to Apply the Concept of an Ongoing Approach to Free Cash Flows Analysis?

To apply the concept on publicly available financial data it is enough to forecast sales, estimate industry specific characteristics of the operating cycle: the length of operating cycle and the length of payment deferral period and build adequate spread sheet financial model. A task that's easy in theory is often complicated in practice. The first and the most severe problem is the unbiased estimation of the above-mentioned periods. In practice, it requires calculating such financial ratios as: the inventory conversion period, receivable collection period and payables deferral period. All these ratios are highly inaccurate, apart from perhaps such an unreal business situation such as constant sales, inventories only in amount of safety stocks and constant working capital policy over whole analyzed past period. Going inside the company the application of these on-going approach complicates even further as the traditional financial model, like the one used in this paper, assumes continuous inflows and outflows resulting from sales which produces a smooth curve of NCF over the whole planning horizon being unfortunately totally inaccurate.

One reason is that such a traditional financial model does not include ordering cycles and delivery cycles that cause cash flows to appear from time to time not every day of company operations. It seems therefore that the application of on-going concern to free cash flows analysis open the waste space for future research.

6 Conclusions

This paper aimed to disclose a bias incorporated into FCF metrics resulting from timing and matching problems that cash flows suffer from compared to EBIT. The sources of the bias are cash investments in OWC, which differ depending on the length of the Cash Conversion Cycle. Under the conditions of negative CCC, the FCF as calculated on the basis of commonly applied metrics ($EBIT(1-T_c)-I_n$) do not satisfy the definition of FCF. That is, they do not sum cash available for distribution to investors as a part of it, namely $\Delta CashOnOWC$, need to be paid to suppliers and workers, which are not company investors parties. The consequences of this bias refer to such areas of corporate financial management as (1) investors preferences comparing FCF to ordinary accounting earnings as a measure of company profitability, (2) application of DCF methods based on FCF for valuation, (3) short-term corporate financial management or (4) liquidity measurement. To obey the bias in the FCF metrics but still satisfy the requirements of financial theory to rely on cash flows for valuation, the alternative valuation based on NPV of net cash flows, NCF, as generated by the operating cycle is suggested in this paper.

References

Arcelus F, Srinivasan G (1993) Integrating working capital decisions. Eng Econ 39(1):1–15

Copeland T, Weston J, Shastri K (2005) Financial theory and corporate policy. Prentice Hall, London

Daves P, Ehrhardt M, Shrieves R (2004) Corporate valuation: a guide for managers and investors. Cengage Learning, Mason, OH

Dechow P (1994) Accounting earnings and cash flows as measures of firm performance. The role of accounting accruals. J Accunt Econ 18:3–42

Estridge J, Lougee B (2007) Measuring free cash flows for equity valuation: pitfalls and possible solutions. J Appl Finance 19(2):60–71

Kim Y, Chung K (1990) An integrated evaluation of investment in inventory and credit: a cash flow approach. J Bus Account 17(3):381–390

Lee LF (2012) Incentives to inflate reported cash from operations using classification and timing. Account Rev 87(1):1–33

Richards V, Laughlin E (1980) A cash conversion cycle approach to liquidity analysis. Financ Manag 9(1):32

Rutkowski A (2000) Podejście inwestycyjne przy udzielaniu kredytu kupieckiego. Rachunkowość, no.1:10–21

Sartoris W, Hill N (1983) A generalized cash flow approach to short-term financial decisions. J Financ 38(2):349–360

Shrieves R, Wachowicz J (2001) Free cash flow (FCF), economic value added (EVA), and net present value (NPV): a reconciliation of variations of discounted-cash-flow (DCF) valuation. Eng Econ 46(1):33–51

Sloan R (1996) Do stock prices fully reflect information in accruals and cash flows about future earnings? Account Rev 71(3):289–315

Szpulak A (2014) Evaluating net investments in the operating working capital: the integrated approach to working capital management. Working paper presented during 15th international conference on financial management: theory and practice, Wroclaw 2014 (available upon request from Author)

Vernimmen P (ed) (2005) Corporate finance. Theory and practice. Wiley, Hoboken, NJ

Wędzki D (2003) Strategie płynności finansowej przedsiębiorstwa. Oficyna Ekonomiczna, Kraków

Do Business Valuation Professionals Need Business Valuation Standards?

Piotr Szymański

Abstract The paper presents results of author's own research on business valuation. The research was conducted among experts in business valuation. A total of 182 experts was surveyed. The article attempts to answer the following questions: whether and to what extent are business valuation standards (BVS) conducive to improving the quality of valuations? Do the experts find business valuation standards necessary? Are there differences in the perception of the phenomena connected with valuation between experts working on the U.S. market, where BVS are well-established, and experts from other countries such as Poland and Romania where these standards have a shorter history?

Keywords Business valuation • Business valuation standards • Business valuation professionals

1 Introduction

Business valuation of privately held companies is an important aspect of economic life. This type of valuation is the basis for settlement between parties in transactions, in court litigation between owners and in other forms of settlement. Theory and practice show that business valuation is a complicated process for at least two reasons. Firstly, the valuation of companies is complicated due to the very nature of businesses. Companies are structures of varying complexity. Moreover, they are mechanisms with a number of internal and external relationships. Secondly, business valuation draws on the knowledge of economics, finance, management and, albeit indirectly, of other social sciences. Such a wide range of knowledge and its varied conceptual apparatus hinders perception and generates numerous problems which translate into practice (see Pratt and Niculita 2008).

Although the first insights and regulations in scope of valuation we can find in XIX century but the business valuation standards have been around for decades. In

P. Szymański (✉)
Wrocław University of Economics, Wrocław, Poland
e-mail: piotr.szymanski.ue@gmail.com

T. Dudycz et al. (eds.), *The Essence and Measurement of Organizational Efficiency*,
Springer Proceedings in Business and Economics, DOI 10.1007/978-3-319-21139-8_18

the United States IRS Revenue Ruling 59–60, issued in 1959, is continuing influence in the business valuation standards that began to appear in the late 1980s (Lieberman and Anderson 2008). The first business valuation standards were created in the United States and Canada in response to the problems of valuation practice and in order to raise the level of valuations (see Hitchner 2006).

In subsequent years, on the one side we observe the process of business valuation standards is being introduced in other countries (e.g. New Zealand, Australia, Hong Kong, Germany, Poland) or will be introduced in the future (Italy and India—still in progress). On the other side international business valuation standards are being introduced (International 2011). Why was BVSs introduced in last few decades? In the preambles of BVS we can find the reason why standards were introduced. For instance, according the American Society of Appraisers, the Standards were adopted in order to maintain and enhance the quality of business valuations for benefit of the business valuation profession and users of business valuations (ASA 2009). Australian APES 225 sets the standards for Members in the provision of quality and ethical Valuation Services (APES 2012). According The Institute of Business Appraisers, Business Appraisal Standards purpose is articulate standards by which those who aspire to participation, and those already established in business appraisal practice may be guided in the ethical and skillful execution of their tasks, and report the results and conclusions of their work in the most effective manner (Professional Standards 2011).

At the same time many countries' economies are changing significantly as a result of globalization and the ensuing liberalization of trade and capital movement. These processes are accompanied by changes in technology that improve the flow of information. In recent years global economy has been shaken by crises: the first crisis occurred in the subprime market and, related to it to an extent, the second crisis—in the public debt market. Both crises have highlighted the problems in the field of risk assessment and, consequently, in the business valuation. Do business valuation standards necessary? According Lieberman whether business valuation professionals need more standards is reasonable question (Lieberman and Anderson 2008). Therefore, in the context of the above events the following questions arise:

- Do the experts find business valuation standards necessary?
- Whether and to what extent are business valuation standards conducive to improving the quality of valuations?
- Are there differences in the perception of the phenomena connected with valuation between experts working on the U.S. market, where the standards of company valuation are well-established, and experts from other countries where these standards have a shorter history as Poland and Romania?

The article attempts to answer these questions.

2 Methodology

The study was carried out under the research project—habilitation No. N N113 261836 funded by the Polish Ministry of Science and Higher Education. The study was conducted in September 2011. An invitation to participate in the study was sent (via email) to 9499 experts whose job description included company valuation, in countries like Australia, China (Hong Kong), France, India, Canada, Germany, New Zealand, Poland, Romania, Singapore, the USA, and the United Kingdom.

It is difficult to estimate the size of the population of experts in company valuation in the countries surveyed. In countries like the U.S. and Canada, where experts in the business valuation are subject to the certification process it is possible to estimate the number of experts fairly accurately. In other countries it is difficult to determine the number of experts because the certification process for business valuation is not carried out. For example in Poland it is difficult to estimate the number of business valuation experts due to the fact that the profession is not regulated and the area of business valuation is in the scope of interest of property appraisers, auditors and accountants. In these professional groups, however, only a small proportion are likely to be involved in business valuation in a systematic way. Many experts are only involved in this area on an ad hoc basis, and a vast majority of experts do not handle this issue at all.

The experts who were invited to participate in the research can be divided into three groups. The first group consists of members of organizations of accountants and auditors which have developed standards of business valuation. The second group consists of experts belonging to organizations of appraisers, who have also developed standards of company valuation. In both these groups experts have a very broad scope of competences, but many or even most of them do not in fact deal with business valuation. They focus on such areas as accounting services or property valuation. The structure of respondent groups was determined by access to contact data available at organizations associating the experts in particular countries. As a rule, public databases of organizations of accountants and appraisers do not provide information about whether an expert who is an appraiser or an accountant is entitled to valuate companies. Even if such information is provided, the risk remains that many of the potential respondents are not practically involved in company valuation. Those fears were confirmed by the respondents returning the questionnaires: many of them do have the right to perform business valuation but they do not use it in their professional practice. The third group consists of experts belonging to organizations which deal with company valuation. The structure of the group of potential respondents dependent on the availability of contact details of the experts in each country. The questionnaire could be filled out on the project website http://bvs.ue.wroc.pl in Polish and http://en.bvs.ue.wroc.pl in English. The questionnaire was open for completion from 19 September to 13 October 2011. The project website was visited 599 times. The survey consisted of 17 closed questions. Respondents were also given the opportunity to offer their comments and suggestions. The questions could be divided into two subject fields: first is the evaluation of standards that experts use and the second is the problems that they encounter.[1] This article is dedicated to the first field.

Three limitations should be taken into account while interpreting research results. They are: limited availability of experts contact data, problems with projecting the size of the surveyed population, and third is tied to the fact that respondents that turned down the invitation to fill out the survey may have different personal traits and opinions than the ones who accepted it.

3 Survey Results

The questionnaire was completed by 182 respondents from many countries and therefore these results are not representative in terms of the multiple criteria of population structure of experts in the field of business valuation. The presented results of the research are merely symptomatic, indicating the problems faced by the experts in the field of business valuation in each country. The largest group of respondents consisted of experts from three countries (Table 1): the USA (26.9 %), Poland (20.9 %) and Romania (17.0 %). Experts from other countries were represented modestly (9.3 % of Canada, New Zealand 8.2 %, UK 2.7 %, Australia 2.2 %). 4.4 % of respondents did not disclose the country of origin (Table 1). Taking into consideration the number of respondents and the representation of each country, the results were analyzed by dividing the population into four groups (experts from the U.S., Poland, Romania and other countries, of which the vast majority are the countries of the Commonwealth). The vast majority of the respondents are experts with over 10 years' experience in company valuation (59.9 %). Experts who have been conducting valuation for 6–10 years accounted for 20.3 % of the respondents, and the smallest group (18.1 %) were experts with less than 6 years' experience. 1.1 % of the respondents did not specify the length of their experience in business valuation, and 0.5 % did not regard themselves as professional experts (Table 2). Chi-square independence test proves that there is a stochastic interdependence between groups of countries and years of experience in company valuation.[2] The group of American respondents was strongly dominated by experts with experience of more than 10 years (92.0 %), while only 8.0 % were experts with experience of between 6 and 10 years. There were not any American respondents in the group of experts with experience of less than 6 years. In the group of Polish experts those with more than 10 years (39.5 %) and less than 6 years' experience (36.8 %) dominated. In the group of experts from Romania experience of between 6 and 10 years turned out to be the most typical (48.4 %). The group of experts from other countries resembled the American group with 59.9 % of experts with professional experience of more than 10 years.

[1] Part of the research embraced problems that experts encounter while conducting valuation, these results are presented in Szymański (2012).

[2] $X^2 = 63.320$ for a critical value of $X^2 = 26.217$ at 12 degree of freedom and 0.01 significance level.

Table 1 Structure of respondents by country of origin

Country	Number of respondents	Structure (%)
Australia	4	2.2
Barbados	1	0.5
Bouvet Island	1	0.5
Canada	17	9.3
Cape Verde	1	0.5
Germany	1	0.5
Guyana	1	0.5
Hong Kong	2	1.1
India	1	0.5
Kazakhstan	2	1.1
Mexico	1	0.5
New Zealand	15	8.2
Poland	38	20.9
Romania	31	17.0
Serbia and Montenegro	1	0.5
United Kingdom	5	2.7
United States	49	26.9
United States Minor Outlying Islands	1	0.5
Jamaica	1	0.5
Virgin Islands, British	1	0.5
No mention of the country	8	4.4
	182	100.0

Source: Author's own research

Table 2 How long have you worked in business valuation?

	USA (%)	Poland (%)	Romania (%)	Other countries (%)	Total (%)
1–5 years	0.0	36.8	32.3	14.3	18.1
6–10 years	8.0	23.7	48.4	14.3	20.3
More than 10 years	92.0	39.5	19.4	66.7	59.9
I am not professional BV expert	0.0	0.0	0.0	1.6	0.5
No answer	0.0	0.0	0.0	3.2	1.1

Source: Author's own research

3.1 Which Business Valuation Standards Do Experts Make Use of?

Due to the fact that the survey was directed mainly the experts affiliated to organisations which promote business valuation standards, it would be expected that vast majority of respondents use these standards in practice (it is one of certified

Table 3 Which business valuation standards do you make use of?

	USA (%)	Poland (%)	Romania (%)	Other countries (%)	Total (%)
IBVE—New Zealand[a]	0.0	1.3	0.0	14.2	4.7
IVS—International[b]	8.1	13.9	65.9	19.8	20.2
PS—US[c]	5.4	3.8	0.0	3.8	3.9
S 110-530—Canada[d]	0.0	7.6	2.4	23.6	9.5
BVS—China[e]	0.0	2.5	2.4	1.9	1.5
VB—US[f]	22.5	5.1	0.0	7.5	11.0
APES 225—Australia[g]	0.0	1.3	0.0	6.6	2.4
BVS—US[h]	40.5	8.9	7.3	7.5	18.7
BAS—US[i]	14.4	3.8	2.4	3.8	7.1
IDW—Germany[j]	0.0	2.5	0.0	3.8	1.8
NI 5—Poland[k]	0.0	32.9	0.0	0.0	7.7
Another business valuation standard	8.1	7.6	9.8	5.7	7.4
I don't use business valuation standards	0.9	8.9	9.8	1.9	4.2

Source: Author's own research

[a]Independent Business Valuation Engagements, Advisory Engagement Standard 2, Council of the Institute of Chartered Accountants of New Zealand, 06/2003

[b]International Valuation Standards. International Valuation Guidance Note No. 6. Business Valuation, The International Valuation Standards Committee, 2007

[c]Professional Standards, National Association of Certified Valuation Analysts, May 31, 2002

[d]Standard no 110-530, The Canadian Institute of Chartered Business Valuators, June 2009

[e]Business Valuation Standards, The Hong Kong Business Valuation Forum, November 2005

[f]Valuation of a Business, Business Ownership Interest, Security, or Intangible Asset. Statement on Standards for Valuation Services, American Institute of Certified Public Accountants, New York June 2007

[g]APES 225 Valuation Services, Accounting Professional and Ethical Standards Board, July 2008

[h]ASA Business Valuation Standards, American Society of Appraisers, 2009

[i]Business Appraisal Standards, The Institute of Business Appraisers, 2008

[j]IDW Standard: Principles for the Performance of Business Valuations (IDW S 1 Version 2008), IDW Verlag GmbH, Institut der Wirschaftsprüfer in Deutschland, Düsseldorf 2009

[k]Nota Interpretacyjna NI 5, Wycena przedsiębiorstw, Powszechne Krajowe Zasady Wyceny (PKZW)

experts' duties). Doubts in this regard where expressed only experts in those countries where national business valuation standards don't exist or national business valuation standards have been implemented recently (Poland is a good example). Research indicates that 92.3 % of the experts use business valuation standards (Table 3). Chi-square test of independence demonstrates that there is a relationship between the stochastic groups of countries and use of business valuation standards in practice. Business valuation standards are used by 98.0 % respondents from U.S. and 96.4 % respondents from other countries. High but much smaller is the proportion of respondents from Romania (87.1 %) and from Poland (81.6 %). Among the Polish respondents is the highest percentage of experts (18.4 %) who do not use business valuation standards. It can be presumed that this percentage is higher in practice, because the experts who do not use the standards may be less willing to participate in these studies. The largest proportion of experts (47.2 %) use one type of business valuation standards, much less (45.05 %) indicated the use of more than one standard. Romanian experts (71.0 %), and experts from other countries (54.5 %) most frequently use one type of valuation standards. Also, the largest group of Polish experts (42.1 %) use one type of valuation standards. However, among the four groups studied it is the American experts (62.0 %) who most often use more than one business valuation standard. On average, Americans use two standards. The analysis shows also that the degree of variation in the standards are used by Polish experts is twice higher than in the case of experts from the U.S. and Romania. Experts indicating business valuation standards can choose from 11 proposals. And if they use the standard, which is not covered by the specification, they could choose the answer "other valuation standard" (which was chosen by 7.4 % of respondents). In the study population the most frequently reported standards were International Valuation Standards (IVS)—20.2 % (see International 2011), subsequently two American standards ASA—18.7 % (see ASA 2009), AICPA—11.0 % (see Valuation 2007), Canadian Standards CICBV—9.5 % (see Standard 2009), Polish standard—7.7 % (see Nota 2010), American standards IBA—7.1 % (see Business 2011), New Zealand standards—4.7 % (see Independent 2013), American standards NACAV 3.9 % (see Professional 2008), the Australian standard APES—2.4 % (see APES 2012), German standard IDW 1.8 % (see IDW 2009), Chinese standards—1.5 % (see The Hong Kong 2005) and other standards (not included in the survey) 7.4 %. Chi square test of independence demonstrates that there is a relationship between the stochastic groups of countries and the types of business valuation standards used by experts. Experts from the United States were mostly choosing ASA—40.5 %, then AICPA—22.5 % and then IBA—14.4 %. Polish experts most often pointed to Polish standard—32.9 %, then IVS—13.9 % and ASA—8.9 %. Among the Romanian experts the vast majority (65.9 %) pointed to the IVS, the next most popular was ASA—7.3 %.

Among respondents from other countries the most popular standards were Canadian CICBV—23.6 %, IVS—19.8 %, and ASA—7.5 %. 4.2 % of the surveyed experts do not use business valuation standards. These results illustrate only the structure of BVS in the context of the study population, hence the answer to this question is not possible to draw far-reaching conclusions with regard to popularity of standards.

3.2 The Need for Business Valuation Standards

One of the survey questions was related to issues concerning the need for business valuation standards. Research shows that the vast majority of respondents (85.7 %) believe that business valuation standards are necessary (Table 4). Chi-square test of independence indicates that there is a relationship between the stochastic groups of experts in the various countries and their indications with regard to the need for business valuation standards. This belief was expressed most clearly by experts from Romania (96.8 %), then by experts from US (90.0 %) and other countries (87.3 %). The most skeptical in this matter were experts from Poland. Although 68.4 % of them believe that business valuation standards are necessary but more often than colleagues from other countries they indicate that BVS are not necessary (15.8 %), or more likely they don't have an opinion on this subject (15.8 %). This is where an additional question arises whether those respondents who do not use the standards also believe that standards are unnecessary? Of the six respondents who declared that they do not use standards, two treat BVS unnecessary, three gave no opinion, and one of them expressed opinion that BVS are necessary.

3.3 Usability of Business Valuation Standards

Another issue researched was the problem of BVS utility. A few questions where dedicated to this matter in the questionnaire. The aim was to find out specific fields in which BVS are useful, discover to what extent BVS fulfill experts' expectations and how well do they fit to the practice of business valuation. One of the questions regarded the impact that BVS have on the security in business transactions. Comparing opinions of respondents from countries less experienced in BVS (Poland) with more experienced ones is particularly interesting. The largest part of respondents (34.1 %) pointed that it is difficult to establish whether BVS increase the security in business transactions (Table 5). Biggest doubts in the matter where expressed by experts from Romania (45.2 %) followed by experts from other countries (36.5 %), USA (34.0 %) and Poland (21.1 %). Second most popular answer was stating that BVS increase the security in business transactions 32.4 %. It was most popular among Romanian experts (48.4 %) and experts from other countries (36.5 %). Significantly less answers like that came from American (22.0 %) and Polish experts (26.3 %). These two groups most often stated that BVS standards do not increase the security in business transactions (respectively 39.5 % and 36.0 %), more often than the overall average (24.3 %) and significantly more often that Romanian (6.5 %) and other countries (17.5 %).

Further detailed questions were aimed at finding out specific fields in which BVS can be useful (Table 6). A significant majority of respondents expresses a conviction that BVS improve the quality of business valuation (67.0 %). This was mostly expressed by experts from Romania 77.4 % and USA 72.0 %, further experts from

Table 4 Do you find business valuation standards necessary?

	USA (%)	Poland (%)	Romania (%)	Other countries (%)	Total (%)
Yes	90.0	68.4	96.8	87.3	85.7
Difficult to say	0.0	0.0	0.0	0.0	0.0
No	8.0	15.8	0.0	7.9	8.2
I have no opinion	0.0	15.8	3.2	3.2	4.9
No answer	2.0	0.0	0.0	1.6	1.1

Source: Author's own research

Table 5 Do business valuation standards increase security in business transactions?

	USA (%)	Poland (%)	Romania (%)	Other countries (%)	Total (%)
Yes	22.0	26.3	48.4	36.5	32.4
Difficult to say	34.0	21.1	45.2	36.5	34.1
No	36.0	39.5	6.5	17.5	25.3
I have no opinion	8.0	10.5	0.0	6.3	6.6
No answer	0.0	2.6	0.0	3.2	1.6

Source: Author's own research

other countries 61.9 % and Poland 60.5 %. Significant part of respondents stated that BVS have a positive, yet small impact on the quality of valuation (22.5 % of the total) and 8.2 % expressed a belief, that BVS do not improve valuation quality. The most critical in this matter are experts from Poland 21.1 %, and much less critical are those from other countries (between 3.2 and 6.3 %).

A majority of respondents from all four groups of countries believe that BVS make their work easier (total 64.3 %), 24.2 % believes that only to a small extent, and 8.8 % that BVS do not make their work easier (Table 6). American experts were those who most often (68.0 %) acknowledged the positive impact of BVS on making the experts' work easier, other countries were slightly less convinced of that (Poland 65.8 %, other countries 61.9 %, Rumania 61.3 %). To a vast majority of all respondents (63.7 %) BVS improve the transparency of valuation reports yet 23.6 % believes that they do so only to a small extent and 6.6 % do not believe that transparency is improved by BVS. Positive impact was regarded by majority of experts from all four groups of countries, although mostly from Rumania (71.0 %). The most skeptical in this matter were experts from Poland, who twice as often as other countries (13.2 %) pointed to the lack of impact of BVS on the transparency of valuation reports.

The researched experts also acknowledge the impact of BVS on raising the methodological level of valuation reports (52.7 % confirming and 26.4 % to a small extent). The biggest optimists in this matter were experts from Romania (80.6 %) and USA (54.0 %) and less enthusiastic were other countries and Poland (42.9 % and 44.7 % respectively). Experts from these two groups of countries were also the most pessimistic because 23.7 % experts from Poland and 17.5 % experts from other countries believe that BVS do not impact the methodological level of valuation reports.

Table 6 Do business valuation standards ...

	USA (%)	Poland (%)	Romania (%)	Other countries (%)	Total (%)
Improve valuation quality?					
Yes	72.0	60.5	77.4	61.9	67.0
Yes, a little bit	24.0	15.8	16.1	28.6	22.5
No	4.0	21.1	3.2	6.3	8.2
I haven't any opinion	0.0	2.6	0.0	1.6	1.1
No answer	0.0	0.0	3.2	1.6	1.1
Enhance experts' work?					
Yes	68.0	65.8	61.3	61.9	64.3
Yes, a little bit	20.0	21.1	32.3	25.4	24.2
No	10.0	10.5	3.2	9.5	8.8
I haven't any opinion	2.0	2.6	0.0	1.6	1.6
No answer	0.0	0.0	3.2	1.6	1.1
Improve the transparency of business valuation reports?					
Yes	66.0	60.5	71.0	60.3	63.7
Yes, a little bit	28.0	15.8	19.4	27.0	23.6
No	4.0	13.2	3.2	6.3	6.6
I haven't any opinion	0.0	7.9	3.2	4.8	3.8
No answer	2.0	2.6	3.2	1.6	2.2
Improve the methodical level business of valuation reports?					
Yes	54.0	44.7	80.6	42.9	52.7
Yes, a little bit	30.0	21.1	9.7	34.9	26.4
No	10.0	23.7	6.5	17.5	14.8
I haven't any opinion	4.0	7.9	0.0	4.8	4.4
No answer	2.0	2.6	3.2	0.0	1.6
Make valuation verification easier?					
Yes	44.0	42.1	61.3	28.6	41.2
Yes, a little bit	30.0	44.7	25.8	41.3	36.3
No	20.0	7.9	3.2	27.0	17.0
I haven't any opinion	2.0	5.3	3.2	3.2	3.3
No answer	4.0	0.0	6.5	0.0	2.2
Decrease the spread of valuation results estimated by an expert?					
Yes	12.0	42.1	22.6	9.5	19.2
Yes, a little bit	40.0	23.7	35.5	33.3	33.5
No	36.0	28.9	29.0	50.8	38.5
I haven't any opinion	10.0	2.6	9.7	6.3	7.1
No answer	2.0	2.6	3.2	0.0	1.6

(continued)

Table 6 (continued)

	USA (%)	Poland (%)	Romania (%)	Other countries (%)	Total (%)
Decrease the spread of valuation results estimated by different experts?					
Yes	18.0	31.6	16.1	7.9	17.0
Yes, a little bit	28.0	34.2	45.2	30.2	33.0
No	46.0	31.6	25.8	524	41.8
I haven't any opinion	8.0	0.0	9.7	9.5	7.1
No answer	0.0	2.6	3.2	0.0	1.1
Increase the reliability of valuation results estimated by an expert?					
Yes	42.0	42.1	51.6	30.2	39.6
Yes, a little bit	40.0	31.6	29.0	50.8	40.1
No	16.0	23.7	9.7	15.9	16.5
I haven't any opinion	0.0	2.6	3.2	1.6	1.6
No answer	2.0	0.0	6.5	1.6	2.2
Decrease the risks of mistakes in valuation which can be made by an expert?					
Yes	28.0	44.7	48.4	20.6	32.4
Yes, a little bit	38.0	28.9	38.7	50.8	40.7
No	34.0	23.7	6.5	27.0	24.7
I haven't any opinion	0.0	2.6	3.2	1.6	1.6
No answer	0.0	0.0	3.2	0.0	0.5
Increase valuation costs?					
Yes	28.0	21.1	6.5	31.7	24.2
Yes, a little bit	44.0	18.4	38.7	39.7	36.3
No	24.0	44.7	48.4	20.6	31.3
I haven't any opinion	2.0	13.2	3.2	7.9	6.6
No answer	2.0	2.6	3.2	0.0	1.6

Source: Author's own research

The biggest group of experts confirms that BVS make it easier to verify valuation reports (41.2 % positive answers). For 36.3 % of respondents this impact is positive yet small. The most optimistic in this matter were Romanian experts (61.3 % positive experts and 25.8 % confirming a small positive impact), 17.0 % respondents believe that BVS do not make it easier to verify valuation reports. The most skeptical in this matter were other countries (27.0 %) and USA (20.0 %). Strongly opposing opinions are expressed while answering the question whether BVS decrease the spread of valuation results estimated by an expert. The majority of answers are negative 38.5 and 33.5 % of respondents confirm a small impact of BVS while only 19.2 % believes that this impact is significant. Thus it can be assumed that according to the majority of respondents BVS do not impact in any significant way the span (the spread) of different valuation results. Answers to this question from experts of different nationalities show significant differences between them. It is also confirmed by the chi-square independence test according to which there is significant stochastic interdependence between experts from specific groups of countries and their answers in terms of how BVS influence the span of valuation results performed by them.[3] Most commonly experts from other countries (50.8 %) point that BVS do not decrease the span of their valuation results. The same opinion is shared by 36.0 % of experts from the US and 28.9 % from Poland as well as 29.0 % from Romania. Yet the most optimistic in this matter are experts from Poland (42.1 % positive answers, and 23.7 % confirming small influence of BVS on the decrease of results span).

To a yet larger group of experts (41.8 %) BVS standards do not decrease the spread of valuation results estimated by different experts. Only 17 % of experts acknowledge this influence and 33.0 % acknowledge a small decreasing influence of BVS on valuation results of different experts. Just as in the last question it was experts from other countries and from the US being the most skeptical (respectively 52.4 % and 46.0 %). Less skeptical were the experts from Poland and Romania, who mostly are convinced that BVS decrease the span of results between different experts (respectively 31.6 % and 16.1 %) although to a small extent (respectively 34.2 % and 45.2 %). Differences in answers of experts from specific countries on this matter are confirmed by the chi-square independence test according to which there is a significant stochastic interdependence.[4]

BVS increase the credibility of valuation according to respondents from all four groups of countries (39.6 %), this influence is positive, yet small according to 40.1 % of experts. It is mostly acknowledged by experts from Romania, Poland and USA (respectively 51.6 %, 42.1 % and 42.0 %). Experts from other countries consider this influence positive but small (50.8 %). Only 16.5 % of experts express a conviction that BVS do not influence the increase of valuation credibility.

According to the majority of experts BVS decrease the risk of mistakes made by the expert while performing the business valuation. 32.4 % of all experts think so and 40.7 % express a belief that this influence exists but is small. A much stronger conviction about the positive effect that BVS exert on the faultlessness of valuation was expressed by experts from Romania and Poland (48.4 % and 44.7 % respectively) while experts from other countries and USA more often believe that this influence exists but is small (50.8 % and 38.0 % respectively).

Majority of experts state that BVS increase the costs of running the valuation (60.5 %) and among them 36.3 % consider this effect small. According to 31.3 % of respondents BVS do not influence the increase of costs. It is worth noting that experts from USA and other countries where BVS exist for a long time much more often point to the increase of costs than experts from Poland and Romania where BVS have a shorter history. Romanian and polish experts point that BVS do not increase cost of valuation (respectively 48.4 % and 44.7 %). It is also confirmed by

[3] $X^2 = 22.938$ for a critical value of $X^2 = 21.666$ at 9 degree of freedom and 0.01 significance level.

[4] $X^2 = 22.494$ for a critical value of $X^2 = 21.666$ at 9 degree of freedom and 0.01 significance level.

Table 7 How does the standard you use identify all relevant areas of valuation practices?

	USA (%)	Poland (%)	Romania (%)	Other countries (%)	Total (%)
To full extent	18.0	0.0	29.0	7.9	12.6
Significantly	52.0	50.0	61.3	57.1	54.9
Slightly	18.0	26.3	6.5	20.6	18.7
It does not relate to important issues	2.0	2.6	0.0	1.6	1.6
Not applicable	0.0	15.8	0.0	3.2	4.4
I have no opinion	6.0	0.0	3.2	4.8	3.8
No answer	4.0	5.3	0.0	4.8	3.8

Source: Author's own research

the chi-square independence test, according to which there is a significant stochastic interdependence between experts from specific groups of countries and their answers in terms of how BVS influence the increase of costs of performing the valuation.[5]

One of the questions (Table 7) dedicated to the problematic utility of BVS was aimed at identifying all the significant fields of valuation (the extent to which they meet practical demands of companies). Majority of experts believe that BVS generally identify all fields of valuation significant to practice (54.9 %). This belief is shared by 61.3 % of experts from Romania, 57.1 % of experts from other countries, 52.0 % of experts from USA and 50.0 % of experts from Poland. Only 12.6 % of respondents pointed to the fact, that BVS identify all relevant fields of valuation to a full extent. The most convinced in this matter were the experts from Romania (29.0 %) and USA (18.0 %). At the same time a significant group of respondents 18.7 % expressed a belief that BVS identify all the practically significant fields but only to a small extent. Among the least satisfied in this matter are experts from Poland (26.3 %), followed by experts from other countries (20.6 %). These discrepancies are confirmed by the chi-square independence test, according to which there is a significant stochastic interdependence between experts from certain groups of countries and their answers in this matter.[6]

The utility of BVS is an issue tackled also by the next question of the survey. Here the respondents determined whether BVS fulfill their expectations (Table 8). A vast majority of respondents provides a confirming answer (61.0 %). The chi-square independence test shows that in this matter there is a significant stochastic interdependence between specific groups of experts.[7] The most satisfied were the American experts (72.0 %), followed by other countries (58.7 %), followed by Romania (54.8 %) and Poland (55.3 %). On the other hand it should

[5] $X^2 = 23.521$ for a critical value of $X^2 = 21.666$ at 9 degree of freedom and 0.01 significance level.

[6] $X^2 = 35.794$ for a critical value of $X^2 = 30.578$ at 15 degree of freedom and 0.01 significance level.

[7] $X^2 = 27.829$ for a critical value of $X^2 = 21.666$ at 9 degree of freedom and 0.01 significance level.

Table 8 Does the standard you are using meet your expectations?

	USA (%)	Poland (%)	Romania (%)	Other countries (%)	Total (%)
Yes	72.0	55.3	54.8	58.7	61.0
Slightly	18.0	23.7	35.5	30.2	26.4
No	10.0	0.0	9.7	4.8	6.0
Not applicable	0.0	15.8	0.0	3.2	4.4
I have no opinion	0.0	5.3	0.0	1.6	1.6
No answer	0.0	0.0	0.0	1.6	0.5

Source: Author's own research

Table 9 Is the range of regulation in business valuation standard

	USA (%)	Poland (%)	Romania (%)	Other countries (%)	Total (%)
Inaccurate?	4.0	23.7	0.0	4.8	7.7
Appropriate?	64.0	31.6	58.1	57.1	53.8
Too detailed?	2.0	0.0	9.7	4.8	3.8
Too detailed in some parts and inaccurate in others?	14.0	18.4	22.6	11.1	15.4
Not applicable	4.0	2.6	3.2	1.6	2.7
I have no opinion	12.0	15.8	6.5	20.6	14.8
No answer	0.0	7.9	0.0	0.0	1.6

Source: Author's own research

be noted that 32.4 % of respondents expresses a belief that BVS fulfill their expectations to a small extent or not fulfill them at all (6.0 % of respondents are unsatisfied with BVS). A significant part of them however believe that BVS fulfill their expectations only to a small extent (26.4 %). The largest amount of such opinions is present among experts from Romania (35.5 %) and from other countries (30.2 %). Hence it is apparent that a significant group of experts is not satisfied. What could be the reason for this lack of satisfaction? The answer is partly provided by the next question of the survey regarding the adequacy of regulations contained within BVS (Table 9). A majority of experts point to the fact that the range of regulation in BVS is adequate (53.8 %). Similar answers are provided by respondents from USA, Romania and groups of other countries (64.0, 58.1, and 57.1 %). Merely 7.7 % of experts believe, that the level of regulation in BVS is inadequate. This view was most popular among experts from Poland (23.7 %), and less popular or not present at all among other countries (4.8 %), USA (4.0 %), or Romania (0.0 %). A significant part of respondents (15.4 %) expresses a conviction that BVS are too detailed in some areas and inaccurate in others (in this matter the most critical were experts from Romania—22.6 % and Poland—18.4 %). Yet to 3.8 % of respondents the standards are too detailed (it was pointed out mostly by experts from Romania—9.7 %). Discrepancies in answers are significant enough to be confirmed by the chi-square independence test, according to which there is a significant stochastic interdependence between groups of experts from specific countries and their answers in this matter.[8]

4 Conclusions

Business valuation standards are used by 98.0 % respondents from U.S. and 96.4 % respondents from other countries. High but much smaller is the proportion of respondents from Romania (87.1 %) and from Poland (81.6 %). Among the Polish respondents is the highest percentage of experts (18.4 %) who do not use business valuation standards. The largest proportion of experts (47.2 %) use one type of business valuation standards, much less (45.05 %) indicated the use of more than one standard. The above presented research results show that among the surveyed experts there is a conviction that business valuation standards are necessary (85.7 %). The most skeptical in this matter were experts from Poland. Although 68.4 % of them believe that business valuation standards are necessary but more often than colleagues from other countries they indicate that BVS are not necessary (15.8 %), or more likely they don't have an opinion on this subject (15.8 %). BVS are necessary because: they increase the quality of valuation, make experts' work easier, raise the transparency of valuation results, raise the methodological level of valuation reports, make verification of reports easier, and decrease the risk of mistakes therefore increasing the credibility of valuations. These advantages are counteracted by higher costs of performing the valuations. Business valuation standards however do not solve all the problems. To a majority of experts standards do not significantly influence the span of results obtained by one expert nor between various experts. The largest part of respondents (34.1 %) pointed that it is difficult to establish whether BVS increase the security in business transactions.

According to a majority of experts (61.0 %) the range of regulation in business valuation standards is adequate and existing standards fulfill their expectations properly identifying all fields significant to everyday practice of business valuation. Additionally a majority of experts point to the fact that the range of regulation in BVS is adequate (53.8 %). Survey show there are differences in the perception of the phenomena connected with valuation between professionals working on the U.S. market, where BVS are well-established, and experts from Poland and Romania where these standards have a shorter history. Especially experts from Poland were the most skeptical in scope of use business valuation standards, positive impact on the quality of valuation, positive impact the methodological level of valuation reports, increase cost of valuation.

[8] $X^2 = 32.748$ for a critical value of $X^2 = 30.578$ at 15 degree of freedom and 0.01 significance level.

References

APES 225 Valuation Services (2012) Accounting Professional and Ethical Standards Board
ASA Business Valuation Standards (2009) American Society of Appraisers
Business Valuation Standards, The Hong Kong Business Valuation Forum, November 2005
Hitchner JR (2006) Financial valuation. Applications and models. Wiley, Hoboken, NJ
IDW Standard: Principles for the Performance of Business Valuations (2009) (IDW S 1 Version 2008), IDW Verlag GmbH, Institut der Wirschaftsprüfer in Deutschland, Düsseldorf
Independent Business Valuation Engagements, Advisory Engagement Standard 2 (2013) Council of the Institute of Chartered Accountants of New Zealand
International Valuation Standards. International Valuation Guidance Note No. 6. Business Valuation (2011) The International Valuation Standards Committee
Lieberman MJ, Anderson D (2008) Will the real business valuation standards please stand up? The AICPA's SSVS compared to USPAP and other business valuation standards. CPA vol. LXXVIII, no. 1, J:22
Nota (2010) Interpretacyjna NI 5, Wycena przedsiębiorstw, Powszechne Krajowe Zasady Wyceny (PKZW), XIX Krajowa Konferencja Rzeczoznawców Majątkowych, Udział rzeczoznawców majątkowych w wycenie przedsiębiorstw. Zasady dobrej praktyki zawodowej, Polska Federacja Stowarzyszeń Rzeczoznawców Majątkowych, Kielce
Pratt SP, Niculita AV (2008) Valuing a business. The analysis and appraisal of closely held companies, 5th edn. McGraw-Hill, New York
Professional Standards (2008) National association of certified valuation analysts
Professional Standards (2011) The Institute of Business Appraisers
Standard no 110 (2009) The Canadian Institute of Chartered Business Valuators
Standard no 120 (2009) The Canadian Institute of Chartered Business Valuators
Standard no 130 (2009) The Canadian Institute of Chartered Business Valuators
Standard no 210 (2010) The Canadian Institute of Chartered Business Valuators
Standard no 220 (2010) The Canadian Institute of Chartered Business Valuators
Standard no 230 (2010) The Canadian Institute of Chartered Business Valuators
Standard no 310 (2010) The Canadian Institute of Chartered Business Valuators
Standard no 320 (2010) The Canadian Institute of Chartered Business Valuators
Standard no 330 (2010) The Canadian Institute of Chartered Business Valuators
Standard no 410 (2010) The Canadian Institute of Chartered Business Valuators
Standard no 420 (2010) The Canadian Institute of Chartered Business Valuators
Standard no 430 (2010) The Canadian Institute of Chartered Business Valuators
Standard no 510 (2010) The Canadian Institute of Chartered Business Valuators
Standard no 520 (2010) The Canadian Institute of Chartered Business Valuators
Standard no 530 (2010) The Canadian Institute of Chartered Business Valuators
Szymański P (2012) What problems does business valuation practice encounter—survey. Bus Valuat Rev 31(1):4–22
Valuation of a Business, Business Ownership Interest, Security, or Intangible Asset (2007) Statement on standards for valuation services. American Institute of Certified Public Accountants, New York

The Effectiveness of Hybrid Organisations: A Purposive Approach

Adam Weinert

Abstract This article has the character of a review to better understand the form of hybrid organisations in the context of their effectiveness. The paper explores how hybrid organisations are defined in many countries, as well as present case studies and the wide range of mixed forms of delivery services. The author suggests that Polish municipal companies could be classified as one of the existing forms of a hybrid organisation. The study is based on foreign and national literatures. In this article, one of the approaches presented is the contemporary interpretation of effectiveness.

Keywords Hybrid organisations • Effectiveness • Purposive approach

1 Introduction

The term "hybridity" is generally defined as being a few distinct logical governances within one organization (Grohs 2014). Hybrid organisations are related to a few academic fields like public administration, organisation and management sciences, economics and similar disciplines. This article focuses on hybridity within the theory of organisation. From this point of view, hybrids are non-pure types of organisations, and combine features from different organisations. There are many examples of hybrid companies: waste management organisations, social housing companies, sheltered workshops or social service deliveries.

This paper begins by introducing different national administrative cultures, which have been moderated by global New Public Management (NPM) trends. This new form has replaced old public bureaucracies. This reform has been characterised in Europe by: the introduction of business management techniques, more customer orientation and competitive market-like mechanisms (Kickert 2001). This situation has also occurred in Poland (Grzymała 2010). The NPM basis results in modern governance with greater effectiveness, and creates new or better ways to organise and provide public services. As indicated by Skelcher and Smith (2014), some public organisations can be conceived as hybrids; for instance,

A. Weinert (✉)
Department of Strategic Management, Poznań University of Economics, Poznań, Poland
e-mail: adam.weinert@ue.poznan.pl

T. Dudycz et al. (eds.), *The Essence and Measurement of Organizational Efficiency*,
Springer Proceedings in Business and Economics, DOI 10.1007/978-3-319-21139-8_19

public enterprises which are profit-seeking, but operate within the public realm. This paper describes municipal commercial companies, which are a special type of public entity. These entities are an example of hybrid organisations, combining features of both private and public organisations. In the light of this idea, the hybrid phenomenon occurs across the Polish municipal industry. The author's research concerns these organisations in the context of their effectiveness.

The theoretical basis of this article consists of three sections, as follows: a review of the research (Sect. 2); the conditions for measuring the effectiveness of an organisation (Sect. 3); and in the last section, the categorisation of the effectiveness indicators (Sect. 3.2).

To select the test methods, a critical literature review has been used. It has been found that there is not any clear way to measure the effectiveness of hybrid organisations, which is why one method has been chosen from among the most popular approaches in the literature. The results of this evaluation may be useful for both empirical research and for business practices.

2 Review of Research

According to foreign literature, organisations of a dual—public and private form—have been categorised in different ways depending on the characteristics chosen by the scholar. The various comparisons are presented in Table 1 below.

The literature clearly shows a lack of consistent terminology. However, in this article, the author will focus on hybrid organisations. Rhodes and Donnelly-Cox (2014) reminds us that organisation theorists have applied the term "hybrid" to organisations practicing in the public sector domain, which are not purely "public". This term has various dimensions, including: public versus private ownership, public versus private funding and polyarchy versus market control (Andre 2010). Besides, the popularity of hybrid organisations has been described with particular density in the public sector (Kickert 2001).

Table 1 Organisations with both a public and private form—different categorisations in the literature review

Scholars	Categorisations of both public and private sectors
Seidman (1975)	Government-sponsored
Stanton (2002)	enterprise
Koppell (2001), Joldersma and Winter (2010), Moe and Kosar (2005), Skelcher and Smitch (2014), Bel et al. (2014)	Hybrid organisations
Hogarty (2002)	Public authorities
Barker (1982) Van Thiel (2001)	Quangos

Source: Author's own

Table 2 Definitions of a hybrid organisation—literature review

Author(s)	Definition
Kickert (2001)	Organisations that exist in the intersection of two distinct spheres—the public and the private
Minkoff (2002)	Organisations that combine different missions—or policy fields—within one organisation
Joldersma and Winter (2010)	Organisations that combine a public orientation with a market orientation
Brandsen et al. (2005)	Organisations that are characterised by a mixture of pure and incongruous origins (heterogeneous arrangements)
Mamoa (2011)	Organisations that attempt to combine the characteristics of three sectors: public (government) private (business), and the third sector (civil society)

Source: Author's own

2.1 Definitions of Hybrid Organisations and Case Studies

A review of the international literature indicates that there is no systematic body of research regarding hybrid organisations (Karre 2011). The literature has not always had a consistent meaning. The definitions of different authors are summarised in Table 2. On the other hand, a lot of work has been done, including case studies, which shows a strong interest in the practical side of the issue (see Table 3).

The concept of hybrid organisations is divergent. As noted by Smith (2010), despite the lack of consensus on a specific definition of a hybrid organisation, many scholars tend to agree that these entities contain mixed sectoral, legal, structural, and/or mission-related elements. Karre (2012) suggests that these organisations operate in a messy and fuzzy reality and it is this that creates the difficulty in studying them. In the next paragraph, the different approaches and possible domains of hybrid organisations are presented.

A wide range of research has been performed, alongside many case studies, which indicates a great deal of interest in this issue from around the world. It is important to be aware that the term "hybrid organisation" can be used in the context of various organisations. Hybrid organisations may involve a conflict of goals, due to multiple societal expectations and business demands (Lindqvist 2013). The majority of examples of hybrid organisations are different types of publicly owned corporations and other companies in the public realm (Koppell 2001).

In the review of the literature on hybrid organisations there are two dichotomous approaches, along with other classifications (Fig. 1).

The classification can also be shown from the point of view of the possible spheres in the sectors, which are shared on two conceptualisations. Brandsen et al. (2009) said that the first conceptualises hybrids as organisations simultaneously operating in the public and the private sectors (i.e. within a dichotomy); while the other defines them in terms of a threefold distinction between state, market and civil society.

Table 3 Case studies on the issue of hybrid organisations

Authors	Field of research	Examples of organisations in the research	Country
Kickert (2001)	Executive agencies from ministerial departments	Ministerial departments: Education and Sciences, Agriculture, Nature and Fisheries, Transport and Public Works, Justice	Netherlands
Koppell (2003)	Credit crunch	Fanny Mae, Freddy Mac	United States
Evers et al. (2002)	Civil society	–	Germany
Kosar (2011)	Quasi government	Fannie Mae, National Park Foundation, In-Q-Tel	United States
Christensen and Laegreid (2010)	Welfare administration	–	Norway
Karre (2011)	Waste management	Dutch waste management	Netherlands
Mamoa (2011)	–	Seventh Generation, Stonyfield Farm, Green Mountain Coffee Roasters (GMCR), Mundo Verde	–
Torre, Fenger, Twist (2012)	Sheltered workshops	Dutch sheltered workshop company	Netherlands
Lindqvist (2013)	Waste management	Municipal organisations	Sweden
Kania (2012, 2013)	Social housing companies	MZGM-TBS Sp. z o.o.	Poland
Grohs (2014)	Social service deliveries	–	Germany
Albalate et al. (2014)	Airport management	European Airport Industry	–
Gradus et al. (2014)	Refuse collection	Dutch municipalities	Netherlands
Girth (2014)	Municipal wireless broadband	Service areas in the U.S. local governments	United States
Rhodes and Donnelly-Cox (2014), Mullins and Acheson (2014)	Social housing companies	–	Ireland

Source: Author's own

Thomasson (2009) has also emphasised that there is a contrast in hybrid organisation in terms from finance, ownership and organisational structure. These differences can be described by an unrelated goals. As shown in Fig. 2, this results in various combinations. In the second approach there are three zones: state, market and community (Billis 2010).

An apparent and strategic dilemma is generated by the combination of public, private and third sector characteristics and objectives. Therefore, combining the organisational features from three different sectors into one organisation is not simple. Hybrids are regarded by many scholars from different fields as companies which generate ambiguity or more difficult choices (Thomasson 2009). Karre

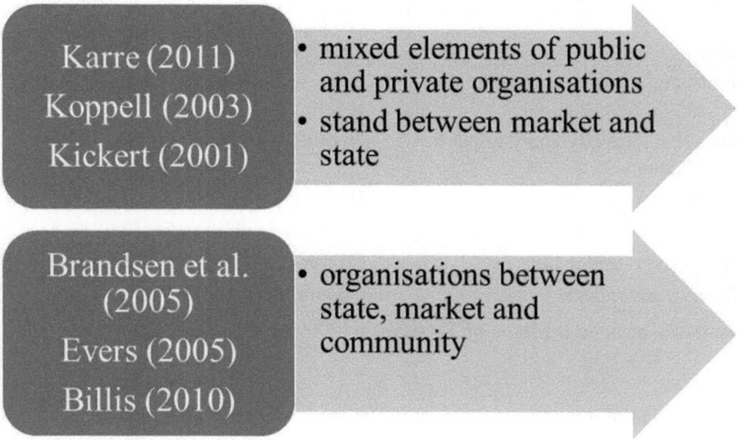

Fig. 1 The approaches to the classification of hybrid organisations in the foreign literature (*Source*: Author's own)

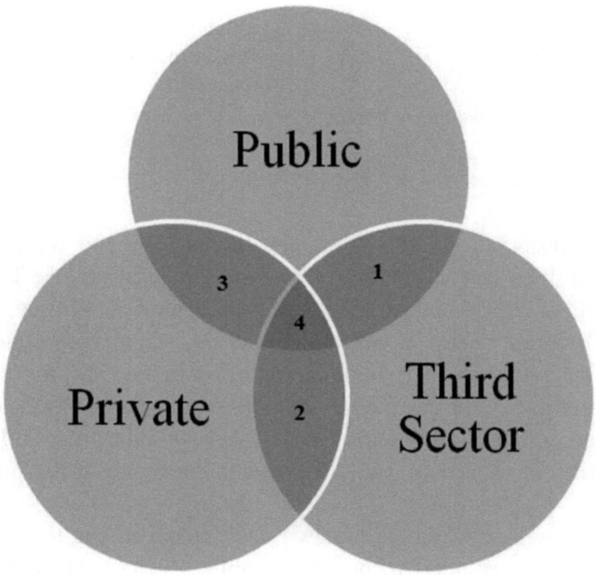

Fig. 2 Possible spheres (zones) of hybrid organisations—combination between the public, private and third sector. 1—Public/Third Sector, 2—Third Sector/Private, 3—Private/Public, 4—Public/Private/Third Sector [*Source*: Author's own on the basis of Karre (2011)]

(2012) visualises hybrid organisations as a few kind of entities. He presents ten dimensions of hybrid organisations, which allows for rating their level of hybridity, as follows: legal form, ownership, activities, funding, market environment, value orientation, strategic orientation, relationship, managerial autonomy and executive autonomy. Based on observations, the author noted that positive and negative

Table 4 Advantages and disadvantages of hybrid organisations—a review of the literature

Advantages	Disadvantages
Autonomous and often exempt from laws	Being not transparent enough and difficulties in securing liability
Regulations that normally apply to public sector organisations	Hybrids generate ambiguity
Increased turnover and profit	Unfair competition
Increased effectiveness and efficiency	Neglect of public tasks
Increased consume-orientation	Cultural conflicts
More effective governance	Opportunistic behaviour

Source: Author's own, on the basis of Thomasson (2009) and Karre (2012)

Table 5 The range of mixed forms of service delivery

Model of mixed forms	
Hybrid organisational forms	• Public corporations
	• State-owned enterprises
	• Mixed public-private firms
	• Public-private/nonprofit partnerships
Mixed contracting forms	• Private, nonprofit or other governmental organisations
Co-production across jurisdictions or between governments	

Source: Author's own, on the basis of Bel et al. (2014)

effects can be observed. In this light, the advantages and disadvantages of a "hybrid" can be distinguished in the form of the organisation (see Table 4).

One example of hybrid entities, which provide a service delivery, are municipal companies. There are many organisational forms, which is vouched for by the various forms of service delivery in other countries. In the U.S., a mixed delivery is an important alternative for the private and public dimension. On the other hand, in many European countries, there are mixed public-private firms and government-owned firms (Bel et al. 2014). Table 5 presents the range of the mixed forms in details.

In accordance with the concept of new public management, the governments of many countries have decided to privatise public services. Hybrid organisations must balance between different objectives to achieve their profit goals. In the literature, attention is paid to the role of hybrid organisations in delivering public services and in representing the interests of citizens (Smith 2010). Mamoa (2011)) showed that hybrids necessarily have to increase their impact to gain a return value for their stakeholders, which are particularly important in this type of organisation.

In view of the considerations relating to the hybrid organisations and the lack of methods of measuring their effectiveness, one of the most popular approaches has been chosen to be used for further research.

3 Conditions for Measuring the Effectiveness of the Organisations

Categories of efficiency in the economic sciences are divided into organisational effectiveness and economic efficiency (Ziębicki 2012). Organisational effectiveness is generally presented in the form of multi-dimensional criteria that relate to the different attributes of the organisations.

In the literature, three dominant contemporary interpretations of the effectiveness of the organisations can be distinguished, which include:

- An approach based on the objectives,
- An approach based on system resources, and
- An approach from multiple aspects (Bratnicki and Kulikowska-Pawlak 2013).

This paper focuses on one of the oldest and most common approaches in the science of organisation—an approach based on the objectives. According to this approach, the effectiveness is defined as the scope to which an organisation achieves its aims, which primarily emphasises the need for the whole organization to achieve results. The theory behind the approach, from the point of view of the objectives, is clear. Hybrid organisations concentrate on combining the features of non-profit organisations with the characteristics of business. Purely-public organisations have multiple variables and often divergent goals. These organisations are set up to meet needs that are socially recognised as important. The measurement of the effectiveness of a public organisation is still at an early stage, in contrast to measuring the effectiveness of business sector organisations (Frąckiewicz-Wronka 2010). Hybrid organisations concentrate on combining the features of non-profit organisations with the features of business or public companies; therefore, we should search for a special method to measure their effectiveness, designed only for hybrids. The approach based on the objectives of the organisation should be measured with the help of indicators from all possible domains of the hybrid organisation. This article focuses on municipal companies as hybrids, and the implementation of their objectives requires the special character of their management in the Polish municipal industry.

3.1 *The Effectiveness of Hybrid Organisations: Dealing with the Objectives of Different Domains and Groups of Stakeholders*

A lot of authors discuss the effectiveness of private sector or nonprofit organisations. However, there is an evident gap of research with regards to hybrid organisations. Synthesizing the main approaches of different authors focusing on profit or nonprofit organisations, it can be stated that hybrid organisations are considered to be more difficult to study, particularly due to their multiple objectives from various groups of stakeholders. This is why, in order to survive, these entities must comply with the demands from the institutional environment.

An example of hybrid organisations with the distinct goals of other interest groups can be observed in the municipal companies in the Polish services market. These entities combine the characteristic features of public, private and nonprofit organisations (Kania 2012; Bartkowiak 2008).

First, the municipal companies have features of private organisations, as a provider of goods and services to citizens (taken into consideration as customers). The customers are regular recipients (consumers) with households, enterprises, local institutions and other entities as the target groups. Secondly, they also have the characteristics of public organisations. The municipal authorities have the legal responsibility for functioning and assigning strategies, as the executors of that company's policy. These organisations are confronted with a hierarchical relationship, with the municipality as the superior political body that they have to obey, but often they can have own development strategy, which should be consistent with the regulations of the community. Thirdly, municipal companies in the Polish service market have the features of nonprofit organisations, because they exist in a public utility sphere. From the point of view of a nonprofit organisation, the municipal companies need to reflect the values of the local community that they serve, and their services must currently and constantly aim to meet the needs of the population. In conclusion, it can be claimed that municipal companies need to realise commercial, public as well as societal goals, which depend on their different environments—market (customers), state (local government units) and community (citizens in general).

Due to the differences between the sectors—private, public and nonprofit—the effectiveness of hybrid organisations becomes a challenge that is difficult to measure. The next paragraph analyses the effectiveness of the indicators, which are considered as the most often used in the context of municipal companies in Poland.

3.2 *Categorisation of the Effectiveness Indicators of Polish Municipal Companies*

Considering the approach based on objectives in the study of effectiveness, there are a few possible fields which can be analysed (Jaki 2011) including: financial effectiveness, technical effectiveness, social effectiveness and environmental effectiveness. According to the described characteristics of hybrid organisations, the indicators can be gathered into the following zones: (1) market-oriented indicators, (2) state-oriented indicators, (3) community-oriented indicators, (4) indicators between two zones—market and community, (5) indicators between two zones—market and state, (6) indicators between two zones—state and community, and (7) fully hybrid indicators. Figure 3 shows the assignment of the effectiveness

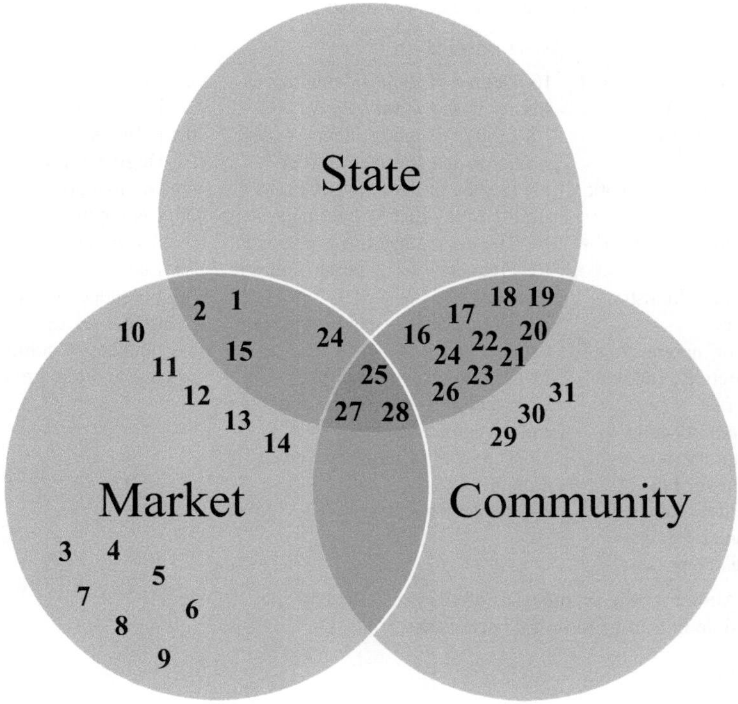

Fig. 3 The assignment of the indicators in three hybrid zones (*Source*: Author's own)

indicators into these zones. The numbers in Fig. 3 correspond with the list of indicators in Table 6.

More indicators could be used, but these would not change the high relation between the state and the community zones. The rest of the effectiveness indicators are dependent on the point of view of various entities. Despite the author's subjective assessment, it is clear that the measurement of the effectiveness of a hybrid organisation is very complicated due to the mixed (conflicting interest) purposes in each of the sides involved. The solution to this situation may be to move as many indicators as possible into the common zones (7) of state, market and community.

This will require a greater commitment from managers, authorities and the local community. Establishing realistic objectives from all groups of stakeholders is also associated with establishing coherent development strategies.

Table 6 The list of effectiveness indicators oriented to the market, state and community

Market-oriented	State-oriented	Community-oriented
1. The volume of sales of municipal products 2. The level of costs 3. Indicators of the intensity of the network load 4. Capacity utilisation rate 5. Technical Industry indicators 6. Rate of income 7. Productivity index 8. Loss rate 9. Profitability ratio 10. Liquidity ratio 11. Turnover rate 12. The debt ratio 13. Financial flows 14. Investment rates	15. Degree of the residents' accessibility to the water supply 16. Degree of the residents' accessibility to the sewage network 17. Degree of the residents' accessibility to the district heating system 18. The percentage of paved roads 19. Frequency of disposal of municipal waste 20. The number of public transportation stops 21. Length of cycle paths 22. Number of communal squares and playgrounds 23. The level of tariffs (avoiding growth) 24. Investment rates	25. The level of tariffs 26. Degree of accessibility to the public sewage network 27. Degree of accessibility to the water supply 28. Degree of accessibility to the district heating system 29. Length of cycle paths 30. Frequency of disposal of municipal waste 31. Number of communal squares and playgrounds

Source: Author's own, on the basis of Grzymała (2010)[a]
[a]All possible indicators have not been used

4 Conclusion

The purpose of this paper is to explore the research regarding hybrid organisations and to better understand the forms of hybrid organisations. Hybrid organisations are variously defined in many countries, and are broadly illustrated by many case studies. This is a phenomenon of growing importance in many countries and in different fields of literature. There has been a lack of studies concerning the effectiveness of hybrids both in domestic and in foreign literature.

Hybrid organisations are located between the public, private and nonprofit spheres. The context of hybrid organisations is discussed in many foreign studies, and research should be continued in Polish conditions. In Poland, municipal companies can be classified as hybrid organisations, because they combine elements of public, private and nonprofit organisations.

In the future, questions should be asked about measuring the effectiveness of hybrid organisations, and how this effectiveness can be evaluated.

References

Albalate D, Bel G, Fageda X (2014) Beyond pure public and pure private management models: partial privatization in the European Airport Industry. Int Public Manag J 17(3):308–327

Andre R (2010) Assessing the accountability of government-sponsored enterprises and quangos. J Bus Ethics 97(2):271–289. doi:10.1007/s1055-010-0509-y
Barker A (ed) (1982) Quangos in Britain: government and the networks of public policy-making. Macmillan, London
Bartkowiak P (2008) Zarządzanie wartością przedsiębiorstwa. Studia i prace wydziału nauk ekonomicznych i zarządzania nr 6, WNEIZ 2008
Bel G, Brown T, Warner M (2014) Editorial overview: symposium on mixed and hybrid models of public service delivery. Int Public Manag 17(3):297–307. doi:10.1080/10967494.2014.935231
Billis D (2010) Hybrid organizations and the third sector. Palgrave Macmillan, Houndmills
Brandsen T, van de Donk W, Putters K (2005) Griffins or chameleons? Hybridity as a permanent and inevitable characteristic of the third sector. Int J Public Adm 28(9–10):749–65
Brandsen T, Karre P, Helderman J-K (2009) The risks of hybrid organisations: expectations and evidence. Paper presented at NISPACEE conference, Budva, May 2009
Bratnicki M, Kulikowska-Pawlak M (2013) Uwarunkowania pomiaru efektywności organizacji. Zarządzanie i Finanse 4/2
Christensen T, Laegreid P (2010) Complexity and hybrid public administration—theoretical and empirical challenges. Public Organ Rev 11(4):407–423. doi:10.1007/s1115-010-0141-4
Evers A, Rauch U, Stitz U (2002) Von öffentlichen Einrichtungen zu sozialen Unternehmen? hybride Organisationsformen im Bereich sozialer Dienstleistungen. Edition Sigma, Berlin
Frąckiewicz-Wronka A (2010) Pomiar efektywności organizacji jako obszar konwergencji metod, narzędzi i instrumentów zarządzania między sektorami biznesowym a publicznym. Organizacja i Zarządzanie 4(12):11
Girth A (2014) What drives the partnership decision? Examining structural factors influencing public-private partnerships for municipal wireless broadband. Int Public Manag J 17(3):344–364
Gradus R, Dijkgraaf E, Wassenaar M (2014) Understanding mixed forms of refuse collection, privatization and its reverse in the Netherlands. Int Public Manag J 17(3):328–343
Grohs S (2014) Hybrid organisations in social delivery in quasimarkets: the case of Germany. Am Behav Sci 58(11):1425–1445. doi:10.1177/0002764214534671
Grzymała Z (2010) Restrukturyzacja sektora komunalnego w Polsce. Oficyna Wydawnicza SGH, Warszawa
Hogarty RA (2002) The Paradox of Public Authorities in Massachusetts: Massport and Masspike. New England Journal of Public Policy 17:19–37
Jaki A (2011) Paradygmat efektywności w zarządzaniu. Przegląd Organizacji 4:3–7
Joldersma C, Winter V (2010) Strategic management in hybrid organisations. Public Manag Rev 4 (1):83–99. doi:10.1080/14616670110101708
Kania R (2012) Zastosowanie mapowania procesów do szacowania kosztów dostaw wynikających z formalnoprawnych obowiązków spółek komunalnych. Studia z zakresu prawa, administracji i zarządzania UKW, t. 2 2012
Karre P (2011) Heads and tails: both sides of the coin. An analysis of hybrid organisations in the Dutch waste management sector. Eleven International Publishers, Den Haag, p 210
Karre P (2012) Conceptualizing hybrid organisations. A public administration approach. Paper written for symposium: neither public nor private: mixed forms of service delivery around the globe, University of Barcelona, 17–18 May 2012
Kickert WJM (2001) Public Management of hybrid organisations: governance of quasi-autonomous executive agencies. Int Public Manag J 4(2):135–150
Koppell JGS (2001) Hybrid organizations and the alignment of interests: the case of Fannie Mae and Freddie Mac. Public Adm Rev 61:468–482
Koppell JGS (2003) The politics of quasi-government: hybrid organizations and the dynamics of bureaucratic control. Cambridge University Press, Cambridge
Kosar KR (2011) The quasi government: hybrid organisations with both government and private sector legal characteristics. Congressional Research Service 7-5700. http://www.crs.gov. Accessed 22 June 2011

Lindqvist K (2013) Hybrid governance: the case of household solid waste management in Sweden. Public Organ Rev. doi:10.1007/s11115-013-0229-8
Mamoa GM (2011) Growth strategy for hybrid organisations: balancing economic, environmental and social impacts. MIT Sloan School of Management, 6 May 2011, p 3
Minkoff DC (2002) The emergence of hybrid organisational forms: combining identity-based service provision and political action. Nonprofit Volunt Sect Q 31(3):377–401. doi:10.1177/089976400231004
Moe RC, Kosar KR (2005) The quasi government: hybrid organizations with both government and private sector legal characteristics. Congressional Research Service, The Library of Congress, 18 May 2005
Mullins D, Acheson N (2014) Competing drivers of hybridity: third-sector housing organisations in Northern Ireland. International Society for Third-Sector Research and The Johns Hopkins University 2013. Voluntas 25:1606–1629. doi:10.1007/s11266-013-9423-0
Rhodes ML, Donnelly-Cox G (2014) Hybridity and social entrepreneurship in social housing in Ireland. Voluntas 25:1630–1647. doi:10.1007/s11266-013-9421-2
Seidman H (1975) Government-sponsored enterprise in the United States. In: Smith BLR (ed) The new political economy: the public use of the private sector. Wiley, New York, pp 83–108
Skelcher C, Smith SR (2014) Theorizing hybridity: institutional logics, complex organisations, and actor identities: the case of nonprofits. Public Adm. doi: 10.1111/padm.1205
Smith SR (2010) Hybridization and nonprofit organisations: the governance challenge. Policy Soc 29(3):219–229
Stanton TH (2002) Government-sponsored enterprises: mercantilist companies in the modern world. AEI Press, Washington, DC
Thomasson A (2009) Exploring the ambiguity of hybrid organisations: a stakeholder approach. Financ Account Manag 25(3):353–354
Torre L, Fenger M, Twist M (2012) Between state, market and community: a study of the slogans of sheltered work companies. Public Manag Rev 14(4):521–540. doi:10.1080/14719037.2011.649974
Van Thiel S (2001) Quangos: trends, causes and consequences. Ashgate Publishing Limited, Aldershot
Ziębicki B (2012) Metodyka oceny efektywności organizacyjnej. In: Mikuła B (ed) Historia i perspektywy nauk o zarządzaniu. Księga pamiątkowa dla uczczenia Jubileuszu 40-lecia pracy naukowo-dydaktycznej Prof. zw. dr hab. Arkadiusza Potockiego, Wydawnictwo Fundacji Uniwersytetu Ekonomicznego w Krakowie, Kraków, pp 381–391

Market Valuation of Innovation-Related Intangibles: The Case of Polish Biotechnology Firms

Aneta Zakrzewska and Tomasz Kijek

Abstract Innovation-related intangibles allow a firm to create and commercialize new knowledge. Intangible assets necessary for innovation are key drivers of a firm's performance and growth in knowledge intensive industries such as biotechnology which is under high pressure to produce new commercial products and processes. Nevertheless, numerous biotechnology firms fail in their attempts to bring on innovations, since the research and development activities are considered to be high-risky in this sector. The aim of this paper is to conduct an analysis of the relationship between investments in innovation-related intangibles, i.e. R&D and patents, and a biotechnology firm's market value. A sample consists of ten biotech firms listed on the New Connect market. This study utilizes the panel dataset over a 3-year period to run empirical analyses using a fixed effects model. The main findings of the research reveal that there is a non-linear effect of patents on the market value in the sample firms. Surprisingly, R&D expenditures appear to have an insignificant impact on the market value.

Keywords Innovation-related intangibles • R&D expenditures • Patents • Market valuation • Biotechnology firm

1 Introduction

Innovation is a powerful drive for gaining and sustaining competitive advantage (Tidd et al. 2005; Castro et al. 2010). New products and processes are primary created by knowledge assets (Sullivan 2000; Lev 2001; Tranfield et al. 2006), thus firms actively invest in innovation—related intangibles, which render services in the processes of new knowledge (innovation) creation and commercialization. According to intellectual capital literature, renewal capabilities of a firm in the form of patents and other intangible assets (e.g. R&D capital) used to create and introduce new products and processes fall into the category called innovation

---

A. Zakrzewska, M.Sc. (✉) • T. Kijek, Ph.D.
Department of Economics and Agribusiness, University of Life Sciences in Lublin, 13 Akademicka St., 20-950 Lublin, Poland
e-mail: aneta.zakrzewska@up.lublin.pl; tomasz.kijek@up.lublin.pl

T. Dudycz et al. (eds.), *The Essence and Measurement of Organizational Efficiency*, Springer Proceedings in Business and Economics, DOI 10.1007/978-3-319-21139-8_20

capital which is used interchangeably with the term "innovation-related intangibles" (Edvinsson and Malone 1997; Lev 2001). The link between innovation capital and the firm's performance is an important area of interest for scientists and practitioners (Pasher and Ronen 2011). Due to uncertainty of innovation process, there is a tendency in economics of innovation literature to use market value for determining the present value of future cash flows generated by innovation-related intangibles (Hall 2000). Under efficient-market hypothesis, the value of innovation capital should be reflected in stock prices. What is more, capital market should react to any changes in the firm's innovation capital stock (Oriani and Sobrero 2008).

Although there is a vast literature on the market value of innovation-related intangibles such as R&D or patents (Hall et al. 2007), the studies on the value relevance of innovation capital in the biotechnology industry are scare and mostly limited to the American biotech firms. The objective of the paper is to fill this gap by conducting a theoretical analysis of the contribution of innovation-related intangibles to the firm's market value and to empirically verify this dependency. In particular, the study uses ten Polish biotechnology firms listed on the New Connect market and included in the Life Science index as a research sample and tests links between R&D, patents and the firm's market value. What is more the study verifies possible non-linearity in these relationships. The remainder of this paper is organized as follows: Sect. 2 provides a literature review and a research question formulation. Sections 3 and 4 present and discuss the methodology and the results of research. Section 5 concludes and closes the paper.

2 Literature Review

2.1 R&D and Patents as Elements of Innovation-Related Intangibles

From the perspective of resource and knowledge based view of the firm (Barney 1997; Spender 1996), innovation capital (innovation-related intangibles) may be defined as a bundle of the firm's resources/knowledge assets that render services in the process of new knowledge (innovation) creation and commercialization. According to Edvinsson and Malone (1997), the set of innovation-related intangibles consists of intellectual property—IP and other intangible assets and it is categorized in the combination with process capital as an element of organizational capital. On the contrary, Chen et al. (2004) argue that viewing innovation capital as an element of organizational capital causes depreciation of this most dynamic component of intellectual capital. The quoted authors call for treating innovation capital as the key element which connects human capital, structural capital and customer capital, and propose its division into the following elements: innovative achievements, innovation mechanism and innovation culture. Kijek (2012) also adopts similar stance and divides innovation capital into two groups of knowledge assets. The former relates to knowledge embodied in the organizational routines, practices, norms and thinking of the employees. The latter pertains to codified technological knowledge in the form of innovative Intellectual Property Rights—IPR (i.e. utility models, patents) and stock of R&D knowledge. In the economic literature, the technological knowledge means the knowledge about the possibilities of transforming commodities (Arrow and Hahn 1971). From a formal point of view, the technological knowledge is knowledge about the arguments (know-what) and behavior (know-why) of the function $Y = f(x)$, where Y is process output and X is a vector of inputs (Bohn 1994). According to Nelson and Winter (1982), the knowledge base underlying technological innovations, i.e. a new process or a new product, is changing over time as a result of an activity called research and development—R&D.

OECD (2002, p. 30) defines R&D as creative work undertaken on a systematic basis in order to increase the stock of knowledge, including knowledge of man, culture and society, and the use of this stock of knowledge to devise new applications. In this approach, R&D consists of following elements:

- Basic research—experimental or theoretical work undertaken primarily to acquire new knowledge of the underlying foundation of phenomena and observable facts, without any particular application or use in view.
- Applied research—original investigation undertaken in order to acquire new knowledge. It is, however, directed primarily towards a specific practical aim or objective.
- Experimental development—systematic work, drawing on existing knowledge gained from research and/or practical experience, which is directed to producing new materials, products or devices, to installing new processes, systems and services, or to improving substantially those already produced or installed.

As noted previously, the output of R&D may be new technological knowledge, which comprises facts (know-what), the connection of facts by a theory (know-why) and the application of theoretical knowledge in combination with personal skills (know-how) (Grube 2009). These different types of knowledge rely upon each other and are partially patentable as a technological invention. As suggested by the reward theory of patents, exclusive rights to new facts (know-what) and new technologies (know-why) in the form of patents are deemed effective for securing the return from inventions and provide sufficient incentives for firms to conduct risky investments in R&D (Zaby 2010). In line with this approach, the increase in commitments to R&D does not precede increased patenting but is simultaneous with it (Basberg 1982). It is important to notice that patent does not always allow the firm to obtain a monopoly over the market. For example, human insulin can be produced either by applying enzymes for eliminating an amino acid from pig insulin or by genetically modified bacteria, so neither of the patents owners of these inventions, i.e. Novo and Genentech, have a monopoly over the insulin market. Moreover, the formal system of IPRs allows the firm to extend its technological knowledge base by the acquisition of external knowledge in the form of patents and utility models or not patented technological know-how.

2.2 *Market Valuation of R&D and Patents in Biotechnology Industry*

The valuation of firms by shareholders is a very important economic phenomenon. The empirical and theoretical studies on the firm's market value assume that a firm can be viewed as a set of assets that are tangible and intangible in nature (Hall 2000). As such, the market valuation approach is comparable to hedonic price models. Under efficient-market hypothesis (Fama 1991), the pool of assets at the firm's disposal, is priced by the financial markets on the level of the present discounted value of the future cash flows generated by those assets. So, expectations about the future performance of the firms are embodied in its stock price. In this approach, the firm's market value is presented by the formula (Griliches 1981):

$$V = q(A + \gamma K) = qA\left(1 + \gamma\frac{K}{A}\right) \tag{1}$$

where: A is the current value of tangible assets (i.e. physical and financial capital), K is the current value of intellectual capital/intangible assets, including innovation capital approximated by different past measures of R&D and patents, q is the asset pricing market coefficient reflecting the monopolistic position and the varied risk of the firm, and γ is the ratio of shadow values of intangible assets and tangible assets. Dividing trough by A, taking logarithms, and assuming that $ln(1 + x) \approx x$, the equation may be rewritten as:

$$\ln\left(\frac{V}{A}\right) = \alpha + \gamma\frac{K}{A} \tag{2}$$

Although evidence on the contribution of R&D capital and patents to the firm's market value is substantial (e.g. Griliches 1998; Hall et al. 2005), the value-relevance of innovation capital in specific contexts such as the biotechnology sector is still a matter of some debate (Xu et al. 2007). The biotechnology sector is characterized by large investments in R&D and other intangible assets. In short, this industry is a testament to the value of scientific research. Hine and Kapeleris (2006) portray the biotechnology sector as one that needs extensive skill sets and technological knowledge. Moreover, intellectual property protection is an essential element of success for it. Biotechnology is generally defined as the application of science and technology to living organisms, as well as parts, products and models therefore, to alter living or non-living materials for the production of knowledge, goods and services (OECD 2009, p. 9). According to the above definition, the application of biotechnology encompasses both traditional application (e.g. fermentation) and modern application (e.g. genetic modification). Modern biotechnology sector can be broadly classified into the following three sub-sectors: the red—biomedical and human health, green—agricultural and

Table 1 Result of studies on the relationship between innovation-related intangibles and the biotechnology firm's market value

Authors	Sample	Main findings
Hand (2004)	606 US red biotechnology firms	The elasticity of biotech firms' equity market values with respect to R&D is significantly larger the earlier is the R&D expenditure in the value chain, and the greater is the growth rate in R&D spending
Ely et al. (2003)	83 US red biotechnology firms	Market value is positively related to research and development expenditures. This relationship is a function of portfolio potential as measured by the number of a firm's in-process drugs weighted by their development status
Callen et al. (2010)	282 US red biotechnology companies	There is a positive and significant relationship between R&D expenditures, patent counts and stock prices
Guo et al. (2005)	122 US red biotechnology companies	Market prices are positively associated with the stage of product development, the number of products under development, R&D expenditures and intellectual property protection

Source: Own compilation

white—industrial biotechnology which differ considerably in innovation activity and performance (Enzing 2011).

On the one hand, Al-Laham et al. (2011) suggest that a biotechnology firm operates in knowledge-intensive, dynamic settings in which R&D expenditures and patents indicate innovative success, on the other hand, there is evidence that uncertainty of R&D projects in biotechnology industry is relatively high (Ely et al. 2003). So, the biotechnology companies often have little or no revenues and consequently generate losses in the short run due to the expensing of R&D. Table 1 presents some findings on the relationship between innovation-related intangibles and the firm's market value in biotechnology industries.

It is worth noting that the relationship between innovation-related intangibles and the firm's market value may not be as simple as has been suggested by the above mentioned studies. According to the S-curve theory (Foster 1986), this relationship may be portrayed by the inverted U-shaped curve which implies an optimal level of innovation capital's stock corresponding to an optimal level of market value. Under this assumption, R&D expenditure positively contributes to the firm's value at the beginning of the investment, but after reaching an optimal level further R&D investment may reduce the firm's market value. A convincing explanation for this phenomenon is the theory of technology limits and uncertainty (Foster 1986; Oriani and Sobrero 2008). As shown by Bracker and Krishnan (2011), firms may overspend on R&D and operate in the area of negative marginal productivity of R&D from the perspective of investors. Diseconomies of R&D may results from the problems of coordination and resource allocation in innovation activities. Also, the stock of patent within the firm may have a curvilinear relationship with the firm's value. As far as patenting is regarded as a tool for recapturing the value of a firm's development efforts, it has positive impact on the firm's performance. However, the increase in patents may be also the result of a competitive positioning mechanism. In this case, patents block a competitor's effort and have little impact on the firm's performance (MacDonald 2004). Consequently, it may lead to a proliferation of broad low-quality patents. This argumentation is partially supported by a Chen and Chang's (2010) study in which they found an inversed U-shaped relationship between patent citations and market value in the pharmaceutical industry.

Based on the considerations in this section with regard to the impact of R&D and patents on the firm's financial performance—market valuation, it is possible to formulate the following research question: What is the relationship between innovation-related intangibles and the biotech firm's market value?

3 Data and Methods

The study uses a panel dataset over 3 years (i.e. 2011–2013) covering data on R&D, patents and market performance of ten Polish biotechnology firms listed on New Connect market-NC and included in the Life Science index. The New Connect is an alternative market which provides dynamic firms with the opportunity to finance their growth. Trading is organized and regulated by the Warsaw Stock Exchange. The R&D figures were derived from the firms' financial statements for each year. It is important to note that we used information on development costs that are capitalized and reported on the balance-sheets, whereas all research activities (applied and basic research), recognized as expenditures, were not included in the analyses. In the case of patents, we used data from the Polish Patent Office. We codified patent applications at the year of publication, since at this time they become fully visible to investors. The market value to book value ratio (MV/BV)—the forward looking measure of the firm's performance—were obtained from firms' annual reports.

So as to find the answer for the research question, we applied the market value function in the following form:

$$MV_{\mathrm{it}}/BV_{\mathrm{it}} = \beta_1 RD_{\mathrm{it}} + \beta_2 (RD_{\mathrm{it}})^2 + \beta_3 Patent_{\mathrm{it}} + \beta_4 (Patent_{\mathrm{it}})^2 + v_{\mathrm{it}} \quad i = 1, \ldots, 10, t = 1, 2, 3 \tag{3}$$

where: β is a vector of parameters, and v_{it} is an error term specific to firm i in period t.

To estimate the market value equation, panel-data models were employed (Baltagi 2005). Since our panel was relatively small and restricted to the set of ten firms, there was a presumption in favor of fixed effects model. The fixed effects model decomposes v_{it} into a unit-specific and time-invariant component, α_i, and an observation specific error, ε_{it}. The individual-specific constant term absorbs the variables which are taken to be constant over time t, such as a firm's specific characteristics, e.g. main business activity, organizational structure and so on. We decided to employ the fixed effects (FE) least squares, also known as least squares dummy variables (LSDV) model (Greene 2003). To avoid the perfect multicollinearity, we included all dummies (for each firm) and, in turn, suppressed the intercept. Besides an arbitrary choice of fixed effects model, we considered the F-test, which makes the null hypothesis that the cross-sectional units all have a common intercept. If this hypothesis is not rejected, one concludes that the simple pooled model is adequate.

4 Results and Discussion

Table 2 contains descriptive statistics of the variables included in the model. The first conclusion to be drawn from the data presented is that financial investors value the biotechnology firms relatively high as indicated by MV/BV ratio. The average firm has the MV 4.67 times higher than its book value. It actively invests in R&D and uses patents to protect its inventions. This finding is consistent with evidence presented in the report on patent activity in Poland (Raport 2014), which shows that biotechnology sector has the highest number of patent applications per inhabitants.

Table 3 presents the empirical results of the market valuation model in the form specified in Eq. (3). The F-test for fixed effects showed that the cross-sectional units did not have a common intercept.

Contrary to our expectations the R&D variable and its squared term became insignificant in the market value function. Although this finding differs from the results of most prior studies on the market valuation of R&D, it is not an exception. For example, Callen and Morel (2005) found very weak empirical support for the value relevance of R&D expenditures. Similarly, Toivanen and Stoneman (1998) showed that past R&D and investment explained very little of stock returns in the sample of UK firms. In our case the possible explanation for this counter-intuitive result may be twofold. Firstly, the valuation of R&D investments in the biotechnology field may be extremely difficult for investors due to their high risk and a lack of sophisticated knowledge in evaluating such ventures. The sample firms are listed on the New Connect market which is a relatively new trading platform. There is a lack of sophisticated investors (institution) (Schweda 2010), who make effective use of financial information, including R&D, to form more accurate profit expectations. Secondly, most sample firms are young dynamic entities at the early stage of development and consequently the value relevance of their financial statements is relatively low.

As far as the number of patents grants is considered, this variable is positively and significantly associated with the market value. However, its squared term appears to be negative and significant. This means that there is an optimal number of patents beyond which further patenting destroys the market value. To determine the optimal number of patents, we computed a peak value of the MV/BV ratio by setting the first derivative equal to zero. Results reveal that the value of the MV/BV

Table 2 Descriptive statistics for the sample of biotechnology firms

Variable	Min	Max	Mean	Std Dev.
1. MV/BV	0.87	24.44	4.67	4.61
2. R&D	0	2.46	0.41	0.57
3. $(R\&D)^2$	0	6.06e + 12	4.85e + 11	1.16e + 11
4. Patent	0	3	0.40	0.77
5. $(Patent)^2$	0	9	0.74	1.87

Source: Own compilation

Table 3 Stock market valuation of R&D and patents

Variable	Coeff.	Std err.	t-student	p-value
R&D	0.00	0.00	−0.22	0.82
$(R\&D)^2$	0.00	0.00	−0.07	0.94
Patent	3.81	1.98	1.92	0.07*
$(Patent)^2$	−1.17	0.68	−1.77	0.09*
u_1	1.57	0.00	0.00	0.00***
u_2	3.75	0.54	6.91	0.00***
u_3	4.07	1.11	3.65	0.02***
u_4	2.65	1.38	1.92	0.07*
u_5	4.24	1.13	3.75	0.00***
u_6	5.08	0.43	11.64	0.00***
u_7	7.85	0.43	18.34	0.00***
u_8	7.18	0.98	7.34	0.00***
u_9	10.87	0.00	0.00	0.00***
u_10	8.41	1.33	6.28	0.00***
Adj. R^2	0.45			

Note: *significant at 10 %; ***significant at 1 %
Source: Own compilation

ratio peaks when the number of patents is two. As mentioned previously, this finding may be connected with the competitive positioning mechanism and the proliferation of broad low-quality patents.

5 Conclusions

This paper produces a few important contributions for the theory and practice on the market valuation of innovation-related intangibles. First of all, it focuses solely on the biotechnology companies. The peculiarities of biotechnology make a debate on the value relevance of R&D and patent in this sector still open. To our knowledge this is first study focusing on Polish biotechnology firms which analyze the market value of innovation capital. Moreover, the paper goes beyond most of prior studies, which assume the linear relationship between the market value and innovation-related intangibles and tests possible nonlinearity in this relationship.

We included both patent data and R&D expenditures as explanatory variables in our market value function. Surprisingly, only the former appeared to be significant. This means that information on patent counts is more valuable for investors than R&D disclosures in the sample firms. The value relevance of patents is peculiar to the biotechnology industry characterized by high R&D costs and by the difficulty of preventing infringers from imitators. These findings suggest that the biotechnology firms should try to apply for patents relatively early in the life of a research project. However, it is important to note that there is a danger of over-patenting at least from the perspective of investors. Interpreting the results obtained in this research, it should be noticed that they pertain to the settings of start-up firms listed on the relatively new trading platform.

The paper is not exempt from some limitations. The main drawback pertains to the limited sample size, which may not be sufficient to adequately estimate the model coefficients at the firm level. It is mainly a result of a narrow set of biotechnology firms listed on the New Connect Market and their short period of quoting. Another shortcoming of the paper concerns missing data on research expenditures which are not publicly available. In order to overcome these limitations future research should be based on a larger sample and incorporate more precise measures of innovation-related intangibles such as research costs and patents quality.

References

Al-Laham A, Tzabbar D, Amburgey TL (2011) The dynamics of knowledge stocks and knowledge flows: innovation consequences of recruitment and collaboration in biotech. Ind Corp Chang 20(2):555–583

Arrow KJ, Hahn FH (1971) General competitive analysis. Holden-Day, San Francisco

Baltagi BH (2005) Econometric analysis of panel data, 3rd edn. Wiley, Chichester

Barney J (1997) Gaining and sustaining competitive advantage. Addison–Wesley, New York

Basberg B (1982) Technological change in the Norwegian whaling industry: a case study of the use of patent statistics as a technology indicator. Res Policy 11:163–171

Bohn RE (1994) Measuring and managing technological knowledge. Sloan Manag Rev 36 (1):61–73

Bracker K, Krishnan R (2011) Examining the impact of research and development expenditures on Tobin's Q. Acad Strat Manag J 10(1):63–79

Callen JL, Morel M (2005) The valuation relevance of R&D expenditures: time series evidence. Int Rev Financ Anal 14:304–325

Callen J, Gavious I, Segal D (2010) The complementary relationship between financial and non-financial information in the biotechnology industry and the degree of investor sophistication. J Contemp Account Econ 6:61–76

Castro G, Verde M, Saez P, Lopez J (2010) Technological innovation. An intellectual capital based view. Palgrave Macmillan, Basingstoke

Chen Y, Chang K (2010) Exploring the nonlinear effects of patent citations, patent share and relative patent position on market value in the US pharmaceutical industry. Technol Anal Strat Manag 22:153–169

Chen J, Zhu Z, Xie HY (2004) Measuring intellectual capital: a new model and empirical study. J Intellect Cap 5(1):195–212

Edvinsson L, Malone MS (1997) Intellectual capital: the proven way to establish your company's real value by measuring its hidden brainpower. Judy Piatkus, London
Ely K, Simko PJ, Thomas LG (2003) The usefulness of biotechnology firms drug development status in the evaluation of research and development costs. J Account Audit Financ 18:163–196
Enzing C (2011) Sectoral innovation watch. Biotechnology sector. Europe INNOVA. http://ec.europa.eu/enterprise/policies/innovation/files/proinno/sector-report-biotechnology_en.pdf. Accessed 4 Dec 2014
Fama EF (1991) Efficient capital markets. J Financ 46(5):1575–1617
Foster R (1986) Innovation: the attacker's advantage. Summit Books, New York
Greene WH (2003) Econometric analysis. Prentice Hall, New Jersey
Griliches Z (1981) Market value, R&D, and patents. Econ Lett 7(2):183–187
Griliches Z (1998) R&D and productivity. The econometric evidence. The University of Chicago Press, Chicago
Grube C (2009) Measuring the immeasurable: valuing patent protection of knowledge-based competitive advantages. Gabler, Wiesbaden
Guo R, Lev B, Zhou N (2005) The valuation of biotech IPOs. J Account Audit Financ 20 (4):423–459
Hall BH (2000) Innovation and market value. In: Barrell R, Mason G, O'Mahoney M (eds) Productivity, innovation and economic performance. Cambridge University Press, Cambridge, pp 177–198
Hall BH, Jaffe A, Trajtenberg M (2005) Market value and patent citations. Rand J Econ 36:16–38
Hall BH, Thoma G, Torrisi S (2007) The market value of patents and R&D: evidence from European firms. National Bureau of Economic Research. http://www.nber.org/papers/w13426. Accessed 4 Dec 2014
Hand JRM (2004) The market valuation of biotechnology firms and biotechnology R&D. In: Mccahery J, Renneboog L (eds) Venture capital contracting and the valuation of high-technology firms. Oxford University Press, Oxford
Hine D, Kapeleris J (2006) Innovation and entrepreneurship in biotechnology, an international perspective: concepts, theories and cases. Edward Elgar, Cheltenham
Kijek T (2012) Innovation capital and its measurement. J Entrepren Manag Innov 8(4):52–68
Lev B (2001) Intangibles: management, measurement and reporting. Brookings Institution Press, Washington, DC
MacDonald S (2004) When means become ends: considering the impact of patent strategy on innovation. Inf Econ Policy 16(1):135–158
Nelson R, Winter S (1982) An evolutionary theory of economic change. Harvard University Press, Cambridge
OECD (2002) Proposed standard practice for surveys for research and experimental development. Frascati manual. OECD, Paris
OECD (2009) OECD biotechnology statistics. OECD, Paris
Oriani R, Sobrero M (2008) Uncertainty and the market valuation of R&D within a real options logic. Strateg Manag J 29(4):343–361
Pasher E, Ronen T (2011) The complete guide to knowledge management: a strategic plan to leverage your company's intellectual capital. Wiley, New Jersey
Raport o stanie patentowania w Polsce. Patenty szansą na wzrost innowacyjności polskich przedsiębiorstw (2014) Crido, Taxand, Warszawa. http://taxand.pl/attachments/Book/Raport%20o%20stanie%20patentowania%20w%20Polsce%20Crido%20Taxand_2014.pdf. Accessed 4 Dec 2014
Schweda M (2010) NewConnect as an alternative trading system. Equilibrium 2(5)
Spender JC (1996) Making knowledge the basis of dynamic theory of the firms. Strateg Manag J 17:45–48
Sullivan PH (2000) Value-driven intellectual capital: how to convert intangible corporate assets into market value. Wiley, New York

Tidd J, Bessant J, Pavitt K (2005) Managing innovation: integrating technological, market and organizational change. Wiley, Chichester

Toivanen O, Stoneman P (1998) Dynamics of R&D and investment: UK evidence. Econ Lett 58 (1):119–126, Elsevier

Tranfield D, Young M, Partington D, Bessant J, Sapsed J (2006) Building knowledge management capabilities for innovation projects. In: Tidd J (ed) From knowledge management to strategic competence: measuring technological, market and organizational innovation. Imperial College Press, London, pp 126–150

Xu B, Magnan M, Andre P (2007) The stock market valuation of R&D information in biotech firms. Contemp Account Res 24:1291–1318

Zaby A (2010) The decision to patent. Springer Science and Business Media, New York

MIX
Papier aus verantwortungsvollen Quellen
Paper from responsible sources
FSC® C105338

If you have any concerns about our products,
you can contact us on
ProductSafety@springernature.com

In case Publisher is established outside the EU,
the EU authorized representative is:
Springer Nature Customer Service Center GmbH
Europaplatz 3, 69115 Heidelberg, Germany

Printed by Libri Plureos GmbH
in Hamburg, Germany